# WESTERN CIVILIZATION

## MAINSTREAM READINGS & RADICAL CRITIQUES

### VOLUME ONE
### FROM THE GREEKS TO THE ENLIGHTENMENT

# JEFFRY KAPLOW

ALFRED A. KNOPF   NEW YORK

THIS IS A BORZOI BOOK
PUBLISHED BY ALFRED A. KNOPF, INC.

First Edition
987654321
Copyright © 1973 by Alfred A. Knopf, Inc.

Library of Congress Cataloging in Publication Data

Kaplow, Jeffry, comp.
    Western civilization.
    CONTENTS: v. 1. From the Greeks to the
enlightenment.—v. 2. From the French Revolution
to the present.
    1. Civilization, Occidental.   I. Title.
CB245.K32   1973          901.9          72-10009
ISBN 0-394-31453-0    (v. 1)

Manufactured in the United States of America. Composed by
Cherry Hill Composition, Pennsauken, N.J. Printed and bound by
The Kingsport Press, Kingsport, Tenn.

Cover design by Bob Silverman

# ACKNOWLEDGMENTS

ERNST BLOCH, "The Millenarianism of the Peasants' War and Anabaptism" from *Thomas Münzer, Theolog der Revolution*. Copyright © 1969 by Suhrkamp Verlag Frankfurt am Main. Reprinted by permission of the publisher.

MARC BLOCH, "European Feudalism" from *Encyclopedia of the Social Sciences*, Vol. VI, edited by E. R. A. Seligman. Copyright © 1931, 1959 by The Macmillan Company. Reprinted by permission of the publisher.

GIORGIO CANDELORO, "Town and Country, Capitalism and Feudalism in the Italy of the Communes" from *Storia dell' Italia Moderna*. Copyright © 1956 by Feltrinelli Editore. Reprinted by permission of the publisher. Translated for this volume by Jill Carlton Manacorda.

NORMAN COHN, "New Masses in Pursuit of the Millennium" from *The Pursuit of the Millennium*. Copyright © 1961, 1970 by Norman Cohn. Reprinted by permission of Oxford University Press, Inc.

BENJAMIN FARRINGTON, from *Greek Science*. Copyright © 1944, 1949, 1966 by Benjamin Farrington. Reprinted by permission of Penguin Books Ltd.

M. I. FINLEY, "Was Greek Civilization Based on Slave Labour?" from *Historia* VIII (1959). Reprinted by permission of Franz Steiner Verlag GMBH, Weisbaden, West Germany.

EUGENIO GARIN, "Interpretations of the Renaissance" from *Science and Civic Life in the Italian Renaissance*. English translation copyright © 1969 by Doubleday & Company, Inc. Reprinted by permission of the publisher.

BERNARD GROETHUYSEN, "The Bourgeois Order" from *The Bourgeois*, translated by Mary Ilford. Copyright © 1968 by Holt, Rinehart and Winston, Inc. Reprinted by permission of the publisher.

CHRISTOPHER HILL, "Protestantism and the Rise of Capitalism" in

*Essays in the Economic and Social History of Tudor and Stuart England in Honor of R. H. Tawney,* edited by F. J. Fisher. Reprinted by permission of The Economic History Society and Cambridge University Press.

R. H. HILTON, "Capitalism—What's in a Name?" from *Past and Present* No. 1 (1952). Copyright © by The Past and Present Society. Reprinted by permission of the author and the publisher.

A. H. M. JONES, "The Social Background of the Struggle between Paganism and Christianity" from *The Conflict between Paganism and Christianity in the Fourth Century,* edited by A. Momigliano. Reprinted by permission of The Clarendon Press.

MAURICE KEEN, "The Outlaw Ballad as an Expression of Peasant Discontent" from *The Outlaws of Medieval Legend.* Reprinted by permission of Routledge & Kegan Paul Ltd.

JOSEPH LORTZ, "The Causes of the Reformation" from *The Reformation in Germany,* translated by Ronald Walls. Reprinted by permission of Herder and Herder.

C. B. MACPHERSON, from *The Political Theory of Possessive Individualism: Hobbes to Locke.* Reprinted by permission of The Clarendon Press.

ROBERT MANDROU, "Some Characteristics of Mass Psychology in Early Modern France" from *Introduction à la France Moderne: Essai de Psychologie Historique (1500–1640).* Copyright © 1961 by Albin Michel. Reprinted by permission of the publisher.

ROLAND MOUSNIER, "The Society of Orders and the Society of Classes" from *Les hierarchies sociales de 1450 à nos jours.* Reprinted by permission of Presses Universitaires de France.

CHARLES PARAIN, "The General Character of Feudal Society" from *Sur le féodalisme.* Copyright © 1971 by Editions Sociales. Reprinted by permission of the publisher and Centre d'Etudes et de Recherches Marxistes.

ROY PASCAL, from *The Social Basis of the German Reformation.* Copyright 1933 by Roy Pascal. Reprinted 1971 by permission of Augustus M. Kelley, Publishers, by arrangement with the author.

ARCHIBALD ROBERTSON, from *The Origins of Christianity.* Reprinted by permission of Lawrence and Wishart.

RÉGINE ROBIN, "On the Definition of the Prerevolutionary Bourgeoisie" from *La Société française en 1789: Semur en Auxois.* Reprinted by permission of Librairie Plon.

M. I. ROSTOVTZEFF, "The Decay of Ancient Civilization" from *The*

*Social and Economic History of the Roman Empire,* 2nd edition 1957, revised by P. M. Fraser. Reprinted by permission of The Clarendon Press.

ELENA M. SHTAERMAN, "The Fall of the Slave Regime" in *Recherches Internationales à la Lumière du Marxisme* No. 3 (1957). Reprinted by permission of La Nouvelle Critique.

E. A. THOMPSON, "The Germans in the Time of Julius Caesar" from *The Early Germans.* Reprinted by permission of The Clarendon Press.

PIERRE VILAR, "Problems of the Formation of Capitalism" from *Past and Present* No. 10 (1956). Copyright © by The Past and Present Society. Reprinted by permission of the author and the publisher.

————, "1598–1620: The Crisis of Spanish Power and Conscience" from "Le Temps de Quichotte" in *L'Europe* vol. 34 (1956). Reprinted by permission of the author.

F. W. WALBANK, "The Causes of Decline" from *The Awful Revolution.* Reprinted by permission of Liverpool University Press.

J. M. WALLACE-HADRILL, "The Bloodfeud of the Franks" from *The Long Haired Kings.* Reprinted by permission of Methuen & Co. Ltd.

ERNST WERNER, "Popular Ideologies in Late Medieval Europe: Taborite Chiliasm and Its Antecedents" from *Comparative Studies in Society and History* II (1959/1960). Reprinted by permission of the author and Cambridge University Press.

# CONTENTS

# THE MEANING OF RADICAL HISTORY

To be radical is to take things at the root. Now, for man, the root is man himself.

> —MARX, *Contribution to the Critique*
> *of Hegel's Philosophy of Law*

It is easy to slide from "let us not oversimplify" into a theoretical justification, or a tacit assumption, of history as just one damn thing after another—a historical nihilism which is becoming fashionable today, for obvious sociological reasons. . . . I am impenitent in my conviction that it is right to try to see society as a whole, and wrong to consider men's work and thought as though they existed in separate self-contained compartments.

> —CHRISTOPHER HILL, in *Past and Present*,
> No. 29 (1964), 96–97

Learning without living doth but breed traitors as common experience too well showeth.

> —ELLESMERE, Lord Chancellor of
> England, early seventeenth century

The purpose of this book is indicated by its title, a confrontation between mainstream interpretations and dissentient radical views of the principal issues of European history. Although my sympathies are clearly with the radical side, there has been no attempt to set up straw men, nor has it been my intent to show the development of historical thought across time. Most of the material reprinted here is of very recent vintage, some 80 percent of it having been published since World War II. I have therefore not included selections from historians who, however great their contributions, have now been left behind because of the discovery of new evidence or because their conceptual schemes no longer attract approval or allegiance. I have focused rather on illustrating the many different ways of approaching the historical past. To do so, it is not always necessary to have opponents engage in direct debate about the significance of this or that trend or event. The confrontation is located at another level, a higher and more abstract one. The crucial question is this: What is important in history—which is to say, in society? What are the agents that, through human actions and their limitations, determine what happens in history? If we all agree, more or less, that causality is the proper concern of the historian, how are we to determine causes—and to establish a hierarchy among them?

The most important development in the historiography of the last fifty years has been historians' gradual assimilation, to a greater or lesser extent, of Marxist thought. At the very least, this has meant a renewed emphasis on what are known as social and economic "factors" in shaping human destiny. But there is a difference between allowing oneself to be influenced by Marx in this way (after all, he was not alone in preaching the lesson) and accepting Marxism as a system of thought. To follow the latter option is not, however, to accept as absolute truth everything that Marx said, much less the obiter dicta of what the Polish philosopher Leszek Kolakowski has called the Office, that is, the ideologists of the Soviet Union. The acceptance of Marxism as a system is the adoption of the method of historical materialism and, more specifically, of class analysis as a means for understanding what has happened in history. The first task men face is to create the conditions of their own survival, that is, the taming of nature and the making of a living, which are inseparable from one another. This is what Marxists call the process of producing and reproducing real life: the carving out of an environment, the perpetuation of the species, and the production of goods. In the course of this activity, men enter into relationships with one another that we call social relations of production, and those social relations most characteristic of a given time and place are said to constitute the dominant mode of production. All areas of human activity are construed to be part of, and dependent upon, these modes. History is thus the study of the totality of human activity, of men in society, of whole men taken at the root. In this light, the traditional distinctions between political, economic, social, and intellectual history, which presuppose the compartmentalization of human life, melt away.

One does not have to be a Marxist to accept the definition of history as the study of man in his total dimension. Marc Bloch, the great French medievalist whose theoretical work was an attempt to come to terms with Marxism while rejecting its basic assumptions, shared this point of view, as do his present-day disciples in the VIe Section of the Ecole Pratique des Hautes Etudes and on the review *Annales: Economies, Sociétés, Civilisations.* It is, however, incorrect to tax Marxism with being an economic determinism. The charge is the result of a basic misunderstanding, which is sometimes knowingly perpetuated. Marxism has nothing to do with economic determinism. It is, indeed, a determinism in the sense that it shows (1) that men are not totally free to do as they wish and (2) that consciousness is neither prior to, nor independent of, real life—that is, the social relations of production. In a narrow sense, one may be justified in speaking of a social determinism, but even then man remains the doer and the measure of all things. Economics and technology remain subordinate to the desires and perceptions of flesh-and-blood human beings who are, in turn, the products of a dialectical interaction between biology and society. For example: It may be said that in the nature of capitalism lies a tendency to expansion and to the maximization of profit. We do not, or should not, say that these tendencies work themselves out automatically. It is capitalists and bureaucrats who actually perform the task. And we cannot maintain that each one of them is motivated in a crude way by rapacity. The archetypal capitalist does not exist; he is always a particular person possessed of an ideology and world view peculiar to his time and place, motivated in complex ways. In short, he is a member of a class, even if he does not recapitulate in himself all of its characteristics.

But then what is a class? The proposed answers are so numerous as to make impossible even an attempt to catalogue them within the framework of this essay. I will content myself with citing what I consider to be the best contemporary definition. It is the work of the historian of the English working class Edward Thompson:

By class I understand an historical phenomenon, unifying a number of disparate and seemingly unconnected events, both in the raw material of experience and in consciousness. I emphasize that it is an *historical* phenomenon. I do not see class as a "structure," nor even as a "category," but as something which in fact happens (and can be shown to have happened) in human relationships.

More than this, the notion of class entails the notion of historical relationship. Like any other relationship, it is a fluency which evades analysis if we attempt to stop it at any given moment and anatomise its structure. The finest-meshed sociological net cannot give us a pure specimen of class, any more than it can give us one of deference or love. The relationship must always be embodied in real people and in a real context. Moreover, we cannot have two distinct classes, each with an independent being, and then bring them *into* relationship with each other. We cannot have love without lovers, nor deference without squires and laborers. And class happens when some men, as a result of common experiences (inherited and shared) feel and articulate the identity of their interests as between themselves, and as against other men whose interests are different from (and usually opposed to) theirs.

The class experience is largely determined by the productive relations into which men are born or enter involuntarily. Class-consciousness is the way in which these experiences are handled in cultural terms: embodied in traditions, value-systems, ideas, and institutional forms. If the experience appears as determined, class-consciousness does not. We can see a *logic* in the responses of similar occupational groups undergoing similar experiences, but we cannot predicate any *law*. Consciousness of class arises in the same way in different times and places, but never in *just* the same way.

We have here in outline the basic tools of Marxist historical interpretation. They ought to be handled with care, bearing in mind, as the historian of Southern slavery Eugene Genovese has said, that class analysis can "only serve as the basis for a much more complex analysis." Marxism is a method of perceiving social reality. Because this is so, there is a priori no single Marxist truth. The results arrived at by the application of Marxist techniques of analysis are liable to the normal rules of evidence and scientific critique. They are never acquired once and for all, but are constantly subject to revision.

The radical historian believes that history should be studied as the sum total of man's activity at a given time and place, and that a liaison must be established between the study of the past and our present concerns. He is a "why" rather than a "how" historian, systematically posing the "big" question about historical change: Why did it happen this way and not that? He challenges accepted ideas when he finds them inadequate and especially when they neglect the dimension of popular movements and class struggle. But the radical historian does not waste his time crying over the victims of past events, no matter how much sympathy he may feel for them. He is not iconoclastic and merely skeptical, nor does he engage in art for art's sake— activities readily tolerated by ruling classes and easily turned by them to their own advantage. The village atheist never did anyone any harm.

History is more than a simple intellectual exercise, a pack of tricks played upon the dead. It is a social science, and therefore the proper field, perhaps even the laboratory, in which to develop the analyses and ideas that form the very stuff of social change. As a social science, it does not pretend to "transcend time and place" in order to permit analogy, generalization, or prediction; only by having one's historical feet planted firmly in a specific context can one learn anything at all. We want not lessons from the past, but learning with which to change the world. Marx, who spoke of philosophers as having done nothing more than study the world, was only expressing in a different way what Ellesmere had said in the early seventeenth century and what today is called the necessity of integrating theory and practice into a revolutionary praxis.

The notion is a very simple one. It means activity aimed at shaping the future in liaison with a theoretical understanding of the basis of change. The man who practices without theory is doomed to failure, for he will be taking pot shots in the dark at an unknown target. The man who theorizes without practice is equally so, for lack of contact with the real world will render him sterile. It is not sufficient to look out on what is going on from the window of an ivory tower. But the conclusion is not that there can be no division of labor in this life, or that the historian is expected to lead the revolution. Even less has it anything to do with sopping up wisdom from the masses. The historian who abandons the study of history to enter the factory is as likely to hinder progress as to advance it.

There are those who argue that to speak of radical history is a contradiction in terms. Truth is one, they say, and our task as historians is to seek it out. For David Landes of Harvard and Charles Tilly of the University of Michigan, editors of the recent *History As Social Science,* ours is an age "that is beginning to fear and mistrust science and technology, that wants to substitute heart for mind, warmth for coolness, passion for reason." Radicals, they argue, wish to subordinate the dispassionate search for truth to political tasks, an attitude which is not only arrogant, but leads them into the dangerous byways of judging the credentials of the historian rather than the results of his inquiry.

To make the search for truth dispassionate is to take the guts out of what a historian does. Truth is a passion, and the fact that the converse is not true has nothing to do with the case. Only the jesting Pilates of this world, for whom truth is of no importance, can adopt an agnostic position. Recent events, of which the war in Indochina has been the most significant and catalytic, have created a new generation of activists who seek explanations of present horrors in historical study. They are no longer satisfied with traditional university fare and demand more meat on the bones of scholarship, by which they mean increased "relevance" to contemporary concerns. Relevance is a tricky and easily abused concept. When it is meant to discredit any scholarly endeavor not directly related to the cure of what ails us, it can be very ugly indeed. Moreover, to use it as a cudgel is in direct contradiction to conscious radical goals. In a "good" society—that is, one free from the imperatives of capital and class—it would presumably be both possible and desirable to allocate resources in such a way as to permit investigations of the most highly abstract and nonrelevant nature; and one cannot prepare the way for that society by suppressing such of its aspects as may already exist. But it is sometimes difficult to separate the error of mindless rhetoric from its context. As Bertolt Brecht once wrote in a poem addressed to future generations:

> Even the hatred of squalor
> Makes the brow grow stern.
> Even anger against injustice
> Makes the voice grow harsh.[1]

The important thing, it seems to me, is to refuse to countenance these errors, but at the same time not to fall into the trap of divorcing oneself from the young people whose responsibility they are. Their protest against the failures of the university, the historical discipline, and the role they are too often made to play in contemporary society is fundamentally healthy. There is a proper and an improper way of attacking the failings of traditional or mainstream history. If relevance is too often senseless and abusive, it nevertheless expresses a real concern and is a direct challenge to the idea of a value-free social science.

For the radical scholar qua scholar, this is the most basic issue. He argues that value-free social science cannot exist in a class society, where all knowledge is to some extent ideological. Although science may under certain conditions attain a measure of autonomy, like everything else it is socially conditioned. In this sense, one can speak of bourgeois science. It is not *bad* science (although one may disagree with it), but science of its time and place. By its very nature, it is a carrier of values. This is what the radical scholar asks be recognized. He demands both lucidity and mastery, the combination of which will allow us continually to deepen our understanding of the past.

Radicalism is not relativism. It does not maintain that one truth (interpretation) is as good as another, in the manner of the American historians Charles Beard (1874–1948), who was led by his view that objectivity was a "noble dream" to maintain that the past was ultimately unknowable, or Carl Becker (1873–1945), who made of Everyman his own historian and insisted on a skeptical distrust of them all. The radical historian refuses to make the question one of individual bias versus objectivity, so the argument that "bias can be overcome" has no significance. The point hinges rather on the question of ideology. Marxists and other sorts of radicals share a conviction that it is possible to analyze the past scientifically according to a set of theoretical principles and that their theory is more consonant with reality than any other. They operate under no illusions about their own objectivity. They recognize themselves as ideologists, and ideology, by definition, as a deformation of objective truth (assumed to exist, even though presently unattainable). But the quality of an ideology is measured by its capacity to furnish a coherent explanation of society and of nature— or in history, of events observed to have taken place in the past.

---

[1] From "To Posterity" in *Selected Poems* by Bertolt Brecht (New York: Harcourt Brace Jovanovich, 1959).

Social science is, then, thoroughly imbued with values, even when its practitioners cry most loudly that their aim is only to be detached and objective. The call for ivory-tower scholarship is itself expressive of a value set, and it is difficult to imagine that the kind of isolation from the outside world it implies will be without effect on the studies so undertaken. The radical maintains that there is something wrong with a system of values that incites professors to publish while others perish. Let me be clear: It is not what you study, but how you study it. No one should want to force a scholar of, say, ancient Greek philology to try to relate his work to the current political situation in Greece. What a radical is against is scholarship that castrates itself by willfully cutting itself off from areas of contemporary concern to which it has a legitimate relation. More generally, radicals oppose scholars who, as a matter of principle, make of their university or discipline a haven from the melee of the problems of this world.

There is also the matter of the perversion of science. Isolation from the real world finds its complement at the other end of the scale among scholars who use their knowledge for dubious ends. I refer, of course, to the kinds of labors that currently go under the name of defense research, in which, for example, the latest techniques of "objective" social science are used to develop counterinsurgency plans for keeping the natives quiet. This kind of thing has been going on ever since Woodrow Wilson, then president of Princeton University, announced the desirability of fostering liaisons between the universities and the state ("Princeton in the Nation's service"—1896). It, too, is a form of commitment, and I would be the last to gainsay it on that basis; I have no desire to consign the university and the state to their separate spheres. But I hold that commitment must not be blind, that the scholar is indeed responsible not only for the quality and accuracy of his work, but for the uses to which it is put. When those uses turn out to be the physical uprooting and even extermination of whole groups of people or the destruction of the physical environment, the refusal to be an accomplice becomes mandatory. To hide behind the skirts of science in order to legitimize—or even refuse to condemn—criminal acts is an act unworthy of a scholar.

The radical scholar is on the defensive these days. He wants the university to be kept safe from manipulation by the state, but he also wants to encourage his fellows to take positions on the major issues of the day not just as citizens, but also as scholars. In other words, he refuses to establish a dichotomy between the two functions of a single individual. In fact, he sees the union between them as the necessary condition of success in either. It is becoming more and more difficult to live as a whole man these days, for the pressures on the members of the university community to conform to the status quo are increasingly great. The price of freedom of thought seems to be the abandonment of freedom of action. But the one cannot survive without the other.

It is at this point that radical activism and radical scholarship meet in a shared concern for revolutionary change. There are many ways to promote that change. In this regard, the historian practices a privileged discipline, for it is one of those most directly related to the building of a new and better world. Without history, there can be no theory, and without theory, there can be no change. The praxis of the revolutionary intellectual takes place most of the time, but not exclusively, in his library and at his writing table. One kind of action is not better than another; although there may be moments when one is more needed than another, each is part of a whole. Everything depends on the attitude of the historian toward his work. If he is radical in his concerns and methods as we have defined them, he is likely to make a significant contribution to the common task. The truth, or what we can know of it, historical as well as actual, is always revolutionary.

This said, there is not necessarily a direct connection between a radical historiography and a commitment to a political movement, however much they might enrich one another. I have little or no idea of the political positions of the authors represented in this collection. It is as yet impossible to present a collection of essays by committed radical scholars that would attempt to offer a coherent overview of European history animated by a common political viewpoint and using the latest techniques; it is a weakness within whose bounds we have to operate. So it is only right to say that what we have here is more a set of challenges and suggestions than a single interpretive system.

# I/ANCIENT GREECE: SLAVERY AND SCIENCE

ANCIENT Greece is usually thought of as the seedbed of Western civilization. Like the term "civilization" itself, the idea is vague and easily abused. To what precisely do we refer? To the tyranny of the rulers of Athens in the sixth century B.C. or to the democracy practiced in that city in the golden age of the fourth and fifth centuries? Is Athens the model, or shall we prefer Sparta? Or perhaps another of the more than a thousand city-states (*poleis*) that enjoyed at least nominal independence at one time or another?

These questions are, in fact, easily answered, but they ought to be posed if only to avoid confusion. Of the four periods into which the history of Ancient Greece is customarily divided, the archaic (800–500 B.C.), the classical (500–322), the Hellenistic (322–31), and the Roman (dated from Augustus's victory over Marc Antony and Cleopatra at the battle of Actium, 31 B.C.), it is the classical one that most draws our attention, and particularly with regard to the Athenian supremacy of its first half. It is the high point of Greek democracy with which we continue to identify.

Athenian democracy is not an illusion, but those who benefited from it were a minority. Only male citizens could participate in the business of government, from which all noncitizens, notably the permanent alien residents known as *metics* and the slaves, were excluded, and it was virtually impossible to become a citizen if one was not born to that status. Women were also refused the right to participate because of their sex. The assembly of citizens (*demos*) was sovereign in all matters, but much of the preparatory work for its discussions was carried out by the *boulé*, a council of five hundred members chosen by lot among all the citizens. There was

1

also a large number of magistrates, usually chosen by lot as well and on occasion elected, to carry out decisions of the *demos* to which each was responsible. Although a system of payments allowed even a poor man to devote his time to public affairs, it should not be assumed that posts were equally distributed among all the strata of the population. Most of the men who directed public affairs were drawn from the ranks of wealthy *rentiers*. They alone had both the means and the leisure, as well as the education, to devote themselves full time to politics. And if they had to defend their policies before the multitude (thus becoming demagogues), this should not be construed to mean that they did not enjoy a considerable amount of latitude in carrying out their own wishes.

Athenian society was based on private property, which meant that classes existed for which words like "rich" and "poor" are only very approximate definitions. It is perhaps better to speak, in general, of persons drawing income from the soil and from commerce as *rentiers,* on the one hand, and the mass of poor peasants working the land themselves with the assistance of one or two slaves, on the other. As there were classes, there were also class struggles, but the extraordinary fact is that they rarely became so virulent as to provoke civil war, as in many other parts of Greece. As M. I. Finley remarks, an equilibrium was established by the middle of the fifth century, with the state providing the mass with considerable material advantages and a share in government, while reserving the honorific and real advantages of leadership positions for the aristocratic elite. This was made possible by economic prosperity and Athenian success in extending its political hegemony over the empire. On this basis, the political system of the *polis* (city-state) functioned to create a sense of identity and allegiance that for a long time enabled the Athenians to resist centrifugal forces at work in their midst and attacks from the outside.

One ought also to note that the very existence of slavery and therefore of slaveholders who had a common interest provided a good part of the cement necessary to keep the Athenian democratic edifice in place. It is often thought that democracy and slavery are incompatible, whereas in fact the latter may be—and in Ancient Greece was—the very basis for the former. Liberty and slavery, which are the real opposites in the matter, are contradictory only when applied to the same people, so that the question must always be: Of whom do we wish to speak? In the article that follows, M. I. Finley, professor of classics at the University of Cambridge, studies the nature of Greek slavery, differentiates it from modern varieties, and concludes that the development of slavery and freedom went hand in hand.

The other problem dealt with in this section is a cultural one. Greek scientists by the end of the archaic period had made many observations and had accumulated an impressive amount of knowledge about the external world in the fields of astronomy, navigation, mechanics, human anatomy and physiology, and agronomy. And their knowledge was applied to practical concerns. Little by little, however, and despite the medical work of the Hippocratic school at the end of the fifth century and the mathematical discoveries of Euclid and Archimedes in the following two centuries, Greek science—in particular, applied science—ground to a halt. It not only ceased to develop but in many instances underwent a clear regression. Why was it that this excellent basis failed to provide the means for a dramatic breakthrough in man's dominion over the universe? Some have attributed the failure to a lack of intellectual curiosity, itself the result of too much progress too early. For a radical historian, this is insufficient explanation, because science, like all other things cultural, has a basis in social life. The question then becomes: What were the particular features of Greek society that kept science from crossing the threshold of modernity? For a Marxist, the cause of this blockage must be sought in the relationship between the productive forces and the social relations of production, to which an ideological formulation is given. If, as is now generally admitted, the Greek aristocracy through their philosophers developed an ideology that scorned the practical application of science in favor of the joys of contemplative knowledge, and took mathematics and metaphysics to be infinitely more worthwhile than any of the "arts," and if no other class of Greek society was capable of providing an alternative conception, science was indeed likely to be relegated to an inferior place. But why did the Greek aristocracy have this change of heart? What in the social setting made the aristocrats turn their eyes inward, as though the real world were not worth the knowing except in highly abstract terms? Benjamin Farrington, professor emeritus of classics in the University College, Swansea (Wales), and the author of several books on Greek science, in the article reprinted here points to the relationship between master and slave and claims that it was reflected in the new dichotomy of thought between technology and science, mind and matter, work and leisure.

# M. I. Finley

## 1

## Was Greek Civilization Based on Slave Labour?

Two generalizations may be made at the outset. First: at all times and in all places the Greek world relied on some form (or forms) of dependent labour to meet its needs, both public and private. By this I mean that dependent labour was essential, in a significant measure, if the requirements of agriculture, trade, manufacture, public works, and war production were to be fulfilled. And by dependent labour I mean work performed under compulsions other than those of kinship or communal obligations.[1] Second: with the rarest of exceptions, there were always substantial numbers of free men engaged in productive labour. By this I mean primarily not free hired labour but free men working on their own (or leased) land or in their shops or homes as craftsmen and shopkeepers. It is within the framework created by these two generalizations that the questions must be asked which seek to locate slavery in the society. And by slavery, finally, I mean roughly the status in which a man is, in the eyes of the law and of public opinion and with respect to all other parties, a possession, a chattel, of another man.[2]

How completely the Greeks always took slavery for granted as one of the facts of human existence is abundantly evident to anyone who has read their literature. In the Homeric poems it is assumed (correctly) that captive women will be taken home as slaves, and that occasional male slaves—the victims of Phoenician merchant-pirates—will also be on hand. In the seventh century B.C., when Hesiod, the Boeotian "peasant" poet, gets down to practical advice in his *Works and Days,* he tells his brother how to use slaves properly; that they will

---

[1] I also exclude the "economic compulsion" of the wage-labour system.

[2] It is obviously not a valid objection to this working definition to point out either that a slave is biologically a man none the less, or that there were usually some pressures to give him a little recognition of his humanity, such as the privilege of asylum or the de facto privilege of marriage.

5

be available is simply assumed. The same is true of Xenophon's manual for the gentleman farmer, the *Oeconomicus*, written about 375 B.C. A few years earlier, an Athenian cripple who was appealing a decision dropping him from the dole, said to the Council: "I have a trade which brings me in a little, but I can barely work at it myself and I cannot afford to buy someone to replace myself in it." In the first book of the Pseudo-Aristotelian *Oeconomica*, a Peripatetic work probably of the late fourth or early third century B.C., we find the following proposition about the organization of the household, stated as baldly and flatly as it could possibly be done: "Of property, the first and most necessary kind, the best and most manageable, is man. Therefore the first step is to procure good slaves. Of slaves there are two kinds, the overseer and the worker." Polybius, discussing the strategic situation of Byzantium, speaks quite casually of "the necessities of life—cattle and slaves" which come from the Black Sea region. And so on.

The Greek language had an astonishing range of vocabulary for slaves, unparalleled in my knowledge. In the earliest texts, Homer and Hesiod, there were two basic words for slave, *dmos* and *doulos,* used without any discoverable distinction between them, and both with uncertain etymologies. *Dmos* died out quickly, surviving only in poetry, whereas *doulos* remained the basic word, so to speak, all through Greek history, and the root on which were built such words as *douleia,* "slavery." But Homer already has, in one probably interpolated passage, the word (in the plural form) *andrapoda,* which became very common, and seems to have been constructed on the model of *tetrapoda.* Still another general word came into use in the Hellenistic period, when *soma* ("body") came to mean "slave" if not otherwise qualified by an adjective.

These words were strictly servile, except in such metaphors as "the Athenians enslaved the allies." But there was still another group which could be used for both slaves and free men, depending on the context. Three of them are built on the household root, *oikos—oikeus, oiketes,* and *oikiatas*—and the pattern of usage is variegated, complicated, and still largely unexamined. In Crete, for example, *oikeus* seems to have been a technical status term more like "serf" than any other instance known to me in Greek history. It was archaic even in Crete, however, and it dropped out of sight there in post-fifth-century documents. Elsewhere these *oikos*-words sometimes meant merely "servant" or "slave" generically, and sometimes, though less often, they indicated narrower distinctions, such as house-born slave (as against purchased) or privately owned (as against royal in the Hellenistic context).

If we think of ancient society as made up of a spectrum of statuses, with the free citizen at one end and the slave at the other, and with a considerable number of shades of dependence in between, then we have already discovered two lines of the spectrum, the slave and the serf-like *oikeus* of Crete. At least four more can easily be added: the helot (with such parallels as the *penestes* of Thessaly); the debt-bondsman, who was not a slave although under some conditions he could eventually be sold into slavery abroad; the conditionally manu-mitted slave; and, finally, the freedman. All six categories rarely, if ever, appeared concurrently within the same community, nor were they equal in importance or equally significant in all periods of Greek history. By and large, the slave proper was the decisive figure (to the virtual exclusion of the others) in the economically and politically advanced communities; whereas helotage and debt-bondage were to be found in the more archaic communities, whether in Crete or Sparta or Thessaly at an even later date, or in Athens in its pre-Solonian period. There is also some correlation, though by no means a perfect one, between the various categories of dependent labour and their function. Slavery was the most flexible of the forms, adaptable to all kinds and levels of activity, whereas helotage and the rest were best suited to agriculture, pasturage, and household service, much less so to manufacture and trade.

With little exception, there was no activity, productive or unpro-ductive, public or private, pleasant or unpleasant, which was not performed by slaves at some times and in some places in the Greek world. The major exception was, of course, political: no slave held public office or sat on the deliberative and judicial bodies (though slaves were commonly employed in the "civil service," as secretaries and clerks, and as policemen and prison attendants). Slaves did not fight as a rule, either, unless freed (although helots apparently did), and they were very rare in the liberal professions, including medicine. On the other side, there was no activity which was not performed by free men at some times and in some places. That is sometimes denied, but the denial rests on a gross error, namely, the failure to differentiate between a free man working for himself and one working for another, for hire. In the Greek scale of values, the crucial test was not so much the nature of the work (within limits, of course) as the condition or status under which it was carried on. "The condition of the free man," said Aristotle, "is that he does not live under the restraint of another." On this point, Aristotle was expressing a nearly universal Greek notion. Although we find free Greeks doing every kind of work, the free wage-earner, the free man who regularly works *for* another and therefore "lives under the restraint of another" is a rare figure in the sources, and he surely was a minor factor in the picture.[3]

---

[3] This statement is not invalidated by the occasional sally which a smallholder or petty craftsman might make into the labour market to do three days' harvesting or

The basic economic activity was, of course, agriculture. Throughout Greek history, the overwhelming majority of the population had its main wealth in the land. And the majority were smallholders, depending on their own labour, the labour of other members of the family, and the occasional assistance (as in time of harvest) of neighbours and casual hired hands. Some proportion of these smallholders owned a slave, or even two, but we cannot possibly determine what the proportion was, and in this sector the whole issue is clearly not of the greatest importance. But the large landholders, a minority though they were, constituted the political (and often the intellectual) elite of the Greek world; our evidence reveals remarkably few names of any consequence whose economic base was outside the land. This landholding elite tended to become more and more of an absentee group in the course of Greek history; but early or late, whether they sat on their estates or in the cities, dependent labour worked their land as a basic rule (even when allowance is made for tenancy). In some areas it took the form of helotage, and in the archaic period, of debt-bondage, but generally the form was outright slavery.

I am aware, of course, that this view of slavery in Greek agriculture is now strongly contested. Nevertheless, I accept the evidence of the line of authors whom I have already cited, from Hesiod to the pseudo-Aristotelian *Oeconomica*. These are all matter-of-fact writings, not utopias or speculative statements of what ought to be. If slavery was not the customary labour form on the larger holdings, then I cannot imagine what Hesiod or Xenophon or the Peripatetic were doing, or why any Greek bothered to read their works. One similar piece of evidence is worth adding. There was a Greek harvest festival called the Kronia, which was celebrated in Athens and other places (especially among the Ionians). One feature, says the Atthidographer Philochorus, was that "the heads of families ate the crops and fruits at the same table with their slaves, with whom they had shared the labours of cultivation. For the god is pleased with this honour from the slaves in

---

a week's work on temple construction; or by the presence in cities like Athens of a substantial number of men, almost all of them unskilled, who lived on odd jobs in the sources do we hear of private establishments employing a staff of hired (when they were not rowing in the fleet or otherwise occupied by the state). Nowhere workers as their normal operation. Public works are frequently adduced as evidence to the contrary, but I believe without sufficient cogency. In the first place, the more common practice seems to have been a contract with an entrepreneur (even if he worked alone), not hire for wages. Second, such evidence as we have—most fully from Delos—argues that such work was spasmodic and infrequent, and quite inconceivable as a source of livelihood for any but a handful of men. All this is consistent with the view that most of the craftsmen appearing in the accounts were independent masons and carpenters who occasionally accepted a job from the state just as they accepted orders from private clients. The key to the whole question is the absence of entrepreneurs whose regular labour force consisted of hired free men.

contemplation of their labours." Neither the practice nor Philochorus' explanation of it makes any sense whatever if slavery was as unimportant in agriculture as some modern writers pretend.

I had better be perfectly clear here: I am not saying that slaves outnumbered free men in agriculture, or that the bulk of farming was done by slaves, but that slavery dominated agriculture insofar as it was on a scale that transcended the labour of the householder and his sons. Nor am I suggesting that there was no hired free labour; rather that there was little of any significance. Among the slaves, furthermore, were the overseers, invariably so if the property was large enough or if the owner was an absentee. "Of slaves," said the author of the *Oeconomica,* "there are two kinds, the overseer and the worker."

In mining and quarrying the situation was decisively one-sided. There were free men, in Athens for example, who leased such small mining concessions that they were able to work them alone. The moment, however, additional labour was introduced (and that was the more common case), it seems normally to have been slave. The largest individual holdings of slaves in Athens were workers in the mines, topped by the one thousand reported to have been leased out for this purpose by the fifth-century general Nicias. It has been suggested, indeed, that at one point there may have been as many as thirty thousand slaves at work in the Athenian silver mines and processing mills.

Manufacture was like agriculture in that the choice was (even more exclusively) between the independent craftsman working alone or with members of his family and the owner of slaves. The link with slavery was so close (and the absence of free hired labour so complete) that Demosthenes, for example, could say "they caused the *ergasterion* [the workshop] to disappear" and then he could follow, as an exact synonym and with no possible misunderstanding, by saying that "they caused the slaves to disappear." On the other hand, the proportion of operations employing slaves, as against the independent self-employed craftsmen, was probably greater than in agriculture, and in this respect more like mining. In commerce and banking, subordinates were invariably slaves, even in such posts as "bank manager." However, the numbers were small.

In the domestic field, finally, we can take it as a rule that any free man who possibly could afford one, owned a slave attendant who accompanied him when he walked abroad in the town or when he travelled (including his military service), and also a slave woman for the household chores. There is no conceivable way of estimating how many such free men there were, or how many owned numbers of domestics, but the fact is taken for granted so completely and so often in the literature that I strongly believe that many owned slaves even when they could not afford them. (Modern parallels will come to mind readily.) I stress this for two reasons. First, the need for domestic slaves, often an unproductive element, should serve as a cautionary sign when one examines such questions as the efficiency and cost of slave labour. Second, domestic slavery was by no means entirely unproductive. In the countryside in particular, but also in the towns, two important industries would often be in their hands in the larger households, on a straight production for household consumption basis. I refer to baking and textile making, and every medievalist, at least, will at once grasp the significance of the withdrawal of the latter from market production, even if the withdrawal was far from complete.

It would be very helpful if we had some idea how many slaves there were in any given Greek community to carry on all this work, and how they were divided among the branches of the economy. Unfortunately we have no reliable figures, and none at all for most of the *poleis* [cities]. What I consider to be the best computations for Athens suggest that the total of slaves reached 80–100,000 in peak periods in the fifth and fourth centuries B.C. Athens had the largest population in the classical Greek world and the largest number of slaves. Thucydides said that there were more slaves in his day on the island of Chios than in any other Greek community except Sparta, but I suggest that he was thinking of the density of the slave population measured against the free, not of absolute totals (and in Sparta he meant the helots, not chattel slaves). Other places, such as Aegina or Corinth, may at one time or another also have had a higher ratio of slaves than Athens. And there were surely communities in which the slaves were less dense.

More than that we can scarcely say about the numbers, but I think that is really enough. There is too much tendentious discussion of numbers in the literature already, as if a mere count of heads is the answer to all the complicated questions which flow from the existence of slavery. The Athenian figures I mentioned amount to an average of no less than three or four slaves to each free household (including all free men in the calculation, whether citizen or not). But even the smallest figure anyone has suggested, 20,000 slaves in Demosthenes' time—altogether too low in my opinion—would be roughly equivalent to one slave for each adult citizen, no negligible ratio. Within very broad limits, the numbers are irrelevant to the question of significance. When Starr, for example, objects to "exaggerated guesses" and replies that "the most careful estimates . . . reduce the proportion of slaves to far less than half the population, probably one third or one quarter at most," he is proving far less than he thinks. No one seriously believes that slaves did all the work in Athens (or anywhere else in Greece except for Sparta with its helots), and one merely confuses the issue when one pretends that somehow a reduction of the estimates to only a third or a quarter of the population is crucial. In 1860, according to official census figures, slightly less than one third of the total population of the American slave states were slaves. Furthermore, "nearly three-fourths of all free Southerners had no connection with slavery through either family ties or direct ownership. The 'typical' Southerner was not only a small farmer but also a nonslaveholder." Yet no one would think of denying that slavery was a decisive element in southern society. The analogy seems obvious for ancient Greece, where, it can be shown, ownership of slaves was even more widely spread among the free men and the use of slaves much more diversified, and where the estimates do not give a ratio significantly below the American one. Simply stated, there can be no denial that there were enough slaves about for them to be, of necessity, an integral factor in the society.

There were two main sources of supply. One was captives, the victims of war and sometimes piracy. One of the few generalizations about the ancient world to which there is no exception is this, that the victorious power had absolute right over the persons and the property of the vanquished. This right was not exercised to its full extent every time, but it was exercised often enough, and on a large enough scale, to throw a continuous and numerous supply of men, women, and children on to the slave market. Alongside the captives we must place the so-called barbarians who came into the Greek world in a steady stream—Thracians, Scythians, Cappadocians, etc.— through the activity of full-time traders, much like the process by which African slaves reached the new world in more modern times. Many were the victims of wars among the barbarians themselves. Others came peacefully, so to speak: Herodotus says that the Thracians sold their children for export. The first steps all took place outside the Greek orbit, and our sources tell us virtually nothing about them, but there can be no doubt that large numbers and a steady supply were involved, for there is no other way to explain such facts as the high proportion of Paphlagonians and Thracians among the slaves in the Attic silver mines, many of them specialists, or the corps of 300 Scythian archers (slaves owned by the state) who constituted the Athenian police force.

Merely to complete the picture, we must list penal servitude and the exposure of unwanted children. Beyond mere mention, however, they can be ignored because they were altogether negligible in their importance. There then remains one more source, breeding, and that is a puzzle. One reads in the modern literature that there was very little breeding of slaves (as distinct from helots and the like) among the Greeks because, under their conditions, it was cheaper to buy slaves than to raise them. I am not altogether satisfied with the evidence for this view, and I am altogether dissatisfied with the economics which is supposed to justify it. There were conditions under which breeding was certainly rare, but for reasons which have nothing to do with economics. In the mines, for example, nearly all the slaves were men, and that is the explanation, simply enough. But what about domestics, among whom the proportion of women was surely high? I must leave the question unanswered, except to remove one fallacy. It is sometimes said that there is a demographic law that no slave population ever reproduces itself, that they must always be replenished from outside. Such a law is a myth: that can be said categorically on the evidence of the southern states, evidence which is statistical and reliable.

The impression one gets is clearly that the majority of the slaves were foreigners. In a sense, they were all foreigners. That is to say, it was the rule (apart from debt-bondage) that Athenians were never kept as slaves in Athens, or Corinthians in Corinth. However, I am referring to the more basic sense, that the majority were not Greeks at all, but men and women from the races living outside the Greek world. It is idle to speculate about proportions here, but there cannot be any reasonable doubt about the majority. In some places, such as the Laurium silver mines in Attica, this meant relatively large concentrations in a small area. The number of Thracian slaves in Laurium in Xenophon's time, for example, was greater than the total population of some of the smaller Greek city-states.

No wonder some Greeks came to identify slaves and barbarians (a synonym for all non-Greeks). The most serious effort, so far as we know, to justify this view as part of the natural arrangement of things, will be found in the first book of Aristotle's *Politics*. It was not a successful effort for several reasons, of which the most obvious is the fact, as Aristotle himself conceded, that too many were slaves "by accident," by the chance of warfare or shipwreck or kidnapping. In the end, natural slavery was abandoned as a concept, defeated by the pragmatic view that slavery was a fact of life, a conventional institution universally practised. As the Roman jurist Florentinus phrased it, "Slavery is an institution of the *ius gentium* [law of nations] whereby someone is subject to the *dominium* of another, contrary to nature." That view (and even sharper formulations) can be traced back to the sophistic literature of the fifth century B.C., and, in a less formal way, to Greek tragedy. I chose Florentinus to quote instead because his definition appears in the *Digest*, in which slavery is so prominent that the Roman law of slavery has been called "the most characteristic part of the most characteristic intellectual product of Rome." Nothing illustrates more perfectly the inability of the ancient world to imagine that there could be a civilized society without slaves.

The Greek world was one of endless debate and challenge. Among the intellectuals, no belief or idea was self-evident: every conception and every institution sooner or later came under attack—religious beliefs, ethical values, political systems, aspects of the economy, even such bedrock institutions as the family and private property. Slavery, too, up to a point, but that point was invariably a good distance short of abolitionist proposals. Plato, who criticized society more radically than any other thinker, did not concern himself much with the question in the *Republic,* but even there he assumed the continuance of slavery. And in the *Laws,* "the number of passages . . . that deal with slavery is surprisingly large" and the tenor of the legislation is generally more severe than the actual law of Athens at that time. "Their effect, on the one hand, is to give greater authority to masters in the exercise of rule over slaves, and on the other hand to accentuate the distinction between slave and free man." Paradoxically, neither were the believers in the brotherhood of man (whether Cynic, Stoic, or early Christian) opponents of slavery. In their eyes, all material concerns, including status, were a matter of essential indifference. Diogenes, it is said, was once seized by pirates and taken to Crete to be sold. At the auction, he pointed to a certain Corinthian among the buyers and said: "Sell me to him; he needs a master."

The question must then be faced, how much relevance has all this for the majority of Greeks, for those who were neither philosophers nor wealthy men of leisure? What did the little man think about slavery? It is no answer to argue that we must not take "the political theorists of the philosophical schools too seriously as having established 'the main line of Greek thought concerning slavery.' " No one pretends that Plato and Aristotle speak for all Greeks. But, equally, no one should pretend that lower-class Greeks necessarily rejected everything which we read in Greek literature and philosophy, simply because, with virtually no exceptions, the poets and philosophers were men of the leisure class. The history of ideology and belief is not so simple. It is a commonplace that the little man shares the ideals and aspirations of his betters—in his dreams if not in the hard reality of his daily life. By and large, the vast majority in all periods of history have always taken the basic institutions of society for granted. Men do not, as a rule, ask themselves whether monogamous marriage or a police force or machine production is necessary to their way of life. They accept them as facts, as self-evident. Only when there is a challenge from one source or another—from outside or from catastrophic famine or plague—do such facts become questions.

A large section of the Greek population was always on the edge of marginal subsistence. They worked hard for their livelihood and could not look forward to economic advancement as a reward for their labours; on the contrary, if they moved at all, it was likely to be downward. Famines, plagues, wars, political struggles, all were a threat, and social crisis was a common enough phenomenon in Greek history. Yet through the centuries no ideology of labour appeared, nothing that can in any sense be counterpoised to the negative judgments with which the writings of the leisure class are filled. There was neither a

word in the Greek language with which to express the general notion
of "labour," nor the concept of labour "as a general social function."
There was plenty of grumbling, of course, and there was pride of
craftsmanship. Men could not survive psychologically without them.
But neither developed into a belief: grumbling was not turned into a
punishment for sin—"In the sweat of thy face shalt thou eat bread"—
nor pride of craftsmanship into the virtue of labour, into the doctrine
of the calling or anything comparable. The nearest to either will be
found in Hesiod's *Works and Days,* and in this context the decisive
fact about Hesiod is his unquestioning assumption that the farmer will
have proper slave labour.

That was all there was to the poor man's counter-ideology: we live
in the iron age when "men never rest from toil and sorrow by day,
and from perishing by night"; therefore it is better to toil than to idle
and perish—but if we can we too will turn to the labour of slaves.
Hesiod may not have been able, even in his imagination, to think
beyond slavery as *supplementary* to his own labour, but that was the
seventh century, still the early days of slavery. About 400 B.C., however,
Lysias' cripple could make the serious argument in the Athenian *boule*
[council] that he required a dole because he could not afford a slave as
a *replacement.* And half a century later Xenophon put forth a scheme
whereby every citizen could be maintained by the state, chiefly from
revenues to be derived from publicly owned slaves working in the
mines.

When talk turned to action, even when crisis turned into civil war
and revolution, slavery remained unchallenged. With absolute regularity, all through Greek history, the demand was "Cancel debts and
redistribute the land." Never, to my knowledge, do we hear a protest
from the free poor, not even in the deepest crises, against slave competition. There are no complaints—as there might well have been—that
slaves deprive free men of a livelihood, or compel free men to work
for lower wages and longer hours. There is nothing remotely resembling a workers' programme, no wage demands, no talk of working
conditions or government employment measures or the like. In a city
like Athens there was ample opportunity. The *demos* [popular
assembly] had power, enough of them were poor, and they had leaders.
But economic assistance took the form of pay for public office and for
rowing in the fleet, free admission to the theatre (the so-called theoric
fund), and various doles; while economic legislation was restricted to
imports and exports, weights and measures, price controls. Not even
the wildest of the accusations against the demagogues—and they were
wholly unrestrained as every reader of Aristophanes or Plato knows—
ever suggested anything which would hint at a working-class interest,
or an anti-slavery bias. No issue of free versus slave appears in this field
of public activity.

Nor did the free poor take the other possible tack of joining with the slaves in a common struggle on a principled basis. The Solonic revolution in Athens at the beginning of the sixth century B.C., for example, brought an end to debt-bondage and the return of Athenians who had been sold into slavery abroad, but not the emancipation of others, non-Athenians, who were in slavery in Athens. Centuries later, when the great wave of slave revolts came after 140 B.C., starting in the Roman west and spreading to the Greek east, the free poor on the whole simply stood apart. It was no issue of theirs, they seem to have thought; correctly so, for the outcome of the revolts promised them nothing one way or the other. Numbers of free men may have taken advantage of the chaos to enrich themselves personally, by looting or otherwise. Essentially that is what they did, when the opportunity arose, in a military campaign, nothing more. The slaves were, in a basic sense, irrelevant to their behaviour at that moment.

In 464 B.C. a great helot revolt broke out, and in 462 Athens dispatched a hoplite force under Cimon to help the Spartans suppress it. When the revolt ended, after nearly five years, a group of the rebels were permitted to escape, and it was Athens which provided them refuge, settling them in Naupactus. A comparable shift took place in the first phase of the Peloponnesian War. In 425 the Athenians seized Pylos, a harbour on the west coast of the Peloponnese. The garrison was a small one and Pylos was by no means an important port. Nevertheless, Sparta was so frightened that she soon sued for peace, because the Athenian foothold was a dangerous centre of infection, inviting desertion and eventual revolt among the Messenian helots. Athens finally agreed to peace in 421, and immediately afterwards concluded an alliance with Sparta, one of the terms of which was: "Should the slave-class rise in rebellion, the Athenians will assist the Lacedaemonians with all their might, according to their power."

Obviously the attitude of one city to the slaves of another lies largely outside our problem. Athens agreed to help suppress helots when she and Sparta were allies; she encouraged helot revolts when they were at war. That reflects elementary tactics, not a judgment about slavery. Much the same kind of distinction must be made in the instances, recurring in Spartan history, when helots were freed as pawns in an internal power struggle. So, too, of the instances which were apparently not uncommon in fourth-century Greece, but about which nothing concrete is known other than the clause in the agreement between Alexander and the Hellenic League, binding the members to guarantee that "there shall be no killing or banishment contrary to the laws of each city, no confiscation of property, no redistribution of land, no cancellation of debts, no freeing of slaves for purposes of revolution." These were mere tactics again. Slaves were resources, and they could be useful in a particular situation. But only a number of specific slaves, those who were available at the precise moment; not slaves in general, or all slaves, and surely not slaves in the future. Some slaves were freed, but slavery remained untouched. Exactly the same behaviour can be found in the reverse case, when a state (or ruling class) called upon its slaves to help protect it. Often enough in a military crisis, slaves were freed, conscripted into the army or navy, and called upon to fight. And again the result was that some slaves were freed while the institution continued exactly as before.

In sum, under certain conditions of crisis and tension the society (or a sector of it) was faced with a conflict within its system of values and beliefs. It was sometimes necessary, in the interest of national safety or of a political programme, to surrender the normal use of, and approach to, slaves. When this happened, the institution itself survived without any noticeable weakening. The fact that it happened is not without significance; it suggests that among the Greeks, even in Sparta, there was not that deep-rooted and often neurotic horror of the slaves known in some other societies, which would have made the freeing and arming of slaves en masse, for whatever purpose, a virtual impossibility. It suggests, further, something about the slaves themselves. Some did fight for their masters, and that is not unimportant.

Nothing is more elusive than the psychology of the slave. Even when, as in the American South, there seems to be a lot of material—auto-biographies of ex-slaves, impressions of travellers from non-slavehold-ing societies, and the like—no reliable picture emerges. For antiquity there is scarcely any evidence at all, and the bits are indirect and tangential, and far from easy to interpret. Thus, a favourite apology is to invoke the fact that, apart from very special instances as in Sparta, the record shows neither revolts of slaves nor a fear of uprisings. Even if the facts are granted—and the nature of our sources warrants a little scepticism—the rosy conclusion does not follow. Slaves have scarcely ever revolted, even in the southern states. A large-scale rebellion is impossible to organize and carry through except under very unusual circumstances. The right combination appeared but once in ancient history, during two generations of the late Roman Republic, when there were great concentrations of slaves in Italy and Sicily, many of them almost completely unattended and unguarded, many others professional fighters (gladiators), and when the whole society was in turmoil, with a very marked breakdown of social and moral values.

At this point it is necessary to recall that helots differed in certain key respects from chattel slaves. First, they had the necessary ties of soli-darity that come from kinship and nationhood, intensified by the fact, not to be underestimated, that they were not foreigners but a subject people working their own lands in a state of servitude. This complex was lacking among the slaves of the Greek world. The Peripatetic author of the *Oeconomica* made the sensible recommendation that neither an individual nor a city should have many slaves of the same nationality. Second, the helots had property rights of a kind: the law, at least, permitted them to retain everything they produced beyond the fixed deliveries to their masters. Third, they outnumbered the free population on a scale without parallel in other Greek communities. These are the peculiar factors, in my opinion, which explain the revolts of the helots and the persistent Spartan concern with the question, more than Spartan cruelty. It is a fallacy to think that the threat of rebellion increases automatically with an increase in misery and oppression. Hunger and torture destroy the spirit; at most they stimulate efforts at flight or other forms of purely individual behaviour (including betrayal of fellow-victims) , whereas revolt requires organization and courage and persistence. Frederick Douglass, who in 1855 wrote the most penetrating analysis to come from an ex-slave, summed up the psychology in these words:

"Beat and cuff your slave, keep him hungry and spiritless, and he will follow the chain of his master like a dog; but feed and clothe him well,—work him moderately—surround him with physical comfort,— and dreams of freedom intrude. Give him a *bad* master, and he aspires to a *good* master; give him a good master, and he wishes to become his *own* master."

There are many ways, other than revolt, in which slaves can protest. In particular they can flee, and though we have no figures whatsoever, it seems safe to say that the fugitive slave was a chronic and sufficiently numerous phenomenon in the Greek cities. Thucydides estimated that more than 20,000 Athenian slaves fled in the final decade of the Peloponnesian War. In this they were openly encouraged by the Spartan garrison established in Decelea, and Thucydides makes quite a point of the operation. Obviously he thought the harm to Athens was serious, intensified by the fact that many were skilled workers. My immediate concern is with the slaves themselves, not with Athens, and I should stress very heavily that so many skilled slaves (who must be presumed to have been, on the average, among the best treated) took the risk and tried to flee. The risk was no light one, at least for the barbarians among them: no Thracian or Carian wandering about the Greek countryside without credentials could be sure of what lay ahead in Boeotia or Thessaly. Indeed, there is a hint that these particular 20,000 and more may have been very badly treated after escaping under Spartan promise. A reliable fourth-century historian attributed the great Theban prosperity at the end of the fifth century to their having purchased very cheaply the slaves and other booty seized from the Athenians during the Spartan occupation of Decelea. Although there is no way to determine whether this is a reference to the 20,000, the suspicion is obvious. Ethics aside, there was no power, within or without the law, which could have prevented the re-enslavement of fugitive slaves even if they had been promised their freedom.

The *Oeconomica* sums up the life of the slave as consisting of three elements: work, punishment, and food. And there are more than enough floggings, and even tortures, in Greek literature, from one end to the other. Apart from psychological quirks (sadism and the like), flogging means simply that the slave, as slave, must be goaded into performing the function assigned to him. So, too, do the various incentive plans which were frequently adopted. The efficient, skilled, reliable slave could look forward to managerial status. In the cities, in particular, he could often achieve a curious sort of quasi-independence, living and working on his own, paying a kind of rental to his owner, and accumulating earnings with which, ultimately, to purchase his freedom. Manumission was, of course, the greatest incentive of all. Again we are baffled by the absence of numbers, but it is undisputed that manumission was a common phenomenon in most of the Greek world. This is an important difference between the Greek slave on the one hand, and the helot or American slave on the other. It is also important evidence about the degree of the slave's alleged "acceptance" of his status.

It is now time to try to add all this up and form some judgment about the institution. This would be difficult enough to do under ordinary circumstances; it has become almost impossible because of two extraneous factors imposed by modern society. The first is the confusion of the historical study with moral judgments about slavery. We condemn slavery, and we are embarrassed for the Greeks, whom we admire so much; therefore we tend either to underestimate its role in their life, or we ignore it altogether, hoping that somehow it will quietly go away. The second factor is more political, and it goes back at least to 1848, when the *Communist Manifesto* declared that "The history of all hitherto existing society is the history of class struggles. Free man and slave, patrician and plebeian, lord and serf, guild-master and journeyman, in a word, oppressor and oppressed, stood in constant opposition to one another. . . ." Ever since, ancient slavery has been a battleground between Marxists and non-Marxists, a political issue rather than a historical phenomenon.

Now we observe that a sizable fraction of the population of the Greek world consisted of slaves, or other kinds of dependent labour, many of them barbarians; that by and large the elite in each city-state were men of leisure, completely free from any preoccupation with economic matters, thanks to a labour force which they bought and sold, over whom they had extensive property rights, and, equally important, what we may call physical rights; that the condition of servitude was one which no man, woman, or child, regardless of status or wealth, could be sure to escape in case of war or some other unpredictable and uncontrollable emergency. It seems to me that, seeing all this, if we could emancipate ourselves from the despotism of extraneous moral, intellectual, and political pressures, we would conclude, without hesitation, that slavery was a basic element in Greek civilization.

Such a conclusion, however, should be the starting-point of analysis, not the end of an argument, as it is so often at present. Perhaps it would be best to avoid the word "basic" altogether, because it has been preempted as a technical term by the Marxist theory of history. Anyone else who uses it in such a question as the one which is the title of this paper, is compelled, by the intellectual (and political) situation in which we work, to qualify the term at once, to distinguish between *a* basic institution and *the* basic institution. In effect what has happened is that, in the guise of a discussion of ancient slavery, there has been a desultory discussion of Marxist theory, none of it, on either side, particularly illuminating about either Marxism or slavery. Neither our understanding of the historical process nor our knowledge of ancient society is significantly advanced by these repeated statements and counter-statements, affirmations and denials of the proposition, "Ancient society was based on slave labour." Nor have we gained much from the persistent debate about causes. Was slavery the cause of the decline of Greek science? or of loose sexual morality? or of the widespread contempt for gainful employment? These are essentially false questions, imposed by a naive kind of pseudo-scientific thinking.

The most fruitful approach, I suggest, is to think in terms of purpose, in Immanuel Kant's sense, or of function, as the social anthropologists use that concept. The question which is most promising for systematic investigation is not whether slavery was the basic element, or whether it caused this or that, but how it functioned. This eliminates the sterile attempts to decide which was historically prior, slavery or something else; it avoids imposing moral judgments on, and prior to, the historical analysis; and it should avoid the trap which I shall call the free-will error. There is a maxim of Emile Durkheim's that "The voluntary character of a practice or an institution should never be assumed beforehand." Given the existence of slavery—and it is given, for our sources do not permit us to go back to a stage in Greek history when it did not exist—the choice facing individual Greeks was socially and psychologically imposed. In the *Memorabilia* Xenophon says that "those who can do so buy slaves so that they may have fellow workers." That sentence is often quoted to prove that some Greeks owned no slaves, which needs no proof. It is much better cited to prove that *those who can,* buy slaves—Xenophon clearly places this whole phenomenon squarely in the realm of necessity.

The question of function permits no single answer. There are as many answers as there are contexts: function in relation to what? And when? And where? Buckland begins his work on the Roman law of slavery by noting that there "is scarcely a problem which can present itself, in any branch of law, the solution of which may not be affected by the fact that one of the parties to the transaction is a slave." That sums up the situation in its simplest, most naked form, and it is as correct a statement for Greek law as for Roman. Beyond that, I would argue, there is no problem or practice in any branch of Greek life which was not affected, in some fashion, by the fact that many people in that society, even if not in the specific situation under considera-tion, were (or had been) slaves. The connection was not always simple or direct, nor was the impact necessarily "bad" (or "good"). The his-torian's problem is precisely to uncover what the connections were, in all their concreteness and complexity, their goodness or badness or moral neutrality.

I think we will find that, more often than not, the institution of slavery turned out to be ambiguous in its function. Certainly the Greek attitudes to it were shot through with ambiguity, and not rarely with tension. To the Greeks, Nietzsche said, both labour and slavery were "a necessary disgrace, of which one feels *ashamed,* as a disgrace and as a necessity at the same time." There was a lot of discussion: that is clear from the literature which has survived, and it was neither easy nor unequivocally one-sided, even though it did not end in abolition-ism. In Roman law "slavery is the only case in which, in the extant sources . . . , a conflict is declared to exist between the *Ius Gentium* and the *Ius Naturale* [Natural Law]." In a sense, that was an academic conflict, since slavery went right on; but no society can carry such a conflict within it, around so important a set of beliefs and institutions, without the stresses erupting in some fashion, no matter how remote and extended the lines and connections may be from the original stimulus. Perhaps the most interesting sign among the Greeks can be found in the proposals, and to an extent the practice in the fourth century B.C., to give up the enslavement of Greeks. They all came to nought in the Hellenistic world, and I suggest that this one fact reveals much about Greek civilization after Alexander.

It is worth calling attention to two examples pregnant with ambi-guity, neither of which has received the attention it deserves. The first comes from Locris, the Greek colony in southern Italy, where descent was matrilineal, an anomaly which Aristotle explained historically. The reason, he said, was that the colony was originally founded by slaves and their children by free women. Timaeus wrote a violent protest against this insulting account, and Polybius, in turn, defended Aristotle in a long digression, of which unfortunately only fragments survive. One of his remarks is particularly worth quoting:

To suppose, with Timaeus, that it was unlikely that men, who had been the slaves of the allies of the Lacedaemonians, would continue the kindly feelings and adopt the friendships of their late masters is foolish. For when they have had the good fortune to recover their freedom, and a certain time has elapsed, men, who have been slaves, not only endeavour to adopt the friendships of their late masters, but also their ties of hospitality and blood; in fact, their aim is to keep them up even more than the ties of nature, for the express purpose of thereby wiping out the remembrance of their former degradation and humble position, because they wish to pose as the descendants of their masters rather than as their freedmen.

In the course of his polemic Timaeus had said that "it was not customary for the Greeks of early times to be served by bought slaves." This distinction, between slaves who were bought and slaves who were captured (or bred from captives), had severe moral overtones. Inevitably, as was their habit, the Greeks found a historical origin for the practice of buying slaves—in the island of Chios. The historian Theopompus, a native of the island, phrased it this way:

The Chians were the first of the Greeks, after the Thessalians and Lacedaemonians, who used slaves. But they did not acquire them in the same manner as the latter; for the Lacedaemonians and Thessalians will be found to have derived their slaves from the Greeks who formerly inhabited the territory which they now possess, . . . calling them helots and *penestae,* respectively. But the Chians possessed barbarian slaves, for whom they paid a price.

This quotation is preserved by Athenaeus, whose *floruit* [creative prime] was about 200 A.D. and who went on to comment that the Chians ultimately received divine punishment for their innovation. The stories he then tells, as evidence, are curious and interesting, but I cannot take time for them.

This is not very good history, but that does not make it any less important. By a remarkable coincidence Chios provides us with the earliest contemporary evidence of democratic institutions in the Greek world. In a Chian inscription dated, most probably, to the years 575–550 B.C., there is unmistakable reference to a popular council and to the "laws (or ordinances) of the *demos* [popular assembly]." I do not wish to assign any significance other than symbolic to this coincidence, but it is a symbol with enormous implications. I have already made the point that, the more advanced the Greek city-state, the more it will be found to have had true slavery rather than the "hybrid" types like helotage. More bluntly put, the cities in which individual freedom reached its highest expression—most obviously Athens—were cities in which chattel slavery flourished. The Greeks, it is well known, discovered both the idea of individual freedom and the institutional framework in which it could be realized.[4] The pre-Greek world—the world of the Sumerians, Babylonians, Egyptians, and Assyrians; and I cannot refrain from adding the Mycenaeans—was, in a very profound sense, a world without free men, in the sense in which the west has come to understand that concept. It was equally a world in which chattel slavery played no role of any consequence. That, too, was a Greek discovery. One aspect of Greek history, in short, is the advance, hand in hand, of freedom *and* slavery.

---

[4] It is hardly necessary to add that "freedom" is a term which, in the Greek context, was restricted to the members of the *koinonia* [enfranchised community], always a fraction, and often a minor fraction, of the total male population.

# Benjamin Farrington

## 2

# Greek Science

In the preceding chapters an effort has been made to think out afresh the meaning of the history of science in the ancient world, and especially in the formative period of Greek thought. The subject is difficult. Opinions on it differ. Our effort in this chapter will be to make as clear as we can what precisely are the lessons we see in it for the modern world.

In the first place, we claim that the human activity we call science did not originate as a mode of thinking about things in order to be able to give verbally satisfying answers on any question that may be raised, but as a mode of thinking about things so as to be able to manipulate them to desired ends. Scientific thought is distinguished from other modes of thought by being proved valid in action. Our opinion on this matter may be expressed in the words of a French writer whose work appears to have missed recognition in this country.

"At the same time as the religious idea," writes Félix Sartiaux, "but much more slowly, because it requires much greater effort, the idea of science separates itself out from the magico-mystical mentality of primitive man. By handling tools, by making objects for a predetermined end, man, in spite of his inclination to represent things in his own image, seizes distinctions, forms ideas of classes, observes relations which do not depend upon his imagination. He comes to see that things do not happen as the rites represent, that they do not behave in the manner of spirits. If he had kept to his magico-religious and his religious dreams, he could never have *done* anything. But in fact, from remotest times he really kills animals and soon domesticates them, he cultivates plants, he extracts metals from ores, he makes objects for ends which he sets before himself. These actions, whatever be the representations which accompany them, succeed. Accordingly, consciously or not, man grasps true relations and submits himself to them. The existence of techniques, which go right back to the palaeolithic age, shows that there exist in the most primitive thought traces of the scientific spirit."[1]

---

[1] *Morale Kantienne et Morale Humaine.* Paris, 1917, p. 254.

In the ancient civilizations of the Near East this scientific mode of thought hardly succeeded in extending itself beyond the sphere of the techniques themselves, but coexisted with a mythological interpretation of the universe. This mythological interpretation of the universe was developed and handed down in priestly corporations, and served very largely a political purpose. The technicians, whose practice contained the germ of science, were engaged in manipulating matter. The priests, on whose shoulders rested the maintenance of the social structure, were mainly occupied in controlling men. In particular the need to control men necessitated the maintenance of mythological interpretations of the major phenomena of nature—the motions of the heavenly bodies, the changes of the seasons, vegetation, irregularities or violences in nature.

The specific originality of the Ionian thinkers was that they applied to the interpretation of the motions of the heavenly bodies and all the major phenomena of nature modes of thought derived from their control of techniques. Fortunate political circumstances made it possible for them to do this. They represented a new element in society, a new class of manufacturers and merchants which brought a temporary peace and prosperity to communities worn out with the struggle between the landed aristocracy and dispossessed peasants. Being dominant in society, they made their mode of thought dominant. While feeling still secure in their possession of political power, they did not hesitate to ridicule the old mythological explanations of nature and attempt to substitute for them explanations of "the things above" derived from their practical experience of "the things below."

The economic basis of this way of looking at the world was introduced into Attica at the beginning of the sixth century by Solon. Solon was a merchant who was called upon to rescue Athens from a desperate *impasse* into which it had fallen in the course of the usual struggle between the landlords and the peasants. He provided an economic alternative to the land by the introduction of the industrial techniques, and tried to secure that every Athenian should teach his son a trade. Athens was an industrial and trading town in the centre of an agricultural area when it became a democracy.

"It is interesting to note," writes W. H. S. Jones, "that the arts were distinguished from the sciences only when Greek thought was past its zenith."[2] In the middle of the great fifth century, at the height of the Periclean Age, this distinction had not yet been made at Athens. This was the age when a working sculptor like Pheidias, or a working architect like Ictinus, were ornaments in the best society. This is the outlook which is reflected in the finest products of the literary art of the time.

---

2 Hippocrates (Loeb Library), IV, p. xxiii.

Aeschylus, for instance, writing just before the middle of the century, puts into the mouth of the fire-bringer Prometheus a splendidly imaginative account of the rôle of techniques in the development of human society. Man, he makes Prometheus say, was in the beginning as witless as a babe. He had eyes but could not see, ears but could not hear, and lived in a dream-world of illusion, until Prometheus planted in him mind and the gift of understanding. In what did the gift of understanding consist? In this, that whereas man had before lived like an insect in sunless subterranean caves without knowledge of brick-making or carpentry, he now lived in well-built houses facing the sun. Previously he could not anticipate the coming of winter, spring, or summer; now he had learned to read the stars, and had made himself a calendar. Previously he could neither reckon nor write; now he had a system of numerals and an alphabet. Previously he had had himself to toil as a beast of burden; now he had subdued wild animals to bear pack and harness. Previously he had not known how to cross the seas, cure himself when ill, or read the future; now he had linen sails, herbal remedies, and an art of divination. To crown all, he had brought up from their hiding place in earth those buried treasures, gold, silver, bronze, iron.[3] Such is the account of the growth of civilization given by Aeschylus. Plainly for him the conquest of the techniques is identical with the growth of intelligence. The idea of a science except as applied does not occur to him.

A few years later Sophocles, in a famous chorus of his *Antigone* (332ff.), again takes up the theme of the technical inventiveness of man. Wonders are many, he sings, but nothing is more wonderful than man. He is the power that crosses the white sea. He makes use of the storm-winds to bear him along under surges that threaten to engulf him. From year to year, the mule, the new strong animal he has bred from the horse, drags his ploughshares through the soil of Earth, oldest of the gods. In his toils, by his superior wit, he snares the birds, the beasts, the fishes of the deep. The shaggy-maned horse and the tireless mountain bull he tames and puts beneath the yoke. He has taught himself how to speak. He has taught himself how to think. He has taught himself the modes of civilized behaviour. He has made himself houses to escape the frost and the rain. For everything except death he has found a remedy. He can even cure disease. His technical ingenuity, though it brings him now to evil now to good, shows a wisdom which defies imagination.

These are but pedestrian paraphrases of the untranslatable poetry of these great tributes to the inventive genius of man, but they will serve to indicate their content. The list of man's achievements in Sophocles is much the same as that in Aeschylus, but whereas the

---

[3] Aeschylus, *Prometheus Bound*, 436ff.

exigencies of his plot compel Aeschylus to refer the invention of all the techniques to Prometheus, Sophocles openly states what, of course, Aeschylus does not intend to deny, that all these are the achievements of man himself. Such, of course, was the opinion of their contemporary, the philosopher Anaxagoras, also a resident in Periclean Athens, who taught that it was through the possession of a capable pair of hands that man became wise.

In the wreck of the ancient literature it is not easy to illustrate as abundantly as one could wish the method of the philosopher-scientists who saw in the techniques the clue to the understanding of the operations of nature. One treatise, however, . . . stressed the contribution made by the cook to the understanding of human nature and of nature in general. And, amid numerous other examples, we have seen the attempt of Empedocles to throw light on the relation of the external atmosphere and the movement of the blood in the human body by an experiment with the water-clock. This experiment also established the conclusion that the fundamental operations of nature, the interaction between the elements, take place on a level below the apprehension of our senses. It became a problem for the scientist to infer the hidden operations from observation of the visible ones.

There is extant another Hippocratic writing[4] which shows us how one scientist attempted to put this method into use. The treatise seems to be the work of the director of a gymnasium who lived about the end of the fifth century. His belief was that human nature was a blend of fire and water. His difficulty was that these elements, on which depend the vital activities of man, are, in their ultimate nature, like the air investigated by Empedocles, too subtle for man to perceive directly. How does he get over his difficulty? From internal evidence it is clear that he was a student of Heraclitus, of Empedocles, of Anaxagoras, in whose thought about the universe we have found many traces of the influence of techniques. As these cosmologists had used ideas derived from techniques to explain the nature of the universe, so our physician turns to techniques for his explanation of the nature of man. He talks a lot of nonsense in doing so, as his predecessors who employed the same method also did. But the point we are concerned with for the moment is the method, not the results.

First he enunciates his general principle. The invisible processes of human nature, he says, may be observed by attending to the visible processes of the techniques. Men miss this point, for they do not understand that the technical processes they consciously control are imitations of unconscious processes in man. The mind of the gods, he explains, has taught men to copy in their arts the functions of their

---

4 *Regimen*, I, chapters xi–xxiv.

bodies. Men understand the arts (*i.e.*, employ them successfully), but they fail to understand what the arts are copies of. They should realize that the arts are a clue to the obscure operations of nature.

Here it is important to consider what the writer means by "understanding." He does not mean the ability to give a verbal explanation. He means the ability to act consciously to achieve a desired end. He wants to act upon the human body with a view to promoting and preserving its health. He thinks he can derive hints from the already established arts for the new art of health he is trying to create. The arts to which he directs attention are those of the seer, the blacksmith, the fuller, the cobbler, the carpenter, the builder, the musician, the cook, the currier, the basket-maker, the goldsmith, the statuary, the potter, the scribe. His master idea seems to be that, if we act rightly in regard to the visible aspect of things, the invisible processes we desire will inevitably follow.

It is in this sense that he sees an analogy between certain physiological processes and seercraft. The seer, by observing the visible, *i.e.*, present events, is able to foretell the invisible, *i.e.*, future events. So a man and a woman by a present act of intercourse begin the process which results in the future in the birth of a baby. In the same way, he implies, we may hope to discover the course of present action which will result in future health.

He tries to get closer to answering this question by consideration of the manufacture of iron tools. In his view of things man is a mixture of fire and water, but fire and water are also constituent elements of steel. The smith, by blowing fire on iron, takes "nourishment" out of the iron, which becomes "rare" and pliable. He then beats it, welds it, and tempers it with water. The tempering with water is a way of putting the nourishment back. The same happens to a man when he is trained. His breath fans the fire in him which consumes the nourishment. When he has been made "rare" he is struck, rubbed, and purged. Then the application of water (*i.e.*, nourishment) makes him strong.

We shall not here follow out the analogies he draws between his regimen of health and the long list of other arts mentioned. They are fantastic enough, but it would be a mistake to regard them as devoid of all scientific value. Only those unfamiliar with the prodigious difficulty of the first steps in any science, and with the tentative and groping thoughts that accompany these steps, will fall into this error. Our author is proposing to *do* various things to men's bodies. His prescriptions of exercises, baths, massage, purgings, and dietings are far from useless. By comparison with other arts he tries to get a clearer understanding of what he is doing. But our main point here is not the value of the results but the nature of the method. The more fantastic the analogies between physiological processes and industrial techniques, the more significant is the fact that our author should have had recourse to this method. At a more primitive level he would have supposed the body to be the abode of spirits and would have prescribed accordingly. Now he thinks human physiology to be like the operations of the smith, cobbler, and potter, and prescribes accordingly. The primitive conception of nature has been transformed by the same force as had transformed primitive society itself, the practice of the techniques of production.

In the earlier period of Greek thought, then, when the sciences were not distinguished from the techniques, science was plainly a way of *doing* something. With Plato it became a way of *knowing*, which, in the absence of any practical test, meant only talking consistently. This new kind of "science," like its predecessor the technical mode of explanation, resulted from a change in the character of society. Historians of society are still disputing the precise degree to which the industrial techniques had, by Plato's time, passed into the hands of slaves. For our purpose it is not necessary to give a more precise answer to this question than to say that for Plato, and for Aristotle, the normal and desirable thing was that the citizen should be exempted from the burden of manual work and even from direct control of the workers. The kind of science they aimed at creating was a science for citizens who would not directly engage in the operational control of the physical environment. Their modes of explanation necessarily excluded ideas derived from the techniques. Their science consisted in being able to give the right answers to any questions that might be asked. The rightness of the answer mainly depended on its logical consistency. This was not all loss. The enormous advances that were made in mathematics largely through the encouragement of Plato and the influence of the Academy transformed the conception of the universe. Whereas the Ionians had such incorrect ideas of the sizes and distances of the heavenly bodies that their astronomy is not to be distinguished from meteorology, the mathematicians soon began to make it clear that our world is but a speck in a vast universe of space. Again, the Ionians, fertile in ideas, had but little developed the capacity to analyse their logical implications. A page of good Aristotelian logic can make their world of discourse seem as primitive as the mathematicians made their world of sun, moon, and stars. But, in spite of these advances in mathematics and logic, the separation of science from the fertilizing and controlling contact with techniques dealt it a crippling blow from which throughout the whole period of antiquity and the Middle Ages it failed to recover.

The new conception of science which came in with Plato and Aristotle demonstrably had its origin in the new form of society which rested on the division between citizen and slave. There is no aspect of Plato's thought which does not reflect a fundamental dichotomy derived from this division in society. In the developed theory of slavery the slave was not regarded as a rational being. The master alone was capable of reason, the slave might hold "correct opinion" if he strictly followed the directions of his master. This master-and-slave relation became fundamental for Plato's thought in every sphere.

First the political sphere. Here Plato conceives of the relation of ruler and ruled in terms of master and slave. He intends government to be for the good of the governed, but it does not require their consent. His golden men, the fully enlightened aristocrats who are to rule, are a small minority of the population. All the rest are in some degree slaves, whose only chance of doing good is to obey mechanically the commands of their superiors. The manual labourer if left to himself could not rule himself, he would be ruled by his appetites. Plato oddly conceived the main activities of the worker to be concentrated, not in his hands, but in his belly and his loins. Artisans are to stand to philosophers in the relation of slaves to masters. There is no difference between the art of the slave-owner and that of the king except the size of their respective establishments. This is the doctrine Plato preached in the city the basis of whose democratic life had been the implanting of the arts by Solon.

Plato's psychology, physiology, and ethics are all three made to conform to this master plan. In the State Plato had conceived of three classes—the Rulers, their Auxiliaries (the soldiers and police), and the Producers. The introduction of a third class does not involve any fundamental departure from the master-and-slave relationship, for the main function of the Auxiliaries is to secure the control of the Producers by the Rulers. On this analogy the soul is made to consist of three parts, the reason, the spirit, and the appetites—the reason corresponding to the rulers, the spirit to the police, and the appetites to the workers. Here we perceive the *social* significance of the rejection of the view of Anaxagoras, that the hand had been the chief instrument in the creation of intelligence. The workers are not embodiments of manual skill, but of *appetite*. Compare Plato with Aeschylus and Sophocles and realize the greatness of the change.

The physiological counterpart of this class-psychology is worked out in detail in the *Timaeus*. The head is separated from the trunk by the neck, because the divine part of the soul, which is located in the head, must be saved from pollution by the mortal part, which is situated in the trunk. Then the trunk itself is divided by the diaphragm, so that the womanish and servile elements in the soul may be lodged apart in the lower chamber, while the manly and spirited element is lodged above, "within earshot," as he says, "of the discourse" of reason which goes on in the head, so that it may combine with reason in suppressing any rebellion of the appetites. The ethical system which flowed from this psychology was harsh and puritanical. There is a sharp cleavage between soul and body. Soul stands to body in the relation of master to slave. The notion that the bodily sensations of pleasure and pain should be attended to by the mind as a basis for ethical action is viewed with the same suspicion as the political proposal that the mob should have a voice in the making of the laws.

To his interpretation of the system of the universe the same key was applied. Mind and matter stand opposed to one another as master and slave. If there is any regularity or beauty in Nature, it is because mind imposes order on matter, which is essentially disorderly. It follows that reason, not sense-evidence, is the true path to science. Reason brings us directly into contact with the mind which imposes order on matter. In the *phenomenal* world, with which the senses hold converse, this order is but imperfectly achieved.

This new view of the relation of mind and matter implies a radical departure from the first premiss of the older school of natural philosophers. The older view had been that there is a necessary order in the material world, and that the human mind grasps truth in so far as it grasps this necessary order. This order could only be apprehended by sense-evidence. To the interpretation of this evidence human experience in the exercise of techniques lent the necessary clue. For Plato, however, true science is teleological. It consists in interpreting phenomena in the light of the ends at which the Mind which strives to direct all things is presumed to aim. These ends are discovered, not by observation, but by reason. Not by trying to act upon nature but by argument about ends will the truth be discovered.

This strange new view of matter as a principle of disorder underlies also the philosophy of Aristotle. "Matter is made responsible for most irregularities," as one of the latest puzzled inquirers puts it,[5] noting at the same time that this involves a radical departure from the Ionian point of view. To the puzzle which he raises this inquirer can give no answer, nor is he likely to be able to do so while he continues to look in the wrong place. The clue to Aristotle's strange view of matter is not to be found in his physical treatises but in his *Politics*. As with Plato, the master-and-slave relation provides the basic pattern for his thought in every sphere.

Aristotle, as is well known, was a defender of slavery on the ground that slavery is natural. By calling it natural he meant, as a recent authority has reminded us, that "it follows a pattern that pervades all nature."[6] In Aristotle's own words: "In every composite thing, there is

[5] D. M. Balme, *Greek Science and Mechanism*, Cl. Q. xxxiii, p. 132.

[6] Gregory Vlastos, "Slavery in Plato's Thought," *Philosophical Review*, May 1941. This very valuable paper gives the references to Plato's text on which the argument of the preceding paragraphs rests.

always found a ruling and a subject factor, and this characteristic of living things is present in them as an outcome of the whole of nature."[7] One must not be put off here by the bad logic. It is difficult to suppose that Aristotle really regarded master and slave as forming a "composite thing." But all the logic of Aristotle's justification of slavery is bad. As Montesquieu long ago observed, "Aristotle undertakes to prove that slavery is natural and what he says does not prove it." What concerns us now is not his attempted justification of slavery, but the effect of the attempted justification on his science. Seeing the master-and-slave relation as a pattern that pervades all nature, he regards matter as being refractory, disorderly, and resistant, and Nature, or Mind, as imposing on matter the working out of definite ends. The attributes which Aristotle applies to matter are puzzling until one understands that they are the same attributes as he applies to the slave.

His famous fourfold theory of causation derives from this conception of the relation of Nature to matter. According to Aristotle, the earlier thinkers, the Ionian natural philosophers, had considered only the material cause and constituted thereby only a primitive, "stammering" kind of science. This was all that could be expected since they considered only the subject, slavish element in any product of Nature. Aristotle himself proposes to add three additional types of cause, the Efficient, the Formal, and the Final. These are the types of cause which explain how Nature imposes ends on refractory matter. This is Aristotle's dominant conception of science—the understanding of the way in which Nature, which resembles a Master in having ends at which it aims, imposes its will on matter, which sometimes resists those ends, and, like the slave, can achieve nothing except under the direction of a superior will. He even goes so far as to claim that the difficulty in distinguishing a natural slave from a natural master is due to a failure of Nature to impose her will on matter. Nature intends, he says, to produce a type of man who will be immediately recognizable as devoid of reason, "a living implement," but fails to do so because matter is refractory. Part of his art of politics is designed to make good this failure of Nature. When men are natural slaves and do not know it, it is, he says, the business of the natural masters to bring it home to them.

In an earlier chapter we saw how the importation of ideas from the politico-religious sphere had affected the development of astronomy. Here we have a further illustration of the same point. The older Ionian conception of an objective order in Nature had been derived from the necessity of conforming oneself to the regular behaviour of matter if one was to be successful in the performance of technical processes. It was not the orderly motion of the heavenly bodies that

---

[7] *Politics*, 1254a.

gave man his first idea of regularity in nature, but the experience, endlessly repeated, that things have their own ways of behaving—that you cannot gather figs of thistles, nor make the hardest bronze unless you put one portion of tin to ten of copper, nor get the octave higher unless you halve the string. The conception of Nature as infinitely various and ingenious but inexorable in its laws is the conception of technicians who attempt to exercise over matter an operational control. The new conception of Nature, as a power with ends in view, which enforces its will on a subordinate but refractory matter, is the conception of a master who governs slaves.

# II/THE END OF THE ROMAN EMPIRE IN THE WEST

A T its height in the second century A.D. the Roman Empire had grown from its point of origin around the Mediterranean (the "Mare Nostrum" of its contemporaries) to cover a substantial part of the known world. Roman hegemony was essentially unquestioned in England, France, Spain, North Africa, Constantinople, and the Middle East. For more than five hundred years Rome reigned supreme, but with increasing difficulty after the great crisis of the third century, which is generally taken as the first sign of its long-term decline. The centrifugal forces of class interest and local ambition were henceforth too strong to be dominated by the central state apparatus, which was eternally involved in assuring the urban food supply and in seeking sufficient revenue to maintain itself. It was this set of circumstances that lay Rome open to the repeated waves of barbarian attack from the middle of the fourth century which culminated in the deposition of the last emperor in 476 A.D. From that day to this, the question of the decline and fall of the Roman Empire has been a vexing one for all historians, the issue on which they have traditionally cut their eyeteeth.

Once upon a time, when history was past politics and the actions of individuals the cause of everything, it would have been possible to erect a memorial tablet to the Middle Ages with the legend: born 476—died 1453, the victim of barbarian conquest. For men to whom history was best viewed as a series of cyclical movements, there must have been some comfort in this formulation, since those same Middle Ages were also born, they reasoned, with barbarians acting as midwife. The barbarians were, indeed, in part responsible for the end of the political unit known as the Western

Roman Empire. A problem arises when the terms of the discussion are allowed to become obscure, and the Roman Empire is equated with the ancient world, the slave mode of production—or, even, civilization.

The traditional notion of decline and fall may be a pernicious one, if we are not careful to state our precise meaning. Rome fell, and the fall was consequent on a long period of internal troubles: economic difficulties, political discord, civil wars, and cultural crisis. But what was the operative cause? For the great Enlightenment historian Edward Gibbon, it was the progress of Christianity and the acceptance by the Romans of unreason and their entrance into the dark night of superstition. M. I. Rostovtzeff, a Russian émigré who taught for many years at Yale University and is generally considered one of the finest classical scholars of recent times, was certain that all else could be traced back to the gradual absorption of the upper classes by the lower, accompanied by an equally general lowering of standards. This was a nonracist but elitist variation on the thesis put forth by Tenney Frank, professor of ancient history at the Johns Hopkins University, that the decay was due to an infusion of non-Roman blood. For Rostovtzeff, the lesson for our time was clear when applied to postrevolutionary Russia: The traditional elites had there been replaced, with the result that the country had fallen into chaos and an economic crisis characterized by a turning "backward from the modern capitalist world to the primitive phase of house [that is, subsistence] economy." His thesis is an excellent example of the intrusion of contemporary concerns into historical study, but I would be the last to criticize him for that. Unfortunately, his opposition to the Bolshevik revolution made him suspicious of the political action of the masses, and he read back some of his fears into Roman history. If this does not necessarily invalidate his approach, it should at least warn us to be careful of the proffered explanations.

There is in the notion of decline or decadence as well a hidden assumption that a well-ordered society is one in which conflict is at a minimum. Essentially, the reasoning is: "Everything was going well, until. . . ." But from the radical point of view this will not do, because conflict is the fundamental rule of all social life. F. W. Walbank of the University of Liverpool tells us that the end of the Roman Empire in the West was a result of the "premises upon which classical civilization arose, namely an absolutely low technique and, to compensate for this, the institution of slavery." It may further be argued, as Elena M. Shtaerman of the Soviet Academy of Sciences does in the article reprinted here, that there comes a time when a given sociopolitical structure is no longer able to resolve the conflicts that arise within it and still continue to function. The disparity between the level of development of the productive forces and the social relations of production becomes too great. It is then that qualitative change must come about. This may take the form of revolution (that is, a change of ruling class), a reinforcement of established authority accompanied by abandonment of existing institutional structures, or conquest by some external enemy. If this is what is meant by decline and fall, well and good. It seems to me that "crisis" is a more appropriate term, and one that allows us to get a good deal closer to the heart of the matter.

The crisis of the Roman Empire was also, or rather, basically, the crisis of a social formation dominated by the slave mode of production, which, for diverse reasons, was unable to continue to support the weight of a bureaucratic state and a parasitic ruling class while also meeting the material needs of the population at large. As the ruling class would not abdicate and the oppressed classes were incapable of making a revolution, the crisis could only continue to deepen and, incidentally, to make Rome vulnerable to outside attack. The barbarian victories, when they came, did not so much resolve the crisis as negate it. By destroying the Roman state and forcing the Roman ruling class into a different role, the barbarians unblocked the process of change and made it possible for slavery gradually to disappear and to be replaced, after a long period of transition, by feudalism.

# M. I. Rostovtzeff

## 3

# The Decay of
# Ancient Civilization

From the social point of view . . . there was no levelling and no equalization. In the late Roman Empire society was subdivided not into classes, but into real castes, each as close as possible, in some cases because of the privileges connected with the caste, in others because of the burdens and hardships, which prevented anybody from desiring to be admitted and made membership hereditary and compulsory. Nor was there even equality in the common slavery to the state. There was indeed equality of a negative kind, for no political freedom was tolerated, no remnant of self-government was left, no freedom of speech, thought, or conscience was permitted, especially after the victory of Christianity; but even this equality of slavery was superficial and relative. The great landed proprietors were slaves of the emperor but masters of the tenant-serfs who lived on their estates. The *curiales* were slaves of the administration and were treated by it as such, but they were masters not only of the tenants of their estates, but also of the population of the city and the city territory, inasmuch as they apportioned and collected the taxes and supervised the compulsory work; and by these they were regarded and hated as masters who were themselves unfree and could not protect but only cheat their own slaves. Little wonder if these slaves appealed for protection to senators, officials, and soldiers, and were ready to pay any price for it and to deprive themselves of the little money and the little liberty which they still had. The working class of the cities stood in the same relation to the members of the various corporations, the owners of ships, shops, and factories. The last were in truth much more like minor supervisors of their own concerns on behalf of the state than their owners; they were themselves in bondage to the officials of the various departments and of the commanders of the various military units. Lastly, the officials and the soldiers of various ranks, though wielding an enormous power over thousands of men, were subjected to an iron discipline of a servile type and were practically slaves of each other and of the agents of the secret police.

General servitude was, indeed, the distinctive feature of the age, but while there were different grades and shades of bondage, there was no equality. Slavery and equality are incompatible, a fact which should not be forgotten by the many modern defenders of the principle of equality.

Above all, there was no equality whatsoever in the distribution of property. The senators, the knights, the municipal aristocracy, the petty *bourgeoisie* of the early Empire were, of course, ruined and degraded. Their patient and creative work, by which they had accumulated their fortunes and built up the civilized life of the cities, had disappeared for ever. But the old propertied classes were replaced by new ones, which even from the economic point of view were much worse than their predecessors. The fortunes of the early Empire were the result of the growing prosperity of the Empire in general. They were derived from commerce and industry, and the capital acquired was invested in land, improving its cultivation and the types of crop produced. The wars of the second century undermined these fortunes and retarded or even arrested economic development. Yet they did not work ruin, and a recovery under more normal conditions was possible. The catastrophe of the third century dealt a severe blow to the prosperity of the Empire and weakened the creative energies of the better part of the population. The reforms of Diocletian and Constantine, by giving permanence to the policy of organized robbery on the part of the state, made all productive economic activity impossible. But it did not stop the formation of large fortunes, rather it contributed to their formation, while altering their character. The foundation of the new fortunes was no longer the creative energy of men, nor the discovery and exploitation of new sources of wealth, nor the improvement and development of commercial, industrial, and agricultural enterprises; it was in the main the skilful use of a privileged position in the state to cheat and exploit the state and the people alike. Public officials, both high and low, grew rich on bribery and corruption. The senatorial class, being free from municipal burdens, invested their spoil in land and used their influence, the influence of their caste—which in this respect was more powerful than the emperors and nullified all their good intentions—to divert the burdens of taxation on to the other classes, to cheat the Treasury directly, and to enslave ever larger numbers of workmen. We cannot here discuss how and under what title they grabbed the large tracts of fertile land, both private and crown property. [They were] at work in Egypt in the third century. In the fourth they proceeded farther on the same path. Purchase, lease, patronage, lease without term, hereditary lease with the obligation to cultivate (*emphyteusis*) were all used to make the senatorial class the class of large landed proprietors *par excellence,* and to form vast estates scattered all over the provinces and resembling small principalities. Few of the members of the senatorial class lived in the capital or in the cities. The majority of them built large and beautiful fortified villas in the country and dwelt there, surrounded by their family, their slaves, a real retinue of armed clients, and thousands of rural serfs and dependants. We are well acquainted with their mode of life from the descriptions of Ausonius, Paulinus of Pella, Sidonius Apollinaris, and Salvian, from the numerous ruins of their villas, and from some mosaics which portrayed on their floors the beauty of their châteaux in town and country. The class was large and influential. Every successful "new" man tried hard to become a member of it, and many succeeded. They were good patriots, they possessed a genuine love of Rome and the Empire, they were faithful servants of the emperors, and they appreciated civilization and culture very highly. Their political outlook was narrow, their servility was unbounded. But their external appearance was majestic, and their grand air impressed even the barbarians who gradually became masters of the Empire. For the other classes they had neither sympathy nor understanding. They regarded them as far inferior beings, in this respect resembling the aristocracy of Rome in the first century B.C. and the first century A.D. The senators of the second century were not nearly so exclusive or so self-confident. Thus, more than ever before, society was divided into two classes: those who became steadily poorer and more destitute, and those who built up their prosperity on the spoils of the ruined Empire—real drones, who never made any contribution to economic life but lived on the toil and travail of other classes.

The social revolution of the third century, which destroyed the foundations of the economic, social, and intellectual life of the ancient world, could not produce any positive achievement. On the ruins of a prosperous and well-organized state, based on the age-old classical civilization and on the self-government of the cities, it built up a state which was based on general ignorance, on compulsion and violence, on slavery and servility, on bribery and dishonesty. Have we the right to accuse the emperors of the fourth century of having deliberately and of their own choice built up such a state, while they might have taken another path and have constructed, not the slave-state of the late Roman Empire, but one free from the mistakes of the early Empire and yet not enshrining the brutal practice of the revolutionary period? It is idle to ask such a question. The emperors of the fourth century, and above all Diocletian, grew up in the atmosphere of violence and compulsion. They never saw anything else, they never came across any other method. Their education was moderate, and their training exclusively military. They took their duties seriously, and they were animated by the sincerest love of their country. Their aim was to save the Roman Empire, and they achieved it. To this end they used, with the best intentions, the means which were familiar to them, violence and compulsion. They never asked whether it was worth while to save the Roman Empire in order to make it a vast prison for scores of millions of men.

Every reader of a volume devoted to the Roman Empire will expect the author to express his opinion on what is generally, since Gibbon, called the decline and fall of the Roman Empire, or rather of ancient civilization in general. I shall therefore briefly state my own view on this problem, after defining what I take the problem to be. The decline and fall of the Roman Empire, that is to say, of ancient civilization as a whole, has two aspects: the political, social, and economic on the one hand, and the intellectual and spiritual on the other. In the sphere of politics we witness a gradual barbarization of the Empire from within, especially in the West. The foreign, German, elements play the leading part both in the government and in the army, and settling in masses displace the Roman population, which disappears from the fields. A related phenomenon, which indeed was a necessary consequence of this barbarization from within, was the gradual disintegration of the Western Roman Empire; the ruling classes in the former Roman provinces were replaced first by Germans and Sarmatians, and later by Germans alone, either through peaceful penetration or by conquest. In the East we observe a gradual Orientalization of the Byzantine Empire, which leads ultimately to the establishment, on the ruins of the Roman Empire, of strong half-Oriental and purely Oriental states, the Caliphate of Arabia, and the Persian and Turkish empires. From the social and economic point of view, we mean by decline the gradual relapse of the ancient world to very primitive forms of economic life, into an almost pure "house-economy." The cities, which had created and sustained the higher forms of economic life, gradually decayed, and the majority of them practically disappeared from the face of the earth. A few, especially those that had been great centres of commerce and industry, still lingered on. The complicated and refined social system of the ancient Empire follows the same downward path and becomes reduced to its primitive elements: the King, his court and retinue, the big feudal landowners, the clergy, the mass of rural serfs, and small groups of artisans and merchants. Such is the political, social, and economic aspect of the problem.

From the intellectual and spiritual point of view the main phenomenon is the decline of ancient civilization, of the city civilization of the Greco-Roman world. The Oriental civilizations were more stable: blended with some elements of the Greek city civilization, they persisted and even witnessed a brilliant revival in the Caliphate of Arabia and in Persia, not to speak of India and China. Here again there are two aspects of the evolution. The first is the exhaustion of the creative forces of Greek civilization in the domains where its great triumphs had been achieved, in the exact sciences, in technique, in literature and art. The decline began as early as the second century B.C. There followed a temporary revival of creative forces in the cities of Italy, and later in those of the Eastern and Western provinces of the Empire. The progressive movement stopped almost completely in the second century A.D. and, after a period of stagnation, a steady and rapid decline set in again. Parallel to it, we notice a progressive weakening of the assimilative forces of Greco-Roman civilization. The cities no longer absorb—that is to say, no longer Hellenize or Romanize—the masses of the country population. The reverse is the case. The barbarism of the country begins to engulf the city population. Only small islands of civilized life are left, the senatorial aristocracy of the late Empire and the clergy; but both, save for a section of the clergy, are gradually swallowed up by the advancing tide of barbarism.

Another aspect of the same phenomenon is the development of a new mentality among the masses of the population. It was the mentality of the lower classes, based exclusively on religion and not only indifferent but hostile to the intellectual achievements of the higher classes. This new attitude of mind gradually dominates the upper classes, or at least the larger part of them. It is revealed by the spread among them of the various mystic religions, partly Oriental, partly Greek. The climax was reached in the triumph of Christianity. In this field the creative power of the ancient world was still alive, as is shown by such momentous achievements as the creation of the Christian church, the adaptation of Christian theology to the mental level of the higher classes, the creation of a powerful Christian literature and of a new Christian art. The new intellectual efforts aimed chiefly at influencing the mass of the population and therefore represented a lowering of the high standards of city civilization, at least from the point of view of literary forms.

We may say, then, that there is one prominent feature in the development of the ancient world during the imperial age, alike in the political, social, and economic and in the intellectual field. It is a gradual absorption of the higher classes by the lower, accompanied by a gradual levelling down of standards. This levelling was accomplished in many ways. There was a slow penetration of the lower classes into the higher, which were unable to assimilate the new elements. There were violent outbreaks of civil strife: the lead was taken by the Greek cities, and there followed the civil war of the first century B.C. which involved the whole civilized world. In these struggles the upper classes and the city civilization remained victorious on the whole. Two centuries later, a new outbreak of civil war ended in the victory of the lower classes and dealt a mortal blow to the Greco-Roman civilization of the cities. Finally, that civilization was completely engulfed by the inflow of barbarous elements from outside, partly by penetration, partly by conquest, and in its dying condition it was unable to assimilate even a small part of them.

The main problem, therefore, which we have to solve is this. Why was the city civilization of Greece and Italy unable to assimilate the masses, why did it remain a civilization of the *elite*, why was it incapable of creating conditions which should secure for the ancient world a continuous, uninterrupted movement along the same path which our modern world is traversing again? Various explanations have been suggested, and each of them claims to have finally solved the problem. Let us then review the most important of them. They may be divided into four classes.

(1) The political solution is advocated by many distinguished scholars. For Beloch the decay of ancient civilization was caused by the absorption of the Greek city-states by the Roman Empire, by the formation of a world-state which prevented the creative forces of Greece from developing and consolidating the great achievements of civilized life. There is some truth in this view. It is evident that the creation of the Roman Empire was a step forward in the process of levelling, and that it facilitated the final absorption of the higher classes. We must, however, take into consideration that class war was a common feature of Greek life, and that we have not the least justification for supposing that the Greek city-community would have found a solution of the social and economic problems which produced civil war in the various communities. Further, this view suggests that there was only one creative race in the ancient world, which is notoriously false. Another explanation, tending in the same direction, has been put forward by Kornemann. He regards as the main cause of the decay of the Roman Empire the fact that Augustus reduced the armed forces of the Empire, and that this reduction was maintained by his successors. The suggestion lays the whole emphasis on the military side of the problem, and is therefore a return to the antiquated idea that ancient civilization was destroyed by the barbarian invasions, an idea which was dropped long ago by the best scholars and cannot be resuscitated. Besides, the maintenance of a comparatively small army was imperatively imposed by the economic weakness of the Empire, a fact which was understood by all the emperors. Still less convincing is the idea of Ferrero, that the collapse of the Empire was due to a disastrous event, to an accident which had the gravest consequences. He holds that by transmitting his power to his son Commodus instead of to a man chosen by the senate, M. Aurelius undermined the senate's authority on which the whole fabric of the Roman state rested; that the murder of Commodus led to the usurpation of Septimius and to the civil war of the third century; and that the usurpation and the war destroyed the authority of the senate and deprived the imperial

power of its only legitimacy in the eyes of the population which was its main support. Ferrero forgets that legally the power of the emperors in the third century was still derived from the senate and people of Rome, that it was so even in the time of Diocletian, and that the same idea still survived under Constantine and his successors. He also forgets that the subtle formula of Augustus, Vespasian, and the Antonines was incomprehensible to the mass of the people of the Empire, and was a creation of the upper classes, completely outside the range of popular conceptions. Finally, he fails to understand the true character of the crisis of the third century. The struggle was not between the senate and the emperor, but between the cities and the army—that is to say, the masses of peasants—as is shown by the fact that the lead in the fight was taken not by Rome but by the cities of the province of Africa. A deeper explanation is offered by Heitland. He suggests that the ancient world decayed because it was unable to give the masses a share in the government, and even gradually restricted the numbers of those who participated in the life of the state, ultimately reducing them to the emperor himself, his court, and the imperial bureaucracy. I regard this point as only one aspect of the great phenomenon which I have described above. Have we the right to suppose that the emperors would not have tried the plan of representative government if they had known of it and believed in it? They tried many other plans and failed. If the idea of representative government was foreign to the ancient world (and as a matter of fact it was not), why did the ancient world not evolve the idea, which is not a very difficult one? Moreover, the question arises, Can we be sure that representative government is the cause of the brilliant development of our civilization and not one of its aspects, just as was the Greek city-state? Have we the slightest reason to believe that modern democracy is a guarantee of continuous and uninterrupted progress, and is capable of preventing civil war from breaking out under the fostering influence of hatred and envy? Let us not forget that the most modern political and social theories suggest that democracy is an antiquated institution, that it is rotten and corrupt, being the offspring of capitalism, and that the only just form of government is the dictatorship of the proletariate. Did not the peasants of the Roman Empire act subconsciously on the same principle?

(2) The economic explanation of the decay of the ancient world must be rejected completely. . . . The Marxians forget that the ancient world went through many cycles of evolution, and that in these cycles there occur long periods of progress and other long periods of return to more primitive conditions, to the phase of economic life which is generally described as "house-economy." It is true that the ancient world never reached the economic stage in which we live, the stage of industrial capitalism. But in the history of the ancient world we have

many epochs of high economic development: certain periods in the
history of many Oriental monarchies, particularly Egypt, Babylonia
and Persia; the age of the highest development of the city-states, especially the fourth century B.C.; the period of the Hellenistic monarchies,
where the climax was reached in the third century B.C.; the period of
the late Roman Republic and of the early Roman Empire. All these
periods show different aspects of economic life and different aspects
of capitalism. In none of them did the forms of house-economy prevail. We may compare the economic aspect of life during these periods
to that of many European countries in the time of the Renaissance
and later, although in no case would the comparison be perfect, as
there is no identity between the economic development of the modern
and that of the ancient world. According to the different economic
conditions of these several periods in the history of the ancient world,
the relations between house-economy and capitalistic economy varied,
and they frequently varied not only in the different periods but also
in different parts of the ancient world during the same period. The
ancient world was in this respect not unlike the modern world. In the
industrial countries of Europe, such as England and some parts of
Germany and France, economic life nowadays is by no means the
same as it is in the agricultural countries, like Russia and the Balkan
peninsula and large parts of the Near East. The economic life of the
United States of America is not in the least identical with the economic
life of Europe or of the various parts of South America, not to speak
of China, Japan, and India. So it was in the ancient world. While
Egypt and Babylonia had a complex economic life, with a highly
developed industry and wide commercial relations, other parts of the
Near East lived a quite different and much more primitive life. While
Athens, Corinth, Rhodes, Syracuse, Tyre, and Sidon in the fourth
century B.C. were centres of a developed commercial capitalism, other
Greek cities lived an almost purely agricultural life. In the Hellenistic
and Roman periods it was just the same. The main fact which has to
be explained is why capitalistic development, which started at many
times and in many places, and prevailed in large portions of the
ancient world for comparatively long periods, yielded ultimately to
more primitive forms of economic life. Even in our own times it has
not completely ousted those forms. It is evident that the problem cannot be solved by affirming that the ancient world lived throughout
under the forms of primitive house-economy. The statement is manifestly wrong. We might say exactly the same of large areas of the
modern world, and we are not at all sure that a violent catastrophe
might not bring the modern capitalistic world back to the primitive
phase of house-economy, as has happened in Russia since the Bolshevik
revolution.

To sum up what I have said, the economic simplification of ancient life was not the cause of what we call the decline of the ancient world, but one of the aspects of the more general phenomenon which I am trying to explain. Here, just as in the other spheres of human life, the political, social, intellectual, and religious, the more primitive forms of life among the masses were not absorbed by the higher forms but triumphed over them in the end. We may select one of these phenomena and declare it to be the ultimate cause; but it would be an arbitrary assumption which would not convince any one. The problem remains. Why was the victorious advance of capitalism stopped? Why was machinery not invented? Why were the business systems not perfected? Why were the primal forces of primitive economy not overcome? They were gradually disappearing; why did they not disappear completely? To say that they were quantitatively stronger than in our own times does not help us to explain the main phenomenon. That is why many economists, who are aware that the usual explanation only touches the surface and does not probe the problem to the bottom, endeavour to save the economic explanation, and the materialistic conception of historical evolution in general, by producing some potent physical factor as the cause of the weakness of the higher forms of economic life in the ancient world. Such a factor has been found by some scholars in the general exhaustion of the soil all over the ancient world, which reached its climax in the late Roman Empire and ruined the ancient world. I have dealt with this theory [previously]. There are no facts to support it. All the facts about the economic development of the ancient world speak against it. Agriculture decayed in the ancient world just in the same way and from the same causes as the other branches of economic life. As soon as the political and social conditions improved in the various parts of the Empire, the fields and gardens began to yield the same harvests as before. Witness the flourishing state of Gaul in the time of Ausonius and of Sidonius Apollinaris; witness the fact that in Egypt, where the soil is inexhaustible and those parts of it which are not flooded are very easily improved by the most primitive methods, agriculture decayed in the third and fourth centuries, just as in the other provinces. It is plain that the economic explanation does not help us, and that the investigations of the economists reveal, not the cause of the decline of the ancient world, but merely one of its aspects.

(3) The rapid progress of medicine and of biological science has had its influence on the problem of the decay of ancient civilization. A biological solution has been often suggested, and the theories of degeneration and race-suicide have been applied to the ancient world. The biological theory supplies us with an apparently exhaustive explanation of the decline of the assimilative forces of the civilized upper classes. They gradually degenerated and had not the power to assimilate the lower classes but were absorbed by them. According

to Seeck, the cause of their degeneration and of their numerical decline was the "extermination of the best" by foreign and civil wars. Others, like Tenney Frank, think of the contamination of higher races by an admixture of the blood of inferior races. Others, again, regard degeneration as a natural process common to all civilized communities: the best are neither exterminated nor contaminated, but they commit systematic suicide by not reproducing and by letting the inferior type of mankind breed freely. I am not competent to sit in judgement on the problem of degeneration from the biological and physiological point of view. From the historical point of view, I venture to remark against Seeck that in wars and revolutions it is not only the best that are exterminated. On the other hand, revolutions do not always prevent the succeeding period from being a period of great bloom. Against Frank I may suggest that I see no criterion for distinguishing between inferior and superior races. Why are the Greek and Latin races considered the only superior races in the Roman Empire? Some of the races which "contaminated" the ruling races, for instance, the pre-Indo-European and pre-Semitic race or races of the Mediterranean, had created great civilizations in the past (the Egyptian, the Minoan, the Iberian, the Etruscan, the civilizations of Asia Minor), and the same is true of the Semitic and of the Iranian civilizations. Why did the admixture of the blood of these races contaminate and deteriorate the blood of the Greeks and the Romans? On the other hand, the Celts and the Germans belonged to the same stock as the Greeks and the Romans. The Celts had a high material civilization of their own. The Germans were destined to develop a high civilized life in the future. Why did the admixture of their blood corrupt and not regenerate their fellow Aryans, the Greeks and the Romans? The theory of a natural decay of civilization by race-suicide states the same general phenomenon of which we have been speaking, the gradual absorption of the upper classes by the lower and the lack of assimilative power shown by the upper. It states the fact, but gives no explanation. The problem this theory has to solve is, Why do the best not reproduce their kind? It may be solved in different ways: we may suggest an economic, or a physiological, or a psychological explanation. But none of these explanations is convincing.

(4) Christianity is very often made responsible for the decay of ancient civilization. This is, of course, a very narrow point of view. Christianity is but one side of the general change in the mentality of the ancient world. Can we say that this change is the ultimate cause of the decay of ancient civilization? It is not easy to discriminate between causes and symptoms, and one of the urgent tasks in the field of ancient history is a further investigation of this change of mentality. The change, no doubt, was one of the most potent factors in the gradual decay of the civilization of the city-state and in the rise of a

new conception of the world and of a new civilization. But how are we to explain the change? Is it a problem of individual and mass psychology?

None of the existing theories fully explains the problem of the decay of ancient civilization, if we can apply the word "decay" to the complex phenomenon which I have endeavoured to describe. Each of them, however, has contributed much to the clearing of the ground, and has helped us to perceive that the main phenomenon which underlies the process of decline is the gradual absorption of the educated classes by the masses and the consequent simplification of all the functions of political, social, economic, and intellectual life, which we call the barbarization of the ancient world.

The evolution of the ancient world has a lesson and a warning for us. Our civilization will not last unless it be a civilization not of one class, but of the masses. The Oriental civilizations were more stable and lasting than the Greco-Roman, because, being chiefly based on religion, they were nearer to the masses. Another lesson is that violent attempts at levelling have never helped to uplift the masses. They have destroyed the upper classes, and resulted in accelerating the process of barbarization. But the ultimate problem remains like a ghost, ever present and unlaid: Is it possible to extend a higher civilization to the lower classes without debasing its standard and diluting its quality to the vanishing point? Is not every civilization bound to decay as soon as it begins to penetrate the masses?

# F. W. Walbank

## 4

## The Causes of Decline

To Gibbon the decline of Rome was something so natural as to require no explanation.

The story of its ruin is simple and obvious: and instead of enquiring why the Roman Empire was destroyed we should rather be surprised that it had subsisted for so long. . . . The stupendous fabric yielded to the pressure of its own weight.[1]

Today that answer would no longer appear adequate. The stupendous fabric sinking beneath its own weight is after all a metaphor. The Roman Empire was not a building, but a state; and a phrase such as "the pressure of its own weight" acquires meaning only when translated into a detailed analysis of various social and economic trends and forces within the Empire.

But in one respect Gibbon's formulation was one of fundamental importance; quite simply and unequivocally it broke with all cyclical, mystical-biological and metaphysical theories of decline, and stated clearly the "naturalistic" view. The cause of decay was to be sought inside the system itself; it was not something transcendental or apocalyptic, the fulfilment of a prophecy, or a link in a sequence, fated to recur throughout eternity; nor was it something fortuitous, like the barbarian attacks (though, as we saw, these were by no means entirely fortuitous), or an error of judgement on the part of one or other of the Emperors or their respective assassins. To Gibbon the cause is something inherent, natural, and proportionate to the effect produced. This view has been amply confirmed by our own analysis. For this has shown that the Roman Empire declined not because of any one feature—the climate, the soil, the health of the population—nor indeed because of any one of those social and political factors which played so important a part in the actual process of decay, but because at a certain point it was subjected to stresses which the whole structure

---

[1] E. Gibbon, *Decline and Fall of the Roman Empire,* Vol. IV, ed. J. B. Bury, 1897, p. 161; appendix following ch. 38.

of ancient society had rendered it unable to withstand. In fact this society was divided by contradictions which are first apparent, not in A.D. 200, nor yet when Augustus Caesar first set up the Principate in 27 B.C., but as early as the fifth and fourth centuries B.C., when Athens revealed her inability to keep and broaden the middle-class democracy she had created. The failure of Athens epitomised the failure of the City-State. Built on a foundation of slave labour, or on the exploitation of non-privileged groups—sometimes a peasantry, depressed or even reduced to serfdom, sometimes the subjects of a short-lived empire— the City-State yielded a brilliant minority civilization. But from the start it was top-heavy. Through no fault of its citizens, but as a result of the time and place when it arose, it was supported by an inadequate level of technique. To say this is to repeat a truism. The paradoxical contrast between the spiritual achievements of Athens and her scanty material goods has long been held up to the admiration of generations who have found that a rich material inheritance does not automatically ensure a corresponding richness of cultural life. But it was precisely this low level of technique, relative to the tasks Greek and Roman society set itself, that made it impossible even to consider dispensing with slavery and led to its extension from the harmless sphere of domestic labour to the mines and workshops, where it grew stronger as the tensions in society grew more acute.

It is not always easy to distinguish cause from effect, when confronted with a closely-knit texture of interacting factors. But briefly it may be said that the Greeks of the City-State, burdened by poverty and subjected to the constant frictions of a frontier large in proportion to the city's area, were by tradition and necessity aggressive and predatory; their strong feeling for autonomy tended, on every opportunity, to slide over insensibly into a claim to dominate others. This led to wars, which in turn took their place among the many sources of fresh slaves. Slavery grew, and as it invaded the various branches of production it led inevitably to the damping down of scientific interest, to the cleavage, already mentioned, between the classes that used their hands and the superior class that used—and was later to cease using—its mind. This ideological cleavage thus reflects a genuine separation of the community into classes; and henceforward it becomes the supreme task of even the wisest sons of the City-State—a Plato and an Aristotle—to maintain this class society, at whatever cost.

That cost was heavy. It says much for the singlemindedness of Plato that he was willing to meet it. In the *Laws*, his last attempt to plan the just city, he produces a blue-print for implanting beliefs and attitudes convenient to authority through the medium of suggestion, by a strict and ruthless censorship, the substitution of myths and emotional ceremonies for factual knowledge, the isolation of the citizen from the outside world, the creation of types with standardized reactions, and, as a final guarantee, by the sanctions of the police-state, to be invoked against all who cannot or will not conform. It is not without reason that a French scholar, writing in 1947, characterized the later Roman Empire with "its allegorising metaphysics, its clerical morality, its liturgical art, its threats of an inquisition, and its instruction by means of catechism, all heralding the approach of the glorious centuries of the middle ages" as "the triumph of Plato."[2]

For this, and no less, was the intellectual and spiritual fruit of this tree, whose roots had split upon the hard rock of technical inadequacy. Materially, increasing slavery made it all but certain that new productive forces would not be released on a scale sufficient for a radical transformation of society. Extremes of wealth and poverty became more marked, the internal market flagged, and ancient society suffered a decline in production, trade and population and, finally, the wastage of class warfare. Into this sequence the rise of the Roman Empire brought the new factor of a parasitical capital; and it spread the Hellenistic system to Italy, where agrarian pauperism went side by side with imperial expansion and domination on an unparalleled scale. In the oligarchic Rome of the senatorial regime, with its intrigues of noble houses for political power, as the gateway to prestige and wealth, a healthy development of productive forces and the deepening of cultural life was an even more remote possibility than it had been amid the turmoil of the city-state democracy or in the capitals of the Hellenistic kingdoms.

From the attempt to control and govern a political unit the size of Augustus's empire on the basis of this relatively backward material equipment arose the typical developments of the social life of the Empire—industrial dispersion, recourse to a partly natural economy within the fiscal system, continuous pressure from the court and army, and a shift of influence from the towns to the countryside—and the final attempt to retrieve the crisis, or at least to salvage whatever could be salvaged from the ruins, by the growing use of compulsion and the machinery of the bureaucratic State. These tendencies we have already analysed [in a previous chapter], and need not repeat them here. Nor should we fall into the error of imagining that each one was inevitable in its particular place and at its particular time. Human skill and weakness played their part in postponing or accelerating the process of decay. The important point however is that the factors we have described fall together into a sequence with its own logic, and that they follow—not of course in the specific details, which were determined by a thousand personal or fortuitous factors, but in their general outlines—from the premises upon which classical civilization

[2] A. Piganiol, *L'Empire chrétien,* p. 401.

arose, namely an absolutely low technique and, to compensate for this, the institution of slavery. It is in these phenomena and, what is equally important, in the mental climate which they induced that we must seek the primary causes of the decline and fall of the Roman Empire.

To this view, which may seem to smack of determinism, as if it were robbing man of the right to make his own history—though in fact it merely defines the conditions within which he is free to act—the objection may be raised: *Why* was there no alternative? *Why* was the process outlined above inevitable? Why could the western Empire not have survived as did Byzantium? To take the last point first, there was, as we have said, no reason compelling the western Empire to founder *there and then*. But if we consider the Empire as it existed at the time of Augustus, and the gradual shift in emphasis from the west to the east, culminating in the final split after the reign of Theodosius (A.D. 379–95), it becomes clear that the survival of the eastern Empire really represents the saving of one part at the expense of the other; indeed the very strength of Constantinople diverted barbarian attacks to the west. It was a rump of the original which survived within the eastern provinces, as a result of the factors already discussed [in a previous chapter]: and though its survival is itself a tribute to the efforts of the third century emperors and to the reorganization of Diocletian and Constantine, a rump it remained. When, after the lapse of several centuries, the next great step forward in European history was taken, it came, as we saw, from the west and not Constantinople. Thus the survival of Byzantium—a part of the Empire—cannot be adduced as a sound reason for thinking that the whole might have been saved.

In fact, as more than one scholar has seen, the only way in which the west might have been preserved and enabled to advance to new achievements was by a radical change in the technical level, including communications, and a consequent transformation of the social structure. How could such a change have been effected? A little reflection will suggest two possibilities and two only. First, the upper classes might have been persuaded to abandon their privileged position, pay higher wages to the artisans, reduce the burden on the peasantry, develop technique and abolish slavery. Alternatively, the depressed classes might have seized power by a violent revolution and carried through the technical changes themselves. What chances did these two methods offer?

As regards the first, there are several valid objections to the paying of higher wages as a solution to a crisis of underconsumption under a system of free enterprise and low productivity, such as characterized the early Empire. But this is a point on which we need not linger here, since the whole history of the ruling class of the Graeco-Roman world rules out the possibility that it could for one moment have contemplated its own abdication. The thesis has only to be stated for its absurdity to become apparent. Slavery, as Aristotle, Plato, and every merchant and landowner in the ancient world knew, was natural and vital to civilization. This view not even the Christians cared to question. Like the Stoics before them they regarded all men as equally free, or equally slaves; and the issue was not one on which they ventured to challenge authority. The early Christian *Didache*, recovered only towards the end of the last century, recommends slaves to submit to their masters as to the images of God; and slaves were not to be admitted to holy orders. Thus, although individual Christians denied the right of man to enslave his fellows, in this they went beyond the teaching of the Church. It is true that manumission continued to ease the fortunes of the slave, despite legal restrictions dating back to Augustus. But by the fourth century the problem had begun to change its character with the gradual depression of other sections of society to the level of the slave. In any case by then the fatal harm was done. For centuries men's minds had been shaped by the conviction that slavery could in no circumstances be relinquished. At this first step they stuck. For the existence of slavery made all other things—improved communications and higher forms of technique—seem superfluous.

What then of the other alternative? In one sense it was a practical issue, and a serious one, throughout Hellenistic times and the last two centuries of the Roman Republic. Social revolution was a powerful dynamic in third-century Sparta, and we know of slave risings in Pergamum, Attica, Macedon, Delos, Sicily and Italy itself, where the forces of Spartacus held the Roman legions at bay for two years (73–71 B.C.). All over the Mediterranean world the misery of the city masses united with the sufferings of the peasants to bring about spasmodic risings, which were put down with the brutality which springs from fear. From one such movement, on which was ingrafted the passion of an intensely patriotic racial minority, was born the last struggle of the Jewish people; conceived within the matrix of this struggle, with its stresses and fanatical belief in the coming kingdom, there was born the new religion of the poor and oppressed—Christianity. Two centuries later, wide-spread popular distress gave rise to similar movements of revolt. As we saw, for over a hundred years dating from the third century the Bagaudae maintained themselves in Armorica and Spain; and in north Africa, during the fourth and fifth centuries, the landless Circumcelliones, under their chieftains, the "leaders of the saints," formed a similar movement with a religious basis—the Donatist schism —encouraging slaves to desert and terrifying the wealthier sections of the people.

On their side, the ruling classes, Greek or Roman, took every possible step to protect themselves and society. Plato had spoken[3] of cities divided as if between two armies watching each other; and his contemporary, Aeneas, who wrote on military tactics (4th century B.C.), urged the setting up of security bands from among the reliable citizens, who had most to lose from social revolution, as a defence against the mercenaries who might (as they did a century later at Carthage) run amok among their employers.[4]

But the depressed sections of society never succeeded in making any real headway, except when some member of the ruling class—an imperialist king like Cleomenes III of Sparta (c. 235–222 B.C.) or the Roman demagogues of the late Republic—exploited them for his own ends. In fact, the material basis of ancient culture was inadequate for the consolidation of such a revolution, even if it could have succeeded; success must have meant chaos, and the end of the classical heritage. Indeed, even granting for argument's sake that the oppressed classes could anywhere have seized power and held it, there is no reason to think that they would have aimed at a more equalitarian form of society; the whole of classical history renders it infinitely more likely that they would merely have attempted to reverse places with their late oppressors. In any case, success was never a possibility. The lower classes were nowhere sufficiently united to make the sustained effort necessary for so gigantic a task as the expropriation of their rulers. The very existence of slavery thrust a wedge between the free artisan and the slave; and there was another cleft between the relatively prosperous domestic slave and the gangs who lived their miserable, short and brutish lives in the mines, and on the plantations and ranches. Hence the possibility of a radical change in the structure of ancient society by either of the methods we have envisaged appears extremely remote. Heitland, indeed, seems nearer the truth, when he attributes[5] the downfall of Rome to the "Roman Fate"—using the phrase not in any metaphysical sense, but to sum up a chain of social and economic factors, which followed one upon another down to the final disintegration.

---

[3] Plato, *Republic*, viii, 6. 551 d.

[4] Aeneas Tacticus, i, 6; xii; xiii.

[5] See W. E. Heitland's three pamphlets: *The Roman Fate; Iterum;* and *Last Words on the Roman Municipalities* (Cambridge: 1922, 1925 and 1928 respectively).

# Elena M. Shtaerman

---

# 5

# The Fall of
the Slave Regime

From what moment can one speak of a general crisis of the slaveholding regime, of a radical violation of the correlation between the productive forces and the relations of production which had become impossible to resolve within the framework of the slaveholding society. . . . How, in general, did the development of productive forces occur?

In the slaveholding society, the improvement of the instruments of production and the development of new techniques were very slow; the more slave labor supplanted free labor, the slower they became. That is why the development of the productive forces took place principally because of improvements in the methods of production and in practical experience.

However, one should not believe that the techniques of agriculture, an essential branch of production, did not develop at all. The most important advances were the invention, in the middle of the first century B.C., of the plow with wheels, colter, and blade, adapted to the working of heavy ground; the introduction of the harrow and special methods for speeding up the harvest; and the improvement of presses for wine and oil, etc. But these changes were made in the provinces of Rhaetia and Gaul where there was still a large number of free peasants; from there they spread to the slaveholders' estates. While on one hand the description of the equipment on the slaveholder's villa (or country property) remains almost unchanged from one century to the next, people did learn to take better care of the crops and animals; specialization in labor developed. This specialization was due not only to the adaptation of individual farms and entire regions to the production of a certain type of agricultural product but also to the division of labor inside the domain. . . . Specialization was combined with simple cooperation, which favored the growth of the work yield. . . . Naturally, cooperation based on slavery was less efficient than cooperation among wage earners, since the slaves were generally not interested in the results of their work. But nevertheless the slave system was effective to a certain degree. First, it made it possible to do more difficult work (clearing of land, draining of swamps, planting of olive trees, etc.). Second, it allowed the pooling of a "mass of labor . . . at critical times in the area of production." The union of the workers in a single agricultural enterprise also played a large role, which Marx presents as one of the principal advantages of cooperative over individual labor; however, in the conditions of slavery, this had more importance in saving labor than in reducing the cost of production (which was not the aim of the slaveholding economy). Thus, in a property of the villa type, a certain number of artisans worked for the slaves; a single cook prepared the food for everyone; a single nurse raised the children of the slaves, etc. On a small farm, all this work had to be done by the farmer himself and by his family. The amount of equipment could be less on a single farm than on several smaller ones which, taken together, were of the same size. It was possible to organize subsidiary tasks: elementary workshops, colonies of bees, saltworks, hunting, etc. Finally, the concentration of a certain number of slaves in a villa made possible a more or less advanced specialization, which improved the labor practices and the experience of the workers; the small landowner, however, was obliged to work in all the branches of his enterprise himself and could not be sufficiently specialized in any of them. It is characteristic in this period that all the progressive treatises on agriculture were designed for slaveholders' country properties of average size, where the more time went on, the more specialization was supposed to advance.

These conditions could not be brought about in all areas of agriculture, as for example with small landowners who specialized in the raising of vegetables, flowers, or fruits, in regions where there could be a demand for these products in an urban market. Although this activity brought them a certain revenue, it drew them into commercial production, and this, sooner or later, led a great many of them into debt and ruin. In the regions far from trading centers the small proprietors farmed their land in a primitive way, sometimes using two or three slaves, sometimes depending on mutual aid (at least this is the way we probably should interpret the aid of neighbors mentioned in the sources; this type is probably linked to survivals of communal agriculture). Here the primitive patriarchic relationships were preserved much longer and the growth of productive forces was much slower because there was neither specialization nor cooperation. These backward methods are to be found also on the latifundia (large landed estates) at the end of the Republican period. There the slaves were employed mostly as shepherds on the great grazing lands, whereas the farmers on the whole were clients, debtors, or tenant farmers who had held on since the decay of the early regime of primitive community and patriarchic slavery. The combination of extensive stock-raising and small-scale agriculture on the great estates hindered the development of productive forces; and only the partial division of the latifundia in the imperial period, both in Italy and in the provinces, opened the way toward later progress.

The most rational economy, for the conditions of the slaveholding regime, was brought about in those slaveholders' country villas or properties possessing several hundred acres of land and several dozen slaves. The extent of the country villa then made possible a simple form of cooperation and solved the problem of supervision, so difficult in a slave regime. This kind of villa was more stable and less dependent on the market than was the small farm; moreover, it could specialize in the production of one kind of product (flax, wine, olives, birds, wool, etc.), which increased the skill of the workers, rendered the property more profitable, and drew the villa into production for the market.

In any region of the Roman world, the growth and ultimate extent of these villas, and of the slaveholders' workshops which corresponded to them in the area of craftsmanship, represented the highest evolution of the system of slaveholding production for that region, its optimum conditions of existence; the relations of production corresponded completely to the level of development of the productive forces. This refers to that period in the history of the slaveholding regime in which, according to Marx, "the action of commerce and the development of trading capital leads . . . to the simple transformation of the system of patriarchic slavery, oriented toward the production of direct means of subsistence, into a system oriented toward the production of a surplus"; it found its most complete expression in the period between the first century B.C. and the second century A.D. One can explain by just this correspondence (between the relations of production and the level of development of the productive forces) the general improvement in the economy which characterizes this period in most of the regions of the empire: new lands are cleared, an irrigation system developed, new crops introduced, crafts improved and new craft centers developed; there is construction of new villas, public buildings, cities, communication routes; cultural and commercial relations are strengthened.

On the political level, these conditions gave the municipal regime its greatest extension, as it did to the *municipii* [free towns], which under the empire had lost the independence of the *polis*, but remained nevertheless a collectivity of landowners and slaveholders. On the ideological level, this greatest expansion of the slaveholding regime was accompanied by the maximum diffusion of Greco-Roman civilization, both material and spiritual.

Thus, it seems, the full development of the slaveholding regime presupposed these conditions: a preponderance of villas whose size permitted the effective supervision of the slaves and where a specialization in different branches could permit the improvement of work habits; the total detachment of the worker from the means of production and his direct and exclusive attachment to the person of the slaveholder, who decided the place of the slave in the organization of his property and who had an absolute power over him—power without which it would have been impossible to force a slave deprived of motivation to work. That is why the essential unit of the slaveholding society was the family, whose chief had the right of life and death over all its members. The slave whom the master could not "buy, sell, kill like livestock" and who, although he had not the right to property, possessed some means of production, was no longer a slave in the absolute sense of that term. Other methods were needed in order to force him to work, to draw a surplus from him. It was as if that slave had escaped from the general economic system of the villa and from the cooperation and the division of labor which had been created there. It is not without reason that the slave established on land, with the rights of a settler (quasi colonus), was not included in the concept of property which the Roman jurists elaborated. . . .

The condition that was essential for the maintenance of this system of slavery was a sufficient level of development in the relationship of goods and money, since the proprietor of a specialized villa had to sell his products and buy what he lacked. It was also necessary to preserve the municipal regime without which, in a collectivity of free men, the conflicts between possessors and non-possessors would grow acute. It was possible to restrain these two groups only by having them participate, more or less truly, in sharing the total surplus extorted by the slave masters from the slaves.

These conditions were threatened during the second half of the second century A.D.: in the greater part of the Roman empire, this was the beginning of the crisis for the slaveholding regime. The slave mode of production could spread, reach new regions, and be perfected internally until it reached the optimum conditions studied above; but these conditions could not be maintained for long because extended reproduction [accumulation of capital] was insignificant and simple reproduction [replacement of goods used] itself diminished little by little. Marx and Engels have stressed over and over again the conservatism of technology in the slaveholding world; they have shown that the preservation of the old method of production was the condition for the existence of its principal classes, because otherwise there would be the destruction of society, of the city, of the collectivity of landowners and slaveholders, all of which were essential to the existence of slave property. . . .

The surplus production was little used for an extended reproduction, precisely because of this technological conservatism. By way of illustration, let us remember that Roman jurists had difficulty in agreeing on the following question: has a husband the right to make certain expenditures in order to improve the working of his wife's property; is that not a way of wasting the assets which are entrusted to him? Finally, the cases where such expenses were deemed necessary or useful were set forth. Considered "necessary" were repairs for the villa, the replacement of dead olive trees and fruit trees, the building of bakehouses and granaries, the preparation of nursery gardens, the enlarging of vineyards, and the care of slaves who were ill; activities considered "useful" were the planting of new trees, the acquisition of livestock for the manuring of the fields, the organization of a shop or a workshop (*taberna*) near the house, and the apprentice training of the slaves. As can be seen, this list is relatively modest. It does not include either the purchase of new tools or new slaves, or the acquisition of new land. It is oriented toward a certain very limited intensification of the economy inside the estate and toward the improvement of the production practices of the workers, and not toward the growth of the economy as a whole.

In reality, the growth of an estate beyond the optimum proportion between the number of slaves and the surface of land devoted to one culture or another had disadvantages. It is not without reason that as a rule the estate with its buildings, farm and livestock (*fundus cum instrumento*) remained a whole which was not broken up, either by the division of property among the heirs or by the acquisition of new and similar agricultural units. . . .

Moreover, it must not be forgotten that an enormous proportion of the surplus value was spent in an unproductive way. The largest part was used to accumulate either treasure (which, as Marx has shown, was one of the characteristic signs of the economy of precapitalist societies) or luxuries. But the essential point is this: as the slave regime expanded, the number of people who broke from their old way of living and were transformed into the proletarians increased, a greater share of surplus value was spent for the upkeep of the parasitic part of society, and the exploitation of the productive part of society was accentuated.

Although the first and second centuries A.D. did not see slave revolts as did the last centuries of the Republic, the class contradictions and the class struggle continued in fact to grow worse. The masters' fear of the slaves became much greater than in the preceding period. . . . This fear had forced the government to promulgate laws that limited the power of the head of the family, which was a blow to one of the principal conditions for the management of the slaveholders' properties.

This struggle by the slaves was relatively inconspicuous, but it occurred constantly, under various forms (escapes, destruction of equipment, the murder of proprietors, robbery), and its results must not be underestimated. The fact that the legal situation of the slaves remained unchanged must not lead us into error. While the general principles remained the same, the exceptions which were gradually introduced rendered them practically meaningless. Thus, for example, it remained forbidden for slaves to testify against masters, but this testimony was accepted if the master was contemplating treason, if he was deceiving the revenue authorities by hiding his income, if he broke the laws on adultery, if he tried to deceive a creditor, a joint heir or someone with whom he had business relations, if he delayed illegally the emancipation of a slave, or if he treated a slave brutally. It is difficult to imagine a case where the testimony of a slave was still refused.

The same thing was true of other relationships; practice went further than legal theory. Extracting one concession after another, the slaves obtained, at the end of the second century A.D. and early third, an effective modification of their situation. The master could not kill the slave nor cast him into a workhouse for offenders. The serious crimes of a slave were not punished by the master but by magistrates. In cases where a master treated his slave cruelly, did not assure his support, and did not give him free time in order that he might earn his living, the slave took refuge in the imperial statutes and applied to a magistrate, who was supposed to examine the case and transfer the slave to another master if the accusation was confirmed. When freedom had once been given, even under the simplified form called *inter amicos,* it could not be taken away. And it was prescribed that cases concerning emancipation should be settled, as much as possible, by the liberation of the slave, setting aside all obstacles raised by the master. Although the marriages of slaves were not recognized by law, the families of the slaves were in fact included in the undivided inventory of the property, and it was considered that the master could not separate them. Although the tenures of the slave remained legally the property of the master, they had in practice become, as it were, a *quasi patrimonium* property. Usually this *peculium* or small property was not sold without the slave, nor the slave without his *peculium.* The debt of the master to the slave was recognized where previously it had been squarely denied, and it was now included as part of his property.

It does not follow from this that Rostovtzeff, Westermann, and the other bourgeois historians are correct when they try to prove that slavery was replaced by the work of free men. The dominant form of exploitation became the dependent worker furnished with minimum means of production (who was consequently no longer a slave in the full meaning of the term), rather than the free wage-earner or farmer.

This change was conditioned not only by economic reasons but also by the struggle of the slaves, which was incessant although unorganized. The concessions that they wrung by this struggle were a crushing blow to the system of slave labor and to the whole structure of the society that it determined. During this period the slaves were the principal force in the class struggle. By changing their class nature, they combined with the mass of subjugated settlers and peasants who then participated in the struggle to destroy all the survivals of slavery.

It is also very important that the growth of market relationships, which at first stimulated the development of slavery, soon began to favor its decline. Marx has shown that at the level where the productive social force of labor was at that time, attempts to convert into liquid revenue, at least the part of the income which was collected in the form of state taxes, were inevitably doomed to fail. They led only to the growth of usury, which rapidly brought great economic harm to the majority and led to the concentration of land and manpower in the hands of a minority.

The effect of the development of commerce worked in the same direction; the owners of the villas, who were not able to produce there everything that was necessary for themselves and their slaves and who also needed money to pay the taxes and meet the expenses linked to municipal office, were obliged to begin to trade. One can suppose, moreover, that the profits they drew from trade were limited in some measure by the attempts made at price control by the government and certain cities, before and after the edict of Diocletian. . . .

The destructive role of market relationships was made manifest by the ruin of the owners of medium-sized villas who constituted the order of the decurions. Some of them freed the slaves they could no longer maintain and became small proprietors, cultivating themselves their parcel of land. Others turned over their land to their creditor as payment for their debts and became its insecure tenants. Others became farmers on private or imperial lands. Still others, having freed their slaves, were maintained by their freedmen obliged to take care of the employers who were down and out. Some fell themselves into slavery. The others lived however they could, struggling to obtain privileges that would liberate them from holding municipal offices. These posts had been sought formerly, when they were not only honorary but lucrative, because they offered the possibility of growing rich through the management of municipal lands. But these offices had gradually become burdensome because, as the number of decurions decreased, the share of expenses that fell to each one increased, while the municipal lands, in spite of the efforts of the emperors to prevent it, passed into the hands of private individuals. The small group of very rich landowners, who concentrated the property of the ruined landowners in their hands, were the only ones to obtain profits. But

they struggled also to detach their holdings from the municipal territory and to break off in that way from the towns. The decline of the
towns as collectivities of slaveholders, which thus brought about the
ruin of the decurion order, was the direct consequence of the decline
of the slaveholding regime; it was a striking symptom of it. As with
the decline of the family, expressed in the laws mentioned above as
limiting the power of the head of the house, the decline of the towns
undermined the social bases of the slaveholding regime and accentuated its contradictions. One of the consequences of this process was
the reinforcement of the state apparatus. This reinforcement is
explained largely by the fact that the "functions of repression," directed
against slaves and poor freemen, passed now from the heads of households and the municipal magistrates to the central government exclusively. But the strengthening of the state and the growth of the state
apparatus led to increased taxes and fees, which hastened the ruin of
the taxpayers and accentuated the processes which were destroying the
slaveholding regime.

Its destruction was all the more rapid since the slave system had
succeeded in breaking up the other forms of property. That is why the
crisis developed with particular violence in the western provinces. It
is significant, for example, that from the middle of the second century
A.D. the number of senators from the western provinces, who were
recruited in the upper classes of the towns, diminished enormously.

In the western half of the empire, the concentration of the land and
manpower gave rise to new methods of farming, different from those
of the slaveholding regime. As was said earlier, when an agricultural
estate had gone beyond a certain size it could no longer be based on
slavery in its classic form. The existence of great slaveholding plantations was impossible for many reasons. First of all, they could not be
profitable except on condition of producing for the market, and this
market was threatened by the increasing breakup of small- and middle-
sized farms and the consequent reversion of the economy to a natural
state. Second, the slaveholding plantations could be maintained only
by using the most pitiless methods to force the slaves to work, and
these methods were already forbidden out of fear of a slave resistance.
There were specialized farms kept up on the latifundia, but these
posed insurmountable difficulties in organizing supervision, which
was, according to Marx, particularly complicated in the slaveholding
kind of enterprise. Thus, on the great domains, although one could,
because of the great number of slaves, more easily maintain highly
qualified artisans (horticulturists, aviculturists, and other auxiliary
workers), one could not apply there the methods which made the
medium-sized farms more advanced than the small ones. On the
latifundia there could not exist either a simple cooperation or the

division of labor which is closely linked to it. The development of productive forces could only follow a new way, namely that of creating in the worker a motivation to work, by giving him some means of production and reserving for him a certain part of the surplus product. In itself, this was radically contrary to the fundamental principles of the slaveholding mode of production. . . .

At the end of the second century a process begins which is directly opposed to the one that developed in the time of the growth of slavery; formerly, the producer was detached from the means of production and linked directly to the owner of those means of production, who owned him and governed him absolutely. Now this link becomes indirect, through the indissoluble unity of the worker with the means of production—the cultivator (slave or farmer) with the land and live-stock, the artisan with the workshop, etc. The old family, a group of people without property rights and subject to the absolute power of its head (who was the only proprietor and enjoyed all rights), is replaced by the domain, a group of workers with the means of produc-tion that are inseparable from them, and at its head the owner of these means of production, who now possesses only a limited power over the people who depend on him. The limitation of his power, as compared to that of the head of a family, was shown by the fact that he did not have the right of life and death over them; later, he no longer had the right to sell or transfer them without the means of production. This was established first by the practice according to which a slave, in case of transmission by legacy, for example, remained on the property where he was assigned and was not deprived of his small personal possessions (his *peculium*); later, this practice was fixed by a series of laws. In the fourth century, the sale of peasant slaves outside the limits of the province was forbidden, and then the sale of colons and peasant slaves without land.

The latifundia of this period knew very different conditions from those on the villas. The dimensions of the villa were necessarily limited; the latifundia could spread in unlimited fashion, always annexing new land and new workers. This expansion even favored their prosperity because, if the villas were linked to the market, the latifundia, on the contrary, were fairly self-contained; the more lands and workers they included, the easier it was to organize exchanges within the whole. The products sold inside the domain to the farmers and the owners themselves were not subject to the taxes on trade. The artisans who belonged to the master of the latifundia made everything that was necessary for him and his farmers. . . . The latifundia with-drew for the most part from the general circulation of trade, and the exchanges that occurred inside them escaped from the control of the state and took place under more advantageous conditions. When the master of the villa increased the number of his slaves, he also increased the expenses for their maintenance; when the owners of the latifundia, on the contrary, acquired new dependent workers, they increased only their revenues, drawn from the rent that these people paid them. That is why we observe a fact that at first seems contradictory: while some of the landed proprietors struggle to get rid of their lands which no longer bring in revenue, others feverishly lay hold of land. The first are proprietors of villas, the second of latifundia.

To yield profits, the latifundia had to have a sufficient number of workers: in the early third century one of the most characteristic facts is the struggle for manpower. In order to obtain it, the magnates resorted to all possible measures: they bought and installed on their land prisoners and freemen who had sold themselves as slaves; they took on prisoners as settlers and enticed away the settlers of others (imperial troops or private individuals); they brought settlers and peasants under their patronage, and settled on their domain their insolvent debtors. The proprietor who was hopelessly in debt turned over to them his parcel of land and then received it as a leasehold; the peasant who was in debt paid the debt by his labor on the land of the creditor; the settler in debt could not leave the land as long as he or his descendants had not paid his debt, which usually did not diminish but, on the contrary, grew constantly larger.

In the West, the economy rapidly became "natural" because the buying power of the population had greatly diminished. The proprietors of villas, who were the principal suppliers and buyers of agricultural and handcrafted products, were increasingly strained and tried to limit their expenses. The settlers and the great landowners generally satisfied themselves with exchanges inside the domain. The European peoples outside the empire had organized their own production and did not need Roman imports, which greatly diminished. The devaluation of coins, caused by the government which needed money, ruined the confidence of the population in wealth founded on money. That is clearly expressed in the edict of Constantine which forbade guardians to sell anything whatever of the property of children. This edict says: "Money, in which the ancients saw all the strength of property, is unstable, uncertain, and often reduces all goods to nothing." In the West, this obliged people to make all payments in kind and no longer in money. To keep up his own farm management the master, who on the land reserved to him directed his enterprise in a more perfected and varied manner than was possible on the small farms, was obliged to add to the rent paid in kind a fee that was paid by forced labor (corvée). But as Marx and Lenin have shown many times, the preponderance of fees paid in kind and by the corvée led inevitably to the attaching of the cultivator to the land and caused the formation of a closed peasant class that was deprived of rights.

Thus, in the western empire, the latifundia were directly opposed

to the slaveholding villas; the villas were a part of the municipal territory (and consequently the property of the master was limited by that
of the town), while the latifundia were independent territories where
property rights were limited only by the state. But the main difference
was that the villas were linked to the slaveholding mode of economic
management, while the latifundia were linked to the feudal mode.

Surely the proprietors of the villas made attempts to adapt themselves to the new conditions, all the more so since for a long time the
renting of the worst land had no longer been practiced. They switched
their slaves to a system of tenures, hired them out, freed some of them,
and rented others; but the changeover to new methods of exploitation
meant a transformation that very few of them could bear. It is true
that in the case of the great landowner the debts of the farmers (slaves
or freemen) led only to the strengthening of his power over them,
while, on the contrary, they ruined the average or small landowner.
He did not have enough means to enslave, by means of debts, the free
workers; instead he built up debts himself. Even after having divided
his lands and allotted them to his slaves and settlers, he could not
break the links with the market because he could not satisfy all his
needs within his small property, nor maintain for himself and his
people a number of qualified artisans. As before, he needed money to
pay the municipal dues, which became constantly more oppressive, and
he could not receive money from either his slaves, his settlers, or his
debtors. Finally, he could not protect those who depended on him
against the tax collectors, soldiers, etc., and this drew people to the
lands of the powerful magnates.

That is why, in the western provinces, the towns declined as soon
as the slaveholding villas collapsed, because the owners of these slave
villas constituted the basis of the towns. If we again consider that in
the West, except in Africa, the imperial domains which were opposed
to the latifundia were relatively small, we understand why the decay
in the slaveholding society's relationships and the birth of feudal
relationships followed the most direct route. The slaveholding villas
were supplanted by the latifundia which were being feudalized; by
breaking up and by annexing new elements, the orders of slaves and
of slave masters were being supplanted by orders of great landowners
and dependent cultivators. In order to found the feudal state, nothing
remained but to sweep away the slaveholding state and the survivals of
slaveholding property which limited the rights of the settlers over
their farm buildings, implements, and livestock, and over a part of
the products of their labor.

The turning point has been called "the crisis of the third century";
this crisis was the expression of struggles between (1) the landed aristocracy in the process of feudalization, which represented the new

mode of production, and the social groups linked to the decaying mode of slaveholding production and to slaveholders' property (the order of the decurions and the army), and (2) the direct producers, who were fused into a single mass of dependent cultivators and reduced to serfdom, and the dominant classes. At this period began the great offensive against Rome by peoples outside the empire, acting further as allies of the great masses but beginning already to be used by the landed aristocracy and other anti-Roman groups. Thus, for example, the Gallic emperors call for the German cavalry, and the Egyptian "usurpers" conclude an alliance with some Ethiopian chiefs, one of whom was even recognized as emperor of southern Egypt. These classes and groups took part in the struggle in all parts of the empire, but their situation and their programs differed according to the general situation in their particular province.

The third century crisis ended with the defeat of the former slave-holding groups. Economically, the slave was replaced by the colons; politically, the empire which represented the large block of slave-holders was replaced by an empire that had become the organ of the great landowners. Constantine legalized the attaching of colons to the land, an attachment that was indispensable for the new methods of agriculture; but he struck a severe blow to the towns, by increasing the responsibility and the dues of the curial assemblymen as well as by sanctioning the differentiations within that order by incorporating its leaders into the privileged order of senators. This was especially important for the Orient, where the great landowners broke away from the curial assembly after having obtained the absolute possession of their lands and inhabitants, and this accelerated the development of feudal relationships, previously checked by the municipal organization.

The usual definition of the government of Constantine as a reaction in favor of the slaveholders completely obscures its true meaning. . . . Constantine's measures had an aim that was quite the opposite. It was at that precise moment that private property finally triumphed over public property, which in this case no longer meant municipal but imperial property, maintained in the East and more and more decadent; even this imperial property was passing gradually into the hands of the imperial householders and the great leaseholders of the landed aristocracy. The government of Constantine was not a reaction for slaveholding but the consecration of the victory of the new class which dominated from the economic point of view—the class of great landowners who exploited the direct producer, the latter possessing means of production and no longer attached to a master but to the land, that is to say, no longer a slave. The state of Constantine was the organ of power for that class, which used it to struggle as much against decadent social groups as against the revolutionary movements of the masses. It is this nature of Constantine's empire, and not the fact that it was a slaveholding reaction, which explains its relative strength and its temporary success, since the state that it created was necessary initially to maintain the new dominant class.

From the time of Constantine onward, one can no longer affirm without reservation that the slaveholding society existed as such. Rather, one can see this period as the beginning of the feudal regime. It was filled with the struggle against the survivals of slavery: the property rights of the colon over his means of production were more limited than those of the feudal peasant, which from the legal point of view brought the settler close to the slave and perpetuated the scorn of work; a parasitic "lumpen-proletariat" in the East laid claim to a part of the surplus product; also in the East a certain number of imperial lands were maintained which had not yet passed to individuals; finally, the bureaucratic state little by little became useless for the ruling class, especially in the West, and weighed heavily on the direct producer. These survivals were destroyed by the revolutionary movements of the masses and by the foreign conquests. The revolutionary movements were temporarily crushed at the end of the third century, and the pressure on all categories of the exploited population was reinforced. From the middle of the fourth century, the revolutionary movements began again with growing force. At the same time the pressure of the barbarians redoubled. However, even the victory of both these forces did not lead to an immediate end of the survivals of slavery. This became possible only after several successive waves of·barbarian conquests and after the rebirth of the primitive commune on the territory of the empire, following the settlement there of Germanic and Slavonic tribes. As has been said above, a contradiction appears here: the new ruling class profited by the result of these movements. This class had been, up to a certain point, in the same camp as the class antagonistic to it, as long as the struggle was against the slaveholding state and against the slaveholding town with its curiae and its lumpen-proletariat, a useless and superfluous burden for the new regime. This is explained by the fact that these two classes of the new society could (within certain limits) march together against the old society; the struggle between them began later and on a new basis, in the form of a struggle for the land and for the rapid end to the survivals of slavery, that is, for the means of development of the new mode of production. The outcome of that struggle depended on numerous interrelated factors: the force of the revolutionary movement; the alliances concluded by the barbarians in the conquered territories and the degree of decomposition of the primitive commune among them; the reciprocal relations between the different groups of the ruling class; the stability of the relationships which dated from the Roman or pre-Roman periods; the development of a mercantile economy and the predominance of one form of rent or another; and, probably, numerous other causes which could be brought out only by a concrete study (yet to be done) of the different regions of the empire during this period. But, whatever the results, the nature of this feudalization process was everywhere the same. It is not contradicted by the preservation in the East of towns and a centralized state, for this was related to the vitality of the commune, the development of commerce, the predominance of rent in the form of money, and, perhaps, the diversity of the kinds of agriculture in the eastern regions, where, in addition to the great domains of the feudal type, there continued to exist an important amount of small peasant agriculture with patriarchic slavery. . . .

But this was not the type of agriculture that predominated and spread; to that type belonged the great domains based on exploitation of colons, whose masters possessed fortresses, prisons, military detachments made up of mercenaries, and armed slaves. The relations between this domain and the state power are very clearly expressed in the edict of 451 A.D. concerning the delivery and seizure of brigands who hid in a domain. The edict ordered that in the case where the masters, the procurators or the *primates possessionum* (no doubt the town administration or the elective officials of the villages on private lands), should refuse to turn them over, the rector of the province should send against them the civil militia (*civilia auxilia*); and if, because of the great number of peasants living on the property, the militia suffered a defeat, the military tribunes should send soldiers. It was also necessary to send soldiers when the masters or the procurators showed that their strength was insufficient to repress the masses of peasants. Clearly, in the picture drawn here, nothing is left from the time of classical slavery.

And so, the general crisis of the slaveholding regime begins in the second century. In the third century, the struggle between the old and the new forms of economy ends with the victory of the latter. From the beginning of the fourth century, one can no longer speak of the existence of the slaveholding society, nor of the classes of slaves and slave masters as the principal and determining classes. A transition period begins, filled with the revolutionary movements of the masses and the struggle against the survivals of slavery which held back the development of the new regime. This period ends with the establishment of the first feudal relationships under a form determined by the concrete historical conditions in each region of the old Roman world.

# III/THE EARLY HISTORY OF CHRISTIANITY

WHY should the historian be interested in the origin and growth of Christianity? The question resembles the one put to the men who climbed Mount Everest some years ago. Why did they do it? And the answer: Because it is there. Surely no ideology has been more "there" throughout European history than Christianity. By its very presence, it has played an enormous part in determining the action of men, which is the historian's essential study. He is therefore duty bound to understand the nature of its influence. This is true of every historian, regardless of his allegiances. The radical historian, or at least the radical who is also a Marxist, brings a particular outlook to his task, for he takes as given that ideology, of which religion is one form, is an expression of a class (or group) interest and as such is a significant weapon in the struggle between oppressor and oppressed.

From the fundamentalist Protestantism of the Tennessee hills to the sophisticated liberal theology of a Hans Kung or a Reinhold Niebuhr, contemporary Christianity is all things to all men. For some, the Bible uninterpreted is the final guide, while others claim allegiance not to the letter but to the spirit of the Gospels. And so it has always been, almost from the moment Jesus became the central figure of the new religion founded in Palestine in the middle of the first century A.D. Indeed, that may well be the secret of, if not the reason for, Christianity's success—that it has proven a suitable vehicle for the expression of the contradictory aspirations of large groups of men. Every time the organized Christianity of church or sect has become identified with the conservation of the status quo, some of the faithful have found it necessary to break away and return to an ideology and worship more consonant with its revolutionary origins.

The object of our study is neither the internal coherence of Christian doctrine nor its ultimate reasonableness, but its early history. Of the many questions around which the discussion might be oriented, three seem to me of primary importance. First, who was Jesus, and how did he come to be designated the Christ? Second, to whom did the young religion appeal? And third, why did Christianity become the official religion of the Roman state?

The answer to the first question will depend very much on the state of one's faith. If Jesus is both the Son of Man and the Son of God, then his life on earth can only be treated as a working out of God's plan, even if one believes, as do some Christians, that the men into whose midst he came were free to welcome or reject him as they chose. If, on the other hand, the assumption is that Jesus, or some person resembling the one who goes by that name in the New Testament, was a man and in no sense divine, his actions and his religious inspiration can only be explained by reference to the social context in which he labored, and his secular history takes on a particular importance. Most radicals nowadays will make the second assumption, for the simple reason that they are likely to be agnostics or atheists. This is not to say that radicalism and Christianity are necessarily incompatible, but only that in recent centuries they have tended to develop in opposition to one another, largely because of the role of the Christian churches as bulwarks of the status quo. A nonecclesiastical Christianity may be radical both in historical analysis and social action, insofar as it is able to give up the idea of divine intervention in human affairs and refuses to become an ideological justification for class rule. By definition, a Christian cannot be a materialist, much less a Marxist. On the other hand, Christianity stripped down to its essentials as a system of ethics need not always be an opiate of the masses, as Marx knew it to be in his time.

The battle over the historical Jesus is essentially a peripheral one, although it has been going on for a long time now. Did Jesus exist? A whole school of German scholars (the "mythic school") has argued that no individual of that name played the role assigned to him in the Gospels. Much of what is related in the New Testament is nothing but myth and fantasy of a variety common to the ancient Near East, but it seems clear that a man resembling Jesus did exist and was active in the early years of the first century. The pretended miracles, death, and resurrection are of less significance than his messianic gospel, whose revolutionary content was not lost on the Jewish masses in their aspiration for liberation from the Roman yoke and the creation of a more just society. The Romans crucified him for his pains. It was left to others, notably Paul and his circle, to make Jesus into the Messiah and to transform his search for the good life on this earth into a promise of eternal bliss in heaven. The content of Pauline Christianity is thus totally different from that of the original. How and why this development took place is the subject of the article by the British Marxist historian Archibald Robertson.

The mythology of Jesus has affected others besides the faithful. Many years ago, the Socialist cartoonist Art Young expressed the left-wing view (particularly widespread in the United States at the beginning of the twentieth century, perhaps because the church-state conflict was never as violent there as in European societies) by depicting Jesus as the subject of a police flyer in the guise of a red-bearded agitator wanted for stirring up trouble among the Judeans. This picture has a certain basis in truth. Early Christianity as preached by its founder was subversive. It appealed to the masses—to laboring men, artisans, and peasants—first among the Jews, later among the Gentiles. And this element has remained strong, despite the later efforts of the established church to domesticate the doctrine by establishing a dichotomy between the needs of the body here below and those of the soul in the world to come. It was with the promotion of the latter concern that Christianity became respectable (or relatively respectable) and acceptable to a wider stratum of the population, itself dissatisfied with things as they were but unwilling to correct them by resort to violent action.

The renunciation of revolutionary politics by Pauline Christians did not save them from intermittent persecution, some of it severe. The Roman state, after the Jewish Revolt of A.D. 66–70, drew the lesson and became increasingly repressive, the more so as it was constantly threatened by the discontent of subject peoples. It was only when Christianity could show itself to be more a unifying than a divisive force (in fact, more unifying than any other available doctrine) that it could be adopted by Constantine as the official state religion. By that time, the transformation was complete, and there was little or nothing left of both the original teachings and the primitive form of church organization. The democratic had been replaced by the hierarchical. Even then, aristocratic Romans resisted the change, and it was not until new men of the urban middle classes began, in the fourth century, to play an ever more important role in the state that Christianity can truly be said to have triumphed over the pagans. The late A. H. M. Jones of Oxford, whose books are standard works in the field of classical history, devoted a great deal of attention in his later years to the study of the later Roman Empire. In the article reprinted here, he explores the relations between late Roman social structure and the spread of Christianity in the post-Constantine era.

Archibald Robertson

# 6

# The Origins
# of Christianity

## THE MYTH THEORY

For over fifty years Freethinkers have wrangled over the question whether "the Gospel Jesus" ever lived or not. Much of the Gospel story can undoubtedly be accounted for as myth. The name "Jesus" is a Greek transliteration of "Joshua" and means "Jah is deliverance." In the Old Testament Joshua is the leader of Israel in the conquest of Canaan. It would be natural to give the name in anticipation to the predestined deliverer of Israel from the Roman yoke. In fact we have evidence that it was so given. In an anti-Roman Sibylline Oracle circulated about A.D. 80 and containing no other evidence of Christian authorship we find the lines:

> Then shall one come again from heaven, an excellent hero,
> He who spread his hands on a tree of beautiful fruitage—
> Best of the Hebrews all, who stayed the sun in his course once.

Here a crucified Messiah is explicitly identified with the legendary Joshua who made the sun stand still. In the *Apocalypse of Ezra,* another anti-Roman work put together towards the end of the first century, the coming Messiah is explicitly called Jesus, though the work is not otherwise noticeably Christian. Evidently many Jewish patriots in the first century hoped for the return of Joshua to inaugurate a new world-order on the ruins of the Roman Empire. The phrase "Messiah Joshua" or (in Greek) "Christ Jesus" was doubtless a revolutionary slogan before it became associated with any historical individual. To any actual claimant to Messiahship the name "Jesus," a common enough Jewish name, would undoubtedly be an asset.

In the Gospels and Acts (but not, it is to be noted, in the Epistles or the Apocalypse) Jesus is called a "Nazarene" or "Nazoraean"; and in the Talmud he and his followers are regularly called *Notzrim.* This name is usually derived from Nazareth, called in Matthew and Luke a "city" of Galilee. But though Nazareth is today a well-known town

73

and has been so since the fourth century, when pilgrimages to the "holy places" began, it is curious that neither the Old Testament, Josephus nor the Talmud mention such a place. If it existed in the first century, it must have been an insignificant village; and it is as a village that Julius Africanus, who lived in Palestine in the third century, refers to it. It is, on the face of it, odd that a sect should be named after a small village in which its founder lived rather than after the founder himself.

Now Epiphanius, a bishop of the fourth century and a native of Palestine, tells us that a sect of "Nasaraeans," existing in Syria and Palestine in his day, had existed before the Christian era; that they were Jews who recognized a Messiah; and that they used the same sacred book as the "Ossaeans." These are our old friends the Essenes, whose part in revolutionary Judaism we have already noted and who hoped, as we have seen, for the return of a martyred leader of their own. Another odd fact is that a sect called the Mandaeans, a few hundred of whom survive today like a historical fossil in Iraq, revere John the Baptist as the true prophet and denounce Jesus as a liar and impostor, but none the less call their chief members *Nasoraye* (Nazoraeans). All this does not look as if "Nazoraean" were derived from Nazareth. The name is more likely connected with a Hebrew word *natzar*, meaning to watch, guard or keep. *Notzrim* or "Nazoraeans" would mean "keepers" of secrets or of some special rules or usages. A pre-Christian sect cannot have been called after Jesus the Nazoraean; but he, if he existed, may well have been so called as a member of the sect. The Nazareth story may have been invented to explain the name "Nazoraean" by people ignorant of Hebrew and hazy enough about geography to make a city of an insignificant village.

There is nothing improbable in the statement that Pontius Pilate, procurator of Judaea under Tiberius from A.D. 26 to 36, crucified Jesus the Nazoraean as a would-be Messiah or king of the Jews. But mythical material has certainly contributed to the Gospel story, which in its earliest shape was not written down before A.D. 70.

We saw [in a previous chapter] that in ancient Babylon it was an annual custom to dress a condemned prisoner in the king's robes, seat him on the king's throne and allow him to enjoy himself for five days, after which he was stripped, scourged and hanged or impaled. This points back to the prehistoric sacrifice of the chief, but it also points forward to the Gospel story, where Pilate's soldiers robe Jesus in purple, crown him with thorns and salute him as king of the Jews before leading him to crucifixion. No followers of Jesus can have been at the Roman headquarters to witness the mockery. In the oldest Gospel source they have "all left him and fled." Not until Luke do we read of any disciples staying to see the crucifixion even "afar off." Not until

John do we read of any standing by the cross. The mock robing and crowning, therefore, will not bear examination as history. But we can see how the story came to be told. Human sacrifice was widespread in ancient society—in Babylonia, in Egypt, even in Greece. Until the second century A.D. human victims were offered on Mount Lycaeus in Arcadia, at Alos in Thessaly, at Salamis in Cyprus. These barbarities must have bitten deep into the consciousness of the exploited classes from whom victims were invariably drawn. Nothing afforded a readier handle to Jewish propaganda. On nothing did the Jewish people more justly pride themselves than on their abolition of the human sacrifices still sanctioned by pagan religion. When the story of a crucified Messiah came to be told, nothing would be more natural than for details to be supplied from those sacrificial rites which were practised in the pagan world at the expense of helpless social outcasts.

The expectation that a martyred Messiah would return victorious over death assimilated the Messianic idea to those of the mystery cults. It is not surprising that those who told the story should have depicted him as crucified, dead and buried, and as raised on the third day—"the first fruits of them that sleep." There is probably a conscious echo of the mystery cults in the analogy drawn in I Corinthians between the growth of a grain of corn and the putting on of immortality by mortal men.

If the earliest features of the Gospel legend have many parallels in pagan cults, still more is this the case with later features. The virgin birth, related only in one dubious paragraph of Matthew and two palpably interpolated verses of Luke, is typical of such accretions. It is a pagan myth ultimately traceable to the prehistoric age when the nature of paternity was unknown and every child, therefore, was reputed to be virgin-born. Hence the gods, made in the image of man, were originally virgin-born too. In one Egyptian myth Isis conceives Horus after her husband, Osiris, is dead. The Babylonian mother-goddess, Ishtar, had originally no male counterpart. A Phrygian variant of Ishtar, Nana, was the virgin-mother of Attis. In the Hesiodic *Theogony* Hera bears Hephaestus, the fire-god, without sexual union. In such myths the mother-goddess was originally earth, the mother of mankind and of all things needful to mankind. Until paternity was understood, she had no need of a consort. Later a father-god was associated with her and, as patriarchal and class society developed, might come to dominate her, as Zeus dominates Hera in Greek mythology. But although the Graeco-Roman pantheon conformed to the pattern of patriarchal society, the tradition of virgin goddesses and virgin births lingered among the masses. Even in the time of Plutarch (about A.D. 100) such births were believed in Egypt to be not impossible. When, therefore, Christianity spread to people holding these beliefs, a story that Jesus had been conceived by the Holy Spirit and born of the Virgin Mary was inserted in Matthew and Luke. That the Fourth Gospel deliberately ignores the story shows that it was not received with unanimity. The words put into the mouth of Jesus, "Woman, what have I to do with thee?" are the evangelist's reproof to those who would attribute to a mere Jewess a part in the salvation of the world.

Similarly the story in Luke of the infant Jesus lying in a manger is traceable to the legend of the pastoral god Hermes, who is represented on an ancient Greek vase and in a Homeric hymn as cradled in a basket and surrounded by oxen. The miracle of turning water into wine, related in the Fourth Gospel, is traceable to a rite performed in more than one Greek city at the winter festival of Dionysus. In the isle of Andros—a short sail across the Aegean from Ephesus, where the Fourth Gospel was written—a fountain in the temple of Dionysus was believed to run with wine every year on January 5. It can hardly be accidental that the Catholic Church commemorates the miracle of Cana on January 6.

Such was the sort of floating legend which went to the building up of the story of Jesus. In part this material was older than history, like the myths of Osiris, Tammuz, Attis and Dionysus. In part it had already been attached to historical figures like Cleomenes and the victims of Alexander Jannaeus and Aristobulus. The exponents of the myth theory could have made their case stronger than it is by paying more attention to the class struggles in the ancient world. Being, with a few honourable exceptions, imbued with a bourgeois contempt for mass movements, they have contented themselves mostly with cataloguing similarities between stories told of pagan gods and stories told of Jesus, and with searching the heavens for astral explanations of both, leaving unanswered the question why people who needed a mystery cult should have gone to the trouble of manufacturing a new one at great inconvenience and danger to themselves instead of availing themselves of the abundant existing facilities.

If we consider that ancient society was the scene of fierce struggles between masters and slaves, rich and poor, imperialists and subject peoples, in which every rebel took his life in his hand; if we consider that one revolutionary leader after another, with his followers, met a violent end, often by the horrible punishment of crucifixion inflicted on rebels in slave societies (eight hundred Pharisees crucified at Jerusalem by Alexander Jannaeus, six thousand slave soldiers of Spartacus crucified along the Appian Way, two thousand Jewish rebels crucified by Varus); if we consider that Jews and Gentiles were not mutually isolated, but mingled daily in the Mediterranean cities, the poorer Jews propagating their vision of a coming Messiah and in the process assimilating it to the poorer Gentiles' dream of a redeeming god triumphant over death—we shall not need to go to the signs of the zodiac for an explanation of the crucifixion and resurrection stories.

We shall understand too why Judaism, rather than any existing mystery cult, had to provide the new movement with its ideology. The existing mystery cults, however popular in their origin, had one by one become part and parcel of Roman State religion. The cult of Dionysus, after a short attempt at suppression in the second century B.C., had been found politically innocuous and amalgamated with that of the Italian fertility-god Liber. The cult of Attis, which the Roman republic had tolerated among aliens and slaves, but banned to Roman citizens, was by Claudius opened to all and incorporated with the State religion. That of Isis, which the republic had suppressed again and again and which even Tiberius forbade in Italy, was soon afterwards freed from restrictions and established throughout the Roman world. All these cults could easily be fitted into the State religion, since all, however transformed to meet the needs of the urban masses, bore unmistakeable marks of their prehistoric peasant origin. Judaism alone had been deliberately expurgated and turned into an ideology aiming at a reign of righteousness on earth. For that reason it could not be fitted into the religion of the Graeco-Roman ruling class, which deliberately exploited ancient ritual and myth as engines of government. For the same reason Judaism, with a little adaptation, was eminently capable of providing an ideology for the uprooted and disaffected masses of the Mediterranean cities. Much of the Gospel story can be explained as a fusion of the Jewish hope of a Messiah with legends of a redeeming god or of some martyred leader which were current among the masses towards the time of the Christian era.

. . .

The earliest strata of the Gospels—proved to be such by internal evidence and by a comparative study of the Synoptics—point back to a revolutionary movement led first by John the Baptist and then by Jesus the Nazoraean, and aimed at the overthrow of Roman and Herodian rule in Palestine and the establishment of an earthly "kingdom of God" in which the first would be last and the last first, the rich sent empty away and the poor filled with good things and given houses and land. The followers of John and Jesus were called *Notzrim* or Nazoraeans, not from the village of Nazareth, but from the Hebrew word *natzar*, "to keep"—either as keepers of secrets or as strict keepers of the Jewish law. This last is rather suggested by the saying preserved in Matthew v, 20:

> Except your righteousness shall exceed
> That of the scribes and Pharisees,
> You shall in no wise enter into the kingdom of heaven.

The Nazoraeans were probably an offshoot of the Essenes. This appears from the close similarity between many of their rules. We have already seen that according to Epiphanius the "Nasaraeans" used the same sacred book as the "Ossaeans." The Essenes, says Josephus, "are despisers of riches. . . . Nor is there anyone to be found among them who has more than another; for it is a law among them that those who come to them must let what they have be common to the whole order. . . . So there is, as it were, one patrimony among all the brethren." Similarly in the Synoptic Gospels:

> Where your treasure is,
> There will your heart be also . . .
> No man can serve two masters . . .
> You cannot serve God and mammon . . .
> Seek first his kingdom, and his righteousness,
> And all these things shall be added to you . . .
> Whatsoever thou hast, sell,
> And give to the poor,
> And thou shalt have treasure in heaven:
> And come, follow me.

The Essenes, says Josephus, "carry nothing at all with them when they travel into remote parts, though they take their weapons with them for fear of thieves. Accordingly there is, in every city where they live, one appointed particularly to take care of strangers and to provide garments and other necessaries for them. . . . Nor do they allow the change of garments or of shoes till they are first entirely torn to pieces or worn out by time. Nor do they either buy or sell anything among themselves, but everyone of them gives what he has to him that wants it, and receives from him again in lieu what may be convenient for himself." Similarly in the Synoptics we read:

> Get you no gold, nor silver,
> Nor brass in your girdles;
> No wallet for the journey,
> Nor two coats,
> Nor shoes, nor staff:
> For the labourer is worthy of his food.
> And into whatsoever city or village you shall enter,
> Search out who in it is worthy;
> And there abide till you go forth.

The Essenes, says Josephus, "dispense their anger after a just manner and restrain their passion. They are eminent for fidelity and are ministers of peace; whatsoever they say is firmer than an oath; but swearing is avoided by them, and they esteem it worse than perjury; for they say that he who cannot be believed without swearing by God is already condemned." Similarly in the Synoptics anger and oaths are forbidden.

Josephus, it will be noted, says that the Essenes carry weapons to defend themselves from thieves. From the part which he assigns to them in the struggle with Rome, it seems that they could put their weapons to other uses too and were less absolute pacifists than is usually made out. Similarly in the Synoptics, in spite of the injunctions to turn the other cheek and love our enemies, we see a movement of which the revolutionary character has been almost obliterated in the extant records. "From the days of John the Baptist the kingdom of God is taken by violence." It is significant that the Gospels, while they often attack the Pharisees and Sadducees, never attack the Zealots, and that a Zealot is included in the lists of the twelve apostles. It is possible for a movement to impose a rigid discipline on its members in the matter of private quarrels without renouncing the use of force in the common cause.

The movement of John the Baptist was nipped in the bud by Antipas. A Nazoraean attempt to seize Jerusalem led to the crucifixion of Jesus by Pilate. The date of these events is unknown; but they must have taken place before 36, in which year Antipas was defeated by Aretas, and Pilate was recalled to Rome. The Essenes, as we have seen, even before the Christian era believed in a Messiah who would return from the dead; and so did the Nazoraeans. According to the Synoptics Jesus was believed by some to be John the Baptist risen from death, and by others to be Elijah or one of the ancient prophets. The whole history of the Messianic idea from Daniel onwards shows that it was the projection of the hopes of a revolutionary movement which had taken root among simple and ignorant people, attaching itself to leader after leader and able to survive the death of many such. We need not wonder that it survived the death of Jesus. In the words of the bitterly conservative and hostile Tacitus, "a most mischievous superstition, checked for the moment, again broke out not only in Judaea, the first source of the evil, but even in Rome, where all things hideous and shameful from every part of the world find their centre and become popular."

This reconstruction in no way diminishes the importance of the mythicist contribution to the history of Christianity. Traditional Christianity, and any attempt to trace traditional Christianity to a unique personal founder, alike break down on the evidence. The religion officially established in the fourth century, for which history has to account, was not the cult of a dead Jewish Messiah, but the cult of a redeemer-god who differed from others only in having a local habitation in first-century Palestine and a Jewish name with Messianic associations. In formulating the creeds of the Church the Pauline Epistles and the discourses of the Fourth Gospel were to play a far greater part than the revolutionary and apocalyptic propaganda of the

Synoptics. The Synoptic Gospels themselves were edited and re-edited ("three times, four times and many times," says the acute critic Celsus) into a ragged conformity with Pauline theology. Somehow a historical individual of whom we know very little, but whose existence we infer from the evidence of Tacitus and the Talmud and from an analysis of the Synoptic documents, became the subject of demonstrably mythical stories—stories of an incarnate God; a virgin birth; a mystical death, burial and resurrection reminiscent of slain gods of prehistoric origin; a mystical feeding of his people on his flesh, turned to bread, and his blood, turned to wine, by which they became partakers in his eternal life. Not only so, but in centres remote from Palestine, such as the Aegean cities where the Pauline Epistles took shape, the myth of the incarnate God, and not the career of a historic Jesus, was the basis of the cult from the first. Paul knows no more of the Nazoraean Jesus than the Synoptics know of the pre-existent Christ. The social genesis of these contradictory factors and the history of their fusion into traditional Christianity constitute the problem to be solved.

. . .

## THE SOCIAL BASIS OF PAULINE CHRISTIANITY

Enough has been said to show that Pauline Christianity as reflected in the Epistles was not a movement of the disinherited classes. Paul himself was a master-craftsman and a Empire. Though most of his converts were poor, the live wires of the Pauline churches were householders like Gaius and Stephanas of Roman citizen, and explicitly repudiated resistance to the Roman Corinth, Erastus "the treasurer of the city," Paul's fellow-craftsman Aquila and the slave-owner Philemon—men perhaps not "wise after the flesh" or "mighty" or "noble," but at least of the middle class and middling education, ranging from small property-owners to artisans in direct contact with the masses. We shall find, so far as the evidence goes, that the same is true of those who continued Paul's work. The question arises why, if they had no quarrel with the Roman government, such men became Christians?

To this question one answer has already been given. Jewish revolutionaries were at this time propagating among the slaves, freedmen and poorer freemen of the Mediterranean cities Messianic hopes which, if not countered, would end in a head-on clash with the Roman Empire. Middle-class Jews like Paul, and such Gentiles as they could influence, though with no illusions about the Roman Empire or its rulers, were interested in averting that clash and tried to avert it by preaching a spiritualized version of Messianism. This accounts for the content of Pauline Christianity. But it hardly accounts for the persistence with which it was preached after it had failed in its immediate object of averting the clash between Rome and Judaism.

To account for this we must consider ancient imperialism under another aspect. Among its principal agencies was pagan priestcraft. For centuries many who were neither Jews nor revolutionaries, and who had no objection to paying tribute to whom tribute was due, had protested against the State religion. That religion had long been open to attack as an organization of imposture for political purposes and had actually been attacked for that reason before the time of Plato.

The strength of this protest may be gathered from the popularity of the Epicurean and early Stoic philosophies. In the fourth and third centuries B.C. ancient slave civilization and imperialism had not yet reached their peak. The successors of Alexander were "multiplying evils on the earth" by their dynastic wars; but Roman rapacity and repression did not yet bestride the Mediterranean. To Greek middle-class intellectuals it seemed possible to palliate the misery of the time by a simple appeal to reason—by organizing a society of people who renounced the struggle for wealth and power, the "hatred, envy and contempt" which that struggle produced, and the superstition and fear of death which it exploited. The teaching of Epicurus, the school-master's son, took the Greek world by storm in the third century B.C.: his adherents were "so many in number that they could hardly be counted by whole cities."

The fact that Epicureanism was a materialistic philosophy and concerned itself only with this life, whereas Christianity called in another world to redress the balance of this, must not blind us to important resemblances. Epicureanism, like Christianity, was a missionary movement rejecting the sanctified magic of official cults and the pretentious learning of rival schools. There is a parallel between Epicurus' advice to a young disciple to "steer clear of all culture" and Paul's dismissal of the wisdom of the world as folly. Like the Christian churches, the school of Epicurus, though its leaders were men of education, admitted women and slaves to membership. Like Christianity, Epicureanism (in spite of the libels circulated by its enemies) inculcated a simple and even ascetic life. The Epicureans held that "the wise man would not fall in love," just as Paul wrote: "It is good for a man not to touch a woman." The Epicurean eulogy of friendship as the royal road to happiness is not unlike the Christian panegyric on comradeship (agapé). Both Epicurus and Paul accepted slavery; but Epicurus taught that "the wise man would not punish his servants, but rather pity them," just as Paul exhorted Philemon to receive the fugitive Onesimus as "more than a slave—a brother and comrade." Epicurus bids his converts seek "peace of mind"; Paul would have his "free from cares." The Epicureans have been well described as "a sort of Society of Friends with a system of natural philosophy as its intellectual core."

Even in religion the opposition between Epicureanism and Pauline

Christianity was not as absolute as we might think. The theism of
Epicurus is no mere lip-service. His teaching that "God is a living
being, immortal and blessed," attested by "the common sense of mankind," and that "not the man who denies the gods worshipped by the
multitude, but he who affirms of the gods what the multitude believes
is truly impious," reminds us of Paul's contrast between the "incor-
ruptible God" manifest in creation and the idols worshipped by the
pagan world—with the important difference that the gods of Epicurus
are part of the material universe, while the God of Paul is prior to it
and created it.

Epicureanism, in fact, in its best days appealed to the same class of
people to whom Pauline Christianity was later to appeal—not to the
ruling class, who found superstition very useful, nor so much to the
slaves and disinherited (though they were not excluded) as to small
middle-class people who were the victims of power-politics which
they could not control, and who, without being revolutionaries,
resented the imposture planted on them by an official religion which
was a mere wheel in the machinery of State.

But ancient social order was incompatible with the emergence of a
scientifically based "society of friends." As Marx puts it, the "duplica-
tion of the world into a religious, imaginary one and a real one" is a
result of "self-cleavage and self-contradictoriness" in the real world.
Not only did the ruling class, as Polybius, Varro and Cicero frankly
tell us, need superstition as an instrument of government, but Greek
science, in which Epicureanism was intellectually rooted, slowly with-
ered away in consequence of mass slavery and the divorce of theory
from experiment. In the last century B.C. Epicureanism (still in the
estimation of Cicero a "plebeian" philosophy) uttered its supreme
protest in the noble poem of Lucretius. Then it began to lose ground
before the religious counter-offensive launched by Augustus, and
from a mass movement eventually shrank to a little-regarded sect. Its
rival, Stoicism, after revolutionary beginnings (the early Stoics had
advocated a world-state without classes or cults) had since the second
century B.C. come to terms with the Roman State and its religion. The
later Stoics were no more than a liberal party (not always so very
liberal) within the ruling class of the Roman Empire.

By the first century A.D. the possibility of either an Epicurean or a
Stoic utopia had disappeared. Whoever else might renounce the
struggle for wealth and power, the Roman ruling class did not. They
were using superstition as their auxiliary policeman, and refuting
Epicurean arguments against the fear of death by a grimly literal
*experimentum crucis* [experiment of torture] on rebel subjects and
slaves. In such a world Epicureanism was no longer a possible creed
for the masses. Opposition to the State religion ceased to be materialistic and became mystical.

Pauline Christianity offered people whose ancestors had flocked to Epicurean lectures an ideology equally opposed to the official religion, but turning its back on the material world and based on elements derived from Judaism, Platonism, Stoicism and the mystery religions. It owed nothing directly to the Epicureans, but it appealed to what had once been their public and had, as we have seen, many points in common with their teaching. The difference between the materialism of Epicurus and the mysticism of Paul is explained by the different historical situations in which the two ideologies arose.

Did any Epicureans join the Pauline churches? We have evidence that some did. In 1 Corinthians xv Paul argues at considerable length against those who "say that there is no resurrection of the dead." These are not pagan opponents, but Christians—"some among you." They do not merely reject a physical in favour of a spiritual immortality. Paul would not have objected to that: he himself repudiates a resurrection of "flesh and blood." The men whom he attacks say that Christian hopes relate to "this life only" and that death ends all. Why did such people become Christians? Probably they were Epicureans who found Paul's other teaching to their liking, but could not swallow the dogma of immortality. The Epicureans had always fought that idea as the mainstay of the priestcraft they abominated. For them the reward of virtue was peace of mind in this life, and the punishment of vice its absence. There was no other life—no reward and no punishment after death.

Now so far as punishment of the wicked was concerned Paul had no quarrel with the Epicureans. We may search the Epistles in vain for the doctrine of hell-fire. For Paul, the "wrath of God" against idolaters is proved by their vicious lives and by the ramifications of wickedness to which they lead. In the end the wicked die, and Paul nowhere suggests that they live again. If he had read it, he would have endorsed the doctrine of Lucretius that "the life of fools becomes a hell here on earth."

What concerns Paul is the fate of Christian believers. Epicurean peace of mind was impossible in the vast slave prison of the Roman Empire. Nothing sufficed except redemption from the material world which had become wholly evil. Such redemption, says Paul, is open to those baptized into the Christian community. They thereby become part of the body of Christ, the indwelling spirit of the community, and share in his eternal life.

Pauline Christianity thus established on a mystical basis—the only basis possible in the conditions of that time—the fellowship of men and women, rich and poor, bond and free, which the Epicureans had tried and failed to establish on a materialistic basis. If they had stopped there, it is possible that Pauline Christians would not have been persecuted any more than the Epicureans. They exposed themselves to persecution when they began to preach their doctrines to the masses and used their funds to attract and capture the destitute followers of the Jewish Messianists. For, as we shall see, Pauline leaders who themselves had no quarrel with the Roman Empire, but only with its cults, thereby found themselves at the head of followers to whom the Empire itself was Satanic, and whom they could not repudiate without undoing their own work and disrupting the "body of Christ."

Christian writers usually show little gratitude to the Epicureans who blazed the trail for them in the struggle with paganism. Tertullian cites with approval a maxim of Epicurus on the endurance of pain; otherwise the Fathers seem to accept the vulgar estimate of him as a voluptuous atheist. In the atmosphere of the Roman Empire men who were trying to supplant the official religion by another could not afford to be connected with avowed materialists. But others saw the connection. In the second century A.D. the fashionable fancy religionist, Alexander of Paphlagonia, used, says Lucian, to warn "any atheist, Christian or Epicurean" to leave his meetings. It has been said of Christianity on its social side that "because Spartacus was beaten, Jesus had to win." We may say of it on its ideological side that because Epicurus was beaten, Paul had to win.

. . .

In this book we have been concerned with the origins of Christianity. The results arrived at differ both from orthodoxy and from most current Rationalism.

Orthodoxy accepts at their face value the books of the New Testament, despite their contradictions. It is thus committed to a creed according to which God, without ceasing to be God, became man in the person of Jesus Christ, suffered death under a Roman governor of Judaea in the first century, rose again, founded the Catholic Church, and will return hereafter to judge the living and the dead.

The Rationalist rightly points out the contradictions in the orthodox creed and in the documents which support it, and the absence of independent historical confirmation of its claims. This commits him to the quest of a credible explanation of the facts. So far Rationalists have reached no agreed solution. The more conservative hold that a teacher named Jesus lived and died at the traditional date and uttered enough of the sayings recorded in the Synoptic Gospels to entitle him to be called the founder of Christianity. The more radical reject an historical founder and regard Jesus as a mystery-god pure and simple. The difficulties of both views have been pointed out. Neither explains all the facts. Neither takes sufficient account of the fact that early Christianity was a mass movement conditioned by the decaying slave society of antiquity. Yet in a sense *both* are true, since both are legitimate deductions from *some* of the available data.

This seeming contradiction disappears when we realize that the texts which support the historical and mythical theories refer to two opposed tendencies in early Christianity. Some, especially in the Synoptic Gospels, refer to a first-century revolutionary movement of the poorer classes, centred in Palestine and connected with the Essenes. Round a crucified leader of this movement or, more likely, round confused traditions of more than one leader the original Gospel story was written. Other texts, especially in the Pauline Epistles, refer to a mystery cult among Greek-speaking Jews of the *diaspora,* whose Christ Jesus was no leader of flesh and blood but a god by whom its initiates were to be redeemed from this evil world, and which attracted rich as well as poor converts. The propaganda of both tendencies was conducted in the underworld of the Mediterranean cities. Their bitter rivalry can be traced in the Pauline Epistles and in the Johannine Apocalypse.

After the Jewish revolt and the destruction of Jerusalem the Pauline leaders set to work to draw the sting of the revolutionary movement and so to prevent, if possible, clashes with Rome in which they too were likely to be involved. They did this, firstly, by using the funds at their disposal to provide benefits which the revolutionaries could not afford, and secondly, by rewriting the Gospel story, neutralizing its revolutionary content and remaking its hero in the image of their own mystery-god. The first process put the control of the churches into safe hands; the second left the Gospels the contradictory patchwork which we see today.

In the second century the church leaders had to turn round and fight another enemy—the ultra-Paulinists who would have cut the Jewish roots of Christianity, and the Gnostics who would have so mystified it as to rob it of all mass appeal. The upshot was the emergence of the episcopate and the formation of the New Testament canon.

Consequently the New Testament exhibits insuperable contradictions—a Jewish Messiah of human descent, who is nevertheless God from the beginning; a material kingdom of God on earth, and yet a kingdom not of this world and not to be inherited by flesh and blood; denunciations of the rich and visions of the fall of Rome, side by side with exhortations to slaves to obey their masters and to all to obey the government. These contradictions illustrate the different points of view rooted in different social classes—the millennial dreams of the poor and hungry, and the mystical escapism of the more comfortable —which went to form the Catholic Church and the Catholic creeds of later centuries. The dogmatic, authoritarian side of the new religion became the ideology of feudalism. Its revolutionary, millennial side, submerged for the time being, helped to shape the popular and progressive thought of ages to come.

# A. H. M. Jones

## 7

## The Social Background of the Struggle between Paganism and Christianity

Christianity has always had its appeal for all sorts and conditions of men. Long before the conversion of Constantine made it politic for the ambitious to profess the emperor's religion, there were Christian senators and soldiers, and even Christian professors. But it remains true that for one reason or another Christianity was at the end of the third century more widely diffused in some areas and classes of society than in others. This fact makes a study of the social background against which Christianity fought its battle with paganism essential for a proper understanding of that struggle.

Christianity was at this date far stronger in the Greek-speaking provinces of the empire than in the Latin-speaking areas. This was, of course, mainly due to the fact that it had originated in an eastern province, and that its earlier missionaries were Greek-speaking. Missionary activity, it is true, was at a very early date extended to the West, but it was at first confined to the colonies of Greek-speaking immigrants in Rome and other large towns. Latin-speaking Christianity first emerges at Carthage towards the end of the second century, but at this period the Church at Lyons was still mainly composed of Greek-speaking orientals, and the Roman Church continued to use Greek down to the third century, and perhaps even later. Even in the fourth century, to judge by the density of bishoprics, the western provinces lagged far behind the eastern. There were areas, such as peninsular Italy and Africa, where Christianity was widely diffused, but in northern Italy, and still more in Gaul, Spain, and Illyricum, many quite important towns still lacked a bishop in the early fourth century.

In the second place Christianity was still in the fourth century a mainly urban religion. This was partly due to the methods whereby Christianity was diffused. The early missionaries moved from city to city and rapidly spread the gospel over a very wide area, but at the

86

expense of leaving the intervening countryside untouched. The early churches were thus urban communities, and they tended to remain so. There was in most parts of the empire a sharp cleavage between town and country: in many areas the peasants did not speak either of the two dominant languages of the empire, but still used their old Coptic, Syriac, Thracian, Celtic, or Berber tongues. Communication must then have been difficult even if urban Christians had taken more interest in their rural neighbours.

But the slow progress of Christianity in the rural areas is also to be attributed to the inherent conservatism of the peasantry. Peasants have at all times and in all places resisted change and clung stubbornly to their traditional way of life. Even in the sixth and seventh centuries, when they had for the most part long been converted, the Church in Gaul and Spain, as repeated canons of the contemporary councils show, had great difficulty in suppressing the old rites whereby they had from time immemorial warded off pests and promoted the fertility of their flocks and fields.

There are, of course, exceptions to this generalization. As early as the reign of Trajan Pliny notes, with some surprise, it would seem, that "the contagion of this superstitution has permeated not only the cities but also the villages and countryside." It would appear that during the latter part of the third century Christianity became dominant in the rural areas of Africa and Egypt. It has been pointed out that in both countries pagan dedications at rural shrines come to an abrupt end in the middle of the third century. This in itself is not very good evidence, for at that troubled period inscriptions in general became very sparse. But it is perhaps permissible to argue back from later conditions. The story of the Donatist controversy makes it plain that by the 340's Christianity was dominant in rural Africa: the Circumcellions, who were certainly peasants, were already by this period a power in the land. In Egypt the scandal of the broken chalice reveals that at a slightly earlier date there was a well-established system of rural parishes in Mareotes. If one goes back a generation to the time of the Great Persecution, Africa and Egypt stand out sharply in our record for the number of their martyrs and confessors, and it might be inferred that the exceptional stubbornness of the Christian resistance in these areas was due to the fact that the peasant masses, who were made of tougher stuff than the townsmen, had adopted the new faith.

The evidence that the African and Egyptian peasantry were already predominantly Christian by the beginning of the fourth century is admittedly tenuous. By contrast there is in other areas strong evidence that at much later dates paganism was still strong in the countryside. The Life of Martin of Tours reveals that in the later decades of the fourth century rural temples and festivals were flourishing in Gaul. Rather later John Chrysostom appealed to the Christian landlords of

Constantinople to take some interest in the spiritual welfare of their tenants, and to win them to the faith by endowing priests and building churches on their estates. Even in the age of Justinian John of Ephesus, as the result of a prolonged missionary campaign in the rural areas of Asia, Caria, Lydia, and Phrygia—districts among the first to be evangelized—found 80,000 pagans to baptize. In the West, at the end of the sixth century, Pope Gregory the Great found that in Sardinia there was a substantial number of peasants, including tenants of the church, who paid the governor of the island a regular *douceur* [bribe] to secure his connivance for their pagan worship.

In the third place Christianity had made relatively little progress among the aristocracy, or indeed among the educated upper classes in general. This was not for want of trying, for the Church early appreciated the importance of winning converts in governing circles. But among the upper classes the education which they had received created a strong resistance to the new faith. It must be remembered that in its early days Christianity was a more uncompromising faith than it later became, and had not yet acquired that wide variety of appeal which made it all things to all men. Christians regarded the old gods with fear and aversion: they were evil and active demons and any contact with them was dangerous. This being so, many believers felt that classical culture, permeated as it was with paganism, was to be rejected *in toto*: to study it was, if not sinful, playing with fire.

There was, it is true, in the third and even in the second century, a number of cultivated Christians who managed to accommodate their faith to classical culture, but the feeling long lingered that the two were incompatible. In Jerome's famous dream the Heavenly Judge answered his plea "Christianus sum" [I am a Christian] by the stern retort "Ciceronianus es, non Christianus" [You are a Ciceronian, not a Christian], and even at the end of the sixth century Pope Gregory the Great severely reproved the Bishop of Vienna for teaching grammar: "one mouth cannot contain the praises of Christ with the praises of Jupiter." This feeling must have been far stronger in the early fourth century, when the synthesis of Christianity and classical culture was still in its infancy, and it formed a very real stumbling-block to men who had been brought up to reverence the poets, philosophers, and orators of Greece and Rome.

In the second place we must not forget that Christianity was in its early days a vulgar religion. Not only were most of its adherents persons of low degree and little or no education, but its holy books were uncouth and barbaric, written in a Greek or Latin which grated on the sensibilities of any educated man, bred up on Menander and Demosthenes, or Terence and Cicero. It is difficult for us to appreciate how serious an obstacle this was. On the one hand, we are accustomed to Biblical language, and venerate the Authorized Version as among the noblest monuments of English prose. And in the second place we find it hard to realize the immense importance attached in antiquity to verbal form. But under the Roman empire higher education was almost exclusively devoted to rhetoric, the art of correct and elegant speech, and the men who were the products of that education naturally tended to attach more importance to the form than to the content of what they read. Jerome himself confesses that when he weakly indulged himself by reading Plautus he found the Hebrew prophets very unpalatable. When Julian forbade Christians to teach the classics, and contemptuously ordered them "to go to the churches of the Galileans and expound Matthew and Luke," only two Christian professors took up his challenge. But even they felt that the Christian scriptures were in their crude form impossible as a vehicle of education and proceeded to rewrite them as epic poems, Attic tragedies, and Platonic dialogues. In this mental climate it was difficult for any educated man to accept the new faith.

For members of the senatorial aristocracy there was yet another obstacle. Senators, believing themselves to be descendants of the republican nobility, and holding the republican magistracies and priesthoods, felt themselves to be the inheritors and guardians of the ancient traditions of Rome. Rome had grown to greatness under the protection of the old gods whom she so piously cherished: "this worship brought the world under my sway," Symmachus pictures her pleading, "these rites repelled Hannibal from the walls and the Senones from the Capitol." It was difficult for men bred in these traditions to believe that Jupiter Optimus Maximus was a malignant demon.

It is very difficult to estimate how far, despite these adverse factors, Christianity had by the beginning of the fourth century penetrated into the upper classes. The edict of Valerian, laying down special penalties for senators and *equites Romani* [Roman knights] who refused to conform, suggests that as early as 257 there were some Christians in these classes. The canons of the council of Iliberris, probably held shortly before the Great Persecution, lay down penances for Christians who as provincial *sacerdotes* [priests] or municipal *duoviri* [magistrates] or *flamines* [priests of a particular deity] take part in pagan rites or celebrate games. This would imply that there were not a few Christians among the curial class in Spain, and, indeed, among its richest and most prominent members, who held not only the highest municipal offices and priesthoods, but even the supreme honour of the provincial high priesthood. But it would seem likely that in the upper strata of society Christians were in a very small minority. The old senatorial families certainly remained predominantly pagan down to the latter part of the fourth century.

The main strength of Christianity lay in the lower and middle classes of the towns, the manual workers and clerks, the shop-keepers and merchants. It is significant that the city of Cyzicus (that is its council) sent an official delegation to Julian to ask for the restoration of its temples, while Eleusius, the bishop who had destroyed them, was supported by the workers in the local mint and government clothing factory. There were also Christians among the humbler decurions. The social range of the curial class was very wide, and while leading decurions of the great cities ranked not far below senators in birth, wealth, and culture, many humbler members of the council, especially in the smaller towns, were modest farmers or craftsmen with no pretension to culture. Diocletian even ruled that illiteracy was no bar to curial status.

But here again it is impossible to generalize, for there were sharp local variations whose reasons we often cannot fathom. There were some towns where the bulk of the population was early Christian, but there were others which long remained solidly pagan. In Mesopotamia Edessa was Christian even in the third century, but at Carrhae paganism was still dominant long after the Arab conquest. In Syria Antioch was strongly Christian in Julian's day, but the Apamenes defended their temples with spirit in the reign of Theodosius the Great. Palestine was in general a Christian province in the fourth century, but at Gaza the Christian community was still only a handful when Porphyry became their bishop in 395, and the temples, despite Theodosius' penal laws, were still open and the pagan cult overtly celebrated.

Let us now consider the bearing of these facts on the conflict of religions in the fourth century. The economy of the Roman empire was to an overwhelming extent agricultural. The vast majority of its inhabitants were peasants, and its wealth was almost entirely derived from their labours. The state drew, it would seem, over 90 per cent of its revenue from taxes levied on land and on the agricultural population. The upper classes derived almost all their wealth from rents paid by peasant tenants. Despite their immense numerical preponderance, however, and their vital economic importance, the opinions of the peasantry did not count for anything. They were merely a vast inert and passive, if stubborn, mass. This is demonstrated by their passive attitude when in the course of the fourth century pagan rites were banned and the temples closed or destroyed. Very occasionally they might lynch a tactless missionary or offer resistance to the destruction of their shrines. But recorded instances of violence are very rare, and pagan townsmen seem to have been far more active in defending their temples. This was no doubt partly because the laws against paganism were even more laxly enforced in the countryside than in the towns, but on the whole the peasantry seem to have submitted quietly to authority. This is not to say that they readily abandoned their ancestral rites and beliefs. Christianity gradually conquered the countryside, it is true, but it was a very slow process, by no means complete even in the sixth century. But the peasantry offered a passive resistance only, stubbornly carrying on their ancient worship, overtly if, as often was the case, the authorities did not bother to interfere, or could be bribed to turn a blind eye, or surreptitiously if the law was enforced.

It follows from what I have said that the proletariat of the towns, and the shop-keeping and mercantile class, were numerically and economically insignificant. They were far outnumbered by the peasantry, and the only tax which they paid, the *collatio lustralis* [a tax levied every five years], was a very small item in the budget. Except for the workers in the mints and the arms and clothing factories, they were not essential to the state. On the other hand, they had greater opportunities for expressing their views and making them felt. They could and did shout slogans in the theatre and at other public gatherings, and if such demonstrations did not produce the desired result, they could riot. In the absence of any adequate police, riots, especially in the larger cities, often assumed dangerous proportions, and troops had to be used to quell them. In this way the urban poor exercised an influence which was not justified by their numbers and economic importance. But they were not more than a nuisance, and could be suppressed whenever the government chose by a relatively small display of force.

An obviously much more important element was the army. The army was in the fourth century recruited, in what proportions we do not know, from three main sources—the sons of serving soldiers and veterans, peasants conscripted from the countryside, and barbarians from beyond the frontiers of the empire. Prima facie, then, it should at the beginning of the century have been overwhelmingly pagan. There were, of course, some Christian soldiers even in the third century. There are a few genuine acts of military martyrs, and in 298 the proconsul of Africa could retort to a Christian conscientious objector: "There are Christian soldiers who serve in the armies of our lords Diocletian and Maximian, Constantius and Maximian." But this, it may be noted, was said in Africa, where, as we have seen, the peasantry were probably already converted to the new faith. The famous Theban legion, if it is not a myth, will also have come from an exceptional area, Egypt. But by and large there must have been very few Christians in the army when Constantine decided to paint the [Chi-Rho] monogram on the shields of his soldiers before the battle of the Milvian Bridge. The barbarians were still pagan, and so were the bulk of the peasantry, especially in the favourite recruiting grounds of the army, Gaul and Illyricum. We have, in fact, a little piece of evidence that the army which two years later, under the protection of the labarum, fought and won the war against Licinius, which was in Constantine's propaganda a crusade against a pagan tyrant, was still pagan. A curious law in the Theodosian Code has preserved the acclamations of the veterans discharged after the victory. "Auguste Constantine, dei te nobis servent" [Augustus Constantine, may the gods preserve you for us] is what they shouted, and the offensive words were not emended to "Deus te nobis servet" [May God preserve you for us] until Justinian re-edited the law for insertion in his Code.

How far the army became christianized as the fourth century progressed it is very difficult to say. Its intake must have remained predominantly pagan. Christianity, as we have seen, made slow progress in the countryside, and the bulk of the peasant conscripts must have continued to belong to the old faith. With the conversion of the Goths and other east German tribes, some of the barbarian recruits will have been Christians, but the bulk of the barbarians in the fourth century seem to have come from the Franks and Alamans, who were still and long remained heathens. The army might have been expected to be a powerful force on the pagan side of the struggle.

Actually it played a purely passive role. It obeyed with equal loyalty Constantine and his sons, Julian the Apostate, and his Christian successors. It may be that military discipline and the habit of obedience were stronger forces than religious conviction. But what little evidence there is suggests rather that soldiers conformed more or less passively to the prevailing religion of the state whatever it might be for the time being. Julian seems to have inherited from Constantius II an army which was superficially at any rate largely Christian. His statement in his letter to Maximus that the bulk of the Gallic army, which he was leading against Constantius, worshipped the gods, reads like a boast of the achievement and implies that in the brief period since his proclamation he had changed the religious tone of the troops. Gregory Nazianzen's description of his insidious propaganda once again implies that Julian found the army of the East full of Christians, and its tone suggests that his success in winning the troops back to the old religion was considerable. Yet when Julian was dead the army accepted the Christian Jovian without ado, if without enthusiasm, and acclaimed Valentinian, who had publicly demonstrated his devotion to the new religion by resigning his commission under Julian.

The religious indifference of the army in an age when religious passions ran so high is a curious phenomenon. The explanation would seem to be that the army consisted of men torn from their normal environment and plunged into a new world where everything was unfamiliar. In his own village the peasant clung stubbornly to the immemorial beliefs and customs of his community, but when he was delivered over to the recruiting officers and marched to a distant province and posted among a heterogeneous crowd of strangers, he lost his bearings. His old gods were far away, and bewildered he accepted the prevailing worship of the army. The situation of barbarian recruits was similar. They too were plunged into an alien environment, and the majority seem to have been assimilated to it, losing touch with their tribesmen at home, and adopting Roman ways, and with them the prevailing Roman religion.

There were still at the end of the fourth century and at the beginning of the fifth some high-ranking German officers who retained their pagan faith despite many years in the Roman service—the Frank Arbogast and the Goths Fravitta and Generid: but the two last are noted as exceptional. Under a succession of Christian emperors the general tone of the army must have become more and more Christian. The sons of soldiers and veterans would have been normally brought up in the new religion, and barbarian and peasant recruits would have been quickly assimilated. It is noteworthy that when Arcadius had to employ military force to effect the arrest of John Chrysostom, he used a regiment of newly recruited Thracians. He may have feared that his more seasoned troops might have had scruples about dragging a bishop from the altar, and therefore have employed new recruits who were still pagans.

To turn to the upper classes, the old senatorial order, though it retained immense wealth and social prestige, had ceased in the latter part of the third century to possess much political influence. Under Gallienus, if we are to believe Aurelius Victor, senators had been excluded from military commands, and Diocletian, in his reorganization of the empire, relegated them to a very minor role. The prefecture of the city and the two proconsulates of Africa and Asia were still reserved for senators, and they could serve as *correctores* of the Italian provinces and of Achaea, but apart from these dignified but practically unimportant posts they took no part in the administration of the empire, which was entrusted to men of equestrian rank. The equestrian order thus became in effect the official aristocracy of the empire, and it was greatly increased in numbers. For not only did Diocletian's reforms involve the creation of many new posts, military and administrative, but many who aspired to the social prestige and legal privileges of the order secured admission to it by the grant of honorary offices or of the titular ranks of *egregius, centenarius, ducenarius,* or *perfectissimus.*

Constantine was less hostile to the senate, increasing the number of posts reserved for senators, admitting them to other high administrative offices, and enrolling them among his *comites* [courtiers]. At the same time he began to expand the order, granting senatorial rank to many of his higher equestrian officers, and to others whom he favoured. His policy was carried on by his sons, and gained momentum, so that by the middle of the fourth century it had become normal for all the higher civilian offices to carry senatorial rank: that is, on the one hand, senators by birth were eligible for them, and, on the other hand, men of lower degree appointed to them thereby became senators. The same policy was under Valentinian and Valens applied to the higher military offices. The result was that the equestrian order, limited to a decreasing number of lower-grade posts, waned in power and prestige, and the socially ambitious no longer aspired to be enrolled in it. The senatorial order, on the other hand, became once more the official aristocracy of the empire, but it was at the same time vastly inflated in numbers and profoundly modified in character. Not only was it swelled by those who entered it by tenure of civilian, and later military, offices. Those who had previously aspired to the equestrian order now strove by the tenure of honorary senatorial offices or the grant of the clarissimate [the status of belonging to the lowest senatorial order] to make their way into the senate. This influx into the senate threatened to deplete the municipal aristocracy of the empire, the curial order, and the imperial government made periodic efforts to check it. But its efforts were not very whole-hearted, and no regulations were proof against interest and bribery. The senatorial order continued to expand, particularly in the eastern half of the empire, where Constantius II, in his efforts to build up his own senate in Constantinople to parity with that of Rome, enrolled thousands of new members.

The new senators were drawn from very various origins. A very large number, as was only natural, came from the upper ranks of the curial class, the old families of the provincial and municipal aristocracy. According to the prevailing standards of the day such men were in virtue of their birth, wealth, and education fitted to hold the civilian offices and eminently eligible for admission to the senatorial aristocracy. Moreover, they possessed the social connexions and the money to press their claims effectively. Both official posts and senatorial rank were normally obtained by the interest of great men about the court, and this interest had often to be bought by hard cash. Men of position and wealth obviously had advantage in making the necessary contacts, and recompensing their patrons adequately for their services.

But a considerable number of the new senators, including many who rose to the highest rank, came from lower in the social scale. There were those who rose through the army by the tenure of the office of *magister militum, comes rei militaris,* or *dux.* Many of these military men were barbarians, but there were not a few Romans, and as the army in the fourth century offered a *carrière ouverte aux talents* [career open to talent], some of these were of quite humble origins. We happen to know of two peasants who rose from the ranks to high commands, Arbetio, who as *magister peditum* was long one of the most influential men in the court of Constantius II, and the elder Gratian, the father of Valentinian and Valens, who achieved the rank of *comes rei militaris.* Such cases were relatively rare, but there must have been a considerable number of senators whose fathers had started life as simple peasants.

The bar was also an avenue whereby able and ambitious men of humble origin could rise. It was the practice for the military and civilian administrators to select rising young barristers to serve as their judicial assessors, and after tenure of two or three such posts they were normally appointed to a provincial governorship, and might rise to the praetorian prefecture. Libanius laments that the law had become such a popular profession that humane studies were falling into neglect. Men of liberal education no longer got the jobs, they all went to barristers; and as a result the young men despised rhetoric and flocked to Berytus to the law schools. Not all barristers, of course, were men of humble origin: wealthy *curiales* and even senators did not disdain the profession. But it was possible for men of very modest status to climb to the top of the tree. Maximinus, who ultimately became praetorian prefect of the Gauls and one of Valentinian's right-hand men, was the son of a very low-grade civil servant, a financial clerk in the provincial office of Valeria.

If the promotion of barristers provoked Libanius' indignation, the rise to power of palatine civil servants, in particular of imperial notaries, roused him to a white heat of fury. What an age, he exclaims more than once, when a shorthand clerk becomes praetorian prefect. It was the function of the imperial notaries to keep the minutes of the consistory, and they were in the early fourth century simple clerks, whose only qualification was a knowledge of shorthand, and were normally men of very humble status. But from their intimate association with the emperor and his ministers they had great opportunities for advancement. They were employed for confidential missions, were appointed to the palatine ministries, and sometimes rose to the highest office of state. In one of his speeches Libanius gives a list of men who had thus risen from stenographers to senators. It includes many of the great names of the eastern half of the empire during the middle fourth century: Ablabius, Constantine's great praetorian prefect, consul in 331; Datianus, consul in 358; and four of Constantius II's praetorian prefects—Philippus, consul in 348, Taurus, consul in 361, Elpidius, and Domitianus. And of these, he declares, Datianus was the son of a cloakroom attendant in a bath, and Philippus of a sausage-maker, while Ablabius started as a clerk in a provincial office, and Domitianus' father was a manual worker.

The senatorial order thus became during the course of the fourth century a very mixed body. Its composition and structure differed in East and West. At Rome there was a strong nucleus of ancient families which claimed descent from the Gracchi and the Scipios. Tenuous as these claims might be, their members regarded themselves and were accepted as aristocrats of the bluest blood, and enjoyed immense inherited wealth. Many of them were content to hold the ornamental offices which they regarded as their due, and took no active part in the government of the empire. But some, like the great Petronius Probus, played an active part in politics. In the West the senatorial order had two main foci. Rome was the titular capital of the empire and the official seat of the senate. Here the old families reigned supreme. But the administrative capital of the emperor was no longer Rome but the imperial *comitatus* [retinue], wherever the emperor might be for the time being, at Milan, Paris, or Sirmium. Here members of the old families were less at home, and were outnumbered by new men who had risen in the emperor's service.

In the East there was no such division. Constantinople was both the centre of government and the seat of the senate, and the *comitatus* and the senatorial order were closely intertwined, with the result that the court dominated the senate. Moreover, at Constantinople there was no hard core of ancient families. As Libanius with rather heavy irony puts it: "the whole senate does not consist of nobles whose ancestors for four generations back and more have held offices and served on embassies and devoted themselves to the public service." Constantius II no doubt enrolled all senators who were already domiciled in his dominions, but they can have been few and undistinguished. The *elite* of the Constantinopolitan senate was formed of men like Philippus and Taurus who had risen to high office from quite humble origins: it was the descendants of such men who in the fifth and sixth centuries were the aristocracy of the eastern empire.

These facts have their bearing on the religious struggle, for the religion of senators was to some extent determined by their social origins. In the eastern parts the upper layer of the order was mainly composed of men who had risen from the strata of society most strongly impregnated by Christianity, the lower middle class and even, if Libanius is to be believed, the proletariat of the towns. In fact most of the leading men in the East in the fourth century were so far as we know Christians; the two principal exceptions were Themistius, who owed his advancement to his repute as a philosopher, and Tatian, a barrister, who after a long administrative career rose to be praetorian prefect. Many of them were no doubt Christians before their rise to power, and those who were not had not been conditioned against Christianity by a rhetorical education, and found little difficulty in accepting the faith of the court.

The great bulk of the eastern senators, who came from the upper layer of the curial order, would have been more divided in their allegiance. They came from families which cherished their Hellenic heritage, and higher education long retained a strongly pagan colour in the East. Most of the great rhetoricians and philosophers were pagans in the fourth century, and even in the fifth and sixth centuries many remained so. Zacharias of Mytilene in his life of Severus of Antioch gives a striking picture of university life at Alexandria, where he and Severus were students, in the last quarter of the fifth century. Not only, it seems, were most of the professors pagans, but so were a large proportion of the students, and he tells lurid tales of the hidden temple where they conducted their secret rites. Even in the sixth century Athens, which remained the leading university town of the East, was still strongly pagan in tone until Justinian expelled the philosophers.

The persistence of paganism among the cultured classes of the East must not then be underestimated. Even in the second half of the sixth century a purge conducted by Tiberius Constantine revealed the existence of many crypto-pagans among the aristocracy. But the furious outcry raised by Julian's law against Christian professors shows how deeply Christianity had penetrated among the educated classes by the middle of the fourth century, especially in the eastern half of the empire. It was not only that there were many Christian teachers, including so celebrated a figure as Prohaeresius, who lost their posts. There were evidently a vast number of Christian parents who regarded a rhetorical education as essential for their sons, but feared that under Julian's regime the schools would become militantly pagan. It is probable that by this time only rather old-fashioned and puritanical Christians felt any objection to a classical education as such, and many pious parents did not even scruple to send their sons to professors who were well known to be pagan; John Chrysostom was sent to Libanius by his mother, a devout Christian. In these circumstances many of the *curiales* promoted to the senate of Constantinople may have been Christians and the influence of the court and of the higher aristocracy must have converted many waverers. On the whole, the senate of Constantinople was probably from its origin a predominantly Christian body.

In the West, on the other hand, the old families remained on the whole faithful to their traditional religion down to the end of the fourth century, and since they dominated Roman society, the senate at Rome was strongly pagan. This is amply demonstrated by the petitions which it officially presented to Gratian and Valentinian II for the restoration of the altar of Victory and of the Roman priesthoods.

How far the senatorial order as a whole was predominantly pagan or Christian it is more difficult to say. Ambrose in 384 claimed that "the *curia* is crowded with a majority of Christians," and in 382 Pope Damasus, as a counterblast to the official request of the senate for the restoration of the altar of Victory, was able to organize a monster petition of Christian senators, who protested that they had given no such mandate, did not agree with such requests of the pagans, and did not give their consent to them. It is obviously impossible at this distance of time to discover the truth behind the rival propaganda of the two sides. From the fact that only two years after Damasus had got up his petition the senate again sent an official request to the emperor it is clear that at Rome the Christian opposition was weak, whether because Christian senators resident in the city were actually in a minority or because they were for the most part relatively humble members of the order, who dared not stand up to the great aristocrats. From the language of the petition it would appear that its signatories had not attended the meeting at which the resolution was voted. This may mean that they had not dared to voice their opposition openly. But it is more likely that Damasus obtained his "innumerable" signatures by sending a round robin to nonresident senators. These would have been for the most part new men, and among them the proportion of Christians would have actually been higher.

At the court at Milan the balance, as the rejection of the senate's pleas showed, inclined to the Christian side. But the decision was by no means a foregone conclusion, and it needed all Ambrose's zeal and eloquence to sway the consistory.

These facts account in a large measure for the very different course which the struggle took in East and West. In the East the pagan opposition was never a serious political force. It was in both senses of the word academic. The leaders of paganism were almost all professors, Maximus, Themistius, Libanius, and the rest. The strongholds of paganism were the university towns, foremost among them Athens. It survived longest among students and intellectuals. Moreover, in the pejorative sense of the word the pagan opposition was academic. It was unorganized and ineffectual, finding expression only in speeches and pamphlets. When Theodosius the Great closed the temples and banned pagan cult, there was no serious opposition apart from the heroic but futile attempt of the philosopher Olympius to hold the Serapeum at Alexandria with a band of enthusiasts. Pagans thereafter contented themselves with furtively practising their rites in secret and nourishing apocalyptic dreams of the return of the old gods. As late as the reign of Zeno great excitement was caused among the pagan intellectuals of Asia Minor when the Neoplatonist philosopher Pamprepius became master of the offices to the pretender Leontius. They began to offer sacrifice openly on his behalf and an oracle was circulated that the span allotted by fate for Christianity had come to an end and that the old gods would come into their own again. Needless to say, their hopes were quite unfounded. Leontius, or rather his patron, the Isaurian general Illus, made no move in favour of paganism.

This weakness of paganism is partly accounted for by their numerical inferiority in the East. More important, however, than the question of mere numbers was that of political leadership. There was in the

East no hereditary aristocracy bred up in the old ways to lead the opposition. The governing class at Constantinople was largely composed of parvenus drawn from the classes where Christianity was strongest, and the senate was from its first formation predominantly Christian in tone.

It cannot be claimed that the pagan opposition was very much more effective in the West, but here the Roman aristocracy did at least make an official stand for the old religion, and its representations, though rejected, were taken into serious consideration. What is more significant, a pretender at the end of the fourth century thought it worth while to make concessions to the pagan sentiments of the senate. Eugenius, though himself a Christian, if not a very fervent one, restored the altar of Victory and handed over the endowments of the Roman priesthood to pagan senators. This rather half-hearted gesture met with a vigorous response, and the Roman aristocracy, led by Flavian, the praetorian prefect of Italy, threw themselves wholeheartedly into the struggle on Eugenius' behalf. They, too, dreamed of a pagan restoration, but their dreams had rather more substance than those of their eastern fellow believers.

It may be claimed that the social changes of the third and fourth centuries were an important factor in the triumph of Christianity in the empire as a whole. When Constantine staked his faith on the god of the Christians in 312, he was on all human calculations making a very rash venture. Christians were on any reckoning a small minority, particularly in the West, where the struggle with Maxentius was to take place, and they mostly belonged to classes which were politically and militarily negligible, the manual workers, shopkeepers, merchants, and lesser decurions of the towns and the clerks of the civil service. The army was overwhelmingly pagan. The senate was pagan. So too in all probability was the bulk of the provincial and municipal aristocracy, and the majority of higher administration, drawn as they were from the army and the curial class. By making himself the champion of Christianity, Constantine can hardly have hoped to win for himself any useful support, and might reasonably have feared to provoke antagonism in many important quarters; and this is incidentally to my mind an important piece of circumstantial evidence in favour of the view that Constantine's conversion was not a calculated political move, but, as he himself consistently proclaimed in his public pronouncements, the fruit of a genuine if crude religious conviction that the Highest Divinity, who had chosen him as his servant, was a more potent giver of victory than the old gods.

The situation was not, however, as unfavourable as it appeared. For at the time when Constantine made his fateful decision Roman society was in a state of flux. The late Roman empire is often conceived as a rigid hierarchical society, in which every man was tied to the station in life to which he was born. The long series of laws on which this view is based seem to me to reveal a very different picture. They show that the imperial government was struggling to impose a rigid hereditary class system, but such legislation would not have been called for had not the familiar structure of society been shaken; and the constant re-enactment of the rules, and the periodical concessions made, show that the government was very imperfectly successful in checking the movements which it regarded as dangerous. There is much evidence which suggests that society was static in the second and early third centuries. The army was to an increasing degree recruited from the sons of soldiers and veterans. The peasants tilled the same farms, whether they were freeholders or tenants, from generation to generation. The decurions were a mainly hereditary class, where son succeeded father to the ancestral estates. The aristocracy of the empire, the senate, and the equestrian order, failed it is true to maintain its numbers and was constantly supplemented from below; but the rate of recruitment was slow, and the new members, who mainly came from the provincial aristocracy, were readily assimilated.

Under the impact of the prolonged crisis of the mid-third century this stable society was profoundly shaken. For a variety of reasons men of all classes became dissatisfied with their hereditary position in life, and the conditions of the time gave opportunities for change. The population had probably shrunk as a result of the wars, famines, and plagues of the years of anarchy, and at the same time the army was making increasing demands for men. The consequence was an acute shortage of manpower, which made itself particularly felt in the empire's major industry, agriculture. Landlords could not find enough tenants to cultivate their lands, and welcomed newcomers to their estates. As a result dissatisfied tenants found themselves able to throw up their farms and move elsewhere with the certainty that another landlord would offer them a home. This restlessness among the peasantry caused grave concern to the government, which saw the basis of its fiscal system imperilled. The poll-tax was based on the assumption that the peasants registered under each village or farm would remain there and in due course be succeeded by their sons. The land-tax too seemed to be threatened, since landlords everywhere complained that their estates had been abandoned by their cultivators. This would seem to be the situation which provoked the legislation tying the agricultural population to the land on which they were registered on the census.

The manpower shortage gave rise to a similar restlessness in other classes of society and provoked similar legislation where, as in the mining industry, the government felt that the interests of the state were threatened. Another disturbing factor was the vast expansion of the administrative services entailed by Diocletian's reorganization of the empire. More and more clerks were required in the growing government offices, and many sons of soldiers and veterans, instead of enlisting in the army as hitherto, preferred a more comfortable and lucrative career as officials; *curiales* of the humbler sort likewise flocked into the ministries. Once again the government, finding the intake of the army reduced and the city councils, on which the administration of the empire and the collection of the taxes ultimately depended, dangerously depleted, endeavoured to tie the sons of soldiers and decurions to their respective hereditary roles.

But the most revolutionary change brought about by Diocletian was the formation of the new imperial nobility of service which I have outlined earlier in this lecture. This change was of crucial importance for the future of Christianity. For it meant that Constantine and his successors did not have to face a firmly entrenched hereditary aristocracy hostile to their religious innovation, but were able to build up and mould a new nobility more subservient to their wishes.

The senate had, it is true, under the principate been powerless to resist a resolute and ruthless emperor. But an emperor could only impose his will by a reign of terror, and while emperors came and went, the senate remained. Through the generations the senatorial order preserved to a remarkable degree a corporate sense of its dignity, and a spirit of independence and even of opposition to the imperial office. The great aristocratic families regarded themselves as superior to jumped-up emperors, and their birth and wealth made them independent of imperial patronage. Such a body might be bullied into submission, but its sentiments could not be easily influenced.

The new nobility of service was a very different body. A heterogeneous collection of individuals, drawn from all ranks of society, it inevitably lacked any corporate sense. And since its members were dependent on imperial patronage for their advancement, it was as inevitably subservient to the emperor's will and took its tone from him. Constantine and his Christian successors were thus able to build up an aristocracy in sympathy with their religious policy.

In the first place they were in a position to show direct favour to Christians. They could choose their ministers and advisers with a free hand from all classes of society, and bestow rank and dignity on whomsoever they wished to favour. They certainly used this opportunity to promote Christians of low degree. Constantine himself, according to Eusebius, was lavish in bestowing codicils of equestrian rank, and even senatorial dignity, on the adherents of his religion. But such a policy had its limits. The number of qualified Christians was too few to fill the posts, and any systematic exclusion of pagans would have provoked dangerous discontent: it was not in fact until the early years of the fifth century that the imperial service was formally debarred to pagans. But it soon became obvious to the ambitious that their chances of promotion would be greatly enhanced if they adopted the emperor's religion, and Eusebius himself deplores that Constantine's open-handed favour to Christians resulted in a large crop of interested conversions.

But it would be a grave injustice to the many upper-class converts of the fourth century to assume that they were all hypocritical opportunists. A more potent cause of conversion than calculations of material gain was the fact that Christianity became respectable and indeed fashionable in high society; and this change of tone came about the more easily because high society was in a state of flux. The old senatorial aristocracy had a strong conservative tradition, and clung firmly to the old religion, even when it was on the wane, from a sense of *noblesse oblige*. They still had great social prestige, and to some extent set the tone of society in the West, but in the East their position was usurped by the new senate of Constantinople, and even in the West it was disputed by the new nobility which clustered around the *comitatus*. In the new aristocracy of service Christians were not perhaps at first very numerous, but enjoying exceptional imperial favour and achieving the highest honours, they set the tone of the whole. The lesser members tended to follow their lead, and the fashion spread in ever-widening circles through the lower ranks of the social order.

Christianity had made great progress during the first three centuries, but it still remained a minority sect: it was still largely confined to the middle and lower classes and had made little impression on the aristocracy. Within a few generations of the conversion of Constantine it had become the dominant religion of the empire. In this revolution the support given to Christianity by the imperial government was without doubt a major factor. But it is significant that the religious change coincided with a social change, which brought to the front men from the middle and lower classes.

# IV/BARBARIAN SOCIETY

THE barbarians were the members of the numerous, mainly Germanic tribes—Goths, Franks, Saxons, Jutes, Huns—who lived beyond the confines of the Roman Empire, principally scattered across the great North European Plain. Probably of Asian origin, their nomadic habits had led them continuously westward and had brought them into contact with the all-conquering Romans in the early years of the Empire. For several centuries Romans and barbarians coexisted well enough, and individual barbarians were sometimes Romanized so successfully that they became important figures in the imperial state. The barbarians as a group, however, did not belong to the Roman world: They were outsiders, and they must indeed have appeared rough and ready, unkempt and uncouth to the Romans who made their acquaintance. But to assume that because this description is accurate, their social organization was necessarily less complex than that of the Romans is unwarranted.

The radical historian accords primary importance to the matter of social organization, for he maintains that the key to an understanding of all aspects of human activity must start by opening the lock of class relationships. Although he recognizes that the social relations of production, that is, the relations men enter into in the process of making their living, may not be, in all societies, the unique determinant of class, he nevertheless starts by examining these relationships and, therefore, the distribution of productive property. Private ownership he takes to be only one historically determined form of property holding, the abolition of which will make it possible, in the future, to create a classless, and therefore more human, society. As one can never plan in a truly serious way for the future without knowing how the present has been conditioned by the past, it is only to be expected that the radical historian should have a particular interest in barbarian society, where private property was rapidly becoming, but was not yet, the dominant mode, and an alternate form of social organization prevailed.

The barbarians were primitive peoples in the sense that, when we first note their appearance on the Roman scene, they were still strangers to the concept of private property in land. They were stockbreeders and hunters; agriculture was only just beginning to be a major occupation. Their land was communally held and allocated annually among the clans to be worked in common. This is not to say that there is no evidence of social inequality among the members of the clans, nor that the structures of authority were purely democratic and participatory, but that stratification was based on something other than the distribution of property. At the same time, we can observe the clear evolution away from communal to private property, partially under the influence of Rome, and the creation of more or less stable and eventually hereditary status groups. In the selection reprinted here, E. A. Thompson, a leading English historian of the barbarian West, uses these concepts to discuss the state of the Germanic tribes in the time of Caesar.

As early as 1877, the American anthropologist Lewis Henry Morgan, in his *Ancient Society*, showed the importance in "primitive" societies, the Greek and the Roman as well as the Iroquois which he particularly studied, of the *gens* or clan. No doubt Morgan's most important contribution was to oppose the then-current theory of the patriarchal family as the original unit of human society, but he gave us as well an emphasis upon the fundamental importance of subsistence needs and the institutions of property arising from them for the development of social organization. In other words, he demonstrated the passage from social organization based on kinship groups to one based on other principles of stratification, notably class. It was for this reason that Morgan attracted the admiration of Marx and Engels, and the latter used his book as the basis for his own *Origins of Private Property, the Family and the State* (1884).

It is true that kinship groups can and do continue to exist even in societies based on private property. They cannot, however, be the exclusive source of power and authority in those societies as they are when only communal property (or no property at all in the strict sense—for example, among nomadic tribes) exists. Historically, kinship groups have tended to hang on for long periods of time in societies based on private property, and at the level of tradition their influence has never been lost. (When I speak of kinship groups in this connection, I exclude consideration of the present-day nuclear family.) The clan and extended family were thus the models for the client relationships of Imperial Rome and the feudal relationships of medieval Europe, which had in common an element of personal subordination (on the model of son-to-father or nephew-to-uncle) of a weak to a more powerful man in return for protection—military, economic, and otherwise. Feud and vendetta continued to exist as major social patterns for centuries, as J. M. Wallace-Hadrill of Merton College, Oxford, makes clear in the following article. But the important thing to remember is that all these forms were eventually made subordinate to class considerations. In more recent times, the ties of kinship have been particularly strong in what may be called one-class communities—that is, communities in which the entire population, despite existing stratification arrangements, not only feels but is, in fact, made one by a threat from the outside. The classic example: peasant communities threatened by the colonial or semicolonial activities of urban capital, especially when it is associated with the apparatus of the state and, even more, of a foreign state.

# E. A. Thompson

## 8

## The Germans in the Time of Julius Caesar

### MATERIAL CIVILIZATION

In the middle of the first century B.C. the Germanic peoples living east of the Rhine were primarily pastoralists, but they were not nomadic pastoralists. They did not drive their flocks and herds northwards in springtime and southwards in the autumn, following the green grass, like the nomads of the Eurasian steppe. In moist and forested Germany the vegetation was not so strictly seasonal as to force the inhabitants into the ways of nomads. The life of the early German was not entirely dependent upon, and conditioned by, his possession of flocks and herds. No doubt these were his principal means of subsistence. These together with hunting supplied him with the greater part of his foodstuffs—meat, milk, cheese. These formed his chief source of wealth and dignity. Yet the care of his flocks and herds was not the sole occupation of his peace-time life. The Romans knew that, although some Germanic peoples resembled the nomads in certain ways, the Germans were nonetheless distinct from the nomads.

Their cattle were stunted and puny in contrast with the enormous oxen which ran wild in the forests, for "the more completely the ox was tamed and deprived of its natural food, the more drastically, under primitive conditions of farming, it diminished in size." In the opinion of the Romans their horses, too, were not remarkable either for beauty or for speed, though daily training could make something of them. It is true that German warriors serving in the Roman army would sometimes be allowed to retain their own unsaddled horses as well as their own inferior weapons. Yet Caesar found it noteworthy that they did not import horses from abroad; and he thought it advisable on one occasion during his wars in Gaul to supply Roman horses to some Germanic cavalrymen whom he had enlisted from beyond the Rhine. Even their livestock, then, the very basis of the Germans' economy, was of inferior quality by Roman standards.

But if the Germans were pastoralists in the first place, their primitive agriculture was by no means negligible, though its importance will have varied from place to place according to local conditions. True, Caesar insists on the subordinate part which it played in the German economy, and he points out that grain was a comparatively small item in the diet of at least the Suebi. But he finds occasion to mention specifically the agriculture of several Germanic peoples; and in the first century A.D. one exceptionally advanced people, the Ubii, practised a method of fertilizing their fields which was akin to marling. Although Tacitus believed that the Germans grew corn crops only, a wide variety of root-crops and vegetables was in fact known to them; and if a more fertile tract of land than their own were found to be lying empty or weakly defended beyond their frontier, a whole people might be expected to migrate into it and build their rude homes there. The Romans believed that this longing for richer land explained the unending pressure of the forest- and marsh-dwelling Germans on the cleared and fertile fields of Gaul. In fact, Caesar himself admits that if a Germanic people were prevented by the raids of a more powerful neighbour from sowing and reaping their crops for a sufficient time, they would have to move away from their homes altogether to some place of greater safety. Their agriculture was no mere digging-stick gardening: even the Bronze-Age rock carvings at Bohuslän in southern Sweden include a picture of an ox-drawn plough. In a word, although crop-raising was subordinate to stock-breeding, it was nevertheless an essential and indispensable part of the Germanic economy.

In Caesar's day the Germans were ardent hunters, and the enthusiasm which they brought to this occupation does not prove that they hunted for sport only. They did so of necessity, and the game which they took formed an integral part of their food supply and provided them with some of their clothing. They were also food-gatherers to the extent that they collected and ate wild fruits and berries as a staple part of their diet; for with the exception of the apple they did not cultivate fruit-trees in Caesar's time. In the days of Tacitus they may have begun to cultivate them, as they saw the Romans do across the Rhine, and later still they certainly grew them in Roman territories which they overran and occupied: they then inherited the fruit orchards which the Romans had planted, and they learned to tend them.

The Iron Age had begun among the Germans several centuries before the time of Julius Caesar, but their use of iron was severely limited, at any rate by Roman standards, even at the end of the first century A.D.; and it is not until the fourth century that we hear of the Romans exacting an indemnity of iron from a Germanic people whom they had defeated in war. Metal of any kind was no doubt a luxury material for domestic utensils, most of which were made either of wood or leather by the menfolk or of clay by the women. Of the larger metal objects used by the Germans, apart from their weapons, most were made of bronze: the bronze industry, though not a bronze arms industry, continued to flourish throughout the Iron Age in western Germany. In the case of many handicrafts technical skill was as high beyond the Roman frontier as it was within it; but the quantities of raw materials, such as iron, which were at the disposal of Roman craftsmen were almost infinitely higher than those available to the northern barbarians.

The bulk of their pottery was made by hand, and pieces turned on the wheel were distinctly unusual. The Germans could use the wheel, but they could not employ it extensively and systematically because of the rarity of large centres of population among them. Only an occasional itinerant potter would make his way from community to community selling wheelmade pots designed for the special needs of the purchasers. Handmade pottery was predominant, and this in itself suggests a very low level of material civilization in the communities which used it.

Finally, there is no certain evidence that the Germans of the times of Caesar and Tacitus could write. Even if the notorious *notae* mentioned by Tacitus were a form of runes it still remains the case that these runes were, so far as can be told, nothing but a kind of private and personal code which was used only in connexion with the casting of lots. Now many Germans learned to speak Latin as a result of living among the Romans as hostages or as mercenary soldiers; and the letters which were sent from time to time by Germanic chieftains to the Romans were written in Latin. But it does not follow that they were written by Germans: they were probably written for them by Roman war-prisoners or Roman traders or in later days by Christian priests.

The Germans of Caesar's time, then, were primarily stock-breeders, although their crop-raising was an indispensable part of their economy. Hunting and food-gathering were still necessary tasks. They had some, but not much, iron at their disposal. They used handmade pottery almost universally; and they were pre-literate.

## SOCIAL ORGANIZATION

Differences of wealth among any one Germanic people were slight in Julius Caesar's time, and the private ownership of land was still unknown. Each year the leading men or "magistrates," as Caesar calls them for want of a better term, would decide which parts of the people's land were to be brought under the plough. They would then allocate these selected parts to the various clans and would settle the extent and site of each clan's holding, leaving the area tilled in the previous year to lie fallow. When they received their allotment the clansmen would plough the land with their ox-drawn ploughs, and reap their harvests; and they did so in common without dividing up the allotment among the various individuals or households included in the clan, and hence they must also have appropriated the fruits of the land in common. The fact is that when the means of subsistence were continuously re-distributed substantial inequalities in the standard of living could hardly arise, and there were few ways in which the leading men could monopolize resources for their own private use. The annual re-allocation of the arable among the German clans would tend to maintain the equality of the different clans' wealth in so far as their wealth was derived from crops at all. On the other hand, although the pastures were unenclosed and common to everyone, we may assume that the herds were held on an individual basis, for it is difficult to believe that cattle acquired as plunder were always owned collectively by the plunderers. This might be the case if the plundering party was composed of the warriors of a single clan; but in fact there were other kinds of raiding bands which would not have owned their booty collectively. It follows that there were differences of wealth in Caesar's Germany, however slight these differences may have been—and in fact they *were* slight, as Caesar clearly implies.

Caesar's comment on the Germanic peoples' system of land-tenure deserves the most careful notice. He is aware of the social consequences which would have resulted had private ownership of land developed fully among them. In extending the area of their property the more influential landowners, if they had existed, would have expropriated the humbler. The accumulation of privately owned wealth would have given rise to class struggles, which he implies were not to be found among the Germans of his time. Wide differences of wealth would have led to tension between the leading men and the common warriors, tension which, as things were, did not exist, for in the actual conditions observed by him each warrior could see that his own wealth, however scanty it might be, was hardly less than that of the most influential leaders. This penetrating analysis, which he says was derived from some of the clansmen themselves, forms the converse of a fact which was later to be remarked by Tacitus: as wealth accumulates in a primitive society, power—and he means coercive power—tends to become concentrated in one central authority.

In peacetime there was no chieftain in Caesar's day whose influence extended over all the clans which made up a people (*civitas*). The leading men of the tribes (*pagi*) into which each people was divided would do what they could to patch up such disputes as arose and to reconcile the contending parties. But in doing so they seem to have been nothing more than mediators: they will have had no coercive power. Moreover, Caesar's words suggest that the leading men of each tribe or "region" acted only in those disputes which broke out between members of their own respective tribe or region: they are not said to have acted in disputes which broke out between persons belonging to different tribes or different regions. For such disputes there was no mediatory body at this date, so far as we know. Further, as we have seen, the arable was allocated every year to the clans by the leading men. Who were these leading men? Did the leading men of the people as a whole meet together specifically for this purpose, or was the allocation discussed and carried out independently by the leading men of each tribe or group of clans? Was the allocation a centralized operation performed by one supreme body with the right to act in all parts of the people's territory, or did it consist of a number of purely local actions? The answer can scarcely be in doubt. It is hardly credible that any clan or group of clans would have consented to have their arable distributed among them by men who might come from a wholly different part of the country and who might know little or nothing about local conditions, the relative size of the various clans, the quality of the soil, and so on. The site of the arable and the allocation of it to the clans must have been decided upon by the leading men of each tribe or group of adjacent clans and not by a central council of the leading men of the whole people. From this it might be inferred that in addition to the general assembly of the warriors of the whole people there was also a tribal assembly in each *pagus,* for the leading men presumably announced their decision on the arable to a meeting of all the persons concerned.

The various clans, then, were not bound together to any detectable extent under one central organ of government in time of peace. Evidently the clans or groups of clans lived more or less independently in their internal affairs, and on at least some occasions they could act independently even in their external relations. Late in the second century A.D. certain Germanic peoples of central Europe, who were in process of surrendering to the Emperor Marcus Aurelius, negotiated with him clan by clan, though others did so people by people; and in the interval since Caesar's time there is not likely to have been an increase in the kindreds' power to conduct external affairs—we shall see that the whole tendency in this period was towards more centralization. There is no reason to doubt that the clans lived on the basis of more or less complete equality. And similarly within the framework of the clan the individual's freedom from coercion and from imposed authority forced itself upon the notice of more than one Roman observer.

A central council of the leading men did come into existence, however, in times of danger; and Caesar shows that in a moment of emergency it could take military decisions and lay down strategical plans. For when the Romans unexpectedly bridged the Rhine in 55 B.C. the leading men of the Suebi "according to their custom" held a council and sent messengers in all directions ordering the womenfolk, the children, and the movable property to be taken from the settlements to the forests, and directing all able-bodied warriors to assemble. What does Caesar mean when he says that this council met "according to their custom" (*more suo*)? Does he refer to their custom in time of emergency, or does he imply that regular meetings of the council were held even in peacetime and that the Roman invasion coincided with one of these regular meetings? If the latter, this is our only explicit evidence for a central council of the leading men of the whole people in peacetime. But if, as we have seen reason to believe, the administration of justice and the allocation of the arable lay outside the scope of any such council, what then were its functions? It is hard to give a wholly satisfactory answer, and hence it is not clear that in time of peace there was any council of elders or leading men which would meet and exert influence over the people as a whole, though such a council certainly met when danger threatened. In peacetime no council higher than the councils of the *pagi* can be said with certainty to have existed.

In time of war an unknown number of confederate chieftains was elected, and Caesar gives no hint that any one of them had greater authority or prestige than the others: they were joint leaders. As long as the war lasted, they are said, whether rightly or wrongly, to have had the power of life and death over the warriors whom they led. It was still the case among some Germanic peoples of Tacitus' day and among the Visigoths in the time of Ulfila that there was normally no one over-all peacetime chieftain. Among some at least of the Franks in the early fourth century the same was true: they, too, elected their chiefs only on the eve of war. The case of the Saxons shows that the type of chieftainship which Caesar describes had not wholly disappeared even in the eighth century A.D. At that date the Saxon war-leader was chosen only on the outbreak of war (though he was chosen, curiously enough, not by election but by lot from among the tribal leaders); and when the war was over he reverted, as his predecessors of Caesar's time appear to have done, to the position of an ordinary tribal leader. The difference between this and what Caesar describes (apart from the use of lot) is that among the Saxons there was only one war-leader, whereas there were several among Caesar's Germans. Nor was the multiple war-leadership quick to disappear in all parts of Germany. It could still be found among the Franks early in the fourth century, among the Burgundians towards its close, and among the Alamanni until the year 536. Even in Caesar's time, however, the tendency may have been growing to limit to two the number of confederate war-chiefs; for in 58 B.C. Caesar heard that a force of Suebi had come down to the Rhine under the leadership of two brothers named Nasua and Cimberius, and in later ages this dual command was exceedingly widespread among the Germanic peoples. But only this one example of it has been recorded from the first century B.C. Unfortunately, we catch only a few glimpses of the war-chieftains in Caesar's time. Ariovistus insisted on being accompanied by ten men when he negotiated with Caesar, who unhappily gives no information about the status of these ten. An important decision concerning the Ubii was expected to be made at a time of danger by their "leading men and their senate," as Caesar puts it; and the two terms are not synonymous. And in wartime the Usipetes and Tencteri came to negotiate with Caesar "with all their leading men and elders"; and again Caesar refers to their chieftains and their council. In none of these cases did the chieftains act without the council. There is no certain evidence for individual, personal authority in early Germany.

Besides the council and the war-chieftainship there was also a general assembly of the warriors. But Caesar gives no description of its powers. . . .

In the middle of the first century B.C., then, a Germanic people was composed of a number of kindreds or clans which were the basic economic units of society, though the acquisition of herds of cattle by individual warriors may have been tending to introduce differences of wealth into the clans and so to detach the individual from his kindred. These clans were grouped together in larger units which we have called "tribes" (pagi). Of these little is known, but it seems that the leading men of each tribe formed a council which allocated the arable land every year and that they acted as mediators in disputes which broke out within the tribe. There is no clear evidence, however, for the existence of a central, confederate council of the elders or leading men of the whole people, except in wartime. In wartime a number of elected chieftains led the forces of the people, for the various tribes federated at least to this extent that they put their military forces under some sort of central leadership. But there is no trace of any institutions of coercion, except perhaps in war; and the evidence seems to point to the conclusion that in peace-time there was nothing which could be called a centralized public power over and above the armed warriors themselves. As for slaves, ancient authors give little information about the nature of Germanic slavery in the period before the Migrations. Their hints suggest that domestic slavery was restricted to females, that the chief function of the slave trade in Germany was to convey slaves from the interior of the country to the Roman frontier for sale to the Romans, that several Germanic peoples killed off their prisoners or at any rate their adult male prisoners after a successful campaign, that it was difficult to hold an adult male German in slavery in Germany, and hence that most of such slaves as existed there were put to work on the land in very favourable conditions: they were given a "home" (penates) of their own and were merely required to pay their owner a quantity of grain, cattle, or cloth. In view of all this and of the constant demand for slaves on the Roman frontier and the ease and profit with which they could be disposed of there, it seems fair to conclude that the number of slaves in early Germany was small (except in one or two places which were exposed to abnormally strong Roman influence) and that such slaves as did exist there were to a large extent of non-Germanic birth. In view of this and of the absence of grounds for serious tension among the free population, organs of repression were not required and did not exist.

## FROM CAESAR TO TACITUS

In Caesar's time, then, Germanic society was more primitive than is sometimes supposed. The fact that the arable was still worked communally by the kindreds and that any given piece of arable was cultivated for only one year suggests that the techniques of agriculture were still at a low stage of development. The kindred and not the monogamous family was still the fundamental entity in society. In the kindreds of Caesar's time descent may still have been reckoned in the female line for many purposes, perhaps for most.[1] The kindreds were only loosely knit together, and in peacetime there seems to have been no public authority to weld them all into a unity. Slavery was still in an incipient stage of growth, and there were no public institutions of coercion. In all, so primitive was Germanic society that we cannot disregard Caesar's remark that the life of the Germans was one of poverty, want, and hardship.

Now in the time of Tacitus a number of changes had come over Germanic society. . . . But there is one change that must be mentioned here. At the end of the first century A.D. the kindred was less decisively the basis of society than it had been in Caesar's day, and one indication of this decline in its importance concerns the distribution of the arable. True, a decision had still to be reached every year as to which tract or tracts of the people's land in each *pagus* or in each village was to be brought under the plough. But when this was done, the land was no longer divided up among the clans to be worked in common

---

[1] On matrilineal descent among the Germans see in English H. M. Chadwick, *The Origin of the English Nation* (Cambridge, 1907), 306 ff.; Bertha Phillpotts, *Kindred and Clan in the Middle Ages and After* (Cambridge, 1913), 265 ff.; R. Briffault, *The Mothers* (London, 1927), i, 414–17; V. Grönbech, *The Culture of the Teutons* (London and Copenhagen, 1931), i, 347 ff. The transition to father-right was still historically recent among the Germans of whom Tacitus speaks and was still incomplete. Before Roman civilization reached the borders of Germany and brought about the rapid social changes which will be discussed later, the matrilineal principle may have been in full force among some at least of the peoples even of western Germany (to say nothing of those of the remote north and east) and perhaps among a majority of them.

by the clansmen, and so its crops cannot any longer have been appropriated in common by the kindreds. The procedure described by
Caesar had been modified; for Tacitus reports that the arable was now
distributed "according to social standing," a phrase which shows that
it was distributed not to kindreds but to individuals, the leading men
of the *pagus* each taking a larger or a more fertile allotment than a
rank-and-file warrior, and the wealthier or more renowned of the
warriors presumably taking more than the less wealthy or the less
renowned. The kindred was no longer of basic importance where the
arable and its produce were concerned. How had this change come
about? And what was its significance?

It may be assumed that such potters as used the wheel—and these
were very few—together with many of the smiths and, where they
existed, the miners and iron-smelters, were full-time specialists at their
work, and did not directly produce their own food-supply. They produced commodities—that is, articles produced for sale or exchange
and not for consumption by the producers—and these commodities
they exchanged for food produced by others. The Germans had also
discovered that men might be treated as commodities: they, too, might
be bought and sold. To what extent the production of commodities
and the trade which resulted from it had developed beyond this point
in the first century B.C. is a matter of equal importance and obscurity.
Leaving aside sporadic cases where the plunder or prisoners taken in
a successful raid were profitably sold or where a crop failed locally or
where the cattle belonging to a community became diseased or were
lost in an enemy raid—leaving aside these and similar local or temporary occasions of plenty or of scarcity, the Germanic village is
unlikely to have used many objects which had not been produced at
home, though a limited number of private individuals certainly
bought metals, including silver. In fact, the private ownership of the
herds and of articles of luxury is proof of private trading between
individuals. But many communities as such were obliged to buy
articles, like iron and salt, which were not produced everywhere.
Indeed, it may be that when the Hermunduri and the Chatti fought
a war in A.D. 58 for the possession of a salt-bed they aimed not merely
at covering their own needs but also at exporting salt at a profit to
those peoples who were in need of it. In the main, then, two kinds of
articles were bartered in Germany in Caesar's time: (a) essential
articles which were required by a community as a whole, and (b)
luxury articles which were owned by individuals. It is not difficult to
guess which of these two kinds of trade was gaining ground propor-
tionately to the other in the years which followed Caesar's arrival on
the Rhine. Soon after Caesar's time exchange between individuals—
for example, cattle or men in exchange for metals or for furs—was
undoubtedly gaining ground relatively to trade conducted for the

benefit of a community. For while the demand of many peoples for articles which could not be made at home may or may not have increased in the period between Caesar and Tacitus, the archaeological evidence shows that the leading men's demand for luxuries increased drastically.

Celtic merchants dealing in Italian as well as Celtic wares were active in Germany in the middle of the first century B.C. and reached some areas in considerable numbers. They supplied the more well-to-do warriors with foreign articles like wine, various kinds of bronze vessels, and so on. But the goods imported by the Germans from the Celtic merchants were much less in quantity and variety than the goods which they bought from Roman merchants in the early years of the Christian era. For with the Roman occupation of western Germany in 12–9 B.C. the German leaders were able to buy whole categories of luxury goods—glass vessels, red table ware, Roman weapons, brooches, statuettes, ornaments of various kinds, and so on— which had not reached them before. And the fact that Roman goods could now be bought stimulated the desire of the leading men of the Germans to have them. These imported luxuries were highly prized and seem to have had an enormous prestige-value. They were privately owned, and from the beginning of the Christian era they existed in great numbers.

From at least the time of Augustus many a Roman trader penetrated deep into Germany hawking his goods from settlement to settlement. There is reason to think, however, that the majority of Roman traders carried on their business with the lands lying immediately outside the Imperial frontier and that many of the Roman goods which reached the interior of Germany did so by being passed from hand to hand among the Germans themselves. If so, they thereby stimulated throughout the whole of Germany and not merely along the frontier the production, or at any rate the acquisition, by the Germans themselves of commodities which could be used to pay for the imported luxuries. The dimensions of this trade must be emphasized. There was even a permanent settlement of Romans residing and earning their living by trade and moneylending in a Germanic chieftain's capital in and about A.D. 19. This was the capital of the Marcomanni in Bohemia, and the goods which these traders imported came in particular from the Danubian provinces, especially Noricum, but also in part from Italy and Gaul. For a time Bohemia imported Roman goods on a scale unparalleled among the Germanic peoples. It is true that soon after A.D. 19 this Marcomannic trade declined and lost its exceptional character—no doubt for one reason or another the community of Roman merchants had been dispersed. But permanent settlements of Roman traders beyond any Roman frontier are very rarely mentioned in Imperial times by our authorities, and no doubt were in fact very unusual; and that traders should have found it worth their while to settle among the Marcomanni illustrates the size of the demand for Roman goods in Bohemia. That the Imperial government itself recognized the importance of this trade would be proved strikingly if it is true that it had secured in a formal treaty with the Marcomanni the right for these traders to carry on their work in Bohemia. But although Bohemia was exceptional in the degree of its demand for imported luxuries, it was exceptional in degree only: the demand for Roman commodities was exceedingly widespread among the more well-to-do tribesmen throughout the length and breadth of continental Germany.

The importance of money in this process must not be exaggerated. The general practice even at the end of the first century A.D., especially in the interior of Germany, was exchange by barter. But in regions near the frontier where trade with Roman merchants was particularly brisk commodities were often paid for in Roman coins in the first century A.D. On the other hand, the vast numbers of Roman coins which have been found in the interior of Germany and which were privately owned by individual Germans were regarded as ornaments rather than as a medium of exchange. Hence, if the general effect of the introduction of Roman money was to hasten the disintegration of the clans, the extent to which it did so must not be overstated. Tacitus notes explicitly that the lending of money on interest was unknown among the Germanic peoples, and the appearance of the Germanic moneylender still lay in the future—though perhaps not in the very distant future, for by the time of Tacitus, both in Bohemia and in the lower Rhine area, the Romans had introduced the practice of lending money on interest.

Between the time of Caesar, then, and that of Tacitus (a) there was a striking increase in the number and value of the goods imported into Germany from abroad, (b) this phenomenon, though more intense in some areas than in others, was universal throughout Germany, and (c) the goods imported were to a large extent owned by individuals and not collectively by the kindreds, for it will scarcely be thought that glass, bronze, textiles, pottery, wine, weapons, coins, and so on, were owned communally. But how did the individual German warriors pay for the commodities which they now imported on a more lavish scale than formerly? Some of them earned Roman money by serving in the Roman army, and some received payments from the Imperial government for good behaviour; but coins, as we have seen, were themselves usually regarded as commodities, and these sources of income will not account for the extraordinary increase in the number of Roman objects which reached all parts of Germany in the early Imperial period. The problem is not simplified by the fact that the general technical level and the division of labour in Germany were such that there could be no large-scale export of manufactured goods to an Empire which had at its disposal far larger quantities of such goods than had any of its neighbours. Amber, of course, was a local product of the Baltic shores, though in so far as it reached the Roman frontier as the result of being traded from one Germanic people to another it will have stimulated the acquisition of commodities among other peoples than those who originally gathered it. But it cannot account for a phenomenon which was universal throughout Germany. On the whole, then, it may be assumed that two commodities above all others were used to pay for Roman goods—cattle and slaves, both of which were privately owned in Caesar's time. The problem is, however: how did the individual warriors obtain enough privately-owned commodities to pay for a quantity of imports *which was vastly greater* than that which they had paid for in Caesar's time? How did they *increase* to such an extent the number of commodities available to them for barter?

It is tempting to think that the increased demand for slaves and cattle must have increased the frequency of wars, of cattle-raids, and of slave-raids beyond anything that had been known before the middle of the first century B.C. As for slave raids, consider the case of the West African coast when slave-dealing Europeans first arrived there. Slavery had been known in West Africa before that time, but it was normally of a mild and patriarchal character, perhaps not much more severe than that which Tacitus describes among the Germans. But the arrival of Europeans with attractive goods to offer in exchange for slaves brought about a disastrous increase in the frequency of slave-raiding among the Africans of the coast. Indeed, it altered the whole nature of native warfare and brought it about that "the coast tribes were nothing more than slave catchers and kidnappers" who left entire regions of the interior depopulated after their raids. It introduced a brutal conception of slavery which had hitherto been unknown among the Africans. The arrival of the Romans on the Rhine and the Danube may not have brought about such calamitous conditions; but is it possible to believe that it caused no change at all?

In any event, their intensified concentration on acquiring goods which could be disposed of privately without the interference of the kindreds turned the eyes of the leading men towards the produce of the arable land. That they exerted themselves to convert the produce of the arable into private property, and that they did so not without success, is proved by the new system of allocating the arable which had come into existence before the end of the first century A.D. The soil was now tilled by individual cultivators each working on his own account, and no more is heard of the collective working of the clan holding. Although private ownership of land was still unknown—it could not develop fully when the one piece of land was cultivated by the one person for a year only—the time of its appearance had now come perceptibly closer than it was in Caesar's day. With further advances in agricultural techniques—with an extension, for example, of the marling which was already practised by the Ubii in the middle of the first century A.D. and which fertilized their fields for as much as ten years—fewer fallow periods would be necessary and the re-siting and re-allocating of the arable would become less frequent. Private owner-ship and inheritance of land would then be possible. But that stage had not been generally reached at the time when Tacitus was writing.

But if his flocks and herds were the main source of a German leader's wealth, would the right to dispose freely of a share of his clan's crops have materially improved his position? It is not certain that the Ger-mans of the late first century A.D. were pastoralists to an equal degree with their ancestors of Caesar's day. True, they still measured wealth in terms of cattle, but it is difficult to resist the impression that the general level of the Germans' agricultural techniques must have been raised substantially as a result of the normal improvement which might be expected in the course of 150 years among a people at this stage of development, especially in view of their contact with the Romans. When the Romans occupied the Rhineland a more intensive agriculture at once made its appearance there far surpassing the pre-Roman, and the crafts and industries in the larger settlements reached a height which had hitherto been undreamed of. Archaeology has shown that even in distant Scandinavia "all the ordinary daily tools, large or small, were made in imitation of Roman technique, which in this sphere was the standard," while the influence of Roman taste extends "in general to all the Germanic forms of ornaments, imple-ments, earthenware vessels, belonging to the [first] two centuries." Moreover, entirely new tools and skills, from the scissors and the distaff to the art of sailing, were introduced about this time into Germany; and it can scarcely be doubted that as a result of technical improvements the value of the arable land was increased appreciably. And Caesar himself admits that even in his day, if a Germanic people were prevented by the raids of a more powerful neighbour from sowing and reaping their crops for a sufficient time, they would have to move away from their homes altogether to some place of greater safety. The value to individual Germans of the produce of the arable, therefore, may not have been negligible.

There are two fixed points in the historical process under discussion: (a) the communal sharing and working of the arable by the kindreds in Caesar's time, which is attested explicitly and indeed emphatically by Caesar himself and (b) the individual working of the arable in the days of Tacitus, which is an inescapable inference from Tacitus' words. Our problem is: why was the earlier system transformed into the later? There was a tendency even in Caesar's day or soon after it for "private" trading to increase relatively to communal trading. The leading men owned cattle privately and so were in a position to add to their well-being, their prestige, and their social standing by buying the silver, the bronze vessels, the wine, and so forth, which traders displayed before them. But this tendency was sharply accelerated by the arrival of Roman civilization on the Rhine and the Danube and for a moment even on the Elbe, for there was now a greater array of goods for the leading men to acquire. The notables in all parts of Germany now distinguished themselves from the rank and file of the warriors and even from their own kinsmen by possessing themselves of imported Roman luxuries on a scale previously unknown. Hence, by the time of Tacitus differences of wealth inside the kindred itself were so substantial that the framework of the clan was undermined, the old communal working of the land disappeared, and the time was nearer at hand when the arable would be freely owned by private persons in Germany.

It would no doubt be possible to overemphasize the part played by the Romans in this process, and a similar result would unquestionably have been reached, though perhaps more slowly, even if the Romans had never appeared on the scene. With gradual improvement of agricultural techniques and the resulting increase in the value of the produce of the arable land the leading men among the Germans would no doubt have found ways and means of ridding themselves of the traditional ways even in the absence of the Romans.

# J. M. Wallace-Hadrill

# 9

# The Bloodfeud of
# the Franks

Among the debts owed by the Germanic tribes to the Romans must be reckoned, with certain reservations, the debt of law. The earliest *Volksrechte* [Germanic Customary Law] bear traces of the complex legacy of Roman Vulgar Law. Few scholars nowadays, students of Frankish history and law, could agree with Waitz that "von Recht kann wenig die Rede sein" [little can be said about law], or would deny that the barbarian successor-states do in fact become the more intelligible as the wanderings of the *Codex Theodosianus* and its western derivatives are kept in mind. And yet a danger lurks here, too; the danger of overlooking the simple truth that the core of all Germanic customary practice was German. This is why it is worth spending a little time upon the most undoubtedly Germanic of all barbarian institutions, the bloodfeud, and to invite consideration of it, moreover, not as an incoherent interlude between Gaius and Glanvil,[1] but as a sociological experiment instructive in itself. We see, as the barbarians did not, the whole panorama of forces, procedural and moral, arrayed against feud, and to some of them this paper will presently draw attention. We note the development from the private feud-settlements of the Germans to public and royal arbitration and intervention, even if we do not always see the corollary, that the legal processes of the *Volksrechte* succeeded just because they derived from feud-processes and closely followed them. We note, too, the continuing pressure of the Church and of Late Roman legal tradition in favour of the abandonment of feud. None of this can be gainsaid. But the death of feud and the better things that replaced it are one thing: the fact of its life, another. Allowing for all these pressures upon it, feud yet lived for centuries in western Europe without frontal attack and

---

[1] Gaius was a Roman jurist of the second century A.D. who wrote a series of important legal commentaries. Ranulph de Glanvil wrote the first systematic treatise of the laws of England at the end of the twelfth century. The expression "between Gaius and Glanvil" thus refers to the legal developments of the first thousand years of the Christian era.—*Ed.*

without stigma. What, then, was its indispensable strength? What actually happened when feud threatened and broke out?

These few pages are limited to the evidence of those who witnessed and described feuds that we can still read about; but before turning to them, there are certain preliminary matters that require clarification.

In the first place, it is not difficult to arrive at what, for these purposes, is a working definition of feud. We may call it, first, the threat of hostility between kins; then, the state of hostility between them; and finally, the satisfaction of their differences and a settlement on terms acceptable to both. The threat, the state and the settlement of that hostility constitute feud but do not necessarily mean bloodshed. Indeed, it is not certain that a legal right to blood, however we understand it, should ever be assumed among the Franks without proof. There is no mention of such right in *Lex Salica,* and the famous rebuke of the *iudex loci* [judge of the region] to the man who avenged his brother's death without leave points in another direction. But of moral right there is no question. Feud is never a crime until it is made so, and cannot till then be studied within the context of criminal law. In brief, it is a way for the settlement of differences, whether through violence or negotiation or both, even though it would be vain to look for any such definition in the sources of the early Middle Ages. We must search for our feuds, incipient or flourishing, in a maze of terms that can mislead: the Frankish *faithu,* latinized as *faidus,* may mean what we are after, or it may mean something different; feud may lurk behind *inimicus, hostis, vindicta, intentio, altercatio, bella civilia,* or it may not. As an institution, feud remains undefined by those who have resort to it. If they help us to distinguish feud from any and every sporadic outbreak of violence, they do so unwittingly. All vengeance is not feud, and all bloodshed is not bloodfeud. If we really wish to see bloodshed practised as a fine art, we cannot do better than turn to Byzantium, mistress of the West in this as in so much else.

Vendetta may be studied, even today, in almost any quarter of the globe, in Arabia or Africa, for instance, or nearer home among patriarchal societies in the mountains of Albania, Sicily, Sardinia and Corsica; and it is so studied by the sociologist. We can learn from him and afterwards look with a new eye to the more particular study of feuding in medieval Europe, and paradoxically may find it easier not to use events of the tenth century to illustrate situations in the fifth, and not to think that Anglo-Saxon laws or Scandinavian sagas are applicable to the Frankish or the Gothic scene. Just here, the great German legal historians came to grief, though it is easy to see why they did so. The concern of this paper is with the Franks of Gaul in the Merovingian age, and it does not take as evidence the feuding practices of the barbarian contemporaries of the Franks, apart from such as were intimately connected with them, like the Burgundians or the Visigoths; neither does it call upon the practices of Carolingian Europe, where feud of a very different sort may be studied. The evidence is Frankish, and specifically literary: the evidence of the historians and the chroniclers and the writers of saints' *Lives*. Why should they have included their tales of feud? Was it as a warning to the furious, or could they not resist a good story? Did they report the exceptional or the commonplace? Why is their evidence sometimes at variance with what the Frankish laws bid us believe?

To the Hun, Attila, there was nothing like a good feud: "quid viro forti suavius quam vindicta manu quaerere" [what is sweeter to a strong man than to seek vengeance with his own hand]? He spoke thus for warriors far beyond, and more civilized by far than, his own Hunnic warbands. All the barbarian invaders of the Empire loved a feud. Not even the learned Cassiodorus could suppose otherwise. We may term it the classical feud of the migrating period, though, of course, it lasted longer; it was that kind of kin-hostility where there was killing in hot blood and with all publicity for the sake of honour, most particularly in avenging an act of treachery. This was the true vengeance, girt about with a magical symbolism that may have remained potent for much longer than we know. Hot blood was never to be overlooked; while in it, a man and his kin might be excused almost anything, and no amount of teaching ever quite persuaded the medieval mind that it was wrong. It will crop up, in various forms, in the evidence. But it is only one kind of feud, and there were many others (at least in the Merovingian era) that arose out of theft, cattle-rustling, accidental injury or mere misunderstanding. The tariffs of the *Volksrechte* warn us at a glance that homicide was but one among many injuries from which feud might spring. The facts hardly suggest that the Franks spent more than a small portion of their time defending their honour. Blood tends to cool. The interesting cases of feud are seldom clear-cut affairs of honour and betray, even then, the natural pulls inherent in feud-society towards settlement and composition. Fighting may be fun, but only a grievous injury or a series of misunderstandings will lead to the destruction of the man-power of a family, let alone of a kin. Composition, offering a natural escape, stretches back far beyond the tariffs of *Lex Salica* to composition in kind in the early Germanic period. The world, private and official, stood ready to arbitrate.

Of the pressures working against whatever traditional forms of feud the Franks brought to Gaul, one was the extreme complexity of Gallo-Frankish society. Already far advanced from the comparative simplicities of Tacitus's *Germania*, the Franks of the fifth and sixth centuries settled in a variety of ways upon the Gaulish countryside. We find them at home in abandoned Roman *villae*, in Gallic *vici* [a quarter of a city], at work in small or large groups upon upland

ranches, mixing in varying proportions and over a long period in
Gaulish and barbarian settlements other than Frankish. How, in these
circumstances, could the kin remain a coherent social force? Kindred
must rapidly have become scattered over wide areas and the ties of
blood within a single settlement become hopelessly intermixed. You
could leave your kin and presumably join another; and the claims of
lordship (already active in Tacitus's time) might well pull against the
claims of kin. How could the kin charged with responsibility for feud,
whether the agnatic kin or the wider circle of blood-relations, be
mobilized for war except as a small *ad hoc* vengeance-group? So we
arrive somewhere near the situation envisaged in another context by
Professor Gluckman, where the mere elaboration and interdependence
of kin-groups may ensure a kind of immobility. Common blood and
propinquity will always make for settlement. This is not to imply that
feud-war will not break out on a minor scale nor that the idea of
fighting is abandoned. Far from it. The sanction of feud-war is the
reality that lies behind every feud-settlement and agreement to pay
and receive composition; but it is difficult to implement and not lightly
to be entered upon, even when a man has a lord to uphold his quarrel
or is himself a lord strong in dependants, whether or not of his blood.
(One may suspect that in practice the assistance of kindred and of such
dependants was often not clearly distinguishable.) The kin, especially
such members as lived within easy reach, must often have been called
upon to meet and act as judges and arbiters in family disputes that
were none the less feud-disputes because unlikely to lead to bloodshed.
They it was who agreed to pay, or to accept, the heavy price of blood,
or to disown the offending kinsman; and other duties too were thrust
upon them, beyond what the *Volksrechte* reveal. The Frankish kin
was probably less often involved as a fighting force than as a composing one. From the mere nature of their settlement, it must be wide of
the mark to conceive of the Franks being at all often engaged in major
kin-warfare.

Against feud also stood the Church, with its teaching and its practice opposed to bloodshed. There can be no doubt that the Frankish
Church was for arbitration and composition; Gregory of Tours himself
describes for us an occasion when he acted in person as arbitrator. Such
is the sense of the well-known words of Avitus on the subject, the plea
of St. Bonitus for *concordia,* St. Germanus on *inhonesta victoria* [dis-
graceful victory], the whole tenor of the fascinating *Liber Scintillarum*
of Defensor of Ligugé, to say nothing of the Church's intimate connection with our earliest manuscripts of the *Volksrechte*. (We can associate
some of these manuscripts with a known church or churchman, as for
instance one fine collection with St. Gallen, or the ninth-century copy
of the *Lex Baiuvariorum,* now in Munich, with Bishop Hitto of
Freising.) But how will you get arbitration without the sanction of

bloodshed? How, if a cleric, can you be sure of putting from your mind the claims of your own blood? One Frankish bishop at least, Badigisil of Le Mans, made no bones about this: "non ideo, quia clericus factus sum, et ultur iniuriarum mearum non ero" [just because I am a clergyman, shall I not be avenged for my personal injuries]? He might, had he known it, have cited in his favour a letter from a pope to an Italian *Magister Militum,* instructing him to avenge the bearer for his brother's murder. More interesting, however, are the difficulties in which less bellicose clerics found themselves. How could they reconcile their views with that *ultio divina* [divine vengeance] that was their own main prop in a wicked world? Look through his writings for the view of Gregory of Tours on divine vengeance and it will be found that he visualizes it as nothing less than God's own feud in support of his servants, who can have no other kin. God will avenge crimes specially heinous in the Church's eyes—parricide for example, crimes within the family generally and crimes involving all who lack natural protectors. The agent of vengeance may be God himself directly intervening to strike down the culprit (for instance, with sickness) or it may be a human agent, as the king. At all events, God's vengeance is of the same nature as that of any head of a family or warband. He strikes to kill, to avenge insult—to himself, to his children or to his property. The Frankish churchmen cannot in any other way see *ultio divina* in a society dominated by the bloodfeud. We may know that Romans xii, 19—"mihi vindicta, ego retribuam dicit Dominus" [vengeance is mine, I will repay, said the Lord]—has nothing to do with bloodfeud, but to the Franks and Gallo-Romans it was not so clear. We must not, then, expect to find Gregory of Tours, brought up to bloodshed, protected by an avenging God and on at least one occasion more than indulgent towards the ferocious treachery of his hero Clovis, opposed to all bloodfeuds merely because they were bloody. His attitude and that of his contemporaries, constituting the attitude of his Church, is, in general, opposed to the sanction of bloodfeud but tends in practice, and for no shameful reason, to be equivocal. He is often opposed to bloodfeuds without seeing the need to state and maintain a case against bloodfeud.

Roman Law, on the other hand, had no need to be equivocal. It had had no truck with feud since the far-off days of the XII Tables. The Theodosian Code and its Visigothic derivatives take their stand on the personal responsibility of the criminal, the *auctor sceleris* [author of mischief]; his kin should not suffer for him: "ille solus culpavilis erit qui culpanda conmiserit" [that one alone shall be guilty who shall have committed crimes]. The Burgundian and Merovingian kings were in varying degrees influenced by their legal advisers in this direction. Burgundian Law in particular tends towards compromise; it admits, for example, occasions when a kin might pursue a killer without, however, pursuing the killer's kin. But even in Visigothic Spain, a stronghold of Vulgar Roman Law, King Wamba was quite clear that any killer was in the *potestas* [power] of the injured kin. If the Visigoths and the Burgundians found difficulties in applying Roman practice among peoples otherwise inclined, we might well look for trouble with the Merovingians.

One question, therefore, on which we must search for light in the Frankish evidence, is the extent to which the Merovingian kings succumbed to these pressures and turned against feud. Some distinguished scholars have had no doubt that they succumbed very largely; but a different case could be argued. What, it might be asked, could the Frankish kings do with a disintegrating kin-system in which the individual more and more escaped from kin-responsibility and kin-protection? What active, legislative support could they lend to a situation where in practice, as Maitland saw in an English context, every new feud demanded an entirely fresh kin-grouping? The Merovingians thus remained independent of, if not unaffected by, the teaching of Church and civilians; it was, as we shall see, still right in Merovingian eyes to enter upon the process of feud, whether it was to lead through bloodshed or composition to ultimate satisfaction. Without the sanction of blood, composition would have stood a poor chance in a world lacking not simply a police-force but the requisite concept of public order. It is easy to imagine that, with the recording of the *Volksrechte* and the publication of instruments like the *Decretio* of Childebert II, the *Pactus pro tenore pacis* [covenant for maintaining the peace] and the documents of the formularies of Marculf and others, we have moved into a new world of royal authority. Useless to deny that the earlier Merovingians were extraordinarily powerful and much feared. But yet, when we come to inquire what it was that made the composition-tariffs of *Lex Salica* work and why wergilds and lesser compositions were in fact paid, the answer is, not fear of local royal officials but fear of feud; or rather, it is both. To be sure, the Merovingians have an interest in intervening in the course of feuds when possible and where they can see profit accruing to the fisc through fine or confiscation; the *fredus* [the percentage of the fine taken by the king] was worth having; this is expressed procedurally; but at what time in barbarian history would chieftains not have intervened in the feuds of their followers for similar reasons? The Romans did much the same. No new principle was at stake. One can detect no blow at the principle of feuding in the famous titles of King Chilperic's *Edictum*: namely *(tit.* 8) that the *malus homo* (that is, professional malefactor), who cannot make composition and whom his kin will not redeem, may be turned over to his accusers, and *(tit.* 10) that the *malus homo* who cannot redeem himself and is beyond the control of his kin may be slain by anyone without incurring risk of feud. Is King Childebert deliberately narrowing the function of feud when he forbids killing *sine causa* [without good reason] and decrees that such a killer shall neither make composition nor have it made for him, and that his *parentes* [relatives] and *amici* [friends] shall suffer for it if they try to do so? Brunner thought he was; but it cannot be proved. At least it gave the king a chance to finish his title with a little Roman flourish: "iustum est ut qui novit occidere discat morire" [it is right that he who knows killing become acquainted with dying]. On the other hand, there are passages that reveal the Merovingians actively defining and approving occasions of feud; for instance, by attempting to sort out the degrees of responsibility for taking vengeance within the kin. As Goebel puts it, the Merovingians were concerned with harsh answers to instant questions: "What is to be done about professional crime? May offenders be executed? Can the fisc take their property?" Groping for answers and grappling with problems that lay outside the kin (a case in point is murder as distinct from homicide), they now and again struck a glancing blow at feud; traces of such will be found scattered in their laws. But this hardly amounts to a deliberate attack upon the principle of feud.

It may be well to state that Gregory of Tours, from whose History much of our evidence of feud is drawn, was not interested in feud as such, and he might have been surprised to hear that some historians have seen in his writings the picture of a society disintegrating through feud. Of one special, because unnatural, kind of feud he particularly disapproved: the civil wars between members of one kin, the Merovingians themselves; and in the prologue to his Fifth Book he exhorts them to slay their enemies, not each other. "Cavete bella civilia" [guard against civil war] he cries, meaning by this that specially heinous type of feud—heinous because self-destroying—the rising of *proximus in propinquum* [kinsman against kinsman]; yet his own evidence shows that this very propinquity of blood was one of the factors that led his warring Merovingians towards settlement. They did not enjoy fighting one another. It is worth looking at some of Gregory's examples of feud within the royal kin or involving the royal kin.

We may take first a feud between the Merovingians and the royal Burgundian house, a feud brought about by a woman. Gregory gives it some prominence. The Merovingian queen Chrotechildis, by birth a Burgundian, urges her sons to avenge the deaths of her parents, not on the murderer, her uncle Gundobad, but on his sons, Sigismund and Godomar. In other words, the Merovingian princes were being required by their mother to attack their second cousins. This they proceeded to do and, defeating the Burgundian princes, imprisoned one of them, perhaps with the intention of obtaining a heavy composition. It is only on a later occasion, after a second attack had become necessary, that the Merovingian Chlodomer decides to kill the imprisoned Sigismund and his family: they are all thrown down a well. There is more to the feud than this; but its features are clear: two royal kins, related by marriage but distinct and separated by a considerable distance, show no hesitation in attacking one another, the one taking vengeance for blood on the second generation of the other. There is something to suggest that complete and early submission by the Burgundians might have induced the Merovingian princes to accept a settlement on terms. But the Burgundians would not submit. Gregory himself has no adverse comment to make on the reason for the feud. We must suppose that he thought it justifiable. What he disapproves of is the slaying in cold blood of the captive prince and family as an act rather of military prudence (to prevent attack in the rear) than of vengeance intended from the first. Chlodomer himself deserved to die by a ruse in the subsequent battle: his head was raised on a spear, so publicly demonstrating the Burgundian viewpoint in the feud.

Gregory has other cases of Merovingian feuds with princes outside the Frankish orbit. One, that between the Ripuarian Franks and the Thuringians, follows directly on the Burgundian feud. The *iniuria* [wrongs] of which the Frankish king here complained was a breach of trust: it did not prevent his killing his Thuringian rival by a trick. Trickery, indeed, was a commonplace of Frankish feuding; it might happen at any stage of a feud short of the final agreement, and particularly in the penultimate stages of arbitration or armistice; and nobody thought any the worse of it. An entire group of Merovingian feuds was waged with their southern neighbours and connections by marriage, the Visigoth kings. We find King Childebert marching to Spain to avenge his sister, wife of the Arian Amalaric. She had sent him a bloodstained handkerchief in proof of the treatment she had suffered for her faith. His motive in marching to kill Amalaric was not brotherly affection; it was duty; and duty normally did dictate such kin-action. But duty could be satisfied short of bloodshed; for, a little later, Gregory tells of the Merovingians sending to the Goth Theodohat for proper composition for the killing of their cousin, a lady who deserved her fate if anyone did; and in fear he paid them 50,000 *aurei* [gold pieces]. Inevitably he had been threatened with destruction if he failed to pay; that was the sanction of the composition. Dalton long ago showed how inaccurate the story was in detail; and yet the point remained for Gregory's readers: the death of Theodohat's victim was shameful, feud was the only answer—and composition was perfectly in order.

. . .

Perhaps enough has been said of royal feud to make the point that . . . there seemed, as a rule, nothing wrong about it to the participants, and often not to Gregory. It would be profitable to pursue the course of later Merovingian feuds in the pages of Fredegar [Gregory's continuator] and to interpret the relations of Pippin III, first Carolingian king, with Ghislemar and with Waiofar of Aquitaine in terms of family feuding. But in this matter we may leave the last word with Gregory. Towards the close of his History he describes the scene at Poitiers when a riotous princess, another Chrotechildis, was brought to account. She stood at bay, begging that no violence be done her: "I am a queen," she says, "and a king's daughter, cousin of another king; take care, for the day may come when I shall take my revenge." The blood-vengeance of a Merovingian, in a word, was to be feared; it could be pursued with great resources; composition might not seem attractive, as it did with humbler folk (provided that they were not asked to pay it). The royal kin, moreover, had a way of sticking together and upholding the feuds of its members against other kins, notably outside Frankish Gaul. Yet the forces making for settlement exist all the time, and are on occasion successful. The conscience that is shocked at feuding within the royal kin is not simply ecclesiastical: it is the conscience of a feuding society that rests, even while it disintegrates, on the idea of the unity of the kin.

A second and no less significant group of feuds we may classify as non-royal; in other words, they do not involve the Merovingians as principals, though they often do involve them as kings. In this group, if anywhere, evidence should be forthcoming of royal intention to suppress feud as an institution. We may start, as before, with Gregory's contribution.

Two courtiers—*retoricis inbutus litteris* [trained in rhetoric], moreover—fall out because of the arrogance of one of them, named Secundinus, towards the other, Asteriolus. The king reconciles them, but a fresh *intentio* [quarrel] breaks out. This time the king makes a judgement, which strips Asteriolus of his honours and places him within the power of Secundinus. However, he is protected by the queen, and not till after her death is Secundinus able to claim his rights and kill him. But Asteriolus left a son who, growing up, made preparations to avenge his father—"coepit patris sui velle iniuriam vindecare" [he has begun to attempt to avenge his father's injury]. Secundinus thereupon fled in panic from one *villa* to another, and finally, seeing no escape, took his own life "ne in manus inimici conruerit" [lest he fall by a hostile hand]. Gregory, relating this, makes no comment; he thought the story worth the telling but had no strong feelings about it. Yet to us it reveals an interesting fact: two families of courtiers, living their lives under the very nose of the king their lord, are able to pursue their differences in feud without the king being able to stop them. First, they ignore the reconciliation he makes, and later, in the second generation, they flout his subsequent judgement by renewing the feud. Nor can Secundinus see any hope of royal protection against the vengeance of his victim's son. Hence he takes his own life. The king can do nothing to stop the feud; indeed, he does something to ensure its continuance. Did he really suppose that the son of the murdered man would hold his peace? It does not look as if the king's part in the matter was at all different from that of any other lord called upon to arbitrate between feuding dependants; he did what he could, but the issue was one of blood and, in the end, passed beyond his power to control. Perhaps he let it pass without regret.

Another feud, having certain features in common with the feud of Secundinus, concerns two well-born families who fall out over a wife's repute. The husband's kin go, as was customary, to her father, requiring him either to prove her innocence or to kill her. He decides to take an oath to her innocence, and this is made in the presence of both kins in the church of Saint-Denis in Paris. But the husband's kin declare this to be a perjury, whereupon swords are drawn and there is bloodshed before the altar, although, as Gregory remarks, both kins were "primi apud Chilpericum regen" [nobles in the power of King Chilperic]. The matter was referred at once to the king, to whom both parties hastened; but he would have nothing to do with them and sent them back to the bishop. They then made composition with the bishop and were forgiven. That is, they were forgiven their riotous behaviour in church; but the feud remained. A few days later, the woman was summoned *ad iudicium* [to court], but strangled herself, so closing the matter. It may well be that she took her life on instructions from her father's kin, who by now knew her to be guilty. Whatever the *iudicium* to which she was summoned, one cannot but be struck by the limited nature of the king's intervention; there is no question, as Dahn points out, of his punishing breach of the law or of the peace or the shedding of blood among those closely attached to his court. His mind is taken up with the act of sacrilege. The right and the duty of kin to clear or punish a member, man or woman, who has impugned its honour is not called in question by the king—nor, for the matter of that, by the church.

Other feuds involving women make the point with equal clarity, as, for example, when a well-born woman goes off with a priest, darkening the insult to her kin by dressing as a man to escape detection. Her kin catches her and, "ad ulciscendam humilitatem generis sui" [to avenge the humiliation of her family], burns her. Then, surprisingly, they accept composition of 20 *aurei* from the Bishop of Lisieux for the priest, who subsequently runs off with another woman, whose husband's kin catch him and torture him, and would have killed him if he had not again been rescued by the Bishop. But the startling feature of the case is the reaction of Gregory of Tours. Does he think the Bishop was right to offer composition for the priest, and the kin to accept it? He does not: to his mind, it was the accursed thirst for gold that caused the first woman's kin to hold the priest to ransom till someone could be found to pay the composition. By implication we are to understand that the priest should have shared the fate of the woman he seduced. All the same, was it no more than the accursed thirst for gold? May it not have been that honour was satisfied with the woman's death and that her kin had no strong feelings about the priest? Wherever feelings are not strong, or are divided, there tends to emerge an inclination towards composition, if only it can be got; and this, it cannot be too strongly insisted, is by Merovingian times felt as part of the feuding process. It crops up in quite unexpected situations, as here, or when Childeric the Saxon paid composition to the sons of the criminal Avius, whom his men had killed in a brawl. Gregory is obviously surprised that he should have paid: "composuit tamen" [compose he did] and the sons accepted it.

There were times, however, when a king would decisively intervene to break an incipient feud. Gregory recounts how a freeborn girl, carried off to the bed of the drunken duke Amalo, struck him with his own sword; and he died, though not before he had had time to admonish his retainers that she had done nothing worthy of death. The admonition did not foreclose feud: that was a matter for the dead man's kin to decide; but it did give her a chance. The girl then fled to the king (not to her own kin, of whom nothing is said). Gregory says that the king was moved by pity to grant her her life and, further, to take her under his written protection against the dead man's kin. This did indeed foreclose feud; and Gregory makes it clear that the *verbum regis* [king's word] and his *praeceptio* [imperial order] were, in this case, adequate protection. But why did the girl go straight to the king? And why did he protect her, instead of leaving her to the protection of her kin? It sounds like a good case for composition; yet of this the king deliberately deprived the dead man's kin. Halban has argued that the king simply felt that feud would be wrong and that, in acting as he did, he overstepped normal practice—and this even if she had no kin and thus a special claim to his protection. Goebel, too, has seen here an extraordinary and early instance of the power of the *verbum regis*. What neither has noticed is that her victim was a duke who would have come under the royal protection. Is not this why she flees straight to the duke's master and why his first act is to grant her what is forfeit, her life? Thereafter he can excuse her the consequences of feud, too. In fact, the girl had a very good case, with the victim's own evidence in her favour. Why should the injured kin have received compensation where the king was prepared to overlook his servant's murder? The king indeed foreclosed a feud; but it is hard to see that he acted in a way that could be interpreted as a blow at the principle of feud.

. . .

Outraged kinship [sometimes] proves too strong for any pacification. . . . We may observe, too, the number of checks to bloodshed that are

met with on the way. There stands the local court of arbitration, to
say nothing of the count, the bishop and the king, ready to throw their
weight into the scales on the side of composition and settlement. There
is nothing clear-cut about it from start to finish; the case drifts from
blood to arbitration, and back again, without ever becoming what
we would call legally clear. Royal intervention and court procedure are
fluid; the transition from one type of procedure to another is bewilder-
ingly easy; and this the *Volksrechte* and the formularies would hardly
suggest. But they settled it in the end.

Without question, Gregory best records the feuds of the Franks; but
we must turn, leaving him still far from exhausted, to Fredegar. First,
the feud of Ermenfred with Chainulf. It is over in a few words.
Ermenfred, son-in-law of the great Aega, kills Count Chainulf at a
court held at Augers. In consequence, his landed possessions are
savagely attacked by Chainulf's kin and many others, all with the
express approval of Queen Nantechildis. Ermenfred seeks refuge in
church at Rheims and thus escapes the royal wrath. That is all. It is a
stray gleam that reveals a powerful and level-headed queen urging on
an injured kin to feud. But Fredegar has a much better feud, that
between Flaochad and Willebad. Nantechildis again, acting as regent,
appoints the Frank Flaochad to be mayor of the palace in Burgundy—
a strongminded if imprudent decision. On his first progress through
Burgundy, the new mayor came upon the patrician Willebad; and he
discovered, says Fredegar, an old hatred that had long lain hidden in
his heart. He planned to kill him. For his part, Willebad lost no chance
of belittling Flaochad. We next move to a Burgundian court held at
Chalon. Willebad arrives with a great following. Flaochad plans an
attempt on his life, which is foiled; instead, he marches out of his
*palatium* [palace] to fight him. Amalbert, Flaochad's brother, inter-
poses to pacify them. Flaochad now calls on the new king, Clovis II, to
help him. Willebad is summoned to appear before the king at Autun
and arrives with a big following, well knowing that Flaochad, Amalbert and others intend to set upon him. The king tries in vain to
entice the victim within the city walls; instead, his enemies again have
to march out against him. The fight is described vividly. It seems to
have been something of a family engagement, with most people sitting
round as spectators. Berthar, a supporter of Flaochad, is narrowly
saved from death by his son Chaubedo. Willebad is killed. Eleven
days later, apparently before the feud had entered a further phase,
Flaochad died of a fever. Fredegar here sees divine judgement. Both
Flaochad and Willebad were robbers and tyrants; what is more, they
had repeatedly sworn friendship on holy relics—that is, had solemnly
agreed to terminate feud. It is an interesting scene described, one
might think, by an eye-witness: the opponents, typical barbarian warriors quarrelling about we know not what, backed by their kins and their

retainers, are each quite ready to make an end of the other by trickery. We are given, too, a straight hint that they had patched up the feud more than once. It ends in a skirmish under the walls of Autun, a skirmish that has something of the flavour of a duel, by which feuds were on occasion terminated. Or rather, it ends in God's judgement on the survivor. Nothing is said of the course of law as it affects the quarrel of such important men; and the king, whether or not present at the final scene, made it possible, even if, a boy, he was the mouthpiece of others.

To work through the seven volumes of the *Scriptores Rerum Merovingicarum* is to be made aware that feuds are like volcanoes. A few are in eruption, others are extinct, but most are content to rumble now and again and leave us guessing. Every so often we pass across the edge of a quarrel that, if only the writer had followed it up, would have turned out to be feud. The language of feud and its assumptions lie in the minds of the Frankish chroniclers and hagiographers, as witness the curious account in the mid-ninth-century *Gesta Dagoberti* of how the sons of Sadregisil failed to obtain their heritage through not having avenged their father's murder; or how the author of the *Vita Anstrudis* preferred not to identify the family that murdered the only brother of Anstrudis, since she sought no vengeance, although they attacked her too: "quorum nomina et stirpem dicere iniuriam esse putamus" [we think we know the names and family to pronounce guilty]; or again, how Ulfus, tortured as he thought through the agency of St Germanus of Paris, flung his swordbelt at the bishop's feet with the cry "my life will be required of you by the king—and by my kin!" It is the same in the story of St Léger and of many another Frankish figure whom it would be pointless to enumerate. None of these writers saw feud steadily giving ground to other and less bloodthirsty processes of law sponsored by enlightened kings.

We have come to the brink of the Carolingian age, the age of Charles Martel and St Boniface. If a new day dawned in the history of feuding, it was concealed from the continuators of Fredegar and the compiler of the *Liber Historiae Francorum*; and concealed too, from Archbishop Hincmar, as he looked back from the vantage point of the next century. Why did St Boniface become doubtful about the propriety of regarding Gregory of Utrecht as a likely successor? Because, it seemed, Gregory might have become involved in feud, his brother apparently having killed the uncle of the *Dux Francorum* [leader of the Franks]; and nobody knew how the *discordia* would end. The *Dux* might decide to avenge his uncle's death fairly widely on Gregory's family. We may assume that this did not, in fact, happen; but the career of Gregory of Utrecht might have been very different had it not been for the threat overhanging his kin at a critical moment. The Mainz version of the *Life* of St Boniface affords a sudden insight into the view of feud held by one of the most powerful Frankish dynasties of the Rhineland. Bishop Gerold of Mainz was killed in a skirmish with the Saxons. His son and successor, Gewilib, did not consider this an unavoidable accident of battle. Instead, he made careful inquiries to discover who actually killed his father, and he succeeded. In due course, while on an expedition against the Saxons with either Charles Martel or Carloman, he sought out his victim and invited him to meet him in the River Weser to discuss terms. And there Gewilib killed him, with the words "accipe quo patrem vindico ferrum" [receive the sword with which I avenge my father]! The writer goes on to say that neither the king nor the nobles considered that Gewilib had done anything blameworthy in avenging his father thus, though he (the writer) clearly did. "Rudi populo rudis adhuc presul" [a rude man held fast by a rude people] is his epitaph for Gewilib, and it sounds well enough; but the great dynasts of the Rhineland would not have thought so, and Gewilib's Carolingian overlord did not think so.

We are not now concerned to consider how far, if at all, the Frankish outlook on feud was modified by Charlemagne. No historian believes that he was particularly successful; the question is simply what his intentions were. Nor, again, must we be misled by developments in court procedure (for example, in the *jurati* [witnesses under oath] being summoned by a judge instead of by the parties to a feud) that tended to strengthen royal resistance to private feud-procedures without necessarily betraying a change of heart. Charlemagne's position, as revealed in his capitularies, may be variously interpreted. If the *Admonitio Generalis* be taken as an indication of policy, then it may be that Charlemagne, viewing his kingly rôle in the light of an Augustinian *pax*, saw feuding as a positive evil and, further, as eminently undesirable by reason of its private nature. But even his friend Alcuin, we must remember, did not always see things thus. What Charlemagne never experienced was a distate for the bloodshed of the process. Royal justice could be savager than feud. There may, then, be a positive change of outlook here, such as no Merovingian evidence can plainly be seen to bear traces of; at once the culmination of a process of practical delimiting of feud that was centuries old, and a special development of the late eighth century. Feuding in the Carolingian world nonetheless had a long future before it.

What this paper has had to express is a view of the feuding of the Frankish age that is the reverse of clear-cut. There is no evidence that contemporaries saw it otherwise. To legal historians feud dies a slow, inevitable death, yielding to the superior equity of royal justice; chaos and bloodshed give place to good order because they must. But it is possible to see the matter otherwise: feud, as a means of obtaining redress, is already a various, elaborate procedure by the time we first meet it in barbarian sources, long since linked with the payment of compositions, in kind or money; the two are inseparable. Records of feud repeatedly betray the drift from fighting to composition, the vagueness of the line separating them. Always it is touch-and-go what will happen; it will depend on what the kins think, how extensively they or their followings are mobilizable, how rich they are or how ready to pay or to receive payment, how much the bishop or the king feels disposed to intervene. The royal position as expressed in legislation is not as a rule clear; and when it is it does not always correspond to practice. Kings may sometimes have judged feuding proper to their immediate followers when they would have disallowed it to a wider circle. Royal justice and the local courts are still far too unsettled in function and fluid in procedure to offer a clear alternative to feud. They are more concerned with compromises than with principles. What, in fact, we do find is the movement of men and their troubles between the two. We may agree with Goebel that the process of composition "remained essentially an alternative rather than a successor to settlement by violence" though the reality of the bloodier alternative was the sanction that made composition possible at any stage. Except generally where honour was obviously involved, kins and families would find reasons and excuses to look to composition first, whether of their own making or under the protection of the courts. Their efforts might break down, and often did; and so might the efforts of the courts. There is no strong and continuous royal pressure against the principle of feud. There is no "Kampf gegen die Fehde" [struggle against the feud]. Even the pressure of the Church should be subject to most careful interpretation. Feuds that wiped out whole kins it is impossible to believe were ever common. Feuding in the sense of incessant private warfare, is a myth; feuding in the sense of very widespread and frequent procedures to reach composition-settlements necessarily hovering on the edge of bloodshed, is not. The marvel of early medieval society is not war but peace.

# V/FEUDALISM

---

THE word "feudalism" was first widely used in the eighteenth century to denote all that was reprehensible in the "gothic" past. As a propaganda weapon in the service of the European bourgeoisie just then engaged, in differing ways and at varying tempos, in the conquest of political power, it became synonymous with oppression, unfreedom, and personal dependency. Like the word "fascism" in too much of the rhetoric of the contemporary left, it designated the enemy whose specific characteristics were less important than the mere fact of its existence and the absolute need for its destruction.

The definitions of feudalism are enormously diverse, and the only thing historians seem to agree on is that something called feudalism existed in western Europe between the fall of the Roman Empire and the fifteenth-sixteenth-seventeenth century, the terminal date to be chosen from among several possibilities. For some, the essence of feudalism is the contract between lord and vassal, the pledge of fealty and service, in return for protection and a fief. Historians of law, who tend to be rather formalist, would refuse the title to any other system. But others, for whom the contract is a means rather than an end in itself, make feudalism (in the words of a current text) "intricate and diverse, but in essence . . . a means of carrying on some kind of government on a local basis where no organized state existed." In other words, it was fundamentally a political system.

Explanations in terms of government and politics isolated from a social context are always suspect, if only because they presuppose a compartmentalization of life that does not correspond to reality. One does not need to be a Marxist to realize as much and that history has to deal, as the late French medievalist

Marc Bloch was fond of saying, with the total man. Bloch was at pains to make up for the deficiencies he found in the work of other historians by situating the failure of the prefeudal state in a context where neither kinship systems (a traditional mode of stratification and political obligation) nor marketplace relationships gave society the cohesion necessary for its survival. He then goes on to associate the social and the political in his definition of feudal society as made up of vassalage, the fief, *and* the manor. The former two are seen as the framework for relations between lords and vassals, the latter for relations between lords and peasants.

Bloch's approach seems to me to remain somewhat artificial, precisely because the various aspects of the system are insufficiently integrated with one another. From a dialectical point of view, the basic fact, as the French Marxist Charles Parain notes in the following article, is the "underlying unity between the relations of production established between lords and peasants around the land, and the feudal hierarchy that so long sanctioned and ensured the very mechanism of these relations." What is fundamental is the class relationships—fluid, ever changing—that grow up in the process of production and reproduction of real life. Thus, feudalism is that system "where the agricultural worker, although no longer a slave, is still subject to a series of extra-economic restrictions that so reduce his freedom and his personal property [but do not separate him entirely from the ownership of the means of production] that neither his labor power nor his product can be true objects of free exchange, true 'commodities.'" The surplus value he produces is, instead, taken from him directly by his landlord, in the form of goods and services having no necessary relationship to the existence of a market.

Feudalism as a mode of production and feudalism as a social formation are not the same thing. The one is an abstraction, the other a description of concrete reality. The connection is that the latter is said to partake of the former. In the event, the social formation called European feudalism developed a specificity of its own, characterized by hierarchical political forms that were the vehicles of a division of power between kings, lords, and bishops in the absence of a centralized, strong, bureaucratic state for the better exploitation of a subject peasantry, the whole supported by the ideological weight of a newly triumphant Christianity in the person of the institutionalized Catholic church.

European feudalism was constantly changing, and first and foremost in the manner of exploitation of the peasantry. Peasants did indeed constitute a single class as opposed to landlords, but this did not preclude the existence of a tangled web of relationships within the manorial villages. From a very early date it was possible for a serf to make money by selling any surplus he may have had on the market. In this way, some were able to buy their freedom. Those who remained in serf status might accumulate additional tenures and eventually have the terms of their servitude commuted in favor of payment in kind or money so as to become for all intents and purposes free. It was a slow process and even in England, where it went ahead most quickly, serfdom did not disappear until the end of the fifteenth century.

The form of rent on land was of great importance. At first, it was usually paid in labor on the lord's demesne or in his household. Those peasants who cultivated their own plots were also obliged to make payments in kind. Later, when market relations were once again sufficiently developed, money payments assumed a new significance. What we can separate so neatly for analytical purposes was, of course, not so in reality. It was quite common for all three types to be practiced simultaneously on the same manor. The substitution of one for the other was not a matter of baronial whim; the increased use of money signaled the presence of an important urban market and a renewal of the ancient social division of labor between town and country. Serf labor was now in crisis because it was no longer sufficient to meet the needs of the feudal lords. Natural economy was being replaced by a market economy, that is, by commodity production. In order for the productive forces to continue to expand (to take advantage of the opportunity, one might say), new relations of production were necessary. They could only come about as the result of a sharpening of the class struggle between lords and peasants, since the former were trying to resolve their problem by increasing the exploitation of the latter on the old model. It is the outcome of this struggle—the fact that the peasants increasingly paid money rents but at a relatively cheap rate—that prepared the way in the long term for the transition to capitalist agriculture.

# Marc Bloch

---

## 10

# European Feudalism

The adjective *feodalis* (relating to the fief) and the French substantive *féodalité,* used in the restricted sense of a quality peculiar to a fief, date the first from the Middle Ages, the second probably from the sixteenth century. But it was not before the eighteenth century that the custom arose of using for the designation of a whole system of social organization either compound expressions like feudal regime, government or system or, a little later, abstract substantives such as *féodalité* or feudalism. German historians in general have adopted *Lehnwesen* from *Lehn,* the German equivalent of fief. The extension of the use of a word derived from a particular institution, the fief, which can scarcely be considered the central and only significant institution of feudalism, to characterize the social regime prevailing widely during the Middle Ages, and more particularly from the tenth to the thirteenth centuries, in the greater part of western and central Europe, is mainly attributable to the influence of Montesquieu. Although Montesquieu considered the establishment in Europe of "feudal laws" a phenomenon *sui generis,* "an event occurring once in the world and destined perhaps never to occur again," modern sociologists and comparative historians have detected in other civilizations the existence of institutions analogous to those of the Middle Ages. Consequently the term feudalism has come to be applied to a mode of social organization that may recur in divers forms in differing periods and environments. Mediaeval European feudalism nevertheless remains the model of all feudal systems as well as the best known.

The origins of the European feudal regime have too frequently been discussed under the form of an ethnic dilemma: are they Roman or Germanic? As a matter of fact the social type that is called feudalism was born in Europe of conditions peculiar to the society from which it sprang. Since feudal society did not stamp itself upon a clean slate, but evolved little by little through the slow adaptation and modification of older usages, it is not difficult to discover in it traces of earlier systems of organization. But these elements were borrowed from very diverse environments. The feudal vocabulary itself, which combines Roman elements—one of them, the term vassal, taken by the Romans from the Celts—with Germanic elements by its very medley represents the singularly mixed character of the society in which feudalism took its rise.

The most remarkable characteristic of the western world at the beginning of the Middle Ages was the fact that it had been constituted by the encounter and fusion of civilizations existing at very unequal stages of evolution. On the one hand, there was the Roman or Romano-Hellenic world, itself hardly a unit in its foundations. For under the apparent uniformity of the imperial façade many local usages persisted which imposed conditions of life at times quite dissimilar upon the various social groups. On the other hand, there was the still comparatively primitive civilization of the peoples of ancient Germany, who had invaded the Roman domains and carved kingdoms out of it.

The bankruptcy of the state represents the most potent fact during this period. Whatever care the kingdoms of the barbarians may have taken to turn to their profit the formidable administrative system of ancient Rome—already, moreover, far advanced in decay at the time of the great invasions—however remarkable an effort at rehabilitation the monarchy of the first Carolingians may have represented after a century of extreme disorder, the powerlessness of the central government to exercise an effective control over a territory much too extensive for the forces at its disposal betrayed itself more and more glaringly, and for a long period after the middle of the ninth century, in a manner truly irremediable. Undoubtedly the reenforcement accruing from the Germanic traditions was not in this regard entirely negligible; the conception of royalty as the appanage of a sacred family, which derived from the most primitive notions of ancient Germany, resulted in a dynastic perpetuity better established than any that the Roman Empire had ever known. The idea of the state—or, more accurately, the idea of royalty—never entirely vanished. Likewise the institutions codified by the Carolingians long continued, more or less deformed, to exercise an influence. Men, however, lost the habit of expecting protection from a too distant sovereign. They sought it elsewhere and supplanted their obedience to the more remote ruler by other ties of dependence. The state tax ceased to be collected and the administration of justice was parceled out among a crowd of local authorities that had little or no connection with a central organism.

Less apparent but not less grave was the disturbance among social groups founded but lately upon a kinship more or less remote and fictitious, such as clan or tribe. It is impossible to ascertain to what degree the tradition of the old clannish relations had been able to survive in Roman Gaul and Italy, although in Great Britain the history of the imperfectly Romanized Celtic lands at the beginning of the

Middle Ages shows them still very strong. On the other hand, it cannot be doubted that this kind of social group was of great importance among the German peoples during the period immediately preceding that of the invasions. But the great turmoil of the conquest, together, no doubt, with certain tendencies from within, weakened these ties. Not that kinship relations ceased during the entire Middle Ages to be a human bond of immense strength. The numerous family feuds which jeopardized the active and passive solidarity of groups in all grades of the social hierarchy bear witness to the strength of these ties. So do various institutions juridical and economic. But these ties came to apply only to a comparatively restricted group whose common descent was easy to establish, namely, the family in the strict sense of the word and no longer the clan or the tribe. This group, which made room for paternal as well as maternal kinship, was not very clearly defined and most of the obligations or modes of living imposed upon its members resulted rather from habits and feelings than from legally defined constraints. The ties of kinship continued to exist very powerfully in the feudal society but they took their place beside new ties after which they tended to pattern themselves and to which they were at times considered inferior.

The social environment in which the feudal relations developed was characterized by an economic system in which exchange although not entirely absent was comparatively rare and in which the not very abundant specie played but a restricted role. It has sometimes been said that at that time land was the only form of wealth. This statement needs explanation and qualification. It cannot be denied that the paucity of commercial relations caused the very existence of every man to depend narrowly upon his possibility of disposing in some way of the resources furnished by a portion of the soil placed under his control. But an important fraction of the population drew its revenue from the land only indirectly under the form of personal service in money or in kind for the use of the land. Moreover, the possession of superior rights to the land was for the possessor in many respects but a means of exercising an effective power of command over the men to whom he conceded or permitted the direct enjoyment of the fields. One of the essential characteristics of feudalism is that prestige and social worth sprang less from the free disposal of property than from the free disposal of human forces. But the difficulty of commercial exchange had a considerable effect upon the structure of society. The absence of an easy flow of sales and purchases such as exists in present day societies prevented the formation of agricultural or industrial salaried classes and of any body of functionaries remunerated periodically in money.

In the absence then of a strong state, of blood ties capable of dominating the whole life and of an economic system founded upon money payments, there grew up in Carolingian and post-Carolingian society relations of man to man of a peculiar type. The superior individual granted his protection and divers material advantages that assured a subsistence to the dependent directly or indirectly; the inferior pledged various prestations or various services and was under a general obligation to render aid. These relations were not always freely assumed nor did they imply a universally satisfactory equilibrium between the two parties. Built upon authority, the feudal regime never ceased to contain a great number of constraints, violences and abuses. However, this idea of the personal bond, hierarchic and synallagmatic in character, dominated European feudalism.

Societies before the rise of feudalism already contained examples of relations of this sort. These did not, however, play the preponderant role that they were to assume later. Rural lordship existed in the Roman world and also at least in germ in the Germanic world. Roman society never ceased to give a large place to patron and client relationship. Around the powerful surged a great crowd of persons—at times themselves of high rank—who commended themselves to them. In addition these "clienteles" included as a general rule numerous former slaves freed by their masters in exchange for certain obligations of an economic nature and a general duty of fidelity (*obsequium*). Celtic society before the conquest also contained similar groups. In Germany alongside the normal relations that united the freeman to his family, his clan and his people others more transitory had grown up in the form of bands of faithful men of every origin gathered around a chief. Nourished in his dwelling, receiving from him horses and armor, they accompanied him to battle and constituted his strength and prestige. In this way people became accustomed to a certain conception of social bonds which developing in a favorable environment were to give rise to feudalism proper.

The leading features of feudalism in its fully developed form are the system of vassalage and the institution of the fief. As early as the Frankish and Lombard periods a great number of freemen of all ranks felt the need of seeking the protection of someone more powerful than themselves or of securing a decent livelihood by offering their military services to a superior. The poorest became slaves or simply tenants. But all who could clung to their dignity as men legally free and preferred not to lower themselves to the less honorable services which burdened the tenant liable to the corvée. They "commended" themselves *ingenuili ordine* [as men of free-born rank]. Exalted persons, on the other hand, sought to surround themselves with loyal people who should be attached to them by solid bonds. Thus arose the contract of dependence most characteristic of the feudal system.

In Frankish law, at least, the relations of vassalage were established by means of a formal act to which a little later the name homage was applied (in German *Mannschaft* or *Hulde*). The future vassal placed his hands in the lord's joined hands while repeating a few words promising loyalty, after which lord and vassal kissed each other on the mouth. As this ceremony, probably borrowed from old German traditions, gave no place to any religious elements, the custom early arose of following it up with an oath of fealty taken by the vassal on the Gospel or on relics.

The obligations created by homage and fealty held as long as both contracting parties were alive. They were extinguished upon the death of either. When heredity later came into play it undermined the whole system of vassalage. But heredity itself, as applying to the vassalic bonds, always remained rather a matter of practise than of law. In case of the death of lord or vassal a new offer of homage was in every case considered necessary to revive the tie. Being attached to concrete forms the vassalic right held bound only the two persons whom the ceremony brought face to face.

The reciprocal obligations of lord and vassal rested upon general simple principles susceptible in their details of infinite modifications and regulated with an increasing precision by local custom. The vassal owed the lord fidelity, obedience in the face of the whole world and aid in all circumstances in which the lord might need it. He supported him with his counsel, assisted him on occasion in his judicial functions and opened his purse to him in case of necessity. Little by little the cases in which this pecuniary aid—also called tollage—was legitimately exactable tended to become more defined and restricted to such occasions as the celebration of the knighthood of the lord's eldest son and of the marriage of his eldest daughter, ransom and so on. Above all the vassal owed the lord military service. This form of aid gradually came to predominate over all others.

In return the lord owed his man his protection; he assumed his defense before the tribunals, when there still were state tribunals; he avenged his wrongs and cared for his orphans until they became of age. Besides he assured him a livelihood in various ways and especially in the form of an economic grant generally known as a fief.

In the absence of a salary system there existed but two means of remunerating services. The master could receive his dependents in his own house, assure them food and shelter (*provende*), even clothe them; or he could assign them a piece of land upon which they might support themselves either directly or through returns received from those allowed to work it.

Of "provided" vassals nurtured in the lord's dwelling there were certainly a great number in the ninth and tenth centuries. They were still to be met with in the France of Philip Augustus. But vassals and lords early agreed in preferring the system of allotments of land, which provided the former with a greater independence and relieved the latter from the responsibility of looking after the support—particularly difficult under a rudimentary economic regime—of numerous and at times turbulent bands. Gradually most of the vassals found themselves "housed" (chasés, casati). The land assigned to them derived its peculiar features from the fact that it carried with it certain clearly defined services that were to be performed for the grantor. The property thus granted was at first called beneficium. Then little by little in the countries of Romanic speech which had adopted Frankish customs this term was supplanted (to such an extent that it has left not a trace in the Gallo-Roman dialects) by a term of Germanic origin: fief (fevum or feodum). The possession of land without obligation to any superior was, after the Frankish period, called alodial tenure. When a freeholder of this kind felt the need of commending himself he was in most cases forced to turn over his holding to the lord and receive it back as a fief. With the more complete feudalization of society these alodia decreased in number.

As the tenure service was a general institution of the economy of the period, there always existed a very great number of fiefs whose holders were not vassals: fiefs of artisans attached to the lord, such as painters and carpenters; of servants, such as cooks and doorkeepers; of officials charged with the administration of the manors, such as mayors and provosts. But any land granted to a vassal could be only a fief. Little by little, in proportion as the class of vassals tended to be transformed into nobility their fiefs appeared of a superior condition to those that were encumbered with humbler services, and eventually the jurists inclined to regard them as the only true fiefs. The institution of the fief, like that of homage, retained its personal character and was effective only for the lifetime of the contracting parties. Whenever either of them died the concession had to be renewed in the form of the symbolic tradition of investiture. With the establishment of the hereditary principle this ceremony became the means whereby the lord collected a sum of money (relief) as the price for the renewal of the fief.

On the other hand, it frequently happened that the vassal himself disposed of the very fiefs he held from a superior lord as fiefs for his own men. This subinfeudation, in principle, presumed the assent of the grantor of the original fief, but social necessities made it more and more customary to dispense with this. Thus alongside of and to a large extent parallel to the chains of personal dependence there arose chains of landed dependence. Mediaeval law in contrast with the Roman and modern notions of landed property conceived the soil as being subject to a great number of real rights differing among themselves and superimposed. Each of them had the value of a possession protected by custom (saisine, seisin, Gewehr) and none was clothed with that absolute character which the word property carries with it.

The seigniory, or manor, was the fundamental unit of the feudal regime. Under the name of villa it was very widespread in Gaul and in Roman Italy and in both cases doubtless went back to very old traditions such as those of village or clan chieftains. The seigniory usually consisted of several small farms. The cultivators were not the owners of the land but owed various duties and services to a lord who exercised over them a general power of command and from whom they held their lands on condition of a renewal of the investiture and the payment of a certain sum with every mutation. Generally in the Frankish period the lord also possessed a vast farm, the demesne, whose cultivation was assured in large part by the corvées due from the tenants. After the twelfth century these demesnes, chopped up into small farms, decreased in importance, first in France and Italy, more slowly in Germany, and the lord tended to become a mere receiver of land rents.

In gathering round the seigniory humble folk obeyed the same need of protection that men of a higher rank sought to satisfy in vassalage. The small peasant handed over his alodium to the lord and received it back under the form of a tenure with dues and corvées attached. Often he pledged his person and that of his descendants by the same act, thus entering into personal service. The life of the seigniory was regulated by custom. As the lords had every interest in keeping their lands peopled, the habit speedily arose of considering the peasant tenures, even the servile ones, as hereditary. Again, the seigniory fortified itself in the feudal period by appropriating a great number of state functions and by assuring the remuneration of the military class, which tended to rise above the others.

The churches figured among the principal possessors of seigniories. Some of them from the end of the Roman Empire obtained the right to retain the taxes levied upon their subjects. These privileges, confirmed and extended to churches more and more by the Frankish sovereigns, were the first form of immunity. This soon carried with it another advantage: the prohibition of representatives of the law—exacting and prone to be tyrannical—from trespassing upon immunized land to exercise their functions, notably their judicial powers. Analogous immunities were early obtained by lay lords.

In theory the men who lived upon a seigniory thus privileged remained answerable to the royal courts; their lord was responsible for their appearance. In reality the lord more and more tended to become a judge; he always had been so for his slaves, who at least in their relations to one another and to their master were answerable by the nature of things only to him. On the other hand, his role as protector seemed to confer upon him the right to maintain good order among his free tenants and his vassals. Under Charlemagne the state itself considered his intervention a guaranty of good order. After the fall of the Carolingian state the judicial power of the lord found a new lease on life in the usurpation of public functions, itself the consequence of the utilization of vassalage by the sovereigns.

In the Frankish period all freemen were liable to military service. But more and more the strength of armies seemed to center in horsemen equipped with complete armor and serving as leaders for little bands of other horsemen and of footmen. To remunerate the services of these knights, who accompanied them to the royal army or aided them in their blood feuds, the noblemen had acquired the habit of distributing fiefs among them; and, to make sure of their fidelity, of requesting homage. The sovereigns soon did the same. Notably Charles Martel, engrossed in his struggle against the Arabs and domestic enemies, created numerous military fiefs, carved largely from the domains of the churches which he usurped. Commendation, which had in the beginning been a sure means for men of every class to find a protector, tended thus to become a social tie peculiar to a class of military vassals (of the king or the nobles), who were at the same time possessors of seigniories. By a parallel tendency the old ceremony of the delivery of arms, a heritage from Germanic traditions originally distinguishing the majority of all freemen, now applied only to specialized warriors. This was the "dubbing"; whoever had received it could give it in his turn and thereby make knights. This class, until the twelfth century still open to adventurers of every origin, had an ethic of its own, a code of honour and fidelity tinged more and more with religious ideas, and felt itself to be virtually an order.

On the other hand, to reward their representatives throughout the country, in particular the counts, the kings, not being able to put them on salary, distributed fiefs among them consisting either of lands or of a share of the royal revenues in the provinces. To bind them by a tie that had some strength they chose them from among their vassals or exacted homage of them. The royal vassals in their turn and the churches surrounded themselves with their own vassals and confided to them a part of their functions and the administration of a part of their property.

Social and economic conditions thus made for decentralization and produced a veritable parceling out of all the powers of the state, such as justice, the right to coin money, tolls and the like. The profits accruing from these powers fell not only to the former direct representatives of the state, such as the counts, or to the immunized churches, but also by a sort of secondary appropriation to the representatives of these first usurpers.

The introduction of the principle of heredity into the feudal system was of paramount importance. The lord, who had need of men, sought to retain the services of the dead vassal's sons. The vassal's son was usually quite willing to do homage to his father's lord, in whom he found a natural protector. Above all it was at this price alone that he could keep the ancestral fief. In fact heredity was adopted little by little as a rule of conduct demanded first by public opinion, then by custom, and the lord who demurred ran the risk of offending his men. Charles the Bald considered it to be normal. In Italy the emperor Conrad II established it as law for fiefs below those of a count. Neither in France nor in Germany was it ever the subject of any legislation. In France it was early made general with but few exceptions and in Germany it was adopted more quickly for fiefs of a lower order and more slowly for fiefs of greater importance.

At the same time that they became hereditary the fiefs tended to become alienable. Of course the lord's assent would always be necessary for alienation. But it became less and less admissible to refuse it. The fiefs, together with the authority attaching to them and with the fragments of state functions that often went along with them, became hereditary, resulting in a confusion of powers over men and things. Heredity, however, while it put a seal on the feudal system certainly compromised its very foundations.

In all consistency the vassal system would have required each vassal to have but one lord. That was the very condition of the entire devotion which was the first of his duties, and the Carolingian legislation had so decided. But it was a great temptation to take fiefs wherever one could get them; when the fiefs had become patrimonial it sometimes happened that a vassal received by inheritance or purchase a fief that was held from some lord other than the one to whom he had first done homage. Cases of vassals of two or more lords are found from the tenth century and they become more numerous in the later period. How was one to apportion obligations to the various masters? In France in the eleventh century the custom arose of choosing one of these allegiances as more binding than the others. This was called liege (pure) homage. But in the thirteenth century this system, in its turn, was rendered ineffectual by the very multiplication of the liege homages offered by the same vassal to different lords. One was then reduced to consider, among the liege homages, which always took the first place, and, among the simple ones, the first homage in date, or sometimes the one attached to the greater fief as the strongest. In Germany and Italy, where the liege homage never took root, these classifications by dates or according to the importance of the fiefs had always been in vogue. But such multifarious allegiances could no longer count for much.

An essential characteristic of the feudal contract was the theory that if one of the two contracting parties broke his pledges he thereby freed the other party from all obligations. But precise definition as to the circumstances under which non-fulfilment of the contract, whether on the part of the lord or of the vassal, justified the rupture was completely wanting. In spite of the efforts of Carolingian legislation this salient point remained vague. The absence of all recognized superior authority left it to the interested parties to arbitrate the particular case. This uncertainty, the unforeseen consequence of the synallagmatic character of the bond, smoothed the way for all kinds of felony.

Although the salient features of the feudal regime were very nearly the same in all countries of western Europe there were, nevertheless, certain national differences and peculiarities. Thus in France the parceling out of the powers of the state, notably the appropriation of justice, was carried farthest. There too the military class became most solidly constituted and developed its chivalrous code, which from there spread over all Europe. In Germany feudal conceptions did not pervade the judicial life so profoundly, and two codes of customary law developed side by side, the general laws of the different countries (*Landrecht*) and the laws of fiefs (*Lehnrecht*). The alodia there, as in Italy and the south of France, persisted in greater numbers than elsewhere. The exclusive right to invest the superior judges who dealt with criminal cases involving the death penalty remained in the hands of the royal power. The emperors also maintained a long and effective struggle against the inheritance of the great fiefs. But they had to accept the obligation to enfeoff again the fiefs having the powers of earldoms when they were left without heirs or had been confiscated. This, unlike the case of France, prevented the increase of the royal domain itself. In Italy the previous importance of the cities and the urban habits of a great part of the knights themselves early created a formidable rivalry to the powers of the landed lords.

In Russia a real feudal regime was in full process of development up to the moment when it was stifled by the power of the Muscovite state. As in the west, the vassalage of the boyars became transformed into a state nobility. They were, however, more strictly subject to the czar since the synallagmatic character of the contract of service had always been less marked than in the west. The seigniory, vigorously constituted, survived for a long time. In the Byzantine state of the first centuries there existed tenures burdened with military service for the state but these were tenures of peasant soldiers. The emperors viewed these free peasants as constituting the strength of the army and struggled against their being crushed by the seigniories. From the eleventh century their resistance weakened and finally the seigniory, favoured with immunities and obliged by way of compensation to furnish soldiers to the state, became the keystone of the military organization. But these seigniories were not themselves subdivided in hierarchical form by bonds of fiefs and vassalage; so that one of the essential characteristics of feudalism—that gradation of obligations which in Europe preserved the homogeneity of the political organization—was always lacking in Byzantium. The Scandinavian peninsula offers a clear case of a country in which for want of one of the primary elements of feudal organization, that of seigniorial economy, a real feudalism failed to arise.

Much more significant is the distinction between countries in which feudalism had grown up spontaneously and those in which it had been planted by conquest. In the former the feudal regime was never able to attain that systematic character that hardly belongs to any but institutions formed fully accoutered and thereby unembarrassed with survivals. It appears, on the contrary, as a much more symmetrical edifice in the countries in which it was planted by conquest, such as the Latin states of the Holy Land, the Norman kingdom of southern Italy and especially England.

The social condition of England at the time of the conquest was in many respects analogous to that of Frankish Gaul at the time when the feudal system began to take shape. Both were marked by a slow absorption of the free peasants in the framework of a seigniory whose dependents still obeyed juridical statutes of extreme variety, by a tendency toward the generalization of dependent relations, by the appropriation of justice by the powerful, by the existence of tenures burdened with military service and called as in Germany *Laen,* and by the importance of the thanes, a class fairly similar to that of the Frankish royal vassals. But all that was poorly coordinated and the fusion of the relations of fief and vassalage had not been effected. The Norman kings imposed upon the country a feudal system conceived to their advantage. The boundaries of the seigniories (called manors) were definitely fixed; a sort of serfdom was introduced which, however, was in the course of time to evolve in a very different direction from the French; in spite of the much greater power of royal justice than in France the English lords were considered the exclusive judges of their tenants in their relations with them, which was finally to prevent the inheritance of tenures. Above all, the kings divided the whole country into military fiefs according to a system brought over from their Norman duchy. The tenants in chief were each to furnish the king with a certain number of knights. To be able to do so they distributed fiefs in their turn. But these chains of dependence soon becoming practically hereditary all led back to the king, from whom in the last analysis all land was held, even that of the church (under the form of the "free alms"). The alodium, a foreign body in the feudal world of the continent, did not exist at all in England. Finally, the king could demand the oath of fealty of his vassals' vassals.

At the end of the twelfth century a profound change took place in European society characterized by the formation of classes, economic transformations and the development of the state. In the tenth or eleventh century society consisted primarily of groups of dependents. As the sense of personal ties wore away, the human mass tended to organize itself in large classes arranged in a hierarchy. Knighthood became hereditary and changed into nobility. In England indeed the noble never had precise lawful privileges clearly separating him from the freeman. In Italy, habituated to a kind of life increasingly urban, he was hardly to be distinguished from the rich burgher. In France, on the contrary, the nobility made of itself a single closed class to which only the king could introduce new members. In Germany a whole hierarchy established itself within the nobility, and according to the theory of the *Heerschild* no member of one of these subclasses could without derogation accept a fief from a man occupying a lower grade.

Beginning in the thirteenth century economic exchange became more active. The cities developed and relations quite foreign to the feudal type came to light. Bound to his fellow townsmen by an oath of mutual aid, which unlike the vassal oath united equals, the towns-man needed no other protector than the community to which he belonged. His social code too was quite different from that of the military vassal. Moreover, the advent of a new economic regime founded upon exchange and money payment permitted the extension of the salaried class and at every step of the social scale took away from the fief and the enfeoffment any *raison d'être* for their functions.

This economic transformation in turn contributed to the rebirth of the state. Hired troops took the place of the vassals, who nearly everywhere had greatly succeeded in limiting their obligations. Corps of salaried officials subject to dismissal were formed. Such concentration of power did not redound solely to the advantage of the kings. In France and Germany certain royal vassals had brought under their control a great number of earldoms and multiform seigniorial rights and exalted their power above the crowd of lesser seigniories. While in France the great principalities thus formed were at last absorbed by the royal power, in Germany they well nigh annihilated it. In Italy the states formed around and by leading cities chiefly benefited from this movement. Everywhere the state, whatever its nature, was henceforth a master and protector. He who now depended only on it without "commending" himself to anyone no longer felt isolated.

The rural seigniory lasted much longer. Being adapted to the needs of the capitalistic era it still continued to flourish throughout the sixteenth, seventeenth and eighteenth centuries; it was transplanted by Europeans into various colonies, notably French Canada. It was not abolished in France until the revolution; it disappeared definitely from Germany—aside from a few survivals—in 1848; in England it disappeared but very slowly from the statute book and left behind a very strong imprint on the constitution of rural society.

The same needs from which vassalage took its rise long continued to make themselves felt, at least intermittently in troubled periods.

The homage, now but an empty rite, had its substitutes. The English liverymen in the time of the Wars of the Roses are reminiscent of the mesne tenants of the early Middle Ages. In the France of the seventeenth century to belong to a great lord afforded the gentry the best means of getting on. The orders of knighthood were invented by the princes at the close of the Middle Ages to insure the fidelity of those admitted to them; Napoleon himself in establishing the Legion of Honour had much the same idea. But those orders that have survived, as well as their contemporary imitations, have lost every role but that of honorific distinction.

In the last centuries of the Middle Ages the states had sought to turn to account the old feudal organization, requiring of vassals if not an active military service at least a compensatory tax. But these attempts had little success. In England a law of the Commonwealth in 1656, confirmed by the Restoration in 1660, abolished all distinction between the fiefs of knights and the free tenures (socages). The fiction that all land is held from the crown, the use of the word fee to designate the highest form of landed rights, are relics of the systematic organization introduced by the Norman kings; primogeniture applied in the absence of a will to all succession in real estate is a legacy of the law of fiefs. In certain German states, such as Prussia under Frederick William I, the fiefs were transformed into alodia in the eighteenth century by legislative action. France waited until the revolution of 1789 to abolish fiefs and vassalage, which had ceased to bring any considerable revenue to the coffers of lords and king. In the nineteenth century these antiquated institutions finally disappeared in Europe. The class of military vassals had given birth to the nobility. In France the latter saw its privileges completely abolished along with the feudal organization itself, and by the same act its social role was doomed to extinction. But in some other countries it has long outlived the fiefs both in fact and in law.

The clearest legacy of feudalism to modern societies is the emphasis placed upon the notion of the political contract. The reciprocity of obligations which united lord and vassal and caused with every grave dereliction by the superior the release of the inferior in the eyes of the law was transferred in the thirteenth century to the state. Practically everywhere, but with peculiar clearness in England and Aragon, the idea was expressed that the subject is bound to the king only so long as the latter remains a loyal protector. This sentiment counterbalanced the tradition of royal sanctity and finally triumphed over it.

# Charles Parain

## 1 1

# The General Character of Feudal Society

### GENERAL CHARACTERISTICS

Between the slave societies, characterized not only by the exploitation but also by the possession of man by man, and the capitalist society, where man is legally free, but the labor of those with nothing to sell but the strength of their arms is exploited by those who possess the means of production, history has witnessed the development in many places of types of society which, regardless of more or less significant variations, display the following general features so far as the relations of production are concerned:

1. The social relations of production are essentially established around the land, since they are based on a predominantly agricultural economy.
2. The workers have rights of use and occupation of the land, but the ownership belongs to a hierarchy of lords, none of whom has the absolute control of the soil, although each has customary appropriation rights over the product and the property of his inferiors on the social ladder.
3. A whole network of personal bonds corresponds to this economic base: part of the workers—the majority at periods of typical development—do not enjoy full personal freedom. There is no longer "slavery" (ownership of the person), but "serfdom" (attachment of the peasant to his master, *homo proprius,* later to his farm *adscriptus glebae*). Even among loads themselves, the property system is linked to a system of duties (particularly military) owed to the person of the superior.

Owing to these factors, the political superstructure of the system is unique. Carried to its logical conclusion, it implies the disappearance of the sovereign state, for authority is exerted from person to person. The essential fact, from this point of view, is that justice is rendered by the suzerain upon his vassals, and by the lord upon his peasants.

The exploitation of economic levies and the judicial-political system are thus closely linked. So long as this complex of traits determines the functioning of a society, we are justified in describing it as a feudal society. A certain number of preliminary remarks are called for, however, either to answer some objections concerning the use of the term, or to avoid oversimplifying the physiognomy of the feudal period.

## THE USE OF THE WORD "FEUDAL"

The word "feudal" is not analogous to the words used to describe either the slave society, the capitalist society, or the socialist society. In these three cases, the word used refers to the basic social mainspring—ownership of the slave, ownership of capital, generalized social property. "Feudal," on the contrary, is a word that applies only to the political superstructure evolved in the typical fully perfected form of the society that forms the transition from the ancient slave society to the modern capitalist society. As a consequence, the word does not always exactly fit the period of early development of that intermediate society, that of its decomposition, or some of its more or less imperfect variations.

In all these cases, the "fief"—the word from which the term "feudal" derives—does not play the main role. Is this a reason for refusing, as do most non-Marxist historians, to use the word "feudal" whenever we are not dealing with the precise legal and political forms based on the fief? I think not, and I regard this refusal as the expression of a dangerous formalism which, in fact, tends to make us forget the underlying unity between the relations of production established between lords and peasants around the land, and the feudal hierarchy that so long sanctioned and ensured the very mechanism of those relations.

At what point, moreover, did it become customary to describe as feudal the whole system, including the basic relations between peasants and lords, and the legal and political remnants of the Middle Ages within the absolute monarchy of modern times? The custom originated mainly in the course of the struggle waged by the rising bourgeoisie against a regime in a state of decadence and already quite different from its typical form. In this struggle, the term "feudal" took on a pejorative and polemical sense (as did the term "capitalist" during the class struggle of the nineteenth century). And that is exactly why the non-Marxist historians prefer not to use it, just as bourgeois economists long refused to use the term "capitalist." But their refusal in no way negates the reality of capitalism or of feudalism.

It should simply be recognized that the type of social relations just briefly defined were established well before the fief itself, which was but its political consummation, and that this type of relations continued long after the political form had disappeared. With these reservations, there is no difficulty in describing as "feudal," as did the men of the eighteenth century, any system in which the agricultural worker, although no longer a slave, is still subject to a series of extra-economic restrictions that so reduce his freedom and his personal property that neither his labor power nor his product can be true objects of free exchange, true "commodities." Thus the Roman colonist of the fourth century already foreshadowed feudalism, and the Hungarian or Sicilian peasant of 1930 lived under restrictions of the same kind. This is the meaning of the Marxist concept of the word "feudal."

## PROGRESSIVE ASPECTS OF THE FEUDAL MODE OF PRODUCTION

It is important, however, to avoid the mistake made by the mechanical materialism of the eighteenth century in the heat of the struggle of the rising bourgeoisie against feudalism. Inspired by an antihistorical conception of history, this materialism unhesitatingly attributed a kind of absolute superiority to the ancient "civilizations" of Greece and Rome and looked upon the establishment of feudalism as a regression. A clear distinction should be made between the feudal mode of production, which implies a definite level of development of the productive forces, and the broader and looser concept of feudal society. It then becomes easier to recognize that in the whole range of historical development, the feudal mode of production represents a forward step in relation to the ancient mode of production.

It is true that, on the economic level, serfdom corresponds to small-scale exploitation, small farms, whereas in agriculture, slavery led to large-scale exploitation. But there are different kinds of small-scale exploitation. In *Capital,* Marx remarks that while small-scale farms and independent trades formed, at least in part, the basis of the feudal mode of production, these features continued to exist alongside capitalist exploitation and already formed the basis of the ancient societies, between the time when the primitive community was breaking down and the time when slavery definitely established its sway over production. But in the feudal mode of production, small-scale farming was practiced at an appreciably higher level of technology, as compared with the small-scale farming connected with the breakup of primitive society. Among other things, the watermill, the wine press, and the bread oven, developed under conditions of large-scale production in the period of slavery, had become the indispensable instruments of satisfactory productivity.

It became necessary under feudalism to combine the advantages of small-scale exploitation, in which the direct producer could show interest in his work and display initiative (unlike the slave), with the advantages of means of production whose development and mainte- nance surpassed the possibilities of small-scale exploitation. These means of production were in the hands of the lord, who became "the organizer and the master of the productive process and the entire process of social life." All this found its expression in the coexistence of the lord's feudal ownership of the land with the peasant's private ownership of the individual means of production and his hereditary tenure. Added to all this (the economic basis of the system), the lord enjoyed other advantages, such as the extra-economic power of coer- cion conferred by his monopoly of offensive and defensive arms and by the class solidarity of the exploiters expressed through the feudal political organization.

The logic of the system resulted in a certain balance, a certain efficiency. In that sense, it was progressive. But from the period of its inception to the period of its breakup, the forms and degrees of the exploitation of the working classes by the ruling classes were many . and various. Simplifications are to be avoided.


THE FORMATION OF THE FEUDAL REGIME:
SERFDOM AND THE VILLAGE COMMUNITIES
                              The destruction of the slave state in Western Europe (that is, the Roman Empire) eliminated a significant obstacle to the emergence of new relations of production, but it did not lead automatically and rapidly to the development of such rela- tions. In the absence of a truly revolutionary class bearing revolution- ary ideas, the passage from one regime to another could come about only very slowly, after long and painful groping. This was true of the feudal regime, which developed as a result of spontaneous uncon- scious adjustments in the face of new necessities of the same type and leading to the same end at a tempo and under forms that varied widely according to local conditions.

For the whole of Western Europe, the outlines only begin to take shape toward the ninth century. The interval of more than four cen- turies stretching from the year 400 to about 850 was a period of great confusion, a real "high Middle Age" in which the historic trend toward the developed form of feudalism was nevertheless clearly perceptible.

In the Late Roman Empire, the *coloni* (slaves or freemen with a plot of land, to which they were bound) were the precursors, but only the precursors, of the serfs of the Middle Ages (not all of whom de- scended from them, however). The German "barbarians," occupying the Roman Empire little by little, settled there—or, more accurately, reestablished—a free peasantry organized in village communities. It is becoming increasingly clear today that the Roman colonial superstructure misled historians by the documents it left behind. Actually, the underlying village and tribal realities had remained very much alive. The disappearance of the Roman cadres and invasions breathed new life into these old peasant structures, which a new system of legal and political relations was to slowly restructure.

At the same time, a new nobility was beginning to take shape: Members of the armed bands gathered around the German chieftains; Romanized natives who had provided the cadres of the administration; the favorites of the barbarian kings from whom they received domains taken from the state lands. A wide variety of combinations must have existed between personal bonds (domestic, military, or religious) and landed property rights (awarded as a "benefice" by the protector or offered by the protégé as a "precarium"). But all these combinations converge toward a single final property structure commanding indirect but not actual ownership by the most powerful lords of vast domains, and more direct ownership (which is not, however, absolute, since it is linked to a series of services and oaths) by small and middle lords. This hierarchy of rights over the land was to extend progressively to the very base, to the level of the peasants working the land, who had nothing more than a precarious possession of the soil.

Indeed, incessant wars—internecine wars, wars of conquest—rapidly ruined the new free peasantry, either because their goods were confiscated, periodically devastated, or destroyed, or because the military service demanded of the freemen was so heavy a burden that it left them no opportunity to work their land. Since the royal power was too weak to protect them, the ruined peasants were forced to put themselves under the protection of either the new nobility or the Church, transferring their property rights in the land to their protectors, as peasants had already begun to do in the Late Roman Empire. The status of the free peasant, even if a legal distinction continued to be made between those born free and those born in slavery, tended toward a status of serfdom, in which each peasant, while possessing work tools and the use of the land, was nevertheless bound to a superior owner—the lord—by all kinds of personal commitments and dues.

The development of serfdom either as a substitute for slavery or by the generalization of the peasant's subordination to his chiefs, defenders, or conquerors appears to be a constituent part of the feudal regime, but serfdom is not everywhere the same, and its function in the feudal ensemble can vary greatly, even to the point of disappearing or assuming new forms. The peasant's dependence, on the other hand, is generally tempered by the maintenance of the rights of the rural community. A double problem then arises: the special role of serfdom, and the place of the village community in the feudal system.

## The Problem of Serfdom

It would be inadequate, even dangerous, to characterize the feudal mode of production as essentially "serfdom" without specifying what kind, what level of serfdom is meant. Engels made this point in several letters to Marx in December, 1882:

Certainly serfdom and subjection to the corvée do not constitute a specifically medieval or feudal form. We find it wherever the conqueror makes the natives cultivate the land for him. It existed very early, for example, in Thessaly. This fact even blurred my own vision—mine and many others—concerning servitude in the Middle Ages. There was such a strong inclination to base it on conquest alone. That would make everything so easy, so uniform.

All recent historical research confirms this warning. Medieval serfdom, in its classic phase, is not the result exclusively either of a sudden imposition through conquest or of a one-sided development originating in a former servile status (*colonate* or ancient slavery). Serfdom results from the spontaneous convergence of varied personal statuses toward an increasingly uniform objective situation, under the combined pressures of reality and of the patient or brutal action of the ruling classes. The law comes after the fact. It crystallizes it; it does not create it.

In the same way, economic conditions may—in various degrees, according to the region—facilitate the trend from serfdom to freedom during the feudal society's period of decline. But this does not happen everywhere, at least not at the same tempo, so there is no possibility of a schematic and universally valid social "profile." Whereas in the tenth century the serf could abandon his farm, but still remain "his master's man," by the fourteenth century the former free man, with no personal bonds to a lord, is tied to the soil which he cannot leave at will. This is what Engels called "the innumerable degrees of subjection to the corvée and to serfdom" in a letter in which, speaking of Germany, he distinguishes between the crushing serfdom of the ninth and tenth centuries, the attenuated serfdom of the thirteenth and fourteenth centuries, and the regenerated serfdom of the sixteenth.

Just as slavery did not cease to exist just because it did not everywhere and always exhibit the same degree of coercion and inhumanity as at the highest point of its development, so it would be a mistake to think that feudalism as a mode of production had radically changed its form because of the disappearance of the classical, typical forms of serfdom. If some of the peasants' wars resulted in the abolition of personal servitude, they did not put an end to feudal rights (for example, Catalonia, in the fourteenth century). If the peasants lost the war (as in Germany in the sixteenth century), serfdom, which had been on the wane, was reinforced. It should not be forgotten that serfdom did not disappear from Eastern Europe until after 1860.

Nor should it be forgotten that the Spanish colonization of America established a form of serfdom through the system of *encomiendas*. Groups of Indians were entrusted (*encomendados*) to a colonist. He was to protect them and catechize them, and they would work for him, while at the same time meeting their own needs. The system is directly inspired by that of feudal Europe, in that it is based on the subjection of those who work to those who bear arms and those who pray. But since the *encomenderos* were set up by the powerful Spanish monarchy or its agents, the political superstructure here is very different from that of the Middle Ages. And in the tropical plantations (Cuban sugar, for example), the return to large-scale property cultivated by slaves rapidly replaced the feudal *encomienda*.

It should not be thought that there was an uninterrupted, direct evolution from ancient slavery to serfdom, and from serfdom to freedom. Serfdom emerged or reemerged more often from the gradual subjection of the free peasant than from the attenuation of the slave condition. Its own attenuation and disappearance depended as much on the objective conditions in each region as on the intensity and outcome of class struggles. The disappearance of legal serfdom did not always eliminate numerous duties and bonds connected with the feudal mode of production.

## The Problem of the Communal Village in the Face of Feudal Authority

In reality, there is one factor which should not be neglected in considering the peasant's means of action against his lord—the existence of a village community, which appears late in the texts and the law, but is indisputably of very ancient origin. The small farms would have lacked a solid basis without the indispensable addition of common rights to the forests, pastures, and uncultivated or only sporadically cultivated heaths. The collective restraints involved by the practice of regular crop rotation and the common use of the pastures united the peasants into a functioning group with possibilities greater than those of any individual. These communities are an integral part of the feudal mode of production and productive relations. This is what made possible the relative emancipation of the serfs as a class, whereas under slavery only individual emancipation was possible. At the most favorable moments, the peasants could thus establish a relative balance between themselves and the lords, limiting the exploitation to which they were subjected and conserving enough resources to increase production not only for their own individual benefit, but for that of society as a whole.

Nothing, however, was more unstable than such a balance. On the one hand, the elements involved changed as the productive forces developed (new land opened up to cultivation, new agricultural techniques, new methods of raising livestock); on the other hand, the relationship of forces was constantly changing according to the degree of determination displayed by the village communities or the degree of strength with which the feudal political organization functioned. Take two opposite examples: In partially or belatedly feudalized countries like Denmark, the village communities were able to display their creative abilities and organize cooperation on a more or less extensive scale, while maintaining a relative autonomy. Conversely, it often happened that the lords exerted and maintained over the peasants dependent on them a pressure that reduced them to total subjection, to the detriment of production.

Even recently, the exploitation of the great landed estates in Sicily corresponded to the worst feudal conditions: To maintain his rights over the land, the big landowner forced his *colons*—the equivalent of the tenants of the Middle Ages—to cultivate continually changing plots and to live in a town often far away from the fields they worked. He thus imposed on them not only extreme poverty, but a state of personal semiserfdom. The *colon,* of course, worked with means of production that were his own property, but they were extremely primitive, and he had neither the desire nor the opportunity to introduce improvements (such as planting olive trees or vineyards) which would have the effect of increasing productivity.

The consideration of the degrees of serfdom and the varying functions of the rural community brings us to the final phase in the development of feudal societies. The cases mentioned are extreme, and it would be well to return to the intermediary stages of development.


THE FLOWERING OF FEUDALISM

The very slow birth of the feudal regime can, of course, be divided into various periods. There is a continuous dialectical interaction between developing material forces (population, agricultural techniques) and legal, political, and moral superstructures which are either dissolving (like the powers of the emperors and kings) or coming into existence (like feudal bonds). This interaction results in some characteristic combinations that vary according to the historical moment.

Distinct phases can be detected within the period between the ninth century, after the failure of the attempted renovation of the Carolingian Empire, and the thirteenth century, when feudal Western Europe reached its climax. The phases we shall discuss are valid mainly for the Burgundy region, one of those that has been thoroughly studied. With the required reservations, they are undoubtedly utilizable for a more general view.

In the tenth century, feudalism is still in its formative period. Feudal links develop between the big landlords and the former high Carolingian officials (dukes, counts) who still preserve a vestige of state authority. At the level of the peasants, there is a clear distinction between the free and the nonfree. The free, who are very numerous, possess *alleux,* that is, completely independent properties. They participate in the administration of justice. They can change their lord, if they have one; the same is true for the vassals. In brief, the feudal bonds are loose. So are family and moral loyalties. Social life continues to bear the stamp of individualism; the features of feudalism are still sketchy.

Between the years 1000 and 1150, we can speak of a rising feudalism. The system becomes more definite. The process of decomposition that had already affected the royal power now extends to the power of the dukes and counts. At the summit, there is danger of anarchy. But at the base, the vitality of free peasant exploitation brings about an expansion of the population—there are many empty spaces, but the easily tillable lands are overpopulated—as well as a technical upsurge: The rigid harness for the horse is in increasingly widespread use, as is the wheeled plough and the flail; barley and oats, recently introduced cereals, are increasingly grown.

Who will reap the benefits of this first upsurge? Those who are able to impose their military protection in the midst of the increasing disorder. This means the independent manorial lords to whom peasants of all ranks, free or nonfree, who have not chosen (or have not been able to choose) the soldier's life, will turn. These manorial lords declare themselves invested with the "ban," the local command, the power at the lowest level of society. This enables them to organize all economic life to their advantage. The counterpart of their "protection" is a series of personal restrictions and economic levies, controls over individuals and communities. The lordship thus establishes itself definitively over rural production and the village community.

The lord, in his turn, constitutes himself the "man" of a more powerful lord, whose power no longer derives from the extent of his lands and the number of vassals who recognize him as their suzerain. It is a system without a state, born of a certain anarchy, but which limits this anarchy and then organizes it.

This organization requires, to a greater extent than in the preceding phase, a framework of loyalties, commitments, beliefs. Family loyalties—lineages—become stricter. Class loyalties are strengthened by rites, customs, oaths—the whole material and moral apparatus of chivalry. Finally, the religious sanction comes into play: The Church, which recruits its higher cadres among the powerful and its troops among the mass of free peasants, imbeds itself deeply in the feudal system; it acquires vast overlordships through donations (feudal in form) given by both peasants and great lords. It limits the violence— mainly violence among lords, which destroys the needed class solidarity —but it ensures the moral subordination of the working classes, who are henceforth obliged to maintain by the product of their labor the fighting class and the praying class. The institutional and spiritual superstructure is now perfectly in place.

This result corresponds to a continuous extension of the economic base of the system through the generalization of technical improvements and the successful opening of new lands to cultivation. In this sense the eleventh century—the century of Romanesque art, of the *chansons de geste*—deserves to be regarded as the rising phase of feudal society in Western Europe. The eleventh century also marks a certain rebirth of commerce and large-scale circulation of money, a new role for the cities with the first communal revolutions, and finally, a tendency toward outer expansion with the Crusades. These transformations bear the germs of the destruction of feudal society in its original forms. But this process is still slow. Toward 1100, even toward 1150, the ascendant phase continues.

From the middle of the twelfth century to the beginnings of the fourteenth, the European feudal regime experiences, in a sense, its flowering and its climax. But the development of the productive forces, in the forms they assumed under feudalism, reaches its limits at this time. The internal contradictions of the system make themselves felt, forcing the institutions and the law to crystallize and become fixed. The fundamental process of development already threatens the very logic of the mechanism.

First of all, in many places, the possibilities of opening up new land to cultivation have already been exhausted by the middle of the thirteenth century. The population upswing results in an extreme division of peasant farms, on increasingly barren land, while the demands of the lords grow increasingly insistent. With every bad harvest, there is increased danger of famine.

Commerce and urban life develop, prices rise, wealth in personal estate grows alongside real estate fortunes. All this brings about several contradictory trends. The peasant mass, now more numerous, is impoverished by its burden of obligations. But the lord, in need of money, converts the corvées, the payments in kind, the franchises, into money payments. Personal serfdom is on the wane. On the other hand, since the poor worker is attracted by the city or by the idea of emigration, the lord uses all his prerogatives to keep him under his control. There is talk of the serf "attached to his plot." The free type of property *(alleu)* disappears. The law declares: "No land without a lord." Thus just at the moment when the realities tend to weaken the already aging feudal system, it tends to become more rigid legally.

The same holds true in the political sphere. The danger of a reversal of fortunes arouses the caste spirit. The nobility is increasingly closed in upon itself. But a higher political authority is taking shape above it. It is the time of the feudal monarchies. They use the old system, rather than destroy it. It is as a suzerain that the king dominates his vassals. The pyramid is more complete, more perfect, than in the eleventh century—but only in appearance. For already the royal power, in alliance with the new forces (the cities), threatens the free play of personal bonds, appropriates justice, reconstructs the state. The feudalism of the years between 1250 and 1350 is legally better defined and psychologically more conscious than in its formative period. It is less free, less creative, more threatened.

Of course, the development described here is mainly valid for a particular region, eastern and northern France. Southern France, Spain of the Reconquest, England (lagging at first, then organized by the Norman Conquest), Germany, where the central power will not be strongly reconstituted—all display definite peculiarities and a somewhat different chronology of feudal development. But the facts are still obvious everywhere. In the East, in Asia, in the Arab countries, the most interesting centuries are not of course the same. And the feudalization process is combined with very different basic structures (maintenance of slavery, nomadism, irrigation). Certain striking similarities (the case of Japan, for example) nevertheless prove that, at a certain stage of development of the productive forces, the modes of production tend to be organized into social and finally political structures in which the system of servitude and duties imposed on the peasant farmer is controlled by a hierarchy of lords (and religious institutions) whose links, commitments, and beliefs resemble our feudalisms.

## THE DEVELOPMENT OF THE RELATIONS OF PRODUCTION IN FEUDAL SOCIETY

The basic character of these societies resides in the relations of production at their foundation: the lord's property in the land, and his limited property in the peasant himself. This property in the person is very important, and without it the lord could not have imposed taxes and corvées (Marx and Lenin stressed this point). But the fact that the property is limited implies a mode of production quite distinct from that of slavery.

At the beginning, the big proprietor divides his land into two parts: the first, vast in extent, is exploited by himself and his direct agents,

and harbors, at its center, the master's house, the agricultural buildings, and various workshops. This is the domain. The second part is
parcelled out into holdings conceded to relatively free peasants. These
peasant tenants owe not only rents from the product of the soil, but
also corvées performed on the land directly owned by the master, who
has virtually no other labor force. These corvées often represent three
days of work a week, and if to this are added various rents evaluated
in labor-days, two-thirds of the entire working year is given over to
the master. Two days for the master, one day for himself—such was
the serf's lot. This labor rent exacted by the lord is the original form
of surplus value and coincides precisely with it, says Marx.

The cultivation of the domain by this corvée system is similar to
that of the Roman *latifundia* [estates] only in appearance. Marx
remarked that it was the relative volume of surplus labor required of
the serf that determined the possibilities of improvements on the
holding:

The output of the remaining days available to the direct producer to
work for himself is a variable factor which will necessarily develop
with the increasing experience of the producer; at the same time, new
needs, as well as the expansion of the market for his new products, and
the constantly increasing assurance that he will be able to use this part
of his labor power for himself—all this will induce him to a greater
exertion of this power. The opportunity for some economic development does then exist here.

Engels adds that this fruitful change in the mode of exploitation is
accompanied by a parallel change in the nature of the exploiting
classes. The big absentee landowner of the Late Roman Empire, with
his taste for luxury and his contempt for manual labor, is supplanted
by cruder but more virile lords living permanently among their
tenants:

The social classes of the ninth century were constituted not in the
stagnation of a declining civilization, but in the birth pangs of a new
civilization. The relations between the powerful landlords and the
enslaved peasants, which had been for the Romans a sure sign of the
hopeless decline of the ancient world, now became for the rising generation the starting point for a new development.

The lord, master of his domain and of the collective instruments of
the ban (mill, oven, and so on) can now indeed appear as the organizer
and director of the productive process as well as a group leader. That
is the starting point.

But from the vantage point of the twelfth rather than of the tenth century, the corvée is seen to have ceased to play the basic role in the feudal mode of production. Only a few days a year, some secondary surviving customs—that is all the lord asks of the peasant. This does not mean that he no longer intends to appropriate a sizable portion of the peasant's labor. But the peasant, supported by the village community, fought fiercely against the corvée. He often won collective franchises, and always worked better on his own land than on the lord's, which therefore vegetated and was finally divided into new holdings. Now the lord's revenues come almost exclusively from annual levies on these holdings. The obligation to use the lord's mill and oven no longer represent anything more than the financial exploitation of a monopoly. The lord is thus more like a rentier drawing an income from the land than an organizer. But the labor rent has become rent in kind [a share of the product]. If the share demanded of them is not excessive (that depends on the time and the circumstances), the tenant and the village community have greater freedom and interest in their work. On the other hand, the lord's prerogatives seem even more parasitic.

A last transformation will take place as the rent in kind tends to be superseded by money rent. But this already corresponds to a phase of dissolution of the feudal society, which occurs at very different periods depending on the region. We have shown how, in thirteenth-century Western Europe, the lords in their desire for liquid cash increasingly preferred money payments to payment in kind. But the rise in agricultural prices which was quite marked throughout the thirteenth century rapidly caused every fixed payment to lose its value. The lord's wealth would therefore be threatened if it consisted mainly of money rent. These two contradictory trends explain the complexity and slow pace of the changes.

## THE DECOMPOSITION OF THE FEUDAL REGIME IN THE COUNTRYSIDE

As with all regimes based on the exploitation of man by man, the periods of formation and equilibrium for the feudal regime were of short duration. A general crisis of feudal society broke out and continued throughout the fourteenth and fifteenth centuries in Europe. Nor was this to be the last one, for while the decline of the feudal world lasted a relatively shorter time than that of the ancient world, it did nevertheless stretch over several centuries (the fifteenth to eighteenth), until a new class—the bourgeoisie—consciously pursued its destruction and replacement.

In the fourteenth century, it became clear in all the countries of Western Europe that the feudal regime had ceased to promote the development of the productive forces. Neither the expansion nor the intensification of agriculture could any longer cope with the increase of the population. No new areas are brought under cultivation; the lands are exhausted. Terrible famines, followed by epidemics, take their main toll among the poorest. The Black Death (1348–1349) is the most famous, but it is not the appearance of these plagues which is so characteristic (there have been many others), but their recurrence and their result: numerous villages depopulated, countless lands abandoned. The emergence, over and above the feudal political structure, of the first national states causes terrible wars (for example, the Hundred Years War between France and England). These destructions are accompanied by great peasant uprisings: in 1358, the Jacquerie in northern France; in 1381, the famous workers' revolt in England. These phenomena are widespread (they can be observed in Spain, in Germany), and often concomitant. They are not the result of local circumstances, but the expression of a general crisis.

The crisis undoubtedly derives from the intensification of the exploitation of the peasant masses—an exploitation no longer accompanied by the development of the productive forces. The lords' levies have become purely parasitic, and they increase with their taste for luxury and the expansion of exchanges within the upper classes. The emergence and development of a royal power, leading to the organization of a modern state, adds a new system of royal taxation to the feudal taxation system. Last but not least, social differentiation, with the resulting struggle of the rich and the poor, begins to make its appearance within the village community.

The peasant revolts, the peasant wars that mark this long period of crisis exhibit a common characteristic despite their varying results: None succeeded in bringing about a revolutionary social change, a new mode of production. In this sense, they resemble the slave revolts of Roman times; they do not possess the requisite means and the conception for a new society.

The most pertinent example is that of the peasants' war which shook part of Germany in 1525. It was a very large part indeed, since it originated between the Black Forest and the Lake of Constance and spread to Alsace, the Palatinate, Hesse, the Duchies of Brunswick, then to the Upper Danube and Franconia, Thuringia, Saxony, and finally to the south: the Tyrol, the Archbishopric of Salzburg, Styria, Carinthia, Carniola. Numerous cities fell into the hands of the insurgents. Mainz negotiated with them; Treves and Frankfort were threatened. And yet everywhere the insurrection was put down in a few months.

The cause of these uprisings was the destitution of the peasants. The concentration of power was carried out in Germany at the level of the princes, who imposed taxes as they pleased to pay for their luxury and their permanent armies. At the same time, the nobility in their castles, ruined by the development of new military techniques, tried to squeeze the peasants by applying to the maximum extent their old feudal rights, by force if necessary. Levies and rents were increased, while the peasants' rights to the use of the woods and communal lands were threatened. The reasons for the generalized insurrection are easy to understand. But the peasant rebels were handicapped by their provincial isolation, and by the narrowness of their views. They constantly refused to go to the aid of peasants in neighboring regions, and their bands were annihilated one after the other in isolated battles by mere sections of armies often representing no more than a tenth of their numbers. The powerful coalition of princes, nobility, and the cities, together with the disavowal by Luther, organizer of the religious revolution, spelled defeat for the peasant revolt. "The greatest revolutionary attempt of the German people," remarked Engels, "ended with a shameful defeat and momentarily doubled oppression."

It was not the same everywhere. For example, Catalonia in the years between 1300 and 1486 was the scene of a sporadic but fierce "hundred years' war" between lords and peasants for the abolition of the *remensa* (the redemption of the peasant's attachment to the land) and the abuses (all sorts of exactions renewed by the lords). The ruin of the lords by the depopulation of the villages and the disagreement between them and the king, who wanted to impose his authority, enabled the peasants to win an advantageous compromise, although it was advantageous, in reality, only for the wealthiest of them. A peasant aristocracy very important for the future of the country was created, but the feudal structure (levies, superior property rights of the lords) remained. This outline is not, however, valid for all of Spain. At Majorca, the peasant revolt was crushed in 1381; at Valencia, in 1526. And wherever the reconquering Christians put down the Muslim peasants, they imposed upon the Moors a status of collective bondage with colonial overtones.

It is clear that the uneasy balance between peasant and lord was often disturbed in one way or another throughout this great crisis of nearly two centuries. The real social revolution was to come from other phenomena, other classes, another kind of revolution, but the role of the countryside in this transformation cannot be underestimated, since it provided the mass of proletarianized workers needed for the establishment of capitalism.

The stabilization of the peasant society, however, was a very slow process that took a wide variety of forms between the sixteenth and nineteenth centuries. Let us recall its principal forms and the extent to which they held back, aided, or guided the advent of capitalism.

When the peasants succeeded in consolidating their possession of the land and when the village community managed, through the maintenance of its collective rights over the common woods and pastures, to retain most of its cohesiveness, the path was clear for the development of free peasant property, but it was very small-scale property. This is exactly what the Revolution of 1789 in France consecrated when it abolished the last remnants of feudal rights. For the future, however, this was to prove an obstacle to the full development of capitalism. "Small-scale property," said Marx, "excludes by its very nature the development of the social productive forces of labor, the establishment of social forms of labor, the social concentration of capital, large-scale breeding, the progressive application of science to agriculture."

When, on the contrary, the peasants found themselves unable to resist the increasing demands of the lords, as was the case in Eastern Europe, a new serfdom was created as the lords reestablished great farms cultivated by means of corvée and independent agricultural laborers. In this case, the medieval property relations proved capable of adjusting to capitalism through the return to large-scale agriculture that amply supplied the outside market. This is what Lenin called "the Prussian path of capitalist development in agriculture," which in no way excludes the maintenance of semifeudal social relations between the landlord and the peasant.

In the Mediterranean regions, especially in those parts of Italy where the money economy was least entrenched, the thirteenth century saw the development of a transitional form between the feudal agricultural economy and the capitalist agricultural economy. This is called sharecropping. The rent in kind paid to the landowner is no longer, as in the feudal economy, merely the price paid for the monopoly of the land, but also partially the remuneration for the landowner's investment. As in the feudal system, however, sharecropping retains the labor payments and, to an extent, the sharecropper's status of personal dependence. In central Italy, sharecropping implies that the entire family of the peasant be required to work on the domain under the supervision of the landlord, who assumes the right to adapt the life of the sharecropper's family, in all its details, to the needs of the domain. The sharecropper is then too burdened to consider improving his productivity, and it is often the landlord who replaces the sharecropper as the owner of the livestock, dead or alive. Little by little, the sharecropper's situation comes to resemble that of the agricultural laborer, paid in kind and very badly. The sharecropper becomes a factor of economic stagnation.

Last, the highest stage in the transformation of productive relations in the countryside after feudalism was tenant farming, whose origins were described by Marx. They are linked to social changes in both the city and the country. In the village community, an increasing differentiation gives rise to a new class of nonpossessors who rent themselves out for money, and are used mainly by the wealthy peasants for their own purposes.

The individual farmers owning their own land become the seedbed of new capitalist farmers. Their rise is particularly rapid in certain situations, as in sixteenth-century England where the progressive devaluation of the coinage enriched the farmers at the expense of the landed proprietors, thanks to the custom of long-term leases. . . .

On the other hand, the land was often rented out to urban capitalists who transferred to the countryside the capital acquired through commerce.

The future belonged to these capitalist farmers; but so long as the feudal society and state structure lasted, they continued to suffer under the weight of tithes and feudal dues, as well as the unjust distribution of royal taxes and various obstacles to commerce. These farmers had an interest in the destruction of the feudal regime for the same reasons as the peasants and the bourgeois. But this brings us to the subject of the development of the bourgeoisie and the emergence of capitalism.

# VI/RELIGION, REVOLT, AND SOCIAL STRUGGLES IN THE LATE MIDDLE AGES

THE late Middle Ages, and particularly the period of secular economic downturn and the general crisis of feudalism (1350–1450), were marked by the outbreak of frequent rebellions in both town and country. The most important were the French Jacquerie of 1358, the Ciompi of Florence and other Italian cities in the 1370s, the English Peasants' Revolt of 1381, and the Hussite Rebellion in Bohemia in 1420; and there were many more, albeit on a smaller scale. If ultimately they failed to secure the kinds of social change to which they aspired, a new kind of community in which the poor, in the name of justice, would inherit the earth, they are still of considerable significance.

Who were the rebels? What did they want? They were the urban and rural poor. The rural poor were all peasants, the majority of them unfree, while the urban poor were a more disparate lot and were to remain so until the coming of industrial society and the constitution of a proletariat: wage earners, domestics, criminals. In the cities, the poor had only their poverty in common: in the country the fundamental opposition between lord and peasant gave them at least some form of structural unity, but one which was already being undermined by increasing class differentiations that were the result of the development of the market economy and the changeover from dues in kind or labor services to monetary payments.

The circumstances of the general crisis of feudalism account for the particular features of these rebellions. They broke out in a society whose rulers were accustomed to peasant passivity and acceptance of their lot. Some historians, following the lead of Alexis de Tocqueville (1805–1859) in regard to the

French Revolution of 1789, would have little trouble in explaining them as so many manifestations of a crisis of higher expectations. The peasants saw for the first time that there was a possibility of significant improvement in their condition. This possibility threatened, they were willing to take extreme measures to defend it. In a sense, this analysis is quite correct, but it is necessary to go further and to seek out the source of the hopes and disappointments, not only in the purely economic sphere of prices and wages but in the domain of peasant aspirations to freedom and property, themselves made possible by the landlords' desires to adapt themselves to changing circumstances.

The rebels of the Late Middle Ages had neither a highly developed class consciousness nor a clear vision of the future. (This is somewhat less true of those who lived in the Italian cities that were at a considerably more advanced stage of social development than the rest of Europe.) They tended to think in terms of individual rather than institutional responsibility, and often tied their yearnings to the idea of a lost order of goodness. Hence the myth of the Golden Age—the return to Domesday, the celebration of the ideal of poverty by the Church. Hence also an expressed hatred for the abuses of justice and the foul deeds of evil men, but no diminution in the sacredness of aristocracy and monarchy. This way of thinking dies hard. In the seventeenth century, English Puritans were still preaching the great heritage of Anglo-Saxon institutions corrupted by the Norman yoke. In the eighteenth, French workers could not believe that the king would not come to their rescue, if only he knew of their misery.

The poor were regularly defeated, for they were incapable of formulating a coherent ideology or of creating an efficient and long-term movement. The only class that might have done so, the commercial bourgeoisie, was more interested in the maintenance of order and in exploiting its own potential within the existing feudal society. For the poor, retreat became the order of the day, but hope was kept alive by religion as well as by the real and imagined exploits of social bandits and other avengers of the good, the true, and the just. In the selection that follows, Maurice Keen, a young English historian, analyzes some popular legends and discovers in them a number of the characteristics just mentioned.

Religion was, throughout the Middle Ages, the vehicle for the grievances of the poor and the oppressed. It was, in fact, the only one generally available to them. Moreover, Christian doctrine emphasized the very virtues—poverty and humility

—to which they might lay claim, and it was often only a short step from the proclamation of those virtues to an attempt to apply them to the problems of this world. Religious revolt took a variety of forms, from simple withdrawal from society in order to prepare oneself for the coming of the millennium, as among the Albigensians in Southern France at the beginning of the thirteenth century, to a crusade for the good society that would conform in part at least to the ideal of a communist utopia, as among the Taborites of fifteenth-century Bohemia. The number and variety of rebels who spoke in Christian accents was very great indeed.

In so doing, they sooner or later came up against the established Church, which provided the ideological cement that kept the stones of the feudal system in place. Its theology implicitly, and sometimes explicitly, described the kingdom of heaven as an extension of feudal obligations. Its personnel was, from the point of view of both origin and interest, totally tied up with the feudal ruling class, in a kind of interlocking directorate. The clerical hierarchy could allow intellectuals within the establishment to debate points of theology ad infinitum, provided only that they did not go beyond the limits of a healthy respect for the Church, its authority, and its role as an institutional bulwark of medieval society. Dissent became dangerous (and was declared heretical) when it grew up outside the ruling circles of society and reached out to embrace problems that were other than purely theological. Until then, it remained merely the expression of individual idiosyncrasy.

"If god did not exist, it would be necessary to invent him" is a statement usually attributed to Voltaire, but it might as well have been said—and, in other terms, was—by members of almost every ruling class in history. The promise of rewards, of the good life in the world beyond, has proven an efficient means of social control. This is what Marx meant when he wrote of religion as the opiate of the masses. He suggested that religious belief, like all other manifestations of the life of the mind, must be analyzed in terms of prevailing social relations of production, that is, class relationships, and that its function historically had often been conservative. But, as we have seen and as Marx would have been the last to deny, in the Middle Ages and perhaps in other historical periods Christianity could be bent to the needs of revolutionary militancy.

Many of the disagreements on the nature of medieval heresy are to be understood as quarrels between diametrically opposed schools of historical interpretation: those who accord primary importance to the power of abstract ideas, and those who seek to explain the force of ideas in terms of social conditions. Ernst Werner, of the University of Leipzig, and Norman Cohn, formerly of the University of Newcastle, selections from whose works follow, both adopt the second point of view, although they may be thought to agree on little else, the former being an East German Marxist and the latter a noncommunist Englishman.

The other point of view is seen most clearly in the classic argument concerning the origins of medieval heresy. Were they or were they not social in nature? Might they not best be understood as survivals (or revivals) of ancient heresies? To answer "Yes" to the last question is to imply a continuum of ideas across the ages and thus to come down heavily on the idealist side of the controversy. This was the position of the celebrated Italian historian Benedetto Croce (1866–1952), who was very much influenced by the teaching of the early nineteenth-century German philosopher G. W. F. Hegel that history was to be seen as the unfolding and development of a spirit of liberty inherent within it. Croce wrote:

These heresies belong, in substance, to the history of moral life, not to the history of the economic life of humanity. This asceticism, this negation of life, this clearly established dualism, all of this was nothing other than a weapon in the revolt, in the moral war declared on the Catholic Church and worldliness, on the lust and greed of its clergy. It was also a means of affirming a need for a truly pure life, which [the heretics] hoped to find in the symbols of poverty, of the apostolic Church and many others of the same sort. Such was . . . the significance of the movements which arose now here, now there in the various countries of Europe or even spread from one to the other. Such was the work of the men of faith and courage, of the heroes and martyrs who made them. It is in this sense that they may be said to have prepared the Protestant Reformation, for which they set the prologue: a Reformation which, picking up their moral activity from a new angle, constituted, so to speak, the passage from an authoritarian Church—thanks to the direct and personal interpretation of Scripture—to freedom of thought and to independence of criticism which the Renaissance, for its part, promoted vigorously, starting out from a humanist, rather than a religious or ecclesiastical, point of departure. From which there follows the slow but sure maturing of the highest ethical concept, that of freedom.

The radical historian will agree that a certain kind of freedom was served by the refusal to recognize external authority implicit in both medieval heresies and the Reformation. But what kind of freedom, and why that kind, are questions that cannot be answered if they are defined as "purely religious" phenomena. In any case, pure religion is a category devoid of meaning, because religion occurs in the minds of men—and men, unless they are ascetic hermits, live in a social world to whose constraints and influences they are subject. They may believe that they are not, but that way lies illusion rather than reality.

# Ernst Werner

---

## 1 2

# Popular Ideologies
# in Late Medieval Europe:
# Taborite Chiliasm and
# Its Antecedents

The basic Chiliastic character of
the Taborite articles was recognized by scholars a long time ago. . . .
When German and Czechoslovakian scholars dealt with the problem
questions of sectarian influence, such as the Waldensian, and of nation-
alism tended to prevail. However after 1945 the young Marxian historiography of the CSR [Czechoslovak Socialist Republic] tried to discover
the social roots of these ideas, focussing attention on certain social and
economic questions which even the bourgeois historians had admitted
to be relevant.

Starting with the perception of Marx and Engels that the existence
of revolutionary ideas in a given epoch presupposes the existence of a
revolutionary class J. Macek came to the conclusion that urban and
rural poverty were the driving forces of the Hussite revolution and that
Chiliasm was the appropriate ideology for the movement. He denied
foreign sectarian influence, and explained Chiliastic Taborism solely
by the Bohemian environment. "The revolutionary ideology of the
popular heretic movement did not depend on a transfusion of ideas
from one sect to another, or from one country to another but could
arise indigenously out of the deep humiliation, oppression and exploitation of our people. . . . What was 'international' in Tabor was a class
war against the common enemy, against the feudal lords and the
church." Likewise, from this point of view, the Picards who were
destroyed in 1421 by Žižka belong to the old Taboritic Chiliasm and
were not a separate sect; they merely pushed its ideal of poverty to
extremes.

Taborite Chiliasm was unquestionably an anti-feudal movement,
supported by the lowest social strata of the towns and the countryside.

Two phases of the Chiliastic movement are clearly distinguishable.

Originally, the movement followed traditional aims which we shall discuss later. Its followers looked for the Second Coming when the Lord would annihilate evil without effort on their part. From February 14, 1420, this pacifist mood turned into frenzied fanaticism, the little town of Usti was destroyed and Tabor was founded. The time had come, it was proclaimed, to launch a militant struggle for the reorganization of the world. All believers were summoned to leave the villages and towns and flee to the mountains, to escape the wrath of the Lord. Prague, like Babylon the great, was to perish in the flames. During this time of wrath the Brothers of Tabor were "the representatives of God, his envoys, called to root out every offense and all evil from the kingdom of Christ"; they were "sent forth to lead the blessed out of Sodom." As avengers, they must move in with fire and sword against the enemies of God, and were to spare no one. This campaign of destruction was directed above all against churches, chapels, altars and against both the houses and the persons of the clergy. Any territory they should enter was to belong to them. Payment of rent or labor service to the enemies of God was forbidden. Preachers went into the villages calling on the peasants to rise against their lords, and to seize the land. "No longer is anything mine or yours; in the community everything is owned in common. So shall it ever be in the community, nobody may call anything his own, otherwise he commits a mortal sin." In Tabor, Pisek and Vodňany newcomers were required to throw their money and jewelry into barrels provided for the purpose before they could be admitted to the community. Thereby the earthly lord-serf relationship was dissolved; from that time forth there were to be only brothers and sisters. The old man-made order of law was to fall: debtors were released from their debts and marriage might be dissolved if it hindered anyone's flight to the mountains. The era of written law was at an end; even the New Testament had lost its validity, since from now on "the divine law was written in the heart of every individual, and that was all the teaching anyone needed." Thus the time had come for Christ to descend to earth in the flesh so that all could see him, and so that he could set up his visible kingdom on the mountains. "Like a king he will move among the banqueters and he will cast out all who have not their nuptial garments, along with the wicked who have not come to the mountains, into outermost darkness." Henceforth the dead "who have already died in Christ will rise," in the first rank being Master Huss, revered of all Taborites. It is obvious that the lordship of Christ was to supersede that of earthly kings. Moreover, it was proclaimed, the state of innocence "as with Adam, Enoch and Elias in Paradise will return; no one will hunger and thirst nor suffer pain in body or spirit, nor adversity." Procreation will be pure, and birth painless, therefore everyone is freed from marriage bonds. Children born of virtuous parents need no baptism, since they received the Holy Spirit in the womb.

This emphasis on the power of the Holy Spirit is typical of the Taborites. The most important preacher of the left wing, the so-called Picards, Martin Húska, saw the Holy Spirit even in Christ, of whom it is written in the Gospel: "He shall send you another comforter" (John 14:16). This Spirit-Christ will dwell with mankind until the end of the world. The sources handed down to us from anti-Picard writers are filled with this theory of the Holy Spirit. At the end of January 1421 the Picards moved to Příběnice on the Luschnitz (southwest from Tabor), after the so called urban-knightly opposition in Tabor, made up of craftsmen, merchants and knights, had obtained the upper hand and were rejecting the far-reaching social and religious demand for the condition of poverty. This obliged the more conscientious to leave the City of Hope and found a new Tabor. The old Czech chronicles mention 300 people, Laurentius of Březová 200 men, women and children, reaching for a new goal. Unfortunately the group was deprived of leadership when Ultraquist lords on January 29, 1421, threw Martin Húska into prison. Macek emphasizes correctly that this was a heavy blow for the cause of poverty, since Húska had education and a political sense, both of which were lacking in the rank and file. In a letter from prison dated February of the same year, Martin warns his followers: "Do not carry anything out hastily, as some have already done. Do not slander anything, that is beyond your understanding." Of what kind of hasty actions was he speaking?

Doubtless he referred to the abolition of the mass and the reviling of the cross. The people were assuming that since God dwelt in them they could not sin. They said: "A time is coming when there will be such love among men that all things will be common, even women. The sons and daughters of God must be free, there shall be no marriage bonds." The Lord's Prayer now ran, "Our Father, who art in us, enlighten us!" The creed they omitted, since they considered the faith of the Old Taborites and Ultraquists to be an error. They observed no holy days, regarding all days as alike except that they interpreted the seventh day as the Seventh Era. They called the heavens their roof and held that God did not dwell there nor the devil in hell, but that good and evil existed only in man. They saw Jesus as a brother, and did not believe in his death, for the Holy Spirit never dies, and the son of God must come forth from the Holy Spirit. Moreover, they apparently indulged in libertine practices, and went about naked like Adam and Eve in Paradise, which had been recreated for them.

In short, these people manifested the most extreme chiliasm. For them, time had come to an end. The graves were to open. The Era of the seventh angel was at hand, as it is written in the revelation of

St. John. Over the whole earth blood was to rise to the bridles of horses. They strove, to the best of their ability, to make these prophecies come true. One must remember that they were oppressed, for they were persecuted not only by the moderate Hussites, but also by the Taborites under Žižka. They spared no one, but killed all—men, women and children—and set fire to towns and villages in the night. To justify these actions they quoted Scripture: "At midnight there was a cry" (Matth. 25:6). In October 1421, under their deified leader Rohan, a smith, they put up a desperate fight on the island of Hamr against the superior forces of the Taborites under Žižka. All of them were either killed or taken prisoner and burned as heretics.

It would be an historical error to write off this Taboristic group as absurd and deluded, without significance in the Hussite revolutionary movement. Its members were flesh of the Taborite's flesh, a product of rural and urban poverty, and the core of their ideology was the same Chiliasm which found a home in Tabor and persisted there until the end of 1420. . . . At the same time this open Spiritualist tendency points to problems in intellectual history which cannot be explained solely by the influence of Huss and Wycliffe.

The hearts of the Picards were filled with the power of the Holy Spirit. This was why they believed God's law to be within, and that it need not be derived from Scripture. This sense of being filled with God produced a state of love, created a community of sons and daughters of God who could nevermore be divided. It was for this reason that the old form of marriage was abolished, for it was based on class divisions now transcended; in the Age of the Spirit, that is, of freedom, it was a contradiction. The reformation of the Lord's Prayer is to be explained in the same way. In the same way the Holy Spirit, dwelling within, made Jesus one's brother, for the Spirit dwelt also in Jesus. It was for this reason that he could not die, for no one could kill the Spirit.

It may have been by the same reasoning that they reached the conclusion that their enemies would become blind if they opposed the bearers of the Spirit, and that these enemies could not prevail against them if they remained firm in the faith. It follows further that because there was a Son of God whose position did not depend on an act of salvation and redemption, they were all sons of God by the fulness of the Holy Spirit which they possessed in common. What seemed to their opponents an unheard of blasphemy was for them a basic truth. Their leaders like Rohan, Moses and Adam justifiably called themselves God or Sons of God. . . . The complete equality of rights of the sexes gave women a chance of leadership, as in the case of Rohan's comrade Maria. Thus all members of the sect were through their possession of the Spirit godlike, and the formula "the Sons and Daughters of God" is to be understood literally, not symbolically.

. . .

In his visions of the third era, Joachim* refers to a monastic order
and the cowl. He makes no attack on the Church or the Pope. He
speaks of the third era as lasting a thousand years; the Taborites on
the contrary gave the kingdom of Christ no time limit. They never
divided the life of Christianity into three periods. According to them
the Holy City of Jerusalem was not to descend from heaven, but was
to be wrought by force of arms. The main task rested not with the
clergy, but with simple believers. However in regard to the time limit
on the kingdom of Christ, Jan Příbram did report that Christ would
rule the world visibly and tangibly for a thousand years. Obviously
there can be no question of a literal taking over of Joachim's scheme,
since the class structure in fifteenth century Bohemia was quite different from that in twelfth century South Italy. The revolutionary
Bohemian populace seized only on those ideas that corresponded to
their needs and they stripped these ideas of all qualifications. The
dominion of the Spirit in the third era meant freedom. "But the Lord
is the Spirit; where the Spirit of the Lord is, there is freedom. We,
however, when we look upon the glory of the Lord with unveiled
countenance, shall be changed into the same image, from clarity to
clarity, as by the Spirit of the Lord." Thus begins the ascent to the
divine person within the contemplative order. The Pneuma appears
as man in whom the fulness of the Spirit is present, in whom God himself has made his home. Spiritualization is deification. In this notion
that what is to come is already secretly at work E. Benz sees the revolutionary impulse of the Joachite view of history. Inexorably it drove
the prophets to take an active hand in overthrowing the present age
and in establishing the promised age that is to come. Joachim himself
did not follow his ideas through in this way; he refrained from any
attack on the existing Church or on the Papacy.

Petrus Johannis Olivi (died 1298) had however been concerned with
the appearance of the mystical anti-Christ, the great Apocalyptic figure,
either as a scion of the house of Hohenstaufen or as an anti-pope.
Although he did not yet dare to identify the devilish, carnal church
with the established Roman Church, Rome was for him nevertheless
the symbol of that church which opposed the Church of the Spirit and
persecuted it. He inveighed against the reigning Pope, Boniface VIII,
for disregard of the ideal of evangelical perfection. This, to Olivi, was
the one supreme value by which the Church, theology, and the papacy

---

*Joachim de Fiore (1145–1202) was an Italian mystic and Cistercian monk. He
divided the history of humanity into three periods: (1) the pre-Christian (the era of
the Fathers), dominated by laymen; (2) the Christian (the era of the Son), dominated
by the clergy; and (3) the era of the holy spirit, when a new monastic order would
dominate the world. The third period was to be preferred and was to be brought
about as quickly as possible. In the thirteenth century, Joachim's system was used by
Franciscan spiritual and heretical groups to attack the official church.—*Ed.*

should be governed. It stood above the papal power because by the law of Christ the Holy Spirit entered into the faithful directly. The Church was thus deprived of sovereign power. Evangelical perfection was the aim of moral and religious life, an imperative from which there was no dispensation. At the end of the fifth era Babylon would pitch her tents in Rome and the "carnal" clergy would form the seat of the Beast of the Apocalypse. The sixth era, the period of transition to the age of the Spirit, was to start with a cruel battle against the carnal church and its adherents. These prophecies too, like Joachim's, were developed on the level of purely passive contemplation. They avoided any challenge to action for any specific group and they kept the monastic orders always in a front rank, attributing to them a desire for reform.

Of those who had taken hold of the spirit of Olivi, the Southern French Beguines were already more concrete and aggressive; they had gathered around the Franciscan spiritualists as Tertiarians. R. Manselli has shown that after the burning of four Spirituals in Marseilles in March of 1318 and the execution of three Beguines in Narbonne in 1319 through the Inquisition, a change came over the outlook of these groups. Whereas before 1318 the ideas associated with poverty had dominated their religious thinking, from that time on eschatological expectation took first place. . . . .

During his activity in Toulouse the inquisitor Bernard Gui dealt with these heretics especially, and through him we get a good insight into their teachings. For them John XXII was the greatest enemy of Christendom, doing more damage to the Church than all the heretics together, for he transformed the *ecclesia Dei* [Church of God] into a *synagoga dyboli* [assembly of the devil]. No wonder the end of the world was approaching. A great war would break out in which many of the defenders of the *ecclesia carnalis* [carnal Church] would fall. The Saracens would press forward and occupy Christendom, coming through Narbonne. They would mistreat Christian women and lead them into slavery. Peter John Olivi prophesied all this in Narbonne, speaking as for God. God had further revealed to him that in the course of the Apocalyptic events the carnal Christians would fall into despair, abandon the faith and die. The *viri spirituales* [spiritual men] would however be unharmed, for God would hide them from anti-Christ. Out of them would be formed a new *ecclesia primitiva* [primitive Church], which would receive an even greater outpouring of the Holy Spirit than the original Church. The Beguines already shared in this fulness of the Spirit, which had taken up its abode not only in their souls but also in their bodies. The victory of the *viri spirituales* is also a victory of the Spirit throughout the whole world. The world will then be *bonus et benignus* [morally good and beneficent]; there will be no evil and except for carnal desire in some men, no sin. Just as among the Bohemian Chiliasts, private ownership and all its attendant evil was to disappear: "omnia erunt communia quoad usum et non erit aliquis que offendat alium vel sollicit ad peccatum, quia maximus amor erit inter eos et erit tunc unum ovile et unus pastor" [all things will be for communal use and there will not be anyone who hurts another or, in any case, stirs him to sin, because there will be great love among them and there will be at that time one sheepfold and one shepherd]. They limited these conditions to one hundred years. During this time love would diminish in the world and evil grow again; therefore Christ himself would have to descend to earth and call a general judgement.

Who were the bearers of these teachings, the people who were persecuted, who were condemned and burned at the stake in 1318 in the province of Narbonne, in 1322 and 1323 in Toulouse and Pamiers?

There is very little evidence in the sources about these events. Inquisitor Bernard Gui differentiated among the heretics according to their grades of consecration. Those with less theoretical knowledge of their teachings stood below those who had full knowledge. Most of them may have had no real understanding of doctrine, merely living as beggars in expectation of a better time. It seems that some among them regarded begging as superior to work. This indicates that the heretics, who in the developed feudal States were quite numerous, came from varying social strata. The large-scale transition to the paying of money rent had resulted in an increase of the non-bond population, working in the country as day-laborers and in the towns as craftsmen or as wage-workers. Separated from production, people formerly industrious gave way to laziness and eccentric dreams. Typical of this is the confession given by the heretic Prous Boneta to the Inquisition in 1325 in Carcassonne. Belief in the work of the Holy Spirit, whose era Peter John Olivi had inaugurated, was enough for her. She saw this faith as uniting Christians, Jews and Saracens, since "qui crediderint in Spiritus Sancti opere salvabuntur" [whoever shall have believed in the work of the Holy Spirit shall be saved]. Christ would descend in the form of a poor virgin, so that he would not be recognized and persecuted. The Word, however, would come from Prous, who was to be elevated as the new Eve, of whom it was said: "Tu eris initium et causa salvationis totius humanae naturae seu humani generis per illa verba quae faction de dicere, si credantur" [You will be the beginning and the salvation for the whole of human nature or of the human race through those words which from speaking become fact, if they are believed]. Visions of this kind might appeal to emotional circles of women, but could not bring broad groups together in a movement.[1] The heritage of Joachim trickled away, so to speak, in such

---

[1] The material from the Doat mss. made available by R. Manselli shows that at Narbonne, Montpellier, Lodève and Bézier there were some craftsmen among the members. Tailors, weavers, clothiers and candlemakers are named, along with a

circles. It roused expectation and a sense of mission and it sharpened the rejection of the Roman church; yet it inspired no action, nor any practical program. The more radical turning of the Southern French Beguines against the established status was theoretical; it looked for deliverance to come from without.

In this they resemble the Northern French-German Sects of the Free Spirit of the Amalrican persuasion, which had probably no direct association with their southern relatives.

The Amalricans, who were condemned by the Paris Synod of 1210, combined the principles of pantheism, Joachite Chiliasm and libertinism in their system. Their central idea was the omnipresence of God. Therefore evil was also divine, and the devil was not repudiated. Moreover all men are of divine essence, and whoever realizes that God controls his life cannot sin. Even harlotry does not fall under the concept of sin since it cannot be attributed to the human beings but to God, who determines all actions. Whoever possessed the Spirit was Christ, yes even the Holy Spirit, and his deeds were divine deeds. The Spiritual, that is, whoever possessed this truth, had no need for sacraments, not even the Lord's Supper, for they were only signs like the ceremonies in the Old Testament; as the latter were given up with the appearance of Christ, so the sacraments can be abandoned on the arrival of the Holy Spirit. The incarnation of the Holy Spirit in a sect member not only produced a state of exaltation but gave the eschatological assurance that is expressed in the following prophecies. In five years all men will be Spiritual, and anyone will be able to say: "I am the Holy Spirit," and "Before Abraham was, I was," in the same way as Christ could say, "I am the son of God, and before Abraham was, I was."

. . .

The Spirituals had marked missionary success in the dioceses of Paris, Sens, Troyes and Langres, especially among the secular clergy and among women. Ley assumes that they turned primarily to artisans, peasants, and in general, to the poor, and the Spirituals' conviction that they had a message may have appealed to the lowly. Their chiliastic hopes continued to be linked with emphasis on becoming godlike

---

butcher, a smith, a parchment-maker, a sawyer and a merchant. There is no mention of peasants; the movement was purely urban. Manselli, because there were clergy in it, thinks the movement had no distinct social profile. This was not so. The records of the Inquisition show that the clergy who participated came from the same kind of urban families as their lay associates. The clergy were bound to the urban environment by a thousand ties, above all when they were active as mendicants. These craftsmen's adoption of Spiritual Franciscan doctrines on poverty clearly reflects the desire of the medieval bourgeoisie for an "accessible" church, without any thinking out of the consequences and without a trace of revolutionary ideas.

and in many Free Spiritual groups with libertinism. Moreover, they democratized Heaven. In their view simple men, by the mere fact of their human nature, had abilities as great as any we can conceive. This turning of man into a God was one medieval way of expressing the doctrine of equality according to natural law.

In his pamphlet *De planctu Ecclesiae* (1330–32), Alvarus Pelagius remarked that the apostles of the Free Spirit sect were welcomed among the lower social classes, especially among peasants, charcoal burners, smiths and swineherds. They attracted these people by promising a life of ease, readily persuading them to abandon their toil and join the sect as wandering beggars. In preaching to the wealthy, on the other hand, the apostles donned the cloak of religion, acting as father confessors to rich burghers and widows and enjoying their hospitality. They sought also to convert laywomen who were under religious vows by discoursing to them in terms of naive piety.

It was A. Jundt's conclusion that the Brothers and Sisters of the Free Spirit probably fascinated the lower classes by holding up to them the idea of a renovation of society. They condemned both marriage and property as imperfect institutions incompatible with godlike union. In this way they condoned theft. The majority of the members of the Free Spirit sect were so much religious driftwood become radical. They wanted to have assurance of individual salvation and to engage in individualistic opposition to the prevailing order of society, religion and morality. They expected to find true freedom in idleness and contemplation. Certain elements of the town populace, such as coopers, carters and porters fell eagerly on the heretics' idea of begging (under the slogan *Brot durch Gott* [bread through God]), and on their notions of unlimited freedom. Uprooted peasants who had suffered the whole gamut of misery, they looked for no more than bare existence. Like the others mentioned above, they fell a ready prey to heretic doctrines. Salimbene tells of vagabonds, robbers, swindlers, seducers, and fornicators joining the Apostolic Brothers under Gerhard Segarelli (1260?–1300), often after a time relapsing into their former life. Once they felt they had achieved salvation, the discipline of an ascetic life lost its attraction.

The *Homines Intelligentiae* [Men of Understanding], discovered in Brussels in 1410–11, are typical. There were two sectarian circles among them, one following the "Theorist" William von Hildernissen, the other following the "Pragmatists" Aegidius and Seraphim. William stood for the spiritualization of man, teaching that no one can understand the Scriptures correctly unless the Holy Spirit is in him. The time is drawing near when its laws will be fulfilled and spiritual freedom will become manifest. Already now the body, the outer man, is powerless to stain the inner man, the soul, for this will not be damned. Such knowledge fills William with joy and confidence. Among his illiterate adherents these doctrines took on a more earthy tone. They spoke openly of the sex act as the joy of paradise. Virginity counted for nothing.

Aegidius, a layman of sixty, said repeatedly to his followers, "I am the Savior of mankind. Through me you will know Christ, as through Christ you know the Father." Along with these doctrines of adoration and salvation went the Joachite theories of time. The period of the Old Testament was the age of the Father, that of the New Testament the age of the Son, and the present was the age of the Holy Spirit. This was connected with Elias, from whom they expected the reconciliation of the Scriptures, that is to say, the Joachite Concordia, harmonizing the two Testaments with the rule of the Holy Spirit. The *homines intelligentiae* thereby stressed the role that Elias was to play in the apocalypse, a figure whom both Bonaventura and Henoch saw symbolically, in Francis of Assisi.

The Brussels heretics therefore repudiated ancient truth and with it Catholic dogma. In the age of the Holy Spirit truth is new, and to preach poverty, chastity, and obedience would run against it. William and the pragmatists were in agreement on this, except that Aegidius and his people spoke their minds more freely. William, however, at his trial rejected libertinism and the idea of the embodiment of the Savior in a member of the Sect, as well as the Joachite theory of time. Yet his tenth theorem, in which he spoke of the beginning of the age of the Spirit, when the true understanding of the Scripture would prevail and the old law be eliminated, shows that he was moving in the same direction as Aegidius. As with the Amalricans the pillars supporting heresy are Pantheism, Chiliasm, and Libertinism, and as with the Amalricans there is a total lack of revolutionary *élan* and large-scale preparation for ushering in the new age. These people were content to found conventicles, large or small, which met together from time to time to demonstrate how filled with God and spiritual strength their members were. They expressed no expectations of change in society. There was indeed no social crisis at the time which could have served as a focus to radicalize their thoughts.

Yet a hundred years earlier in Italy there had been a kind of anticipation of the Bohemian revolution, the insurrection of Fra Dolcino. The Soviet historian S. D. Skazkin has written a short sketch of economic and social conditions in the territory which served as Dolcino's base of operations, that is, Trento, the South Tyrol, and the dioceses of Bologna and Modena, Brescia and Bergamo. Skazkin sees the extension of trade in the countryside as the key to the depression of the peasantry at the end of the 13th century and in the 14th century. The victorious cities, displacing the feudal nobility as landlords, sought to increase feudal rent as much as possible. This is evident in short leases and in forced manumission, that is, in the dissolution of the peasants' personal relationship of dependence. The sum required was as a rule so high that only a few could pay it all at once. Most fell into debt and were forced by their creditors to make them a yearly payment in addition to their rent for the land they worked. In short, the sale of freedom was only a subtle way of raising feudal rent.

It is therefore understandable that it aroused indignation among the peasants, who rightly identified it as a new form of pressure by the lords. The latter were seeking to absorb the profits that accrued to the independent peasant economy through the growing ties with the city market. In the 14th century uprisings began in almost all Europe in opposition to attempts to raise feudal rents and in defence of traditional custom. [Skazkin]

In addition to this, during the city communes' struggle for emancipation from the feudal nobility the peasants succeeded in building their own organization of rural communes. These were the peasants' own administrative bodies serving to protect their interests. The successful cities which were building their Contado at the end of the 13th century threw their whole energy into the subjugation of these rural communes. It was a question not only of establishing the right of lordship, but above all, of the subjugation of rural interests to those of the city. This affected the peasants' production and marketing interests. Everywhere the cities interfered with the rural economy, and exploited it to their profit, for instance, in the price of food. This aroused discontent and opposition among the peasants especially in the territories where the rural communes were most strongly developed, in Northern Italy. The communal lands were confiscated by cities like Cremona and Vicenza as security for the peasants' debts, and in every way they curbed drastically the rural communes' powers. For the use of their land they introduced special taxes to be paid to the cities. Above all they interfered with the established system of land tenure. Forests, meadows and pastures were let to villagers temporarily for payment. Thus a group of well-to-do peasants developed who paid for the lease and then sublet the land to poorer members of the village.

With the extension of the power of the cities over the countryside, middle-class landowners replaced the "village aristocracy," putting the system under their own management, accelerating and aggravating the process of differentiation. It was in this atmosphere of ferment that Dolcino, a pupil of Segarelli's developed his Chiliastic doctrine. Although he leaned strongly toward Joachite spiritual views he thought along thoroughly practical lines. He saw the historical process not in terms of abstract periods, but in actual possibilities of existence. He placed the emphasis on the apostolic way of living; therefore he introduced four realms. The fourth era would bring a complete renovation of life. The clergy and the monastic order would be eliminated because they no longer met the needs of society, especially not in the simplicity and freedom of the apostolic age. Frederick of Sicily, son of Peter of Aragon, would act as emperor of the last age, and he would kill all priests, monks, and prelates, beginning with Boniface VIII. This event would occur in 1305. The fourth era had already started with Gerhard Segarelli. Dolcino was commissioned by God to explain the prophecy. Therefore he issued proclamations designed to turn the Christians to him so that they could reintroduce the apostolic life during the time of change, a life of freedom and common ownership. This return to the *vita apostolica* [apostolic life] was the basic motivation of his sect, the essential heritage of Segarelli. Out of this he derived his authority and that of his followers, since it also embodied for him the *ecclesia spiritualis* [spiritual Church].

Dolcino rallied 4000 followers to fight against the old age in the belief that they possessed divine right, founded on property and freedom. The struggle against the bishop and the communes of Novara and Vercelli, which lasted several years, demanded organizational measures, above all material resources, which Dolcino wanted to procure through church tithes; although tithing as such in the apostolic Utopia was a contradiction. E. Dupré-Theseider has however argued that while the heretic preacher was in the mountains there were no such social needs. There is no sign of any militant push, it is as though he had simply fled with his followers. When he appeared in Gattinara he was unarmed but after his retreat over the Pietra Calva he warned his people to prepare for the defence of the true faith. He himself had as yet no social program but was merely building up the eschatological expectations of the faithful.

No doubt Dolcino was influenced by the fact of enemy encirclement. It is however impermissible to argue that his policy was the fortuitous result of being joined by peace-loving enthusiasts of the type of the Provençal Beguines. Dupré-Theseider forgets the social milieu, without which the movement remains unintelligible. His lack of detail notwithstanding, it is Skazkin's merit that he has made the social environment clear. What is new in the behavior of the Apostolic Brothers is the turning of eschatological expectation and prophecy toward revolutionary action. The fact that Dupré-Theseider finds no articulate social program in the sources does not prove that the sect had no ideas on the subject. The ideal of the primitive church and the hope that the year 1305 would transform the entire scene constitute a Utopia. Behind this were specific ends such as economic equality and the abolition of class divisions.

The Church knew what it was doing when it launched a Crusade against these "fanatics." Dolcino's shrewd and cunning tactics show that he and his followers were realists and did not lean entirely on hope and expectation. In speaking of the revolutionary phase, Dupré-Theseider adduces the acts of the Inquisition in Bologna, which show the participation not of proletarians and serfs but, almost exclusively, of the middling bourgeoisie (*medio ceto*), namely, petty merchants, craftsmen, and small property-owners. To derive the whole social character of the rising from individuals who were dispersed after its suppression is methodologically wrong. It is however significant that dissident members of the bourgeoisie should have adhered to Dolcino. This shows that he became a rallying-point for all forms of discontent, that he was threatening to expand his purely rural base of operations into the little towns of Northern Italy and was obviously a menace to the ruling classes. But one cannot overlook the fact that he attracted a mass following among the peasants of the Alpine region. Why would the feudal lords of that region have been so anxious to suppress him if he was attracting only the middling bourgeoisie? The fact remains that in the Apostolic Brethren we have a heresy determined essentially by peasant conditions, a heresy looking not to reform, but to militant combat with State and Church. Radicalization proceeded from this core, not from the peripheral strength among craftsmen and traders; these latter were satisfied with reforms aiming at an "accessible" Church.

As the military situation worsened, libertinism and an exalted Spiritualism came to be intensified, as occurred among the Bohemian Chiliasts when their hopes were frustrated. The strict asceticism that Dunken calls "the revolutionary discipline of the masses" and which had marked the Old Taborites as well as the Apostolic Brothers in the first phase of their operation, came to be abandoned. The sect members, under the sense of achieving perfection, linked community of property with free love. In my opinion the charge of libertinism cannot be put down to mere clerical slander. Such an interpretation disregards the extreme consequences of a sect community which relates chiliastic fulfillment with death or destruction, and seeks to accomplish the latter by sloughing off all that is old. Traditional morality becomes totally inadequate. The sense of community within the sect comes to rest on the needs of defence and on hatred of the enemy. In the ultimate phase the heretics' diminished consciousness of self will often incline them to practices and theories which at first played no role or only a subordinate one.

Both Apostolic Brethren and the Bohemian Chiliasts connected Joachite phantasies with social reality and created for themselves a unique ideology adapted to the class demands of the peasantry and the lower strata of the towns. There is no question here of confused reception of philosophical-theological theorems as in pseudo-Joachism and Spiritualism. Rather, we see the medieval populace of town and country at a certain stage of development, building a new ideology out of traditions which as a rule had not dealt with them or with their interests at all. Dolcino himself represents only a vague beginning. The Chiliastic Taborites, on the other hand, produced a well-thought out program which sharply reflects the fifteenth century people's self-consciousness.

Does this mean that wherever the poor appear as an independent faction their aims and wishes will be grounded in Chiliasm?

By no means. When the Ciompi revolted in Florence in 1378, temporarily overthrowing the *Populo Grasso* [the bourgeois employers who stood immediately below the great noble and mercantile families on the social ladder], we hear nothing of Chiliastic expectations; indeed, the insurrection had no religious ideology. And yet prophecies were current in Florence foretelling the destruction of tyrants and traitors by the *popolo minuto* [the working masses, both artisanal and proletarian]. An anonymous writer who wrote a day-to-day chronicle of the insurrection says that a Minorite had circulated these prophecies ten years before, predicting their fulfilment in 1377–8. The serpents of the earth, it was said, would devour the lions, the leopards and the wolves as well as all birds of prey, and simultaneously the people would put all tyrants and traitors to death. A great epidemic and famine would follow, with many fatalities. The church would lose its temporalities and the people would be swayed by false deceivers. In the end the clergy and people would unite, cast out the wicked and live happily with enough to meet their needs. Ideas of this kind did not suffice for the Ciompi, who set up guilds and took measures to raise their standard of living. It was the same with the insurrection of the workers in Siena in 1371. They formulated their demands thus: "Pay according to the orders of the Commune of Siena and not of the guilds." At the same time they put their own men in the government. Religious ideals played no role. The same was true of the Community of Zealots in Thessalonica in 1342–9, which from 1345 was supported almost exclusively by the urban and rural populace. It was swayed by political ideas which left no room for heretic (bogomil) doctrines, nor showed any trace of Chiliastic tendencies.

The great Peasants' Revolt in England in 1381 was strongly influenced by Wycliffe's ideas, but John Ball was concerned only with the social elements in these, that is, with the doctrine of common ownership. The dispossession of mortal sinners among the lords was to be carried out by the people. There were no Chiliastic tendencies. The peasants were sufficiently well-organized to put forward economic and social demands without any religious husk, and made use of Wycliffite heresy only to strengthen their will to fight. There are other examples at hand as in the 14th century (the Jacquerie, 1358, and Etienne Marcel, 1356–8).

It is thus clear that Chiliasm represents only one ideology of the late medieval populace, and was not the only one. This was no accident. The people did not form a solid class. In the towns they hardly formed a party. Until the great German Peasants' Revolt they were dependent on the support of peasants. They were outside bourgeois and feudal groups. The town populace had neither privileges nor property; they had no small holdings of land as the peasants and the petty bourgeois had. In every relation they were possessionless and rightless. As Engels wrote, they were a living symptom of the dissolution of feudal and guild society, and, at the same time, the forerunners of modern bourgeois society. This position explains their radical point of view, their Utopian speculation about a classless society, and their uncompromising practicality. It was understandable that the first attempt to realize their fantastic dreams of the future were doomed, under the conditions of feudal society, to subside into the absurdities of their prophecies. Therefore we see their aspirations in pure form only where the rural and urban proletariat went its own way, where the middle-class townspeople either split off or played no part, where the land-owning peasants disassociated themselves from the rural poor or where an unsuccessful insurrection collapsed in despair. The organized craft workers in Siena and Florence, the strongly-united sailors in Thessalonica, were too occupied with the immediate struggle for better living conditions, higher wages, and political equality to be concerned with Chiliastic dreams like those of the Apostolic Brothers or the left-wing Taborites. In Bohemia, where in founding their own party alongside the bourgeois and knightly opposition, the people were in process of becoming conscious of their position, Chiliasm doubtless had some influence over them. But the first step was not followed by a second, indeed could not be, for the time was not yet ripe for the classless society. Any further step would have to lead into pure Utopia, into illusion, and end in a complete fiasco. Žižka destroyed the Chiliastic community in order to save the revolution. The poor allied themselves with the bourgeois opposition, bowed again to its leadership.

As Thomas Müntzer developed into the ideologist of poverty in the German Peasants' War, he dropped the career of a prophet, after a little hesitation, and founded a political party, or *Bund*. But the poor were not yet strong enough to win. A new residue of Chiliastic expectations remained, as expressed in Müntzer's speech before the Battle of Frankenhausen. The solution to the problem—the political party— could only be realized after the overthrow of feudal society.

# Norman Cohn

---

## 13

# New Masses
# in Pursuit of
# the Millennium

Although revolutionary movements of more or less eschatological inspiration were numerous during the Middle Ages they did not occur in all periods or in all regions. There seems to be no evidence of such movements having occurred before the closing years of the eleventh century; and even thereafter (so far as northern Europe is concerned) it is only in the valley of the Rhine that one can detect an apparently unbroken tradition of revolutionary chiliasm continuing down to the sixteenth century. In some areas of what are now Belgium and northern France such a tradition can be traced from the end of the eleventh to the middle of the fourteenth century, in some areas of southern and central Germany from the middle of the thirteenth century down to the Reformation; after which the beginnings of a tradition can be observed in Holland and Westphalia. On the fringe of far bigger upheavals, a chiliastic commotion occurred around London and another in Bohemia. With one or two minor exceptions all the movements with which the present study is concerned arose within these fairly precise limits. Nor can this be merely an impression produced by defective sources, for from the eleventh century onwards the sources are plentiful enough; and even for earlier centuries they are not so scanty that they would contain no reference to such movements if there had been any of appreciable size. However hazardous it may be to pursue the causation of social phenomena in a society which cannot itself be directly observed, the incidence of revolutionary chiliasm is here far too clearly defined, both in space and in time, to be without significance. A bird's-eye view suggests that the social situations in which outbreaks of revolutionary chiliasm occurred were in fact remarkably uniform; and this impression is confirmed when one comes to examine particular outbreaks in detail. The areas in which the age-old prophecies about the Last Days took on a new, revolutionary meaning and a new, explosive force were the areas of rapid social change—and not simply change but expansion: areas where trade and industry were developing and where the population was rapidly increasing. Life in such areas differed vastly from the agricultural life which was the norm throughout the thousand-year span of the Middle Ages; and it is worth considering in what precisely the difference consisted.

It was certainly not that the traditional life on the land was easy. Agricultural techniques, though they improved, were never such as to keep the peasantry in a state of plenty even under favourable circumstances. For most peasants life must always have been a ceaseless struggle, and for many a losing struggle. In every village there were numbers of peasants living near or at subsistence level; and agricultural surplus was so small and communications so precarious that a bad harvest often meant mass famine. For generations on end large areas of northern and central Europe were devastated by invading Northmen and Magyars and for centuries on end much larger areas were repeatedly thrown into turmoil by the private wars of feudal barons. Moreover the bulk of the peasantry normally lived in a state of permanent and irksome dependence on their lords, ecclesiastical or lay. The serfs, who seem mostly to have been descended from the slaves and prisoners of war of Roman and Carolingian times, carried their unfreedom in their blood and transmitted it from generation to generation; a serf was subject to the absolute authority and arbitrary will of the lord to whose patrimony he belonged by birth. But if serfdom was felt to be a uniquely degrading condition, there were others which were often as hard to bear. During the long centuries of constantly recurring warfare, when no effective central government existed, most small landowners had found it necessary to surrender their lands to the local lord who, with his band of mounted retainers, was alone in a position to offer protection. The descendants of these men were also dependent on a lord; and although their dependence was regulated by a permanent and hereditary contract, it was not necessarily less onerous than that of a serf. In an age when the most effective guarantees of personal independence lay in the possession of land and in the ability to bear arms, the peasants were at a great disadvantage; for only nobles could afford armour, and almost all the land in the agricultural regions was held either by nobles or by the Church. Land on which to live had to be rented, protection had to be earned; and this meant that most peasants had to supply their lords with a formidable amount of labour services, of regular dues in kind and of special fines and levies.

Admittedly the conditions of peasant life were extremely varied. The proportion of bond and free in the peasant population differed greatly from century to century and from region to region, and again within these two main categories there were to be found infinite

variations both in juridical status and in prosperity; even amongst
the population of a single village there were usually great inequalities.
But when every allowance has been made for these complexities it is
still true that if poverty, hardships and an often oppressive dependence
could by themselves generate it, revolutionary chiliasm would have
run strong amongst the peasantry of medieval Europe. In point of fact
it was seldom to be found at all. A marked eagerness on the part of
serfs to run away; recurrent efforts on the part of the peasant communities to extract concessions; brief, spasmodic revolts—such things were
familiar enough in the life of many a manor. But it was only very
rarely that settled peasants could be induced to embark on the pursuit
of the Millennium. And when they did so it was either because they
were caught up in some vast movement which had originated in quite
different social strata, or because their own traditional way of life was
becoming impossible, or—which was the commonest case—for both
these reasons together.

It is possible to see why, despite all the poverty and the hardships
and the dependence, the agricultural society of the early Middle Ages
—and of the later Middle Ages too in many regions—should have
been so unreceptive to the militant eschatology of the unprivileged.
To an extent which can hardly be exaggerated, peasant life was shaped
and sustained by custom and communal routine. In the wide northern
plains peasants were commonly grouped together in villages; and
there the inhabitants of a village followed an agricultural routine
which had been developed by the village as a collectivity. Their strips
of land lay closely interwoven in the open fields, and in ploughing,
sowing and reaping they must often have worked as a team. Each
peasant had the right to use the "common" to a prescribed extent and
all the livestock grazed there together. Social relationships within the
village were regulated by norms which, though they varied from village
to village, had always the sanction of tradition and were always
regarded as inviolable. And this was true not only of relationships
between the villagers themselves but of the relationship between each
villager and his lord. In the course of long struggles between conflicting interests each manor had developed its own laws which, once
established by usage, prescribed the rights and obligations of each
individual. To this "custom of the manor" the lord himself was subject; and the peasants were commonly most vigilant in ensuring that
he did in fact abide by it. Peasants could be very resolute in defending
their traditional rights and even on occasion in extending them. They
could afford to be resolute, for population was sparse and labour
much in demand; this gave them an advantage which to some extent
offset the concentration of landed property and of armed force in the
hands of their lords. As a result the manorial *régime* was by no means
a system of uncontrolled exploitation of labour. If custom bound the

peasants to render dues and services, it also fixed the amounts. And to most peasants it gave at least that basic security which springs from the hereditary and guaranteed tenancy of a piece of land.

The position of the peasant in the old agricultural society was much strengthened, too, by the fact that—just like the noble—he passed his life firmly embedded in a group of kindred. The large family to which a peasant belonged consisted of blood-relatives by male and female descent and their spouses, all of them bound together by their ties with the head of the group—the father (or, failing him, the mother) of the senior branch of the family. Often this kinship-group was officially recognised as the tenant of the peasant holding, which remained vested in it so long as the group survived. Such a family, sharing the same "pot, fire and loaf," working the same unpartitioned fields, rooted in the same piece of earth for generations, was a social unit of great cohesiveness—even though it might itself be riven at times by bitter internal quarrels. And there is no doubt that the individual peasant gained much from belonging to such a group. Whatever his need, and even if he no longer lived with the family, he could always claim succour from his kinsfolk and be certain of receiving it. If the ties of blood bound they also supported every individual.

The network of social relationships into which a peasant was born was so strong and was taken so much for granted that it precluded any very radical disorientation. So long as that network remained intact peasants enjoyed not only a certain material security but also— which is even more relevant—a certain sense of security, a basic assurance which neither constant poverty nor occasional peril could destroy. Moreover such hardships were themselves taken for granted, as part of a state of affairs which seemed to have prevailed from all eternity. Horizons were narrow, and this was as true of social and economic as of geographical horizons. It was not simply that contact with the wide world beyond the manor boundaries was slight—the very thought of any fundamental transformation of society was scarcely conceivable. In an economy which was uniformly primitive, where nobody was very rich, there was nothing to arouse new wants; certainly nothing which could stimulate men to grandiose phantasies of wealth and power.

This state of affairs began to change when, from the eleventh century onwards, first one area of Europe and then another became sufficiently peaceful for population to increase and commerce to develop. The first areas in which this occurred lay partly in French, partly in German territory. In the eleventh, twelfth and thirteenth centuries, in an area extending almost from the Somme to the Rhine and centering on the great principality which the counts of Flanders were governing with singular firmness and efficiency, population expanded very rapidly indeed. Already by the eleventh century north-east France, the

Low Countries and the Rhine valley were carrying a population so dense that the traditional agricultural system could no longer support it. Many peasants set about reclaiming land from sea, marsh and forest, or migrated eastwards to take part in the great German colonisation of lands hitherto inhabited by Slavs; and with these pioneers things generally went well enough. But many remained for whom there were no holdings, or whose holdings were too small to support them; and these had to shift for themselves as best they could. Multitudes of such people streamed into the commercial and industrial society which was beginning to develop in the very area where population was densest.

The Vikings, having brought ruin upon many parts of Europe, gave the first impetus to the development of industry in and around the County of Flanders, which at that time extended from Arras to Ghent. Weaving had been carried on there since Roman times and it had become a considerable industry when, in the tenth century, the import of English wool began. With their great wealth and their trade-routes which stretched deep into Russia, the Vikings offered a splendid market for high-quality textiles, just at the time when effective government was bringing sufficient peace and stability to the land to make industrial development possible. During the eleventh, twelfth and thirteenth centuries a great cloth industry grew up and spread until the whole of what is now Belgium and north-east France had become a single manufacturing district, the most highly industrialised part of a predominantly agricultural continent. With this concentration of industry the Rhine Valley was closely linked. In the twelfth century Flemish merchants were trading along the Rhine; by the thirteenth the merchants of the Rhine valley themselves were dominating the international commerce of northern Europe and Flemish cloth was passing through their hands on its way to the new markets in central and southern Germany and in the Levant. In Cologne, the meeting-point of many trade-routes, flourishing textile and copper industries had grown up.

The new industrial centres exerted a powerful attraction on the peasantry—primarily no doubt on the surplus population, but also on those who wished to escape from the restrictions and exactions which harassed them on the manor, on those who were restless and eager for a change, on those also who happened to have exceptional enterprise and imagination. For life in those centres certainly offered to the common people opportunities and satisfactions such as they had never known on the land. Industry was concentrated in towns, and any serf who was received into a town shed his servile status and became free. Moreover it was far easier there, especially in the early stages of economic expansion, for a poor man to improve his position than it had ever been on the manor. A penniless immigrant with a flair for business might always end as a rich merchant. And even amongst the artisans, those who produced for the local market developed, in the craft-guilds, associations which fulfilled many of the functions which the village community and the kinship-group had fulfilled for peasants, and did so with considerably more profit. As social and economic horizons expanded, hardship and poverty and dependence ceased to appear the ineluctable fate of common folk.

There were however many who merely acquired new wants without being able to satisfy them; and in them the spectacle of a wealth undreamt-of in earlier centuries provoked a bitter sense of frustration. In all the over-populated, highly urbanised and industrialised areas there were multitudes of people living on the margin of society, in a state of chronic insecurity. There industry even at the best of times could never absorb anything like the whole of the surplus population. Beggars crowded in every market-place and roamed in gangs through the streets of the towns and along the roads from town to town. Many became mercenaries, but in those days of short campaigns mercenaries were constantly being disbanded. The very word *Brabançons* came to signify the marauding bands of unemployed soldiers of fortune who were for ever coming down from Brabant and the neighbouring territories to devastate whole provinces of France. And even amongst artisans in employment many found themselves more defenceless than peasants on the manor.

It is of course true that medieval industry is not to be compared, either in degree of rationalisation and impersonality or for sheer scale, with the giant enterprises which were to transform the social structure of Europe in the nineteenth century. But neither did it consist simply of small workshops in which the "master," himself a man of modest means and no great ambition, exercised a benevolent patriarchal supervision over some three or four assistants and apprentices who together formed almost a family group. This familiar picture is valid only for the industries which produced for the local market. Industries which made goods for export, on the contrary, had their economic basis in a rather primitive form of uncontrolled capitalism. Notably in the great cloth industry it was merchant capitalists who provided the raw materials and who owned the finished product, which was sold in the international market. There the position even of skilled workers—the weavers and fullers—was precarious; though they had their guilds, these could not protect them as artisans working for the local market were protected. These men knew that at any moment a war or a slump might interrupt trade and that then they too would be thrown into the desperate mass of the unemployed; while the many unskilled workers, who were miserably paid, owned no equipment and had no guild organisation, were wholly at the mercy of the market.

In addition to poverty as great as that of any peasant, the masses of journeymen and casual labourers suffered disorientation such as could scarcely occur under the manorial *régime*. There was no immemorial body of custom which they could invoke in their defence, there was no shortage of labour to lend weight to their claims. Above all, they were not supported by any network of social relationships comparable to that which sustained a peasant. Although by modern standards the largest medieval towns seem small, there can be no doubt that in conglomerations of towns such as were to be found for instance in Flanders, in which each town had a population of from 20,000 to 50,000, the unfortunate could go under in a way which would not be possible in a village of perhaps fifty, perhaps a couple of hundred souls. And if in the upper strata of the urban population kinship-groups were still important, in the lower strata they dwindled away to the point of insignificance. The migrations from the over-populated countryside into the industrial centres began by disrupting and ended by destroying the large peasant families. Amongst the industrial population on the other hand kinship-groups of any considerable size hardly had a chance to form—partly because, given the high death-rate, that population had largely to be recruited anew each generation; and partly because poor families were unable to acquire more than a small amount of living-space in any one quarter.

Journeymen and unskilled workers, peasants without land or with too little land to support them, beggars and vagabonds, the unemployed and those threatened with unemployment, the many who for one reason or another could find no assured and recognised place— such people, living in a state of chronic frustration and anxiety, formed the most impulsive and unstable elements in medieval society. Any disturbing, frightening or exciting event—any kind of revolt or revolution, a summons to a crusade, an interregnum, a plague or a famine, anything in fact which disrupted the normal routine of social life—acted on these people with peculiar sharpness and called forth reactions of peculiar violence. And the way in which they attempted to deal with their common plight was to form a salvationist group under the leadership of some man whom they regarded as extra-ordinarily holy.

In this they were following a very usual medieval practice, and one which obtained in the most diverse social strata; at least from the eleventh century down to the close of the Middle Ages the laity was constantly throwing up salvationist movements of one kind or another. To appreciate with what passionate fervour perfectly orthodox Catholics could throw themselves into such movements one has only to read the account given by the Norman abbot Aimo in the middle of the twelfth century. He describes how multitudes of both sexes and all ages, including some of noble birth and great wealth, helped in the building of a church. Having banded together in communities under the leadership either of a priest or of a layman noted for his piety, these people yoked themselves like oxen to wagons loaded with building-materials and dragged them across mountains and rivers to the site of the church. During halts the leaders, working themselves into a frenzy, called their followers to repentance; and the followers scourged themselves, weeping and crying to the Virgin for forgiveness of their sins. "Hatreds were lulled to sleep, discord put away, debts forgiven, the union of minds restored. But if anyone refused to obey the priest and to put sin from him, his offering was thrown off the wagon as something unclean and he himself expelled with ignominy from the Holy People." When the teams came to the mouth of a river, led by God they marched straight ahead and lo! the sea was held back for them as it had once been for the Children of Israel. And in their carts they carried sick and dumb and insane people, whom they cured by their prayers. A holy people indeed, chosen by God and endowed with super-human, thaumaturgic powers.

In such descriptions as this there is a good deal that would apply equally well to the salvationist groups which proliferated amongst the poor in the over-populated, urbanised areas. For these groups too holiness was a quality which was to be attained through renunciation of the world and the flesh, through self-abnegation and even through self-torture. For them too the outward sign of holiness was the power to bring down divine blessing upon the world, and in particular the power to perform miracles. Yet from the point of view of the Church these groups were heretical sects; and it is easy enough to see wherein the heresy lay.

Amongst the surplus population living on the margin of society there was always a strong tendency to take as leader a layman, or maybe an apostate friar or monk, who imposed himself not simply as a holy man but as a prophet and saviour or even as a living god. On the strength of inspirations or revelations for which he claimed divine origin this leader would decree for his followers a communal mission of vast dimensions and world-shaking importance. The conviction of having such a mission, of being divinely appointed to carry out a prodigious task, provided the disoriented and the frustrated with new bearings and new hope. It gave them not simply a place in the world but a unique and resplendent place. To a far greater extent even than groups such as that described by Abbot Aimo a fraternity of this kind felt itself an *élite,* set infinitely apart from and above ordinary mortals, sharing in the extraordinary merits of its leader, sharing also in his miraculous powers. Moreover the mission which most attracted these masses from the neediest strata of the population was—naturally enough—a mission which was intended to culminate in a total transformation of society. In the eschatological phantasies which they had inherited from the distant past, the forgotten world of early Christianity, these people found a social myth most perfectly adapted to their needs.

This was the process which, after its first occurrence in the area between the Somme and the Rhine, was to recur in later centuries in southern and central Germany and, still later, in Holland and Westphalia. In each case it occurred under similar circumstances—when population was increasing, industrialisation was getting under way, traditional social bonds were being weakened or shattered and the gap between rich and poor was becoming a chasm. Then in each of these areas in turn a collective sense of impotence and anxiety and envy suddenly discharged itself in a frantic urge to smite the ungodly —and by doing so to bring into being, out of suffering inflicted and suffering endured, that final Kingdom where the Saints, clustered around the great sheltering figure of their Messiah, were to enjoy ease and riches, security and power for all eternity.

# Maurice Keen

---

## 14

## The Outlaw
## Ballad as an Expression of
## Peasant Discontent

The characteristic plot of the Robin Hood ballads, and indeed of all the later outlaw stories, is very simple. It is a tale in which wicked men meet a merited downfall, and the innocent and the unfortunate are relieved and rewarded. As the wicked are always the rich and powerful and the innocent the victims of poverty and misfortune, they may be said to be in essence stories of social justice. Though an occasional episode may have nothing to do with this theme, this is only the result of uneclectic borrowing by authors who only half understood the demands of their material. In fact the general drift of nearly all the stories is the same; clearly it was not only their traditional source which was shared by the ballad makers, the circumstances which inspired them were common to them also.

Their theme is the righting of wrongs inflicted by a harsh system and unjust men. It is this that raises the stature of Robin Hood above that of the common thieves who lurked about every highway in a lawless age; he was no ordinary robber:

> "Strong thievys were tho childerin none
> But bowmen good and hende."

He stole from the rich only to feed the poor. It is this that gives point to his ferocity; he was dreaded only by those whose wealth was undeserved. It is also this that gives point to his liberality; there is more in it than the traditional medieval loyalty of master to man, for he was open-handed also to all those in real need, the victims of misfortune and the oppressed poor. For he was essentially the people's hero. His friends were to be found among the pindars and potters of the world, or with knights whom fraud or mischance had reduced to penury; he belonged to a different social world to exiled nobles like Hereward

and Fulk Fitzwarin, whose companions were high born like themselves. The lowly people whom he befriended responded to his cham-
pionship of their cause; always in the ballads and stories they are the
outlaws' staunchest allies. Richard atte the Lee lowered his draw-
bridge to let in Robin Hood's men as they fled from the sheriff, though
by his act he risked his life and lands; it was the swineherd's boy whom
they had helped who slipped away to the forest to warn Adam Bell
and Clym of the Clough that Cloudisley was a prisoner in Carlisle. So
it was too with Gamelyn; the simple folk stood steadfastly by him:

> "There was no lewde man in the hall that stod
> That wolde do Gamelyn anything but good."

It was people such as these that were embraced in Robin Hood's "good
yeomanry," and their rewards were tangible. The potter went away
paid for his wares three times over; Sir Richard had again not only his
four hundred pounds but the interest thereon that doubled it. Alan-a-
Dale in another ballad had back his bride who had been "chosen to
be an old knights delight"; the widow in the ballad of *Robin Hood
and the Three Squires* not only saw her sons who had been condemned
to die for poaching free once more, but also avenged upon their
enemies. Robin Hood was true to his own maxim, "Look ye do non
housbonde no harme"; he was the man to right the wrongs of the
poor:

> "What man that helpeth a gode yeman
> His frende then will I be,"

he declared. Where he acted, moreover, justice was not only done but
was seen to be done.

Martin Parker, who compounded his *True Tale of Robin Hood* out
of old ballads, was near enough to the mark when he sketched the
character of his hero:

> "The widow and the fatherlesse
> He woulde send means unto,
> And those whom famine did oppresse
> Found him a friendly foe."

But the poor man of Robin Hood's story is not the traditional toiling,
suffering peasant of so much medieval literature, whose cry of woe,
unheard on earth, goes up to heaven where his reward is prepared
for him. There is hardly a hint of pathos in the ballad makers' treatment of those victims of want and injustice whom the outlaw helped
in need. The peasant people with whom Robin Hood mingled were

yeomen, independent and with a pride in themselves and their free status, who would brook interference from no man. Robin himself was a yeoman "corteys and free"; Little John when he first met his master was a young giant, "brisk" and "lusty," already famed far and wide for his strength; Alan-a-Dale was a bold youth clad in a scarlet cloak and with a bow in his hand. When in the ballad of *Robin Hood and the Tinker* the outlaw asked the man what knave he was, the answer was proud and defiant:

> "No knave, no knave," the tinker said,
>   "And that you soon shall know;
> Whether of us hath done most wrong
>   My crab tree staff shall show."

It was his independence of speech, his demand that he be not trifled with, that won the potter Robin Hood's friendship and the freedom of his and the outlaws' society:

> "By my trowet, thou says soth" sayde Roben
> "Thou says goode yemanrey."

There is nothing menial about the bearing of Adam the Spencer in *Gamelyn;* Adam Bell and Clym of the Clough "had dread for no man," even in the King's hall. Their independence of spirit is an essential part of the atmosphere of the outlaw ballads; the whole theme of the "free forest" revolves around it. The life of those who dwell in the woods may be harder than that of hermit or friar, as the *Geste* declares, but at least it is free; the men of the forest choose their own law and live untrammelled. With their bows in their hands and the waste of woodland about them, these are the freest spirits in the land; they are not bound to any soil or to the whim of any master:

> "Mery it was in grene forest,
>   A'mong the leves grene,
> Where that men walke bothe east and west,
>   Wyth bowes and arrows keen."

They belong to a society of their own, and in their own territory they speak on equal terms with whoever comes, be he bishop or baron. There is nothing humble about the yeomen of the ballads; poor they may be, but they hold themselves erect and proud, "comely, corteys and good."

On the one side in the ballads stands Robin Hood and the great brotherhood of good yeomen, independent and defiant. Against them on the other side are ranged all those who use their rank and possessions to cheat and oppress, to hold down the poor in unwilling thraldom. Two classes of men in particular earn the undying enmity of the outlaws, the officers of the law and the rich churchmen. The retribution which always overtakes them in the end reveals their incorrigible villainy. It is in the ferocious verse of the *Tale of Gamelyn* that the bitterness of the hatred in which these men were held finds its fiercest expression; in it we can almost hear the groans of the maimed clergy who were carried home from Gamelyn's hall in "carts and waynes," and the rattle of the bones of the sheriff and justice upon their windy gallows. But the same theme runs consistently through all the outlaw poems.

It is strange to find in the guardians of the law the villains in a poetic cycle whose undercurrent theme is the triumph of justice. Yet it is consistently so: the sheriff, the King's justice, and the foresters who enforce the arbitrary precepts of the law of the King's forest, are the men who are singled out to be the victims of an exemplary retribution. It is significant, therefore, that the ballad makers are always careful to particularize the abuse which these men have made of their position. The sheriff is a man in whose word no one can put the slightest trust; no trickery or injustice is too despicable for him to stomach. Though the case between them is *sub judice* and Sir Richard atte the Lee has sworn to answer for his conduct before the King, the sheriff will have him ambushed when he is hawking alone by the river, and do his damnedest to see him hanged before any questions can be asked. If he takes an outlaw in the wood, there will not even be the mockery of a trial; Guy of Gisborne or the first-comer may crave his death for a boon and will be satisfied. The sheriff in *Gamelyn* does not shrink from shedding the innocent blood of his own brother:

> "If he have not that oon, he will have the other."

It is the same with the justice. His judgements have been bought almost before a tale begins. What hope had Sir Richard of obtaining a delay at the law when his judge was already the abbot's man?

> "I am holde with the abbot" sayde the Justice
> "Both with cloth and fee."

Judge and jury alike in *Gamelyn* had been hired to hang Sir Ote; the process in their court provided not justice but a legal travesty thereof. These men have earned the fate that overtakes them in long careers of crime, and when the end comes no pity is wasted on them, for only by their death will men ultimately be free from their oppression. So when finally in the ballad of *Robin Hood and the Three Squires*, the Sheriff of Nottingham is hanged on his own gallows "in the glen," we may speak justifiably of the poem having a happy ending. The tale of his misdeeds has already revealed him to be incorrigible in wickedness.

This care to particularize the crimes of sheriff and justice explains the curious attitude of the outlaw poems towards the law's officers. They are not hated because of the law which they administer, but because their administration of it is corrupt. Before justice's guardians are attacked it is made clear that their justice is a mockery. There is no animus against the law itself; did not Sir Ote in the *Tale of Gamelyn* himself end his days as the King's justice? Significantly in the case of the foresters the treatment is not the same. They are slain indifferently; Adam Bell and his companions had forty dead foresters to account for, and Robin Hood is said to have killed fifteen of them single-handed as he went to Nottingham:

> "You have found mee an archer" saith Robin Hood
> "Which will make your wives for to wring."

There are no tears shed over Guy of Gisborne or Wrennock of the Dunne, though the story of their crimes remains untold. The reason is not far to seek, and it lies in the nature of the law the foresters administered. The forest law was arbitrary and tyrannical; it threw men into prison on suspicion to await trial at the convenience of the forest justices. It knew no equity, and those who lived on lands where it ran had no recourse to common law to protect them from its injuries. For the venial sin of poaching the penalty could be death. It was not for any real crimes committed, the widow told Robin Hood, that her three sons were condemned to die; it was:

> ". . . for slaying of the King's fallow deer,
> Bearing their long bows with thee."

It was because they enforced without mercy a merciless law which had its foundation not in custom nor equity but in arbitrary will that the foresters were hated, as the dying words of the Scots outlaw, Johnnie Cock, whom they shot as he hunted in the woods, tell us:

> "Woe be to you, foresters,
> And an ill death may you die!
> For there would not a wolf in a' the wood
> Have done the like to me."

Here it is the law itself which is resented, because there was no shadow of justice in it. The crimes of sheriffs and men of law are retailed because in the ballad makers' ideal world the sheriffs and justices would be better men; those of the foresters are not because their calling itself is unjust and in an ideal world they would be out of work.

The case of Robin Hood's other traditional enemies, the rich churchmen, is very similar to that of the men of law. Once again their misdeeds are particularized. Their greed, their frauds and their lying have been proven to the hilt before they come to grief. Indeed there is not much of the priest about them in the ballads. They are hard, pitiless men, who in their covetousness have forgotten the Christian quality of mercy. To the pleas of Gamelyn, chained to the post of his brother's hall, they were deaf as the post itself; Sir Richard atte the Lee begged in vain to the Abbot of St. Mary's for a delay to pay his debt:

> "The abbot sware a full grete othe;
>  'By God that dyed on tree,
> Get the londe where thou may,
>  For thou getest none of me.' "

It was no wonder that Robin Hood gave his famous bidding to his men:

> "These bishoppes and these arche bishoppes
>  Ye schal hem bete and bynde."

Their conduct deprived them of any claim which their religious calling might make on his mercy, or that of any other of their fellow Christians. But once again, as in the case of the men of law, it is noticeable that Robin Hood's animus is against particular churchmen and not the Church itself. When the King came to Sherwood disguised as an abbot, Robin would only take half the alms that he offered him, and his conduct was courtesy itself; he took the abbot "full fayre by the hond" and spread a royal feast before him "under his trystel-tree." He himself was always the model of conventional piety. His own sorrow in the forest was his enforced absence from the mass:

> "Yea, on thyng greves me" seid Robin,
>  "And does my hert mych woo;
> That I may not no solemn day
>  To mass or Matyns go."

According to the *Geste,* he built a chapel in Barnsdale dedicated to the Magdalene. Our Lady was his patron saint; when Guy of Gisborne wounded him, his prayer to her "that was both mother and may" gave him strength for the riposte. It was not against religion that he fought, as the mythologists who see in him a devotee of the witch religion would have it; it was against the rich cleric whose insatiable hunger for land would not stop short at fraud. It is as landlords, not as priests, that abbots and monks play a part in the outlaw ballads, and it is as unjust and ungenerous landlords that they are robbed, beaten and bound.

It is the churchmen of rank whom the outlaws persecute, the bishops and archbishops, the abbots and the officers of the great monasteries. Against the lesser clergy they have no animus, and in the friars, significantly, they find their friends. Though he does not come into any of the early outlaw ballads, Friar Tuck seems to have been long associated with the outlaws. In the fragment of a play of Robin Hood among the Paston papers, which dates from 1475, he has a part to play, and before that in the reign of Henry V, there was a real outlaw, Richard Stafford, who went under the alias of "Frere Tuk." The friars were just the kind of persons whom one might expect to be the outlaws' friends. They were vowed to poverty, and their rule made them the natural critics of the monks who could enjoy privately the profits of their wide estates in the seclusion of their cloisters. As mendicant preachers they mingled with the poor, and many of them shared the same humble origins with the people of the countryside. Whether or not he was really the same man as Tuck, it need not surprise us that the *Ballad of Robin Hood and the Curtal Friar of Fountains Abbey* should end with the latter bound for the greenwood in the company of Robin's merry men.

Though it is among those who have riches and high rank that Robin's enemies, both in the religious and in the secular worlds, are to be found, it is important to note that the poems about him reveal no animus against wealth or rank as such. The poems do not just divide the world into rich and poor, and describe the struggle of their champions. To hereditary rank Robin Hood payed the respect which his age regarded as appropriate. Richard atte the Lee was justly proud that he was a knight, and what the ballad maker is anxious that we should know is that he enjoyed that rank by a right of birth which he does not attempt to question:

> "A hundred wynter here before
> Myn auncestres knyghtes hath be."

For him there was something essentially wrong about the idea that the son of an old family should lose his inheritances, and the attempt to wring it from him is contributory to the injustice of the abbot's part. Robin Hood and Little John by contrast honoured Sir Richard as was due:

> "It were great shame" sayde Robin
> "A knight alone to ryde"

and for just that reason he gave him Little John to be his knave and go with him. Knights and lords seemed to the ballad makers to be an essential part of the social system, and they did not question their right to a high social status. They even reproduced in the ranks of the outlaw's own society a graded hierarchy; Gamelyn was "King of the Outlaws," and the crown that he is said to have borne shows that this was not an empty euphemism for the leadership of a robber band, but a title which set him apart, giving him duties towards his men as well as the right to their obedience. As soon as he was free of prison he must hurry back to his subjects in the wood, to see how they went about their business and to judge their quarrels:

> "To see how my yonge men ledyn her lif
> Whether thy live in joye or ellys in stryf."

Gamelyn, like Sir Richard, belonged to the hereditary knightly class, and he too was proud of his breeding. His brother's slurs on his legitimacy roused him to the quick: he was no "gadelyng,"

> "But born of a lady and gotten of a knyght."

It was only meet that the king of the outlaws should be a man of high birth. In some stories Robin Hood himself is made out to be a noble, though he is more usually a proud yeoman. One tradition makes him an outlawed Earl of Huntingdon; another makes him the child of "Earl Richard's daughter," born in the greenwood, out of wedlock it is true, but of a father who was also of gentle blood:

> "O Willie's large O'lith and limb
> And come o' high degree"

The object of the ballad maker here is quite clearly to increase the stature of his hero, and like others of his age he took it that nobility of blood gave a man a right to special status and consideration. The middle ages were profoundly respectful to hereditary rank and they did not question its title to homage. They did on the other hand question the right of those whose actions belied any nobility of mind to the enjoyment of the privileges of noble status. They were not indignant against an unjust social system, but they were indignant against unjust social superiors. The ballad makers accepted this contemporary attitude and echoed it in their poems.

This explains why the ballads have nothing to say of the economic exploitation of the poor, of the tyranny of lords of manors whose bondmen were tied to the soil and bound by immemorial custom to till their land for him. For we might expect, from what we know of the social system of the countryside in the middle ages, to find Robin, as the champion of the poor, freeing serfs from bondage, harbouring runaway villeins in his band, and punishing the stewards of estates whose conduct was every whit as harsh and unjust as that of the officers of the law. But the middle ages did not view social injustice, as we do, in terms of the exploitation of one class by another; they admired the class system as the co-operation for the common well-being of the different estates of men. They recognized three different classes in their society; the knights and lords, whose business it was to protect Christendom in arms, the clerks who had charge of its spiritual well-being and whose duty was prayer, and the common men whose business it was to till the soil. Each rank had its obligation to discharge its proper duties without complaint, and, in the case particularly of the first two classes, not to abuse the privileges which its function gave it. That they were made to "swink and toil" gave the peasants no ground for complaint; their occupation, as one preacher quaintly put it, lay in "grobbynge about the erthe, as erynge and dungynge and sowynge and harwying" and "this schuld be do justlie and for a good ende, with-oute feyntise or falshede or gruechynge of hire estaat." But those who failed to discharge their duties and abused their position had no right to a place in the system, nor to the profits of association. "They neither labour with the rustics . . . nor fight with the knights, nor pray and chant with the clergy; therefore," says the great Dominican, Bromyard, of such men "they shall go with their own abbot, of whose Order they are, namely the Devil, where no Order exists but horror eternal."

The law's object is ultimately to uphold social justice, and to the middle ages social justice meant a hierarchical social system. The trouble came when those who belonged to a high class used the wealth, which was given them to uphold their proper rank, to corrupt the law and abuse it for their own profit. Their ultimate sin was the use of their originally rightful riches to purchase more than was their due. For this reason, those who were shocked by flagrant injustice into at-tacking the accepted system criticized not the economic oppression which it almost automatically implied, but the corruption of evil men whose personal greed destroyed the social harmony of what they re-garded as the ideal system. The method which these men employed was to buy the law, and to control by their position its application. It is for this reason that the outlaw ballads, whose heroes are the champions of the poor, are silent about the multitudinous economic miseries of the medieval peasant, and are concerned only or at least chiefly with an endless feud against the corrupt representatives of the law. Contempo-rary opinion diagnosed the disease which was gnawing at society as the personal corruption of those in high rank; that such disease was the inevitable accompaniment of their hierarchic system they simply could not see. This is why the animus in the outlaw ballads is against oppression by those who own the law, not against exploitation by those who own the land.

The cast of contemporary thought also explains the immunity from criticism of one particular lord in the outlaw ballads, that is, the King. Because they accepted that the law, with all its hierarchical implications, was ultimately just, and confined their attacks to those who administered it to wrong ends, men had to accept the justice of the law's ultimate fountain head, the King. Reverence for the King stood upon a basis even firmer than respect for high rank in medieval thought. He stood apart from the social system, in it but not born of it like the baronage, hallowed and anointed but not of the hated race of clerks, God's minister in the land, made sacred by the mysteries both of religion and tradition. He was its guardian, God's vicar in whose hand was placed the sword of temporal power, and from whose court no appeal lay in this world. We are trespassing here upon the edge of one of the great unsolved problems of medieval thinking, that of the powers of the King who in person is human, but the authority of whose office is divine. Whether as the Roman law declared the laws were in the King's mouth, or whether, as ancient custom implied, he was but the guardian of a law to which he and his people alike owed obedience, was a question over which the subtle doctors of the schools were themselves divided. The fiction of the King's two bodies, the corporal body which was mortal, the phenomenal shell of regality, and the mystic body which was undying, explained the problem posed by his office but did not solve it. About the answer a thousand problems revolved, as the question of tyrannicide and the right to depose an erring monarch, and the question of prerogative and the force of the King's arbitrary will; but these were problems far beyond the understanding of the humble minstrels who sang the outlaw ballads and of the simple men who heard them. They only knew that the King was the ultimate repository of a law whose justice they acknowledged, and they saw treason against him as a betrayal of their allegiance to God himself. If they could only get past his corrupt officers, whose abuse of the trust reposed in them amounted to treason in itself, and bring their case before the King, they believed that right would be done. Their unshakeable faith in the King's own justice was the most tragic of the misconceptions of the medieval peasantry, and the ballad makers and their audiences shared it to the full.

Thus it is that just as the outlaws love the God whose servants they persecute, so they honour as truly as any of his subjects the King against whose officers they war:

> "I love no man in all the worlde
> So well as I do my King"

declares Robin in the *Littel Geste*. In that ballad, indeed, comely King Edward is treated as almost as much a hero as Robin Hood himself. There is another ballad on this same theme where it is "King Henry" who comes to the forest in disguise and is made welcome by the outlaws. All sorts of variant stories of the King's mixing in disguise with poachers of the forest and being entertained by them were once known, and several survive. There is one which tells of how Edward IV met with a tanner when he was out hunting, which has significantly opening lines very similar to the traditional summer setting of the scene in the ballads of Robin Hood; another tells of the King's clandestine feasting on poached meats with a shepherd in Windsor forest, in which the King adopts the name of Joly Robyn; another, which is incomplete, of his meeting a friar in Sherwood who combined the roles of hermit and forest archer. All these men are ultimately forgiven for their offences by the King and admitted to his intimacy. So also, when they finally come to him, the King always sees the justice of the outlaws' case and pardons them. He took Robin Hood with him to serve at his court; he pardoned, at his Queen's entreaty, Adam Bell and his companions; he forgave Gamelyn. Over the deaths of his servants he seldom shed any false tears. To Sir Richard he returned his lands which were confiscated; Ote and Gamelyn became his justices; Robin Hood and Adam Bell became his yeomen and exchanged their Lincoln green for the King's livery. The King is the *Deus ex machina* of the outlaw stories; by his authority the righting of wrongs done which has been the theme of the poems is stablished fast, and those who have served him loyally, if illegally, are rewarded. Occasionally, as in the ballad of *Adam Bell,* pardon is wrung from him unwillingly, but one knows that his word, unlike the sheriff's, cannot be broken when it is once given. Robin Hood in the ballads is the arbiter of an unofficial justice which accords with the unrecognized moral law; the King is authority, which ultimately endorses the moral law and makes its justice official.

The concept of justice is one which has held different meanings for different ages, and we should not, because it is said to be based in the moral law, read too modern an interpretation into it. The medieval picture of the day of judgement, with its vivid, hideous detail of the suffering of damned souls in a nether world of bestial demons, stands to remind us that for this age justice was retributive. It is this that explains the callousness, amounting almost to brutality, of some of the outlaw stories. Medieval man saw nothing tragic in the downfall of the wicked; awful and exemplary it might be, but not poignant. Justice, moreover, was in no way impaired by the fact that it could only be achieved by violent means, for the resort to force was ultimately nothing less than an appeal to the judgement of God, which does not err. The levying of war in a just cause was a duty, not a last resource forced on one by dire necessity. The shedding of innocent blood was of small moment provided the cause had absolute justice; had not God himself forced by the exigencies of nature, when he visited his wrath on the sins of Sodom and Gomorrah, to consume three other cities in the same storm of fire, although their inhabitants had not run up a more than average debit balance of sin? After all, the innocent had their reward laid up for them in heaven. If through mischance their fate was caught up on this earth in the retribution which overwhelmed the wicked, it was not a matter for undue regret, since death to them was but the gate to a better world. For an age of faith such as was the medieval period, their was nothing incongruous about justice and violence going hand in hand: they were familiar bedfellows.

The wildness of their life and the violence of their deeds cannot therefore be made a reproach to the outlaws. In taking the law into their own hands they were only falling back upon the ancient right of those who could not obtain justice to use force, and to use that force in the cause of others could only be altruism. When they shed the blood of their enemies, they were performing meritorious acts of retributive justice. Hence the endless tale of death and bloodshed which runs through the ballads. There are few holocausts so dramatic as the blood-bath with which the *Tale of Gamelyn* is rounded off; but it will not do to forget the forty foresters of the fee killed by Adam Bell, or the bloody mutilated head of Guy of Gisborne which Robin set on his bow's end, or the rotting corpses of the monk and his "little page," hidden in the moss by the wayside in Barnsdale in *Robin Hood and the Monk*. Nor should one forget Gamelyn's words of triumph over the body of Wrennock of the Dunne, or Robin Hood's exultant cry in the *Geste,* as he stands over the sheriff's body in the square of Nottingham:

> "Lye thou there, thou proude sheriffe,
>   Evyll mote thou cheve!
> There myght no man to thee truste
>   The whyles thou were alyve."

Face to face with their enemies, one will find the outlaws pitiless enough, for one cannot spare thought for pity in the cause of justice.

This streak of violence does not, of course, run through all the ballads. There are some, like that of *Robin Hood and the Potter,* which preserve the gay mood of their opening lines throughout. But it is important not to overlook it in other ballads, because it is so much taken for granted that it can quite easily pass unnoticed. There are the exultant moments which strike one, as those quoted above, but there are plenty of deaths which are recorded without comment. The monk and his page are assassinated and quickly forgotten; the sheriff in *Guy of Gisborne* is shot down running and his death is dismissed in a line; in the ballad of *Robin Hood and the Three Squires* the drama of the sheriff's execution is quite undeveloped (by contrast, for instance, with the same scene in *Gamelyn*). This might be taken for callousness, but it is hardly even that. It is simply the recognition of the fact that in the cause of justice, blood must most probably be shed; indeed, that it ought to be. This is the second tragic misconception of the common man of the middle ages, that because his cause was just and force was an appeal to the judgement of God, his ends would be served by recourse to violence.

Behind the matter of the later outlaw stories, therefore, there seems to lie the common man's demand for social justice. This is the only consistent theme which runs through most of the poems. We have seen that the manner of its presentation accords well with what we might expect to be the prevalent attitudes of the times. What we have still to see is whether history will bear out this interpretation and show that in the fourteenth and fifteenth centuries, the period which seems from their background to be the setting of the ballads, there was a real demand from the common people for social justice. If there was, we must further examine whether or not it was framed in terms which accord with the recurrent grievances urged in the ballads.

By and large, the earlier middle ages seem to have been a period of oriental passivity among the common people. We know a great deal about the terms of their bondage, about the number of days in a week on which a villein had to work on his lord's land and about the fines and reliefs which he had to pay; we know plenty too about the economic organization of manors, the methods of tilling the soil, the function of lords' officers such as bailiffs and reeves and haywards. But of the peasants' attitude to all this we know very little. We can imagine that he grumbled, for the burdens put upon him seem to us to have been almost intolerable, but history has left no witness to his complaining of his hard fate. Once in a while we hear of the angry tenants of some specially tyrannical lord suddenly breaking into revolt and assassinating their master or burning his house; or of some body of peasants withdrawing their services from their lord in protest against some particularly harsh innovation. But these revolts and protests are confined to one estate at a time, and one and all seem to fizzle out in failure. They are not part of any great movement. The average peasant does not seem to have had much to say to the conditions which bound him to poverty and ancestral thraldom, and in the history of the age he plays his passive role in sullen silence.

But in the last centuries of the middle ages the giant who strides through modern times, the labouring man, collective and impersonal, seems to be stirring for the first time in his sleep. He is only half awake as yet, and with only glimmerings of political consciousness his efforts are doomed to failure. But from all over Europe comes the same story. Suddenly the passive peasant is in arms, and his wrath breaks upon his oppressors like a thunderstorm. In 1359 it was the peasants of France who rose in revolt in the hour of national disaster, when the King was a prisoner in England and the country was riven with civil war, and for a moment they caught their masters off their guard. The quelling of this rebellion of the *Jacquerie* was the one good deed for France of Charles the Bad, King of Navarre. In 1381 it was the peasantry of England who rose in the great Peasants' Revolt, and marched with Wat Tyler and John Ball to London. Their rising too was relentlessly put down. In 1525 it was the peasants of Germany who took to arms, inspired by the preaching of Luther, only to be betrayed when their hero, horrified at the effect of his words, threw in his hand with the princes. In England at the end of the middle ages there seems to have been a permanent subcurrent of popular discontent; 1381 was the first occasion when it flamed up into widespread revolt, but there had been rumblings of the coming storm for years before that, and there had been scattered outbreaks of violence up and down the land. Stories were abroad of gatherings of recalcitrants in the woods at night, and of men banding together to support one another in a struggle for justice. In the very year after 1381 there were rumours of revolt in the West Country; there was open revolt in Cheshire in the 1390s, and there were many scattered local outbreaks over the succeeding years. Jack Cade's revolt in 1450 saw peasants marching on London once more, though there were others too, of higher rank, among the rebels. In Robin of Redesdale's revolt in the North in 1469 poor men again had their part. Down to the time of the Pilgrimage of Grace in 1536 and Kets rebellion in 1549 there seems to be a constant simmering of popular discontent just below the surface. But the same tragic sequel of repression follows all these outbreaks. They are bursts of sleepy-eyed wrath; half-blind, the peasant does not quite know what it is he is fighting for, except for a world in which his lot shall be less harsh. There is no realism about the aims he professes, and his leaders have not the understanding of politics to make realistic plans for the event of success. But though these risings were doomed to failure before they started, they do reveal just that background of widespread popular unrest which would make men listen, and admire the stories of an outlaw whose defiance of the law was more successful than their own.

# VII/THE CULTURE OF THE RENAISSANCE

**T**HERE are more renaissances than one can shake a stick at, if one reads the work of enough historians. The Carolingian Renaissance is supposed to have lit up the Dark Ages; the twelfth-century Renaissance to have relieved the dreariness of the pre-Crusade era. A few years ago, in an article entitled "Still Another Renaissance," the economic historian Robert S. Lopez dealt with the revival of trade and culture in the tenth century. With so many centuries clamoring for recognition, one might wonder whether the concept still has any validity. It is a question that can be answered only in terms of the study of concrete historical events.

Although chronologically the last, the Italian Renaissance of the fourteenth and fifteenth centuries is the oldest because it was discovered first, by the men who lived it. They were wholly conscious of all that was new in their break with the traditional past, even if they were prone to express themselves in terms of renovation and renewal of an ancient heritage. As Marx once remarked, it is a habit of men to present the new in the clothing of the old, so that they may have greater legitimacy.

The modern concept of the Italian Renaissance dates back to Jakob Burckhardt and his *Civilization of the Renaissance in Italy,* published in 1860. Burckhardt, who taught history for many years at the University of Basel, defined the Renaissance as having three principal attributes: the state as a work of art, a special brand of individualism, and a humanistic emphasis on classical antiquity. Although he eschewed the ordinary sort of political history, it was to politics that he attributed the motive force. A *Volksgeist* or Folk

Spirit peculiar to fourteenth-century Italians had produced a state which was "a calculated, conscious creation," unscrupulous in pursuit of ends assumed to be independent of those of the community. The existence of such a state gave rise to a certain type of individual "wholly dependent on his own resources and therefore developing them to the fullest extent, seeking only egocentric ends, and uninhibited by sentimental or traditional standards." This was the essential point that marked the true break with the corporate, community-oriented individual of the Middle Ages.

There are many criticisms that can be made of Burckhardt. First of all, as Wallace K. Ferguson has noted, his was much too static a view of the period it was meant to delineate. More important still, he made no concerted effort to relate cultural to socioeconomic changes, although he was perfectly well aware of the uniqueness within feudal Europe of the milieu with which he was dealing. Yet, when all is said and done, Burckhardt's thesis at least has the virtue of pointing to a fundamental truth: that there are privileged moments in history when the combined drives of slowly maturing historical forces all converge on a given set of people in a given place to make of them the bearers of enormous change, and of the moment, a qualitative leap forward into the future.

Burckhardt spoke in terms of a *Volksgeist*, a more than dubious concept. It is meant to designate a kind of spirit or animus welling up from the depths of the soul of the Italian nation, but everything points to the conclusion that it is a fiction, or at best a means of designating a set of beliefs and assumptions shared by a very small section of the Italian ruling class in the principal urban communes or city-states, which had grown up in opposition to the power of both the Church and the Empire from the end of the eleventh century onward. It certainly was not the heritage of all Italians, or even all Florentines, nor did it precede the creation of political-economic enterprises and institutions.

The setting for the Italian Renaissance was the Italian city-states of the north. With the expansion of international trade from the eleventh century, a "first" or "partial" capitalism had been created there and had soon taken the place of an immature feudalism. City once again dominated country, as the great merchant families combined in their own hands control of foreign commerce and ownership of a substantial part of the land in the *contado* or rural hinterland. They also established control over the artisans of the craft guilds and even succeeded in setting up large manufacturing enterprises, particularly in the woolen textiles field where a proletariat appeared for the first time since the fall of the Roman Empire. These merchants were certainly bourgeois within the meaning of the age: men of quality, rich and, although commoners, having some claim to social recognition. But at the same time they formed a special stratum within the bourgeoisie known as the urban patriciate, a term meant to designate those who, personally or through their families, actually participated in town government, that is, were members of the group that exercised direct political authority. A patriciate continued to exist throughout this period, its personnel changing more or less rapidly according to circumstances. The class structure of the towns remained substantially the same until the emergence of new forms of capitalism and the consolidation of "despotic" rule in the fifteenth and sixteenth centuries. In the twelfth and thirteenth centuries, it was the patriciate, with help and pressure from the classes that stood below it on the urban social ladder, that led the communal movement to victory and a greater measure of autonomy from king, lords, and clerics.

While I would not wish to say that Renaissance thought is the logical expression of these material developments, it is clear that there is a relationship between the two, whether it showed up as civic humanism or took some other form. More than a simple coincidence of personnel (the same families) between merchants, rulers, and philosophers, Renaissance culture expressed the confidence of a growing society transforming everything with which it came into contact, from goods to people to art. It was the ideology of man the maker. To the slogan-question: "What is man that thou should be mindful of him?" the Renaissance answered: "Man is the measure of all things." In Eugenio Garin's words, the task was to establish a metaphysics of man the creator, and it is small wonder that the metaphysics, an expression of the ideal world that is always surer of itself than is the material one, sometimes overshot the mark and came up with formulations about freedom and individualism still out of place in an economy oriented, as before, to consumption rather than production.

Was the Renaissance really new? Most definitely, yes. There were forerunners who, on an individual level and in the privacy of their minds, had come up with similar thoughts, but they had never made the breakthrough into the new world of the fourteenth-century Italians. The times had not been ripe for them to discover the "indifference of the universe," much less to react to it in positive fashion. And no amount of discovery of intellectual continuities between the Middle Ages and the Renaissance can alter that fact. The Renaissance men were the first to get down to the business of understanding the world in order to change it. Later, the periodic loss of that kind of energy often gave rise to protests from those who, like Marx, thought the true vocation of philosophy to be the shaping of human destiny in a world that, so far from being finite, it was up to man to make. Marat, in Peter Weiss's recent play *Marat/Sade,* expressed the Renaissance ethos perfectly when he said:

> Against Nature's silence I use action
> In the vast indifference I invent a meaning
> I don't watch unmoved I intervene
> and say that this and this are wrong
> and I work to alter them and improve them
> The important thing
> is to pull yourself up by your own hair
> to turn yourself inside out
> and see the whole world with fresh eyes[1]

The article by Giorgio Candeloro reprinted here gives us a Marxist interpretation of the changeover from feudalism to early capitalism in the Italian cities, seen as the basis for both the growth of the communes independent of the traditional power-holders and for the cultural flowering of the Renaissance. Following the theses of the Italian Communist leader Antonio Gramsci (1891–1937), he lays great stress on the relationships between town and country and shows how the incompleteness of change was responsible for the eventual stagnation of the communal economy in the fifteenth and sixteenth centuries. This is an important point, for it demonstrates that great cultural progress may continue to take place even in the face of economic and political difficulties and, more generally, that economic, political, and cultural developments related to one another do not necessarily operate on the same time-scale. With Candeloro's arguments in mind, one may then turn to the work of Eugenio Garin of the University of Florence, one of the most respected students of Renaissance philosophy and humanism, who here tries to present a picture of the distinguishing characteristics of the Renaissance world-view.

---

[1] From *The Persecution and Assassination of Jean-Paul Marat as Performed by the Inmates of the Asylum of Charenton Under the Direction of the Marquis de Sade* by Peter Weiss. English version by Geoffrey Skelton. Verse adaptation by Adrian Mitchell. Copyright © 1965 by John Calder Ltd. Reprinted by permission of Atheneum Publishers.

# Eugenio Garin

## 15

# Interpretations
# of the Renaissance

There is today a lively interest in the problem of the Renaissance which impells many people to take another look at Renaissance Humanism. This new interest is not entirely due, it seems to me, to the fact that after so many attempts all purely historical interpretations of the Renaissance have been exhausted. There was a time when many of us were seduced by these historical interpretations. But now there is not a single such interpretation which satisfies our methodological demands. Too many new problems have come to our knowledge. They define and help us to understand a great many aspects and motifs which used to be either neglected or obscured by the purely historical approach. There can be little doubt that any purely historical interpretation of the Renaissance creates more problems than it solves. But in the last instance, the crisis through which all purely historical interpretations of the Renaissance are going results from our need to give an account of the essential and directive lines of thought in western civilisation. This need continuously turns us back upon what is, after all, a crucial period in the history of the west. The Renaissance was indeed a crucial period—not only in the history of philosophy in the narrow sense in which philosophy is a discipline concerned with the technical discussion of certain defined problems, but in the history of the view of the life of man. For it was precisely during this time that the horizons of the most serious of all researches began to alter. As a result there disappeared, even though many people were not fully aware of it at the time, a well-established and venerable form of philosophising. The truth is that at this time there emerged, once and for all, a new manner of seeing the world, and an ancient way of seeing it disappeared. True, the old manner of seeing it disappeared in a blaze of glory, for the old manner had aspects which gave rise to the new manner. But all in all it did amount to a solemn burial of a dead, if noble, interpretation of reality. The only thing is that that burial was not accomplished all at once. The knowledge that the old world was dying matured very slowly and agonisingly. And it is perhaps only today that we can fully understand the catastrophic conclusion of this process. The centre of interest was shifted from one method of research to another. A complete change in the relationships between man and the ultimate realities, between man and things, between man and human institutions took place. And all this bore witness to a total change in man's attitude. If one goes to the bottom of things, these changes indicate the end of a sense of security and the beginning of an age of torment. The direction the new search was to take was at first not clear, for the new conception of the "free" man was placed in the very margin of the destruction of all preconceived forms: "you, who are neither a citizen of heaven nor a citizen of the earth, neither mortal nor immortal, you are, by yourself almost free and a sovereign creator. You must shape and hew yourself in an image which you must choose for yourself."

There was a way of writing history which pictured this rebirth of the free man as something like a triumphal march of certainties and resounding achievements. But if one peruses the most important testimonies of that age, and I am thinking chiefly of the fifteenth century, one will all the time discover that people, instead of being conscious of a beginning, were dimly aware that something was ending. The ending they sensed, though glorious, was nevertheless an ending. True, there is no lack of reminders that something new was being constructed. And there were assurances that man is indeed capable of carrying out a reconstruction of the world and of himself. But there was also an awareness of the fact that the secure tranquility of a homely and familiar universe, ordered and adjusted to our needs, was lost forever. Even where the most ancient themes lingered on, they changed in tone and flavour. Thus people kept believing that perhaps our illnesses are written in the stars. But in such cases they ceased to think of astral communications as the work of benevolent celestial deities and interpreted them as signs of man's sad enslavement to obscure and indifferent forces, beyond man's grasp. For this reason, people came to think of the liberation from astral destiny as a liberation from man's annihilation by things. To free man from the tyranny of the stars meant to free him from the anxiety of not being able to achieve anything or be anything.

Today we derive great pleasure from reading those new praises of nature and hymns to the infinite. But this is only because we somehow imagine that there was a tranquil confidence which kept shining through; or at least because we keep having a confident hope that the infinite which was promised was something positive. The sense of loss which ran through the whole of that civilisation thereby escapes us. For that civilisation, once it had smashed the ancient idols, was aware of the boundary it had reached, and knew of its own responsibility before unknown possibilities. A fine example of this is the spiritual itinerary of Ficino, who had come to the infinity of nature through Lucretius. In that infinite nature, man, because of his substance, has no prerogatives. Later he discovered that same loss and that same indifference to the meaning life once was supposed to have had in the immobile and timeless rigidity of the thought of Averroës and in the Aristotelianism of Alexander of Aphrodisia. It was then that he donned the garments of a priest and turned towards Plato and Plotinus in order to find someone who might transform into hope the restlessness that troubled him, and to assure him that the meaning which we are unable to discover here on earth, the positive certainty of things, is in reality up on high where it will be revealed to us in the end. Both his Christianity and his Platonism helped him to keep alive at least one comforting doubt: "perhaps things as they appear to us are not true; perhaps, at present we are asleep." Hence emerged the Ficino who was more sincere and more lively than the one who arranged everything in well-ordered and systematic concepts and substances which he could then place as a screen between himself and his bewilderment. His systematic universe was as fictitious as it was comforting. It was solidified in a reassuring hierarchy in which even the much celebrated dignity of man tended to vanish, for there was always the risk that the idea that man stood in the centre would reduce itself to the mere determination of a spatial locality.

There was another sense and another courage in the rich appeal to human virtue, to a virtue capable of overcoming destiny, capable of changing that destiny and constructing its own world and of giving a new shape to things with the help of that human artfulness which joins science and poetry. This, indeed, was the meaning of the civic humanism of Florence in the fifteenth century. This meaning inspired both Alberti and Pico when they transformed rhetorical and philological humanism into the metaphysics of man the creator. This metaphysics, I believe, was the most profound part of the whole of the Renaissance.

If we regard the ideas of Alberti as typical it would be wrong to see in his idea of virtue nothing more than the joyful certainty of a man confident of his actions and unaware that he is standing on the edge of an abyss. Just because Alberti is always a poet, and that means a creator, he was well aware of the risk involved in all creativity, in every construction which amounts to bringing about a fundamental change in what is given to us and indeed in the whole world. He was very aware of how unstable all constructions are and how in the very end all virtue will be vanquished. Campano wrote that there is no man whose virtue is not defeated in one last battle, be it only the one with death, for all human beings and all things are destined to perish. One ought to remember that Alberti's sadness was not a well-articulated pessimism. It was simply nourished by the knowledge that everything must change. Alberti had experienced many economic and political changes in his own home and had watched a whole mode of life disappear before his eyes. All this made him extremely thoughtful about the insecurity of life. His beautiful dialogue *Fatum et Fortuna* is one of the most deeply serious works in our whole moral literature; it eliminates all chances of optimism. The man who wants to know too much is aware of the shadows that darken the tempestuous river of life, and they remind him how vain it is for beings who are allowed to know only through sense experience to seek to understand God. And just as there is a limit to knowledge, there is also a limit to action. One cannot escape the rapids and falls of the river *Bios* [Life]. They form stumbling-blocks and ambushes which will sooner or later break every ship, even when a calm and free mind, with the help of the arts, can maintain it within certain limits and guide its course safely for a certain distance. The ultimate truth is harsh: "I have understood that fate determines the course of everything in the life of man and that it runs its course according to its law . . . I have also understood that for us, *Fortuna* is hard, if we have to be drowned in the river at the very moment when we ought to be fighting the violence of the wave with a strong arm: nevertheless we cannot ignore that in human affairs prudence and industry count for much."

These reservations insistently recall the obscurity of the foundations of life and its uncertainties. They are a reminder of the ineluctable limits set on all our efforts to determine our fate. Everything in this vision reminds one of the myth of Er in which the element of fortuity that is present at the launching of every fate is emphasised by the blindness that is at the very root of the human condition. The wise builder, the master of architecture was to tell us, constructs solid buildings, capable of withstanding the ravages of time. The many calculations by which he has dealt with even the most minute natural forces are hidden. For the artist's dreams are not dreamt in a state of intoxication. On the contrary, the artist builds on the basis of a detailed and prudent plan; and he builds things that will be fruitful and useful. He will always bear in mind his own interests and those of his friends. But in spite of everything, the edifice must one day fall to pieces. There can be no such thing as absolute stability. Everything decays: even the things that have taken their inspiration from absolute stability, stable goodness and stable truth, including those things which pretend to have been built according to absolute rules. And when they decay, they do not decay because of the malignity of men or because of the adversity of matter. They decay because in our world there is no such thing as a fixed rule and an absolute certainty. "There was a time . . . when I was in the habit of basing my views on truth, my zeal on considerations of utility, my words and expressions on my innermost thoughts. . . . But I have learnt now to adapt my views to the prevailing superstitions, my zeal to caprices, and to frame all my words so as to be capable of deception." These myths console us and create the illusions and seductions of our daily life. They are like the many branches of the ivy into which Momus transformed himself so as to be able to embrace, possess, and corrupt the beautiful daughter of virtue.

One could say that Alberti's mood was no more than a pleasantry, a bitter way of telling a tale, an expression of contempt, perhaps a joke. But the very opposite is true. The full flavour of his *Momus* comes out in the way that gaiety is made to appear serious. The *Momus* is meant to demonstrate the validity of a caprice, the philosophy of a mere poet, the non-philosophy of the philosopher. In reality, the philosopher himself is an extraordinary myth-maker. He calls these myths "systems." As Telesio was to observe in all seriousness, these systems fashion whole worlds according to his arbitrary will in competition with God. The worst aspect of these philosophical constructions is that they are so often ugly, inconsistent, sterile, and serious to the point of boredom whereas the artist has at his disposal the imagination of very life itself, and he builds even as life builds and makes no claims for his creations over and above their own inherent value. The world of the artist is the world of living imagination just as the world of nature is the living imagination of God. The artist is a creator and his forms take shape, rejoice and appear among us, live with us and transform our lives as the fables of ancient superstition were wont to do. In the *Momus,* Charon says something which is on the face of it quite trivial but he gives it immediately a new subtle interpretation: "you, who know the course of the stars but are ignorant of human affairs, you are indeed a fine philosopher! I will not report the opinions of a philosopher—for all your science, you philosophers, is limited to verbal subtleties. I will relate instead what I have heard from a painter. That painter, when he observes the shapes of bodies, sees more things than all you philosophers together have ever seen in your efforts to measure and explore the skies." Charon then shows us what it is that the painter has seen when he prefers the loving observation of flowers to rational and speculative discourse. When he hears of subtle doctrines, he is stupefied and demands to know why "you neglect flowers when in a single flower all things combine into beauty and gracefulness . . ." Alberti's main theme is life in its spontaneity. He talks about the function of artists and poets as it was to be understood later by Vico. Hence he finds nourishment for his disconcerting praise of the vagabond, of the man who breaks all bonds and restraints and who refuses to accept any position as absolute; of the man who is free and who is, in spite of his gay caprices, fundamentally serious—for he is aware of the non-value of all sacred values as well as of the value of what seems mere folly. Alberti's *Momus* is much less famous than Erasmus' *Praise of Folly*. But often enough it touches upon very profound matters. In the end, it furnishes a lavish proclamation of the importance of myth. It includes a critique of religious myths and recognises the validity of myth-making for the life of man. But in spite of all this not one of the venerable forms of the most authoritative traditions is salvaged—neither philosophy (except perhaps Socratic irony) nor religion, which is finally demolished by Charon: "If I were by myself I would just laugh at it. But among so many people I pretend to respect it." If Momus had continued his tales, the gods would have been dispersed in next to no time. For this reason Alberti silenced him by a curious final reminder of the limit—a reminder which recalls his *Fatum et Fortuna*. Hence, Alberti's "dispersal," contained in this kind of irony and therefore essentially ambiguous, is very different from the enthusiastic and confident "dispersal" of Bruno. Bruno's "dispersal" came close to blasphemy but ended up by reassembling in its own way all the gods, all the laws, and all the old certainties—amounting, therefore, perhaps to no more than the rebellion of a penitent. Alberti's dispersal, in spite of its vague tone, is a very terrible one in that it reminds man of the full responsibility with which it is fraught. For after the dispersal the consoling and well-systematised world of the metaphysicians, as well as the no less tranquil and reassuring world of the gods, is gone forever. Even if an infinitely far-away and unknowable absolute God were to be invoked or rejected, man's situation in the universe could never be changed again. Lefèvre d'Étaples was to give us a description of Pico della Mirandola. When he was carried away by the most powerful wave of Savonarolan faith, Pico intoned a moving prayer in the Lucretian manner and bemoaned the fact that God was so far away.

Bruno was solidly confident that he would be able to open a passage through the shattered walls of the world and that that passage would lead towards the all embracing One, the absolute which was well worth one's infinite love and the truth of which was a guarantee of the positive sense of reality. Bruno, and Cusanus before him, supply good arguments against those who reason that the culture of the Renaissance was a continuation of traditional culture. Both thinkers were men who had undertaken the construction of a metaphysical system and had thus taken up the traditional themes inherent in the logic of every speculation. They had not succeeded in determining the structure of reality by fixing necessary and stable forms. A truly "humanistic" standpoint, rather, has to be a poetical one. It proceeds by ignoring scholastic philosophy, or at least by considering it as something foreign. It has to remain deaf to it. A humanistic approach has to refute scholasticism as something which exhausts itself in the elaboration of rational schemes and paradigms that not only fail to explain or unravel reality but also have absolutely nothing to do with it. It is for this reason that Alberti never speaks of the actual infinity of man or of his substantial dignity, either of which might serve to reassure man about his transcendental destiny. He always speaks instead of the infinite number of human possibilities which, in the manner of a good humanist, he emphasises. These possibilities are the many mundane possibilities of the architect, the poet, the builder and the administrator of the city, the merchant and the householder. In the last analysis we are to be consoled in our melancholy position by beautiful fables and myths. Every time we approach the Renaissance we sense that its truth is to be found in Valla, Alberti, and Poliziano, in its Massaccios, Brunelleschis, Leonardos, Michelangelos, and Galileos—that is, in the artists, poets, historians and philologists, scientists—and last but not least in politicians and historians like Guicciardini and Machiavelli as well as in a prophet and reformer like Savonarola. It is not that this period is without its philosophers and could not have made its contribution to philosophy or that if it did, it only impinged upon the most obstruse parts of metaphysics, ontology, and gnoseology. It is rather that the most conscious form of human speculation took place in the sphere of philology, history, and science, all of which were opposed to the traditional ways of philosophising, which were busy "competing with God" instead of seeking to understand the world in order to change it and subject it to human requirements. This was the manner in which Telesio, for one, defined the difference between the old and the new way. It was no accident that the historico-philological attitudes, in the widest meaning of the term, proved a critical consummation and consolidation of the ancient way of viewing the world. While the old Aristotelian physics, in one last and fatal crisis, was dying of exhaustion, there emerged into full daylight a body of magical and alchemical doctrines consisting of techniques which could change the world. And in their wake came the irreverent experimental arts designed to break all laws and subvert all order. They were destined to move the stars from their courses, to transform all living beings, and to bring the dead to life. Men like Francis Bacon, Giordano Bruno, and Tommaso Campanella were to be among those who were seduced by the fascination of the experimental arts. It is worth recalling that in this environment there was nourished the theory that truth is the daughter of time; for, as magicians and astrologers were only too quick to notice, the certainties of today can only be slowly built by conquering the errors of the past. This was not likely to be done by people who seek to deduce once and for all the rational order of the world *a priori* but only by people who are engaged in the laborious pursuit of experimentation.

Towards the end of the fifteenth century, in a work which could well be compared with the *Discourse on Method* and the *Novum Organum,* Giovanni Pico della Mirandola defined the implications of the new image of man with great precision. He considered that the essence of the new image was man's independence of every predetermined species of 'form, as if man were breaking the bounds of the world of forms, as if he were the lord not only of his own form but also, through magic, the lord of the whole world of forms which he might combine with one another, transform, or remake. At the same time, reinterpreting the very ancient doctrine that the universe was a grand book of great originality, he demonstrated how historico-philological research coincided with the investigation of nature and how the world of man coincided with the world of nature provided the latter was transfigured and humanised by the effort of man. On the other hand he tended to intrude a religious element into this vision of man. He managed to achieve this through his historical critique of astrology as an astral religion and through his attempt to explain the biblical narratives by precise methods. In this way humanism attempted to become aware of its own radically new implications. It laid down the precise limits of the validity of a philosophy which, in Italy, was to continue along the royal road of historico-philological research. On this road we find Galileo, Vico, Muratori, to mention only the greatest names. This refutes Spaventi's theory that after the Renaissance philosophy emigrated from Italy. The theory, with all due respect to the subtle philosopher that Spaventi was, was due to a failure to understand fully the meaning and the inheritance of the humanistic ideal of the Renaissance.

We are bound to misunderstand the genuine significance of the Renaissance if we do not appreciate the proper meaning of humanism and keep on seeking its secret in the writings of a belated grammarian or in an alleged continuity with the middle ages. At the same time, the humanistic praise of the dignity of man can easily lead to a facile rhetoric if one does not bear in mind the price which had to be paid for it. The price was indeed high: one had to pay for the freedom to fight in a world that was stubbornly opposed to any effort and in which progress was difficult by relinquishing the reassuring idea that a given order existed. One also had to abandon the belief in a justice which would always in the end, albeit sometimes by very obscure means, triumph. What emerged instead was a political life without illusions, in which people were buffeted by forces without pity and in which the vanquished were eliminated without compassion. Similarly, people began to sense that everything in the world was frail and that God, if a God remained, was terribly faraway and ineffable and likely to issue unintelligible decrees to punish the just and save the sinner—a God to Whom it was vain to address prayers. If it is necessary to mention names, one need only think of Machiavelli and Pomponazzi, of Luther and Calvin as well as of the faces sculpted by Michelangelo. And finally, with Copernicus, Bruno, and Galileo, there came the end of the homely and well-ordered Ptolemaic system.

Once this is understood, one can give proper emphasis to the question of what precisely was new in the thought of the Renaissance. From a number of different standpoints attempts have been made to push back the Renaissance to the twelfth century or even to the Carolingian age and even to deny that apart from literary and artistic development, there ever emerged anything that was really new. It would be no exaggeration to say that much of modern historical writing about the origin of modern thought is devoted to the attempt to demolish the conventional view that there was anything like a break between one way of thinking about the universe and another way. Admittedly this reaction was encouraged by the fact that the upholders of this view used to take their stand on arguments which are only too easily discounted. It is perfectly true that such things as a love for pagan antiquity and the classical writers, a lack of piety or of religion, atheism, naturalism, and radical immanentism can without difficulty be traced back into the middle ages. In this sense it has actually been helpful to stress and illustrate the continuity between the middle ages and the world of humanism and, for that matter, between the ancient world and the middle ages. In this way it has been possible to document the fact that humanism did not amount to a rebirth of ancient culture because ancient culture had always been alive throughout the middle ages, at least since the twelfth century. This view, when all is said and done, was not even very new, for it had been a not infrequent habit among the writers of the fifteenth and sixteenth centuries to trace the Renaissance back to Dante, a position that was propounded with some solemnity in the *Commentari urbani* of Raffaele da Volterra. Similarly, the argument that the Renaissance goes back to the days of Charlemagne and Alcuin was not invented by modern French medievalists; it was put forward by Filippo de' Medici, Archbishop of Pisa and Florentine ambassador to Paris on the occasion of the coronation of Louis XI. . . .

However this may be, it is certainly one of the merits of modern historical research to have understood that the myth of rebirth, of the new light, and hence the corresponding conception of a preceding darkness was the result of the attacks made by the humanists themselves upon the culture of the preceding centuries. There can be no doubt that the writers of the fifteenth century insisted with exasperating repetitiveness on the fact that they had revolted against an age of barbarism in order to bring about an age of humaneness (*humanitas*). It is equally beyond doubt that in the preceding centuries the sense of rapid historical development had never been as lively. From every corner emerged the idea that an old world was on the wane, and wherever people looked they found confirmation of the view that an established vision of the world was being abandoned. The new discoveries broke the traditional image of the world, and the old conception of the universe was shaken long before Galileo. Ever since criticism had destroyed the psychological premisses of the Ptolemaic system, it had become necessary to face the consequences of the idea that the universe was infinite, that there were other inhabited worlds and that the earth was not in a privileged position. There is no need to enlarge upon the effects that ideas and observations of this kind had on theology. The curious thing is that modern historiography, in its attempt to grasp the idea the Renaissance had of itself, has managed to stand this idea on its head by denying that it included any element of newness. If it is true that the light-darkness opposition is very old and goes back to an ancient religious tradition, and if it is therefore true that the alleged contrast between the darkness of the middle ages and the consequent rebirth was nothing more than an occasion for a conventional controversy, then all insistence upon a break and the emergence of something new is of doubtful value. As a result of much critical work it has now been clearly established that much of what we believed to belong to the Renaissance goes back to the middle ages. People in the middle ages loved the classics no less than people in the Renaissance. Everybody knew their Aristotle in the middle ages—and perhaps they knew him better than the people of the fifteenth century. Even Plato was known in the middle ages and by no means only indirectly. Ancient poets, historians, and orators were known and appreciated. Bernardo Silvestre had written philosophical poems worthy of Bruno; Bernard of Chartres had been aware that truth was the daughter of time, and jurists had been busy reconstructing the whole essence of Roman wisdom. The revaluation of man had been more powerfully and profoundly conceived by St. Thomas than by Ficino. Furthermore, the naturalism and lack of piety of Machiavelli, Pomponazzi, and Bruno, even where they seemed most bold and most new, turned out to be quite old. In fact, these men were the heirs, more or less consciously so, of medieval Alexandrism (condemned as early as 1210) and of Averroism and, through Arabic science, of other Hellenistic currents.

In this way the recognition that both in content and in problems there was nothing very original in the Renaissance as far as the history of thought was concerned forced some people to regard humanism as an aspect of *studia humanitatis* understood in a narrow sense as grammatical studies. They alleged that such studies assumed in the fourteenth century a major importance. But not even here did these people allow that something really new had happened. At most, they assigned to the rhetorical arts a somewhat more dignified place than

they had occupied before. One is tempted to say that with this conclusion the academic controversy resounded in favour of the grammarians.
Grammarians, it was held, had simply continued their customary
labours which they had never interrupted; but now they were trans-
lating more accurately and more widely—though even this is doubted
by some. Thus they were said to have diffused a more solid knowledge
of both Latin and Greek, but indirectly, with a consequence which
was always purely marginal. It is curious that this argument completely obscured the importance of the Salutati, the Bruni, the Poggio,
of men who had been the great exponents of the highest culture and
of a grand epoch, of citizens, magistrates, thinkers, and all this in order
to vindicate in a facile manner the continuity of the scholastic habits
of a whole lot of second-rate compilers of knowledge. Looked at from
this angle, even Valla's philology, instead of bearing the imprint of an
era of rebellion, is reduced to a burnt-out case.

It was quite justifiable to make an attempt to understand the slow
process by which a grand period of culture had blossomed and
matured. But in the end this attempt misfired so completely that the
preoccupation with minute forms crowded out all sense of proportion.
The same error which had been at the basis of the old interpretations
had proved fatal in this case. The old interpretations sought to discover what exactly was new in the Renaissance by comparison with the
middle ages. It might have been useful to observe that there was a
correspondence between the bodily gestures of a fifteenth-century
Madonna and the astrological representation of the *facies* of the
Virgin, but it would be absurd to claim that such a comparison could
be elevated into a judgment about the meaning of a whole period.

The glorious myth of a rebirth, of a light which shattered the darkness, of a return of the ancient world, has great polemical strength.
But as such it is not essentially linked to any special content. It stresses
the fact that there was a new soul, a new form, a new way of looking
at things and, above all, it emphasises that this new birth made man
conscious of himself in a new way. The ancient world, classical
antiquity, which as a result of this new birth had come to be regarded
with much nostalgia, came now to be loved and cherished in a completely new manner. There is no denying that the ancient world had
been known and loved in the middle ages as well. The ancient gods
peopled the dreams of the anchorites and appeared to them as tempters,
and at times they turned up in the old places to demand solemn sacrifices
from the people. We have all read about the rages of Gunzone and
the dreams of Vilgardo da Ravenna. They are full of classical scenes
and in some of them people are invited to nothing less than an
apostasy of the Christian gods and a return to pagan rites. We know
of countless verses that are full of a profound love for ancient Rome,
and Dante allowed the ancient poets to intrude into the economy of

sacred history. He even brought in the ancient gods, turned demons, and made them live in the caves of hell.

Humanism, however, though full of love for Vergil and Cicero, no longer accepted Vergil as a prophet, and if humanists had faith in him, it was a completely new kind of faith. They believed in him in the sense that one believes in every human being who partakes of the light of truth. In this sense, the humanists were very far from worshipping the ancient gods—so much so that at times they gave the impression of not even believing in the new ones. The humanist's passion for the ancient world was no longer based on a barbarous confusion of his own culture with that of the ancient world. On the contrary his attitude was one of critical detachment. He saw the ancient world in historical dimensions and contemplated it as something which was situated in the august temple of the past. The myth of Renaissance paganism may have a certain justification for the purposes of argument; perhaps it can even be supported by reference to one of the decadent writers. But only historians lacking in wisdom can uphold it. As soon as we start to study the profound seriousness of humanistic philology, the myth is exploded. Gentile well observed that philology was the essential feature of the culture of humanism. By philology is meant a study so rich and complex that it includes a complete critical survey of the totality of man. It was not a pseudo-philosophy put forward by people who were not philosophers to use in their fight against genuine philosophy. It was a true, new, and serious philosophy. It amounted to both a restoration and a discovery of antiquity. But for this very reason it implied that antiquity was taken as something other, as something completely distinct from the thought of the humanists who did the discovering. The discovery was the result of laborious reconstruction; and for this reason antiquity was no longer seen as part of contemporary life. Antiquity, therefore, came to be defined as something that confronted the humanists. Its discovery was the discovery of an object which had to be placed into a valid relationship with the people who discovered it. The humanists thus found themselves *vis-à-vis* a historical past that was very different from their own world. It was precisely in this field of philosophy that there took place the conscious detachment from the past of which the humanists were so proud. It was a critic's detachment. The humanist wanted to learn from the classics not because he imagined that he shared a world with them but in order to define his own position as distinct from theirs. For this reason there arose a veritable gulf between those people who had loved the ancients because they thought they shared a common culture with them and the people who now realised that antiquity was something that had to be restored. The former, to make their belief come true, had often been forced to do violence—loving violence—to antiquity; and the latter sought to restore it with a

for accuracy which bordered on pedantry. Thus a whole world
up; and it was rediscovered at the very point where it was most
d. The face of ancient culture could no longer be simply rein-
reted. It had become once and for all part of history. It had ceased
be part of people's lives and had to be contemplated instead as a
torical truth. There was detachment; and as a result of this detach-
ent a classical author ceased to be part of me and I began to define
my own identity as something different from him. I found my own
identity by discovering his. The Renaissance myth of ancient civilisation was based upon a definition of the character of that civilisation.
And in defining that character the Renaissance reduced that civilisation to something dead. There was not much of a break between
antiquity and the middle ages—certainly less of a break than there
was between the middle ages and the Renaissance. For it was precisely
the Renaissance, or better, humanistic philology which made people
conscious of the fact that there had been a break. It was here that the
most important requirement of our culture came to the fore. We had
to define our own identity by defining the identity of another civilisation. Thus we had to acquire a sense of history and a sense of time.
We had to learn to see both history and time as the dimensions proper
to the life of man. We had to abandon for good the idea that the world
was solid and fixed, that it exhibited a graduated order and a permanent hierarchy—in short, that it was something definitive. We had to
give up the notion that the world was a cosmos which could be contemplated, indifferent to the passage of time, secure in eternity and
forever rotating in continuing circles. This old reality had been supposed to be utterly solid and to have a timeless subsistence—so much
so that its very solidity had crushed all prophets of man's liberation.
It had led instead to the grand manner of medieval speculation and to
the diabolical temptation to absorb the disquietening Christian message into the security of the Aristotelian world.

From Petrarch onwards, humanism took up an entirely different
position. A genuinely fruitful renewal, it sought a way out of an
insoluble problem, in the areas of poetry and philology, ethics and
politics. In the end it even sought a new way in a field which might
appear hostile to humanism but which was nevertheless intimately
connected with it: the field of the arts which godlessly attempted to
change and subvert the world. Philology and poetry, understood in
the sense of Vico, gave birth to the new philosophy.

Giorgio Candeloro

# 16

# Town and Country,
# Capitalism and Feudalism
# in the Italy of
# the Communes

The development of communes was a European phenomenon which was particularly rapid and intense in Italy. Therefore, it had a more profound impact there than elsewhere on the social structure and on political and cultural developments. This was due to favorable circumstances deriving both from the general condition of the world at that time and from the particular socio-political conditions in Italy, which were themselves a result of preceding Italian history. Above all, it is important to remember that the Mediterranean was still the main center of commerce among the various countries of the world. Thus, as soon as trade between the Romano-Germanic world on one hand and the Byzantine and Islamic worlds on the other became intensified (about the year 1000 and especially after the first crusade), Italy found itself in a position particularly favorable to maritime commerce with the Orient and overland commerce with central and western Europe. Even when, beginning in the thirteenth century and still more in the fourteenth and fifteenth centuries, another important trade route developed in the Baltic, in the North Sea, and in the English Channel (the first step toward a future shifting of the trade routes), Italian commerce was able to maintain—until the time of the geographical discoveries—an almost complete monopoly of certain goods which were in great demand in Europe and which at that time came to the Mediterranean Levant from the Middle and Far East. Moreover, one must bear in mind that in Italy, even in the barbarian and early feudal periods, urban life, albeit on a somewhat small scale, never ceased to exist, for in Italy feudalism itself had, to a certain extent, an urban character. Therefore, a tradition of mercantile, maritime, and artisan activity was maintained. Finally, the existence in Italy of the Papacy, a cosmopolitan center which attracted people and wealth, especially from the middle of the eleventh century, had an equal importance for the development of commercial and financial activities.

The rise of the communes brought about first in Italy before anywhere else a strong growth of commerce and an accumulation of capital, which in turn made possible the growth of intense banking activity that later developed around the Papacy and in the countries of western Europe. At the same time, there was a considerable development of industry, at first in the form of crafts and then, in some towns and for some industries (above all, textiles), in a partially capitalistic form as well. Furthermore, notable social changes in the country and significant progress in agriculture went along with the development of towns. The freeing of the serfs in many parts of Italy, the transformation of the old feudal relationships from customary to contractual ones, the development of new agrarian contracts, the passage of a large part of the landed property to the hands of the urban bourgeoisie together with the farming of previously swampy and wooded lands, the embankment and the canalization of rivers in some areas of the Po Valley, and the introduction and the spread of new crops are likewise characteristics of the communal period (and in some areas also of the subsequent period of the *signorie* and the principalities[1]) that gave to the Italian countryside a social structure and often also an exterior appearance which remained unchanged for centuries, and in many cases and in certain aspects are still in existence.

This rapid and intense progress, which took place almost without interruption from the eleventh to the fourteenth centuries, guaranteed to those parts of Italy where the development of the communes was greater, that is, northern Italy and Tuscany, an economic primacy in Europe which lasted until the sixteenth century, despite the decline, which had begun at the end of the fourteenth century, of certain industrial and mercantile activities. From this economic primacy arose a cultural primacy which culminated in the great flowering of the Renaissance. But during this very flowering, precisely at the moment when Italy was the leader of Europe in art, literature, science, and philosophy, it was hit by a very serious crisis which initiated a period of political decadence, economic recession, and then cultural decline that lasted until the eighteenth century. In order to understand the reasons for this crisis, it is necessary to consider various external factors which at the end of the fifteenth century and the beginning of the sixteenth had a seriously negative influence on Italy. Among these factors were the shifting of the main trade routes (determined by the geographical

---

[1] *Signoria* (pl. *signorie*) refers to the rule of despots, that is, direct rule by one man, which in the fourteenth century in Italian cities began to replace the oligarchies of the communal era. Where the despots took the title of duke, count, or prince, as they often did, we speak of principalities.—*Ed.*

discoveries), the Turkish expansion in the Mediterranean, and above all the French and Spanish conquests in Italy and the wars that ensued, which transformed Italy into a battlefield and ended with the establishment of Spanish rule. But one must also remember that these events had momentous consequences for subsequent Italian history also, because they took place when Italy had for some time been in a phase of social and political stagnation which had originated during the communal period. Thus, there are certain social and political characteristics of Italian history in the communal period which one should bear in mind in understanding the Italian crisis of the sixteenth century and many important aspects of the subsequent history of Italy.

First of all, one must recall the particular shape that the relationships between town and country took in the Italy of the communes. The conquest of the countryside by the commune was a general phenomenon which engendered a permanent subordination of the countryside to the towns and a juridical inequality between inhabitants of the towns and of the countryside. This was maintained, although somewhat attenuated, in the *signorie* and the principalities as well. In addition, the subordination of country to town was not just of a political and administrative nature, but was also characterized by a feudal or semifeudal dependence of the peasants on the urban ruling class. Certainly in the twelfth and thirteenth centuries, the development of towns stimulated the overthrow of feudal relationships in the country, which involved to a considerable extent the peasantry itself. This led to those progressive changes to which we have already referred. But on the whole, the communes aimed at undermining the political power of the feudal lords but were only partially successful, so there was a resurgence of feudal jurisdiction in the period of the *signorie* and the principalities. Furthermore, the freeing of the serfs was in effect an incomplete emancipation and did not completely sever the peasants' dependence on the landowners. The formation of "free towns" (*Borghi franci*), inhabited by completely free peasants, was relatively limited and quickly interrupted, and the creation of small peasant landholdings was very limited except in a few areas. In general, it can be said that in northern and central Italy most of the cultivated lands passed from the feudal lords to the urban merchant bourgeoisie, to which families of feudal origin, rural landowners of long standing, also belonged. In addition, it seems that a considerable part of church property passed in various ways during the communal period into the hands of merchants and bankers. There was among the communal bourgeoisie a permanent trend, which intensified with time, to invest a part of the income from commerce, banking, and industry in land.

But the ruling urban class maintained feudal or semifeudal relations of production on their acquired lands, which crystallized into forms which lasted for centuries and in part still survive. This is evident from even a cursory examination of the agrarian contracts prevailing in northern and central Italy during the age of the communes, *signorie*, and principalities. These contracts can be reduced to two principal types: the *livello* (long leaseholding) and the *mezzadria* (métayage or sharecropping).

The *livello* was originally a long-term contract (nineteen or twenty-nine years), according to which the leaseholder enjoyed a piece of land upon payment of a *censo*, or rent, generally fixed, in kind or in money, with the option to sublease but with the obligation to reside on the land and to supply specific services to the landlord, who, on his part, was generally obligated to renew the contract when it expired. In essence, one can say that the *livello* maintained, in written form and shorn of certain services, the relationship of production typical of feudalism, because the farmer worked the land with his own means of production and owed the proprietor the rent without the latter having any obligation to advance capital, and because the subordination or *commendazione* (commendation) of the *livellario* (long leaseholder) toward the landlord continued to exist. But with the passing of the land to the urban merchant bourgeoisie, which began to invest its capital in land reclamation and improvement works, the *livello* underwent an evolution. On the one hand, the owners succeeded in transforming many *livelli* into short-term rents, increasing the rents and taking away from the farmers the right to sublease and those guarantees of tenure which they had previously enjoyed. On the other hand, the owners almost always succeeded in rendering more burdensome the ties of subordination by increasing the obligations of real and personal services.

The *mezzadria*, however, much more than the *livello*, was a step in the transition from a feudal to a capitalistic economy. It was in its origins strictly related to the investment in agriculture by the merchant class. This involvement of the merchant class was perhaps initially stimulated also by the need to increase agricultural production in order to provide for the needs of the growing urban population. In sharecropping, the means of production for cultivating and improving the land are in part provided by the owner and in part by the sharecropper, in such a way that the portion of the crop (usually half, at least originally) that the farmer owes the owner represents in part a land revenue of a feudal type and in part a return on the capital invested by the owner in the enterprise. However, sharecropping had other feudal characteristics from the very beginning and acquired still more with the passing of time. This was due to the fact that sharecropping involved the rendering of free services and produce by the farmers and that in many cases they got seriously into debt to the owners and were forced to pay off their debts with extra services and were often reduced to a state of partial servitude.

One can generally say that in northern and central Italy, that is, in the areas of the greatest development of the communes, the condition of the peasantry, after a period of improvement in the eleventh, twelfth, and thirteenth centuries, underwent a slow but steady deterioration in the fourteenth and fifteenth centuries, when a close dependence of the peasantry on the landed merchant class, ruling in the towns, was established. However, it seems that even during these centuries agricultural production kept on increasing and became, in addition, more varied because of the introduction of certain crops in the central and northern areas which had before existed mainly in the south (such as the mulberry tree with the related raising of silkworms, rice, etc.). This increase in and improvement of production might have slowed the worsening of the conditions of the peasantry to a certain extent. In fact, there were no peasant revolts in the fourteenth and fifteenth centuries in northern and central Italy comparable to those that were taking place in other countries of Europe. But the *politica annonaria* (food supply policy) of the communes helped to aggravate the problems of the countryside and to crystallize in it the relationships and the type of production which would further worsen the condition of the peasants. The food policy, continued by the *signorie* and the principalities as well, was dominated by the preoccupation of guaranteeing the food supply at a relatively low and steady price to the urban artisans and wage laborers, whose unrest was greatly feared by the dominant merchant class. Legislation restricting the sale and export of the principal agricultural products was developed to this end. The owners made the burden fall mainly on the peasantry, precisely by means of those tenant contracts already mentioned.

The crystallization of the burdensome dependence of the country on the town must, however, be considered in the greater context of the economic development of the Italy of the communes. One must, therefore, take into consideration another important point, that is, the development of industry in the communes and the forms it took. The handicrafts industry, typical of the first period of communal development and still the prevailing form of production, certainly was not capitalistic in nature. In belonging to guilds, which greatly limited competition, the master craftsmen produced basically for the local market, working in their own shops with a few associates and apprentices and often some journeymen. It was not possible, therefore, to accumulate capital comparable to that in commerce and usury. An evolution toward capitalism took place, however, in those industries in which merchants (who initially in some cases were the more enterprising artisans) intervened and established a supremacy over the artisans. This took place especially in the textile industries, which in the thirteenth century began to process important quantities of imported raw materials and supplied a considerable amount of exports for that time. The development of the Florentine textile industry, with the subsequent supremacy of the *calimala*,[2] wool, and silk guilds, all three dominated by merchant groups, is typical in this respect. But it seems certain that also in Lombardy, whose textile industry was not inferior to that of Florence, the same phenomenon of domination of the artisans by the merchants took place, sometimes associated in their own particular corporate guilds.

At first the merchant had two roles in industry: acquiring the raw materials and distributing them to the artisans for processing, and then acquiring the finished product from them for export. Therefore, the artisans, instead of working only for the local customers with whom they were in direct contact, worked mainly for the merchants, on whom they came to depend. But it soon happened that, because of the complexity of the processing, which was a result of the quantitative and qualitative progress of industry, the merchants became directly involved in the productive process. A part of the manufacturing process was concentrated in factories which employed a considerable number of wage laborers, and a part remained in the hands of the artisans who worked at home with their own instruments of production but who were by now reduced to a mere link in a productive chain, directed and exploited by merchant-entrepreneurs. One can therefore say that some industries, in the age of the communes and of the *signorie* and principalities, passed from the artisanal to the capitalistic stage of production, but only in an incomplete fashion. This was because part of the instruments of production remained in the hands of certain groups of workers and because centralized manufacturing was only a partial phenomenon; instead, the *decentralized* or *scattered* system of manufacture prevailed in the productive process. In addition, the merchant-entrepreneurs did not break down the corporate guild system, but remained part of it and exploited it for their own ends, by guaranteeing their guilds a political supremacy in the towns, by establishing within their guilds the supremacy of the major members over the minor ones, and by quelling the attempts of the wage laborers to organize themselves in their own guilds.

Italian industry did not go beyond this stage at that time. The silk industry, developed as an export industry in the fifteenth century (when the wool industry was dying) and still flourishing in the sixteenth century, also took on the form of decentralized manufacture. The Flemish textile industry, which in the fifteenth century took the western European markets away from Italian industry, also had somewhat similar characteristics. Only in the fifteenth and sixteenth centuries,

---

[2] The guild of dealers in raw wool.—*Ed.*

and mainly in England, did superior, more clearly capitalistic, forms develop. The lack of development of these more advanced forms in Italian industry and the constant decline could easily be attributed to the political crisis of the Italian states in the first decades of the sixteenth century and to the shifting of the trade routes. Certainly these facts had their importance, but one must not forget that the development of decentralized manufacturing had taken place previously, and that in general there was not a sudden economic crisis which coincided with the political crisis or was an immediate result of the changing of trade routes. There was instead a slow decline from the end of the fourteenth century to the beginning of the sixteenth century, which in the course of that century became total decay. One must therefore conclude that the phenomenon of the stagnation and regression of Italian industry, like the analogous and contemporaneous one which took place in agriculture, was mainly the result of an internal trend of the Italian economy in the last centuries of the Middle Ages.

We are confronted here with a very complex problem, which until now has not been sufficiently studied. However, one can safely state that in the Italian economy of the Late Middle Ages capitalistic industry was in reality a marginal phenomenon, subordinated to commercial activities and to usury. The general conditions of the world at that time and the low degree of financial development of the major European countries made it possible for the precociously developed Italian bourgeoisie to realize large profits through the trade (very lucrative, but rather limited in volume) of precious or very refined goods and through banking activities connected with the finances of the western monarchies and the Papacy. The typical capital of the communes came, therefore, from commerce and usury; the rudimentary and limited development of industrial capitalism and the limited penetration of capitalism into agriculture were only partial and secondary phenomena. The merchant bourgeoisie, having come to dominate the artisan classes because of the peculiar development it had given to the corporate guild system, and having come to rule over the countryside because of the elimination and absorption of the feudal class and the adoption of feudal or semifeudal systems of exploitation of the peasantry, was also able to easily crush the agitation of the wage laborers, who constituted a minority even in the most advanced towns. Therefore, the merchant bourgeoisie became a privileged class everywhere; it was essentially conservative, tending to become a closed and restricted oligarchy, and was not interested in introducing new economic forms. Thus, Italian society crystallized rapidly, and there was a stagnation in the development of the productive forces which resulted in a general decline of the economy.

The same phenomenon of stagnation after a time of dynamism also took place in the political arena. In the first part of the communal period, the presence in the towns of feudal groups, their increase with the immigration of other feudal lords from the countryside, the turning of feudal families to commerce, and the acquisition of land by enriched merchants, led in the majority of the communes to the formation of a landed and merchant ruling class known as the *grandi*, the *magnati*, or the *nobili*, which maintained many feudal customs in its way of life, but which tended to give commercial and banking interests greater and greater importance. This class, restricted but not completely closed as it slowly absorbed newly enriched families, was divided into cliques and rival factions. In reaction to it, a widespread movement of smaller merchants and artisans took shape in the thirteenth century, a movement which in a certain sense can be considered democratic since it aimed at broadening the basis of the government of the commune. But, although such a broadening occurred in many towns and although many rich noble families were destroyed or greatly weakened, a new class did not come to power at that time. There was only a turnover and broadening of the existing ruling class, which was in fact able to absorb the richest of the merchants and artisans who were exerting pressure from below, while the poorest masses were driven back to a subordinate position. In some cases, as previously mentioned, the ruling landed merchant class was able to use to its own advantage the corporative system and the particularism of the individual guilds by establishing both a hierarchy among the various guilds and a sort of hierarchy in the membership of each craft. Generally, one can state that the dominant class in the communes was able to behead the popular movement through a policy which, to borrow a typical term of modern Italian politics, can be called transformist.[3] In any event, the oligarchic tendency prevailed in the end over the democratic one. The political development was analogous to the economic development that was taking place at the same time.

This development, nevertheless, did not take place in a peaceful manner. The always-resurgent unrest of the common people and the continuous struggles among the factions of the ruling class created a permanent political instability in the majority of the communes, which was aggravated by the exclusive and often terroristic way in which the factions that followed one another in government exercised power. In the majority of the communes, the discontent of the common people on one hand and the fear and weariness of the ruling class on the other facilitated the taking of power by individual political leaders who generally belonged to the ruling class itself. It was in this way

---

[3] "Transformist" is a term used in Italian politics from the 1880s onward to indicate the growing rapprochement between the left and right parties of the Risorgimento (the period of struggle for Italian unity), until ultimately little difference remained between them.—*Ed.*

that the *signorie* arose, some of which were later transformed into principalities.

The birth of the *signorie*, nevertheless, did not lead to a transformation of the existing social relations. In fact, although the *signori* [the holders of power in the *signorie*] often succeeded in winning the support of the common people and in crushing the power of the most important families, the socioeconomic preeminence of the landed merchant class was in substance maintained. Indeed, this preeminence was stabilized, thanks to the subjugation of the popular masses, which by now had become permanent in the *signorie* and the principalities. Moreover, despite the efforts of the *signori* to improve the conditions of the countryside and the smaller subordinate towns, mainly by attenuating the serious fiscal inequality typical of the government of the communes, the privileged position of the ruling towns was maintained both in the *signorie* and in the principalities. In addition, some princes, like the Visconti and the Sforza in Lombardy, extended feudal jurisdiction to the countryside again by granting land as fiefs to their *condottieri* (soldiers of fortune) or by selling feudal titles or rights to families of merchant origins.

However, in order to understand clearly the sociopolitical situation of Italy at the end of the Middle Ages, it is necessary to bear in mind that even in northern and central Italy there were large areas where the development of the communes was either weak or nonexistent Piedmont, for instance, with the marquisates of Monferrato and Saluzzo, the large possessions of the House of Savoy, and other smaller fiefs remained predominantly feudal. In the Papal States also the baronage remained powerful, especially in Latium, which was almost entirely enfeoffed to the main Roman families; in Umbria, the Marches, and Romagna as well, the many communes were almost all ruled by noble oligarchies or by *signori* of feudal origin. This still feudal part of Italy remained predominantly agricultural and constituted an economic complement to the Italy of the communes. Furthermore, when the use of mercenary armies became widespread, these poorer and more backward regions, especially in the Papal States, whose relatively dense populations had been made warlike by the incessant communal and feudal petty wars, supplied large numbers of soldiers and captains of fortune to the big communes and the big *signorie*. In this aspect as well, therefore, these regions were a complement to the more-advanced Italy of the communes and of the *signorie*.

# VIII/THE TRANSITION FROM FEUDALISM TO CAPITALISM

WAS there ever a word more abused, more variously defined than "capitalism"? As R. H. Hilton points out in the reading that follows, the result has been a headlong rush into confusion, with capitalism and capitalists here, there, and everywhere, and a middle class eternally rising like yeast in a baking cake.

Everyone has a right to define his terms as he sees fit, but one of the cardinal rules of the game is that the definition should help us to understand the phenomena under analysis. It must therefore be broad enough to encompass change over time, but narrow enough to respect the principle of historical specificity. War is war, armed conflict between belligerent collectives and particularly, in modern times, between nation-states. Such a definition does not get us very far; if we want to explain an actual confrontation of, say, the mid-twentieth century, we need a deeper, broader concept. The same may be said of the terms "capitalist" and "capitalist investment." They refer only to the act of using money in order to make a profit, and as such, they have always existed to one degree or another. To be sure, they were less evident in the autarkic, subsistence economy of feudal Europe than they had been earlier. Capitalists and capitalist investment reappeared extensively in the eleventh century and set in motion a new process, one that needed a new conceptualization. Here we have the beginnings of capitalism properly so called. But what does that mean?

Everyone will admit that the application of capital on a large scale to the sphere of circulation of goods disturbed the balance of feudal society. Markets, never wholly lacking in the earlier period, expanded greatly, and men produced more goods for them. This simple commodity production (that is, production of goods for exchange on the market) was much different from the artisanal household economy. As a result, the productive relations of the feudal system began to change to a considerable extent with the introduction of money rents and the increased employment of labor in the agricultural sphere.

It is to the transformation of the relations of production that Marx draws our attention. His concept is based on only two assumptions: first, that goods must be created before they can be exchanged; and second, that in the course of producing the goods, men enter into certain social relations with one another, social relations which are independent of their will. A fully formed capitalist mode of production is one in which capital has penetrated into all areas of social existence and subjected everything to its control. This occurs only in a "society producing commodities for exchange on the market, whose principle classes [are] capital owning entrepreneurs and [free] propertyless wage-earners." In other words, it occurs only when labor itself has become a commodity.

This highly abstract formulation, which is not intended to describe existing reality but to make its analysis possible, is dynamic and capable of accounting for long-term historical development. Centuries were required for capitalism to mature fully, as the contradictions within feudal society worked themselves out in crisis after crisis. None of this was automatic, and much of it depended on the action of men, on the interaction between their conscious desires and the opportunities that lay at hand, between their insertion into the feudal system and their attempts to step outside it. We do not yet know all the circumstances of this development even in the several European countries. The articles by R. H. Hilton and Pierre Vilar that follow seek to be no more than guideposts to the questions we must ask and the methods we may employ for their resolution. Hilton argues the need for a rigorous definition of capitalism along Marxist lines. Why is it, he asks, that "in spite of the expansion of production, of population and of trade in the 13th and early 14th centuries, the main features of the old social and political framework remained, not to disappear until the 17th and 18th centuries?" And the answer, he insists, must be found not in economic considerations alone, but in the persistence of habits and ideologies inherited from the earlier period which played a most important role in altering the balance of class relationships.

Vilar of the University of Paris questions the validity of the Keynesian thesis found in the work of E. J. Hamilton, late of the University of Chicago, and of numerous other historians of the economy of early modern Europe. The English economist John Maynard Keynes (1883–1946) was no doubt best known for his conviction that the cyclical crises of modern capitalism might be avoided, or considerably ameliorated, by an inflationary policy based on government spending and manipulation of the money supply. This theory, well adapted to the circumstances of the Great Depression of the 1930s, influenced the policy of numerous governments, including that of the United States, at that time and since. It was only natural that historians should have been tempted to apply it to the past as well. But Vilar points out that, aside from the empirical objections to so doing, there are theoretical reasons to be alarmed. Keynesian theory leads us to believe that "once a price movement has been established, we could immediately deduce a definitive corollary from it," which is to ignore the specific historical circumstances in which the movement took place. Moreover, to attribute profit to monetary manipulation rather than to exploitation of labor (surplus value) is to negate the most basic of Marxist theses on the matter of social organization. In Vilar's view, interpretations that make much of the price revolution of the sixteenth and early seventeenth centuries (the extraordinary rise in the price level between 1550 and 1650 usually ascribed to the influx of American gold and silver and particularly harmful to persons living on fixed incomes while inflating the amount of wealth available for investment) do not go much beyond a rather sophisticated version of the quantity theory of money to the effect that prices will be determined by the relationship of the amount of money in circulation to the number of goods offered for sale. And money, for Vilar, no matter what the quantity, is never in and of itself of any significance unless it is understood in connection with the social relations of production.

It has been suggested that there is a correlation between capitalism and Protestantism. More specifically, in Max Weber's formulation the connection was between the Protestant ethic and the spirit of capitalism, both of which require a definition. For Weber (1864–1920), whose sociological work has without any doubt constituted the principal non-Marxist pole of attraction in the field, modern Western capitalism was distinguished by the drive for the unlimited accumulation of profit by means of the rational organization of labor, quite independent of any consideration of the ownership of the means of production or the transformation of labor itself into a commodity—primary characteristics attributed to the capitalist mode of production in the Marxist formulation. The spirit of this capitalism lay in the idea that accumulation was not a means, but an end in itself. The Protestant ethic (that is, Calvinism as interpreted and corrupted in daily use) supported the spirit of capitalism by concentrating on the ideas of predestination and the calling, which in turn justified wealth acquired through methodical, unremitting labor as a proof of election or eternal salvation. In a word, Calvinism provided the ideological cover and encouragement for capitalist enterprise.

Weber has been much criticized over the years on many different grounds. He has, first of all, been interpreted as saying that the Protestant ethic caused capitalism. He never made any statement so patently absurd. He was an idealist in his philosophical options, and he was therefore able to believe that, given an already existing capitalism, Protestantism contributed substantially to changing its content from the old-fashioned speculative or commercial variety of the Late Middle Ages and Renaissance to the new, rationally acquisitive capitalism of his definition. According to his partisans, Weber wished to draw attention to only one side of the equation, but had no intention of denying an analysis whereby the development of the spirit of capitalism would be seen as essentially the result of capitalist practice.

It seems to me that it is difficult to dispute Weber's basic insight if we accept his definitions, or even if we modify them a good deal. There's the rub. If the chronological coincidence between the Reformation and the introduction of new forms of capitalism is too extraordinary for us to give up the connection entirely, it is nonetheless important that the question be posed in the proper way. It is untenable to argue that ideas make the man, and the challenge issued by the late Christian socialist historian R. H. Tawney of the London School of Economics in his *Religion and the Rise of Capitalism* (1926) was successful on this point. More important to us now, however, is to find out why and how Protestantism, or Calvinism in particular, might justify the rapidly evolving changes in the relations of production and by so doing appeal to the bourgeoisie *as a class*. It is at the institutional and ideological level that the subject must be studied, for, in the words of the Swiss historian Herbert Lüthy, it is impossible to reduce the question to the "relationship between the individual adherence to a religious doctrine or ethic and individual efficacy in the economic sphere." It is not necessary to show that Calvinism held a monopoly on the expression of bourgeois class interests in order to establish the connection between it and capitalism. Catholic countries did, of course, eventually "go capitalist," and they developed the matching ideologies of which they had need. That they did so at a later date than Protestant countries does not justify the inference that Protestantism was the unique variable in the mix, but only that it played some role. In the article that follows, Christopher Hill, the distinguished Marxist historian of seventeenth-century England, puts the matter most sensibly when he writes: "There is nothing in protestantism which leads automatically to capitalism: its importance was rather that it undermined obstacles which the more rigid institutions and ceremonies of catholicism imposed." In other words, it was one among many sets of beliefs that could be adapted to carry bourgeois ideology.

# R. H. Hilton

---

## 17

## Capitalism —
## What's in a Name?

          The history of capitalism was once studied by its supporters and its critics on the basis of reasonably common agreement as to what both meant by the term.

"The subject of capitalism" wrote Professor M. M. Postan, "owes its present place in political and scientific discussion to the work of Marx and the Marxians." Many historians substantially follow him. Mr. E. Lipson in his *Economic History of England* on the whole adopts Marx' definition of capitalism. He agrees that its essential feature is the division of classes between propertyless wage-earners and entrepreneurs who own capital, in contrast to the characteristic medieval organisation of industry and agriculture on the basis of the small producer who owned his own means of production.

Definitions, both implicit and explicit, which are much less precise have become fashionable in recent years. A characteristic definition is given by Professor Pirenne describing "the tendency to the steady accumulation of wealth which we call capitalism." Two leading French historians refer to capitalists and capitalism when writing of large scale landed property in the Carolingian era. And it is surely a looser definition than that of Marx which leads Professor Armando Sapori, the historian of Italian industry and commerce in the middle ages, to write of a "capitalist revolution" in the time of Thomas Aquinas.

Pirenne's definition referred to the activities of European merchants in the 12th and 13th centuries. Such definitions face the history teacher and student with the puzzling phenomenon of "the rise of the middle classes" (associated of course with the growth of trade), which seems to start so early, to go on for so long, and to be the explanation of so many different historical movements and events. For although the urban middle class of medieval Europe is said to have begun its notorious career as early as the 10th century, the teacher is faced with the problem of explaining why it was not until the 17th and 18th centuries that this class became the dominant force in society. Why did it take more than 700 years to reach this position if during the whole period it was "rising"?

Not all historians equate the expansion of a class based on trade in a predominantly agricultural society with the expansion of capitalism. Nevertheless the assumption that the two movements were identical is generally made. It is made with care and reservations by the specialists, but usually more unreservedly by those who feel it necessary to simplify for general teaching purposes. The latter do in fact get plenty of justification from some of the eminent specialists writing on medieval trade. For example, Professor de Roover, an outstanding contributor to our knowledge of medieval banking, speaks of the "commercial revolution at the end of the 13th century" which paved the way for "mercantile capitalism, which in most European countries was not replaced by industrial capitalism before the middle of the 19th century." And most of the contemporary contributions by historians of medieval industry and commerce rest on the (usually implicit) assumption that what is being discussed is "capitalism."

Recent researches have shown that an older generation of economic historians who regarded the middle ages as a period of "natural economy" were mistaken. These historians minimised the extent to which commodities were produced for the market. They also underestimated the volume of international trade and the repercussions which it had on economic activity. Pirenne, both in his studies of the growth of medieval towns and in his more general works has had a considerable influence on the teaching and study of medieval economic history. He emphasised that the growth of international trade played a key role in the transformation of feudal society. Many current assumptions about medieval capitalism are derived from his work, and his conclusions have been supported by a number of subsequent studies. Only a few need be mentioned here. The most important have been those which have explored the development of trade and industry in the most advanced economic regions of medieval Europe—Flanders and Italy. The researches of Espinas have shown how great was the industrial activity of the Flemish cloth manufacturing centres, adding detailed material to illustrate the more general remarks of Pirenne. Doren, Davidsohn, Sapori and others have shown how the industrial and commercial activity of the Tuscan towns was even further advanced than that of Flanders. These centres were producing cloth for an international market. They bought their raw material far from the place of manufacture. Wool was imported from England, Spain and elsewhere. Dyestuffs were brought from as far afield as the Black Sea. Naturally this shipment of raw materials and the export of finished goods brought into being an elaborate trading mechanism. Up to the end of the 13th century, the great fairs of Champagne formed the greatest among a number of international emporia where buyers from the south met sellers from the north. In the 14th century merchant importers (Italians especially) established permanent agencies in the manufacturing and trading centres. To avoid the transport of bullion and to overcome the difficulties of currency exchange in coin, letters of exchange were elaborated. This permitted the development of credit not to speak of facilitating large and small scale usury and international public finance.

Investigations which revealed the importance of international trade have been accompanied by studies of agrarian life which again have corrected the older impression of a world composed of closed "natural" economies. The disintegration from the 11th century onwards of the big estates of the Carolingian era, the sub-division of manorial demesnes, the reduction in the numbers of completely servile peasants and the growth of rent paid in money, rather than in labour or in kind, have been described in works written half a century and more ago. Since then economic historians have tended to link up these features more definitely with the contemporary commercial expansion. Yet less detailed study has been made of the market aspects of agriculture than of industry or trade. One reason for this is that evidence for production for the market in agriculture is comparatively scanty, except for England. The break-up of the big landlord estates was delayed longer in England than in France and Western Germany; and so they were the main participants in market production when the demand came, above all in the 13th century. Consequently records of this production for the market have survived in England, as they have not on the continent. Annual manorial and central estate accounts dating from about the middle of the 13th century exist in abundance. But although many valuable monographs concerning individual estates have been written, comparatively little systematic investigation of the exact scope of production for the market has been undertaken. Even so, one modern historian at least has concluded that the 13th century English estates were examples of agricultural capitalism.

There is clearly no little confusion in the study of early forms of capitalism. It is therefore well to look back to what Marx understood by the word. He used it to denote what he described as a "mode of production" of the material wealth of society. He believed that social and political institutions, the ideas and achievements of any society ultimately derive from its "mode of production." He therefore saw the heart of the change from feudal to capitalist society in the change from a primarily agrarian society of petty producers, whose most important social classes were the landlords and their unfree tenants, to a society producing commodities for exchange on the market, whose principal classes were capital-owning entrepreneurs and propertyless wage-earners.

Marx' general views are well enough known, and his chapters on the "primitive accumulation of capital" in Vol. I of "Capital" (Part VIII) are familiar to most economic historians. But of more special interest to the medievalist are three chapters of Vol. III which summarise his less well-known views on the genesis of capitalism.

His main argument is that commerce, in money or goods, however widespread, and however productive of accumulations of money capital, does not *by itself* transform feudal society. The speed and forms of the disintegration of feudal society, on the contrary, "depend[ed] on its solidity and internal articulation" as a "mode of production." It was rather the inherent contradictions within the society than the impact upon it (as from without) of commerce which were the prime causes of its downfall.

In his view, the only form of capital in the ancient and medieval world was the money capital accumulated by merchants and usurers. The typical medieval capitalist was the merchant who drew his profit from the monopoly of the carrying trade between economically backward and geographically remote areas. This profit might be derived from the import of articles of small bulk and high prices (such as spices) from the east; or from the exploitation of the different prices of commodities of everyday consumption as between one local market area and another. The usurer's profit also depended on the backward, rather than on the advanced features of the economy. It was drawn from the extravagance of the landowning classes, and from the perpetual bankruptcy of the peasant and the small artisan. It is only when capital "takes hold of production" that merchants' and usurers' capital becomes subordinate to industrial capital, and only then that it becomes possible to speak of a capitalist "mode of production."

This attitude to medieval money capital led Marx to view with scepticism the claim that the growth of money rent in itself had any direct connection with the decay of feudal relationships. He distinguished "feudal rent" from capitalist ground rent with the same care that he distinguished merchant from industrial capital. The "feudal rent," paid by the peasant to the landowner, whether in labour, kind or money, is analogous to the "surplus-value" which the capitalist derives from the wage earner. Ground rent under capitalism is not the main source of the income of the ruling class. It is merely a "super-profit," derived by the landlord from the capitalist farmer by virtue of his monopoly of a force of nature, the land.

Marx emphasised the corrosive effect of money on the economy of feudal society, whilst he also pointed to some of the retrograde effects of the action of merchants' and usurers' capital. In the cloth industry, the domination of merchants' capital simply deteriorated the conditions of the artisans, so that in some respects they were worse off than the wage earners. Usury, especially in the countryside, caused a depression without altering the character of existing society. "The indebted feudal lord becomes even more oppressive, because he is himself more oppressed." But Marx regarded the growth of merchants' capital as one of the preconditions of the capitalist mode of production.

The most important of these preconditions, especially for the development of capitalist industry, was the concentration of moneyed wealth. In agriculture, the development of money rent assisted the stratification of the rural population, and the growth of capitalist farming. When money rent replaced labour rent, the peasants were able to devote all their time to their own holdings, and the richer among them were able to accumulate surpluses. The poorer peasants, on the other hand, were ruined by the effect of continuous demand for money rent, and by usury. When the rent from land was expressed in money, it became possible to put a money price to the land. This promoted the buying and selling of land; and, as more land came on to the market, the resulting disintegration of traditional holdings further assisted the social differentiation of the peasantry.

The test of any such analysis is not whether or no it sounds convincing, but whether it helps to interpret the facts and solve some of the problems which confront the historian of the middle ages. One of the foremost among such problems is how far older forms of economic structure and social organisation persisted, and how far they remained dominant.

The main new developments in the agrarian life of the later middle ages in Western Europe are well enough known. The legal claims of the lords over the persons of their tenants were reduced; a majority of tenants were freed from the obligation to labour on their lord's demesne; money rent predominated; and the total amount of rent paid over to the landlords decreased. In short, the landlords' control over their peasantry was weakened. Ignoring for the moment the exact relationship between these new developments and increased market production, let us briefly consider how far they involved a fundamental change in the character of society. The big demesnes tended to disappear or to shrink, but they had never constituted more than a fraction of the land under cultivation nor did the techniques used on them differ significantly from those which the peasants used on their own plots. Small scale peasant production continued as before. It is true that, from the 14th century onward, a number of richer peasants, and, a little higher in the social hierarchy, many of the lesser nobility, were beginning to farm on a larger scale. Both needed a certain amount of wage labour. But the amount was not yet enough to change the old system. Furthermore, although a landlord-tenant relationship based on the payment of money rent can be seen in the light of later events to have been an important transitional stage in the decline of medieval agriculture, the main features of feudalism persisted. The landlords continued to take rent from peasants by non-economic compulsion.

The peasants handed over to their lords a portion of their surplus under the same sort of legal and military sanctions as before (though the growth of the state machine made them much more efficient). The fact that the surplus had to be converted by the peasant into money instead of being rendered directly in labour or in kind did not *yet* alter the class relations.

Small scale production operated also in industry. It was a great change when to the activities of the scattered artisans in the villages was added the productive effort of large numbers of workshops concentrated in towns and organised in gilds. This was part of the general economic expansion of the 12th and 13th centuries. In certain centres producing for export, primarily cloth, groups of wealthy merchants seized hold of both ends of the process of production: the provision of raw material, and the marketing of the finished product. In so doing they destroyed the independence of the artisan. But the big merchants of Douai, Ghent or Florence did not revolutionise production. Although some centralisation of the preparation and finishing processes was achieved, the greater part of the work of manufacture was done in the family workshops of the master craftsmen. Furthermore although a proletarian labour force of some dimensions existed in both the Flemish and Italian cloth centres, they were normally concentrated in groups of no more than four or five apiece in the central warehouses of the merchants. For the most part they were employed in the artisan workshops by the master craftsmen, by whose side they worked.

In some respects the big merchants actually retarded the development of production. They were afraid of production for the market by the artisans themselves. Consequently they forbade any collusion between artisans at different stages of the production process. If weavers passed their product straight on to the fullers and dyers, there was risk to the merchant that an element among the craftsmen might control the process of production from within. This almost happened in Flanders in the 14th century. When the political power of the old merchant-draper patrician caste was broken, the weavers of towns such as Ghent threw up an entrepreneur element which would have taken over the organisation of the industry, had not political factors, the rise of the country industry and the decay of the Flemish cloth industry prevented them. It was to avoid this that in Northern Europe and in Italy, the merchants supplying the raw materials insisted that after the completion of each stage of the production process, the product should be brought back to the central warehouse for re-issue to the next craftsman in the chain. Whilst the artisan remained subordinated to the merchant in this fashion, no change in the traditional small scale methods of production was possible.

As in agriculture, so in industry and finance, there was conservatism

as well as change. Great concentrations of merchant capital and elaborate credit and exchange mechanisms were a new feature of the 13th
and 14th centuries. They arose when European industrial exports
restored the balance of trade between Western Europe and the East.
The human agents of this development were those great merchants
of whom the Italian bankers were the finest flower. Yet, in spite of
their seeming power as international financiers, they adapted themselves like their ancestors of the 11th and 12th centuries to the existing
social structure. The very diversity of their interests as bankers, money
lenders, and traders, in any and every commodity, made them the more
adaptable, both politically and socially, to the feudal ruling circles.
For these rulers were their principal market for their luxury commodities, the recipients of private and government loans.

Old methods and old relations of production must be emphasised.
But there were none the less very great changes within medieval
Europe between the 11th and 15th centuries. Without these changes,
subsequent development would have been impossible. The point is
that *in spite of* the expansion of production, of population and of
trade in the 13th and early 14th centuries, the main features of the
old social and political framework remained, not to disappear until
the 17th and 18th centuries. Of course, forms of government and social
relations did change greatly during the middle ages. But the states of
Europe continued to be ruled by and for territorial aristocracies
represented by feudal monarchies. They were not ruled by or for
merchants or industrialists. That is why there had to be bourgeois
revolutions before the full expansion of capitalism was possible. Our
insistence on the persistence of the old structure in industry and
agriculture has been to show the economic basis for the continued
dominance of the old classes. This is one reason why an uncritical
acceptance of the view that capitalism gradually expanded from the
13th century onwards may lead to a falsification of the real history of
capitalism as well as of the preceding epoch.

It follows from the line of criticism outlined above that a changed
direction of research into capitalist origins is needed. This does not
minimise the great value of work done by the various specialists in the
history of commerce, banking and industry. The point is that a number of questions with which the contemporary historians have not
dealt remain to be answered.

In order to promote the solution of the problems both of the
chronology of capitalism and of its earliest characteristics, an approach
might be made under two main heads. First a chronology of the
*predominating* methods and relations of production should be established, and co-ordinated with the much better known chronology of the
growth of commerce. Secondly, the inter-relationships of the economic,
social and political aspects of society should be studied. In particular,

the significance and consequences of the unevennesses in the development of these varied sides of human life require investigation.

We are likely to obtain the truest insight into the end of feudal and the beginning of capitalist society if we pay attention first to the techniques and relations of production. Naturally the commercial expansion of the middle ages must be examined in the closest association with the investigation of changes in the mode of production. But the history of trade alone will not tell us how and when the characteristic relations of feudalism gave place to those of capitalism, how peasant agriculture and artisan industry gave place to large concentrations of capital and of wage labourers, profit by rent to profit drawn from the value given to the finished product by the worker.

Political conditions need closer attention. The political structure and political movements ultimately arise out of the social relations based on production, but economic and political changes do not develop hand in hand. Though they develop unevenly, they are integrally connected. It is not possible to talk of a capitalist *society* when political power is still in the hands of a feudal aristocracy. It is unwise to speak of a capitalist system when the political and legal superstructure of society is still one shaped by pre-capitalist economic conditions. Political power, even in the hands of a ruling class whose economic basis is decaying can still retard the development of new economic and social forms. The history of England under the Tudors and Stuarts and of central and eastern Europe in the 19th century illustrates this point.

What kind of problems demand the attention of the research historian? The growth of capitalist production cannot be measured simply by estimating the level of commodity production. Developments in technique, the growth of the volume of total production, and the manner of application of labour to production also require study. These problems are common to both agriculture and industry; indeed it must not be imagined that in studying capitalist origins, attention should primarily be concentrated on industry. The history of England up to the revolution of 1640 would be but half told if it ignored the growth of capitalism in agriculture.

Questions of technique ought not to be considered simply as problems of technological evolution. What matters is their economic and social effects. One of the main obstacles to the accumulation and investment of capital was the small scale of the units of production in agriculture and industry. Therefore one of the central problems for the student of capitalist origins is to find out about the number, size and methods of operation of the larger farms held in the late 14th and 15th centuries by the thriving elements in the country-side—the big peasants and the smaller gentry. All that we yet know about such farming units is that they were considerably larger than the traditional average peasant holding of the 13th century, being often more than 100 acres in arable area; that they were heterogeneous in composition, including the farmer's ancestral holding, fragments of other peasants' lapsed holdings, and leased-out demesne; and that they must have required hired labour for working them. We also need to know more about the chronology and scope of the turn-over to sheep farming for wool production. It is probable that in the middle of the 15th century England was producing less wool than at the beginning of the 14th century. Yet there has been much loose writing about England being "covered . . . with sheep farms in place of corn fields."

Problems of size of farms and type of farming immediately raise the question of the agrarian labour force of the later middle ages. Was there a proportionate decline or increase in the number of wage labourers in the country-side after the middle of the 14th century? In a recent article Professor Postan has challenged the usual view that wage labour increased in importance during the period. From figures of rising real wages, he deduces a decline in the numbers of wage earners compared with other sections of the population. Landless labourers and small-holders were able, he believes, to move after the Black Death into the vacated holdings of victims of the plague. But who provided the labour on the enlarged holdings of the top stratum of the villeins, the yeomen and the lesser gentry? Whilst 14th and 15th century rentals and surveys confirm that the small-holding class had diminished relatively to other peasant groups, this type of evidence is naturally useless for estimating the number of totally landless. The best English evidence bearing on the subject is not entirely reliable. This is the Poll Tax return of 1381. Unlike earlier returns it gives the occupations of practically all of the taxed personnel. The lists are very incomplete, for there was a mass evasion of the assessors.

But those who hid and were not counted were more likely to be the landless than those whose houses and holdings could not be concealed. The returns are therefore likely to minimise rather than to exaggerate the proportion of wage workers. Such returns as have been examined show a surprisingly high proportion of wage workers, but much further investigation of the returns needs to be done before any firm conclusions can be reached.

An estimate of the amount of wage labour in the late middle ages gives more than an indication of the growth of capitalist social relations. It is in addition indirect evidence for production for the market. As the peasants became landless, they not only became labourers. They became consumers with an income entirely in the form of wages (not all, but mostly money) who needed to buy in the market the goods which previously had not gone through the market. The quantitative significance of the home market in early times is so difficult to measure that international trade (for which there is much better evidence in the form of customs and toll figures) tends to dominate our ideas about production for the market to the exclusion of a sufficient consideration of internal demand. Furthermore, in order to estimate the significance of the production of commodities for the home market in its relation to the productive system as a whole, it is advisable to attempt an estimate of the relative quantities of goods produced for direct use and for the market. A useful addition to what we already know about regional variations in English history would be a survey of how much of the total peasant product in different districts was consumed by the producer, how much went on to the market, and how much was left to spend when the rent was paid.

Some of these considerations apply also to industry. Here too the size and nature of the productive unit is of great importance. The continuing organisation of production on the basis of the artisan family unit prevented the development of capitalist relations of production. But simply to estimate the distance travelled on the road to capitalism from this factor alone would be insufficient. One of the most fruitful ways of tackling the problems of the earliest stages of capitalism in industry would be to compare the history of the cloth manufacture in medieval Flanders and Central Italy with that of England in the 16th and 17th centuries. The concentration of capital and labour, the organisation of the supply of raw material, and of the sale of the finished product by capitalists in the Flemish and Italian towns at the end of the 13th and beginning of the 14th centuries was such that one could almost say that here were societies trembling on the brink of the capitalist mode of production. Yet modern capitalism derived its initial impetus from the English textile industry and does not descend directly from the principal medieval centres. Its foundations were laid in the rural domestic industry which had fled from the traditional urban centres. We know of course that gild restrictionism was one reason for the shift in the centre of gravity from town to country. But this is only one of many aspects of the problem.

One of the principal attractions in studying the failure of medieval Flanders or Italy to develop the capitalist mode of production is that it not only permits, but demands, the widest treatment. The problem is insoluble on the basis of a narrow concentration on technical and economic factors, for social and political developments were all important. How different were the Boinebrokes of Douai and the Bardi and the Acciaiuoli of Florence from the English entrepreneurs of the 17th century! These earlier capitalists had unspecialised commercial interests; they had close financial associations with the leading feudalists; they were disinclined to invest in industrial or agricultural production; they were so enmeshed in the political and social relationships of European feudalism that no break through to a new form of society was to be expected under their leadership. In Flanders at the beginning of the 14th century they lined up with the king of France and the feudal nobility against the urban craftsmen and the peasants. In 14th century Florence, the classic pattern of the bourgeois revolution in its least heroic aspects is anticipated like the spectre of the future— the bourgeoisie allying itself to its defeated feudal enemies out of fear of the workers and artisans, and in so doing destroying its own future as a class.

To use Marx' phrase, the "solidity and internal articulation" of feudal society was still sufficient, even during this period of economic and political crisis, to prevent the new mode of production from establishing itself. But exactly how and why is a matter for further investigation.

It is not enough to study capital, wage labour, and units of production in their economic aspects. Since men make their own history, the historian must know what part the political and social consciousness of the various classes played in advancing or retarding the tempo of capitalist development. Since that consciousness is by no means a direct reflection of the economic activity of these classes, the historian cannot but concern himself with law, politics, art and religion. Neither feudalism nor capitalism are understandable simply as phases in economic history. Society and its movement must be examined in their totality, for otherwise the significance of uneven developments, and of contradictions, between the economic foundation of society, and its ideas and institutions, cannot be appreciated. A failure to appreciate their significance is fatal not only to the understanding of the growth and final victory of the capitalist mode of production, but to an insight into the principal motive force of all human development.

# Pierre Vilar

---

## 18

## Problems of the
## Formation of Capitalism

Do we know more about the origins of capitalism today than we did thirty years ago? Statistical information has accumulated, but our understanding has not always advanced. The crisis of economic thought, not unconnected with the general difficulties of capitalism since 1929, has led some historians into theoretical over-simplifications which are necessarily unhistorical. Their models are not based on reality. I would suggest that, if we are to make the best use of the recent quantitative and statistical discoveries, we ought to return to Marx' approach to the problem of capitalist development. In a sense, this would be merely a return to the original tradition of economic history. Only since 1917–25 have scholars discussed problems of historical methodology and economic development without mentioning Marx. Hence what we need is an *explicit* return to him.

### KEYNESIAN THEORY AMONG THE HISTORIANS: 1929–1950

#### (a) The Starting Point: Earl J. Hamilton

I propose to discuss the influence of the ideas of E. J. Hamilton, though not to attack his work as a scholar, which is above criticism. In 1926 Hamilton undertook to reformulate the old question which had haunted historians and economists since the sixteenth century: what was the precise nature of the link between three obviously connected series of facts: the flooding of Europe by American bullion, the general price-rise of the sixteenth century, and finally the contemporaneous transformations of economic, social and sometimes political relations? Let us briefly sketch in the background.

*In the sixteenth century*, men observed and interpreted at one and the same time. I am thinking less of Bodin, who has been too exclusively studied, than of the theologians of Salamanca and Seville, who were both subtler, and better placed to study "the phenomenon as it emerged."

*From the seventeenth to the nineteenth centuries*, interpretation rather than observation held the field. This is the period of the economists—Petty, Cantillon, Adam Smith, Marx.

*In the last quarter of the nineteenth century*, the desire to measure economic phenomena exactly appeared in Germany. . . .

Hamilton's merit, in 1926, was that he went to the original sources: to that inexhaustible *Archivo de Indias* in Seville, where the smallest piece of gold and silver which passed through the "arca" of the "Casa de Contratación," the organ of Spanish monopoly, was registered. There the logbooks make possible a reconstruction of the life of the sailors, and the economy of the galleons and treasure-fleets. The nearby Andalusian convents and hospitals supply admirable price-series. The first results of these explorations were published in three articles in 1928–1929. As we shall see, Hamilton's later work makes it necessary to begin the discussion of his views with these articles.

They contain (i) a statistical reconstruction of the bullion arrivals (gold, silver) at Seville, of Andalusian prices and wages for a long period, 1503–1660; (ii) a brief critique of customary views on the rise of capitalism (improvements in the techniques of exchange, agrarian transformation, rise of the modern State); (iii) a much more definite critique of Sombart's and Weber's explanations in terms of "capitalist spirit," preferring the analysis of objective conditions. But Hamilton found the decisive conditions neither in the rise of merchant capital, nor in that of ground rent (which he believed to have been less than that of prices in the sixteenth century). Lastly, the articles contain *Hamilton's own hypothesis*: *capitalist development in the sixteenth century derived essentially from the lag of wages behind prices.*

Three curves illustrated this: that of Andalusian prices and wages, based on his own researches, that of French ones (after d'Avenel), and that of English ones (after Wiebe). Hamilton concluded as follows:

In France and England the vast discrepancy between prices and wages, born of the price-revolution, deprived labourers of a large part of the incomes they had hitherto enjoyed, and diverted this wealth to the recipients of other distributive shares . . . For a period of almost two hundred years, English and French capitalists (and, presumably, those of other economically advanced countries) must have enjoyed incomes analogous to those American profiteers reaped from a similar divergence between prices and wages from 1916 to 1919.

Admittedly, in Spain, capitalism did not take root. However, in Spain precisely the gap between prices and wages was closed after 1530. Hamilton's explanation of Spanish decline was the traditional one: medieval outlook, religious expulsions, even "Iberian idleness." Nevertheless, the decisive factor in his view was the narrowing gap between prices and wages.

Important as they were, and great as was the repercussion of Hamilton's 1929 articles, it is only fair to add that they were written up rather hurriedly.

### (b) Critique of Hamilton's Original Presentation

From 1932 Simiand raised queries about the relation between the influx of bullion and the price-rise. Was it legitimate to correlate the absolute quantity of bullion arriving in Seville with price-indices on a single graph? Did not the parallelism of their movement reflect merely the choice of scale? Moreover, the quantity of metal in circulation must be presented on a *cumulative* graph.

Since then other objections have been raised. Carande has shown the importance of the gaps in the documents (1521–25), of the monumental frauds (1557). Other scholars have contested the general value of figures based purely on the "Casa de Contratación." At least one factor has not been measured: the exports of bullion, which imperial debts compensated by an enormous system of internal, and often forced, credit. However, let us not be hypercritical: Hamilton's estimate still stands. But his 1929 graphs present a misleading simplification, though this is the picture which has become accepted to the point of entering textbooks, such as Heaton's, from which the general public derives a most elementary view: *prices rose in proportion to the mass of bullion entering Seville*. Bodin, Azpilcueta, Mercado, in their first stammering formulations of the quantity theory of money, never defined it as crudely as that.

We should be equally cautious about *the gap between prices and wages*. The curve of Andalusian wages is less reliable than that of prices. For England and France the graphs depend on very old figures (Thorold Rogers) or doubtful ones (nobody relies on d'Avenel in France to-day). One may, of course, defend these approximations. Hamilton himself pointed out that his own immense effort at reconstructing prices only confirmed the facts already observed by Tooke and d'Avenel. This is, however, not an argument against hard statistical work, which can alone penetrate the detail of regional, chronological, and concrete historical differences. But if we are to confine ourselves to broad general statements, Hamilton's 1929 thesis was hardly a revelation. As early as 1847, Marx wrote:

In the sixteenth century the amount of gold and silver in circulation in Europe increased as a result of the discovery of American mines, richer and easier to exploit. The result was that the value of gold and silver diminished in relation to that of other commodities. The workers continued to be paid the same money-wage for their labour-power. Their *money-wage* remained stable, but their *wage* had fallen, for in exchange for the same amount of money they now received a smaller amount of goods. This was one of the factors which favoured the growth of capital, the rise of the bourgeoisie in the sixteenth century.

Moreover, Cantillon described the backwardness of Spain as due to the wage-rise in a masterly page, which all the eighteenth-century Spanish economists knew, though they also seem to have arrived at this explanation independently. Thus an unpublished "Discurso," of 1780, says:

The conquest of America caused wages to rise from the fifteenth and sixteenth centuries, the price of foodstuffs having, at an estimate, quadrupled in the course of the century of Charles V and Philip II. Since other countries had not increased the mass of their money, their wages did not rise to any great extent, and they could develop their industry happily, while ours declined. Spain gained momentary wealth in currency, but lost her manufactures and gradually her treasure also migrated to those areas where we find those articles which are consumed, and then produced again for consumption.

Thus Hamilton's article "American Treasure and the Rise of Capitalism" was a fine statistical illustration of a classic hypothesis, but not a new discovery. Beyond this, however, he shocks us by his comparison of two centuries of capital accumulation with four years of American super-profits in 1916–19. Historians are well aware that the seventeenth century differs from the sixteenth, and France in 1688 is not the same as the England of the second Revolution. Economists are aware that four years are not comparable to a secular movement. But in 1951 F. Braudel could still describe the "demonstration" of 1929 as one of "the most remarkable" carried out by the great American economist-historian. If I regret my inability to join him, I do so precisely because Hamilton's "demonstration" had such far-reaching results. It appeared in November 1929, a bitter month for "the rise of capitalism," and this affected its fortunes. Among the economists (who were later to neglect the findings of Simiand, Labrousse, and of Hamilton himself), the most famous, Keynes, drew from the small article of 1929 what I shall call, for the sake of simplification, the germ of inflationist thought. On the eve of the devaluation of the pound sterling, his *Treatise on Money*, basing itself with some reservations on Hamilton (as was legitimate), propounded some generalizations (which were less legitimate). These must be quoted in full, for they dominated future discussion, in spite of being patently only an imaginative digression.

## (c) Keynes and the Danger to History

It would be a fascinating task [wrote Keynes] to re-write Economic History in the light of these ideas, from its remote beginnings—to conjecture whether the civilizations of Sumeria and Egypt drew their *stimulus* from the gold of Arabia and the copper of Africa, which, being monetary metals, left a *trail of profit* behind them in the course of their distribution through the lands between the Mediterranean and the Persian Gulf, and, probably, further afield; in what degree the greatness of Athens depended on the silver mines of Laurium—not because the monetary metals are more truly wealth than other things, but *because of their effect on prices they supply the spur of profit*; how far the dispersal by Alexander of the bank reserves of Persia, which represented the accumulated withdrawals into the treasure of successive empires during many preceding centuries *was responsible* for the outburst of economic progress in the Mediterranean basin, of which Carthage attempted, and Rome ultimately succeeded to reap the fruit (Note: after Hannibal's conquest of the Sierra Morena), whether it was a coincidence that the decline of Rome was contemporaneous with the most prolonged and drastic deflation yet recorded; if the long stagnation of the Middle Ages may not have been *more surely and inevitably caused* by Europe's meagre *supply* of the monetary metals than by monasticism or gothic frenzy, and how much the Glorious Revolution owed to Mr. Phipps . . . Such is a rough outline of the course of prices. But it is the teaching of this Treatise that the wealth of nations is enriched not during Income Inflations but during Profit Inflations— at times, that is to say, when prices are running away from costs.

The phrases italicized show how the notion of *stimulus* insensibly turned into that of *responsible factor*, then into that of *cause*; similarly *flow* of metals became *supply* by the end of the passage. What is meant, in any case, by "the medieval stock of metals"? Moreover, was this "new view of economic history" as new as all that? In 1859 Marx had already written:

The references to the price-rise in ancient Rome following the conquest of Macedonia, Egypt and Asia, dear as they are to the disciples of Hume are of no importance whatever. Neither Hume nor any other eighteenth-century writer disposed of the material which a detailed study of monetary fluctuations calls for: on the one hand a precise history of commodity prices, on the other hand adequate official statistics of the expansion and contraction of the volume of currency and the influx and flight of precious metals.

Both those who deny the importance of historical statistics for economics and those who attempt to invoke them for periods where they can probably not be, and have certainly not been, compiled might profit from these observations.

Hamilton interpreted his first hasty curves thus: "Prices rise in proportion to bullion arrivals." Then Keynes said: "When bullion arrives, prices rise above costs, profits take a turn upward, civilization follows." A curious game of hide-and-seek now began. "History shows . . ." wrote Keynes, reviving Hume's (and Saravia de la Calle's) old arguments, as modernized by Hamilton (who followed Wiebe and d'Avenel). "Keynes, using Hamilton's material, has confirmed one of his best-established theses . . ." "In this argument I follow Keynes . . ." "As Keynes shows . . ." So the historians now wrote. We enter the realm of illusions.

. . .

But History continued to exercise the theoreticians. The monetary experience of the interwar years led Aftalion into his "psychological theory of money." Simiand proposed a "sociological theory"— a sort of Durkheimian money-myth. In spite of some controversies, interpretations converged to prepare the victory of psychological monetary theory and its penetration into history. The publication of the *General Theory* (1936) improved the fortune of Keynesian historical discussion. The prestige of the conservative-revolutionary thinker turned prophet led historians to accept views which I hardly apologize for presenting schematically, for that is how they invaded history. Here are some of them.

(1) *Profit, not savings, stimulates enterprise and hence production.* When the rate of interest falls, while the entrepreneurial profit rises, times are good.

(2) *Price-rises create profit-expectation*, by widening the distance between prices and profit on one hand, interest and wages on the other, and by devaluing the debts of the "active" entrepreneur to the "passive" lender. We ought therefore to favour the rise of prices (if need be by means of managed money).

(3) *Employment* became an urgent pre-occupation in view of contemporary mass unemployment. This led thinkers back to Marx, and demographic studies.

(4) *Mercantilism*, the doctrine of the influx of metal and creative function of luxury, was rehabilitated. Cantillon's views on the decline of Spain were rediscovered, and quoted.

Unfortunately, the last two themes, which might have inspired some fruitful rethinking, had less effect on historians than the first two. After 1940, Hamilton, strengthened by Keynes' support, returned to the schematism of 1929:

The secular downswing of Valencian prices in 1659–89 was steady enough to be predictable and moderate enough to be absorbed in most commercial transactions, but the decline transferred purchasing power from energetic and dynamic debtors to lethargic and passive creditors. Through inventory depreciation and the impact of relatively inflexible costs, falling prices also depressed business profits, the chief source of capital at the disposal of the rising entrepreneurial class.

This conclusion did not confirm Keynes; it invoked him. It suggested an hypothesis for passing from the study of prices to that of society; but it encouraged the dangerous belief that, once a price-movement had been established, we could immediately deduce a definitive corollary from it. Again:

Philip V (1700–1746) increased the price of fine gold in terms of money of account by twenty-five per cent., and of fine silver by approximately thirty-seven per cent. This mild monetary inflation helped to insulate Spain against the world decline in commodity prices during the first third of the eighteenth century, that both reflected and contributed to economic stagnation. Although lacking great talent and occasionally exhibiting traces of mental derangement, Philip V was incomparably superior to any of his predecessors of the seventeeth century. Early in the eighteenth century the uninterrupted decadence of more than a hundred years' standing was arrested and by 1725 stability was achieved . . . An important element of better government that promoted economic recovery, was the cessation of alternate monetary inflation and deflation, that had deranged prices, stifled initiative, frustrated hope, and wreaked havoc during the preceding century.

Here Hamilton assumed, in spite of an important qualification about the *interaction* between prices and economic activity, that a government can "isolate itself" from the effects of a world decline in prices, create stability at will (but the stabilization of 1725–28 was international), or conversely "derange prices," "frustrate expectations" (i.e., expectations of entrepreneurs). In fact, kings are to be classified according to their capacity to be Keynesians, not merely in theory, but in policy.

A third example: in an article of 1942, Hamilton took up the schematic idea that the Industrial Revolution of the eighteenth century resulted exclusively from the gap between wages and prices. This time the statistics (English and Castilian) were extremely solid. On the other hand, the conclusions were cruder than ever:

The high level of profits raised large incomes, which always have supplied practically all the savings in a capitalistic society. As Professor J. M. Keynes has pointed out, savings without investment not only would have proved fruitless, but would have depressed business and thus limited savings. By keeping the normal rate of profit far above the prevailing rate of interest, the lag of wages behind prices stimulated the investment of savings as they took place.

In 1946, Hamilton similarly concluded his great work "War and Prices":

By involuntary sacrificing real incomes *through the price-wages squeeze,* the labouring class bore the burden that implemented material progress, just as labourers and peasants in Soviet Russia, sacrificing through governmental directives have largely financed the mechanization of industry that was instrumental in the recent expulsion of the German invaders.

Postponing criticism, let us note the thesis: whatever the régime, capital investment requires a fall in real wages, which a capitalist régime achieves through price-rise. We shall see how this view was generalized, sometimes presented as self-evident, sometimes as a new discovery of merit.

. . .

## OBJECTIONS TO THE KEYNESIAN INTERPRETATIONS
### (a) The Statistical Method
No criticism of the statistical method is intended here. I believe it to be alone capable of defining fundamental historical processes precisely. What climatologist can claim to work with material as reliable as price based on 20,000 quotations? History should work like a natural science: that was Marx' ideal. But there are times when figures become dangerous.

(1) *When our mathematical apparatus is not justified by the statistical material.* . . .

(2) *When we generalize unduly in space.* Hamilton believes the eighteenth century industrial revolution to be due to the price-wage squeeze. Example: Castile. But Castile did not industrialize. Never mind, Catalonia did. Alas—in Catalonia the "price-wage squeeze" was smaller.

(3) *When we generalize unduly in time.* What does an analogy between the inflation in Italian towns of the thirteenth–fifteenth centuries and Venice in the sixteenth prove? Can we speak of a "rise" in France during the Fronde and under Colbert, merely in order to establish a picture of two centuries of positive movement, as Hamilton does?

(4) *When we generalize on the basis of unequal material.* Hamilton has reservations about Labrousse's statistically irreproachable price series, but talks of "industrial revolution" in France on the basis of Sée the Germain-Martin. He illustrates his views on the Spanish eighteenth century by the claim (no sources are given) that the real wage of the Soviet workers fell during the first five-year plans. Throughout we have the attempts to evolve a unique pattern, applicable to all times and places, and to all economic categories, which are always defined with excessive crudity and little analysis.

### (b) Economic Categories and the Connexion between Them

(1) *Profit and profit expectation.* Historians, like economists, statesmen or trade union leaders, may usefully observe the movement of prices which encourages or discourages production. But "profit-expectation" is not the same thing as profit. "Economic man" does not long remain content with promises such as the short-lived illusion created by unstable currencies. We must therefore study total profits concretely and directly. All attempts to measure profit in terms of its variable components presupposes a theory of profit, which ought to be clearly set out.

(2) *Interest.* Can we say that "interest" and "profit" are antagonistic since both may increase as a result of the greater exploitation of labour? Who was right before the nineteenth century: the old economists who confused interest with "rent of money," and believed that its rate fell with monetary abundance, or the banker Cantillon, who believed the opposite? But can we investigate this matter satisfactorily at a time when different forms of interest are still intermingled: the usurer's loans for consumption purposes, loans to early capitalist production (often camouflaged as exchange operations), and loans to States and Princes, which may be both one and the other? Let us add that from the seventeenth century onwards, private enterprise rests on well-analysed combinations of loans at fixed interest and risk-and-profit-sharing investment. To oppose the "dynamic" debtor to the "lethargic" creditor is to fall into convenient abstraction.

(3) *Rent.* In societies where ninety per cent. of the population lives on the land, can we pass lightly over agricultural incomes? Hamilton holds that in periods of expansion, rents rise more slowly than prices. All Labrousse's results contradict him, as do my own for Spanish Catalonia (1716–1806): there, in spite of complications, it is clear that lords and their farmers accumulated wealth faster than prices rose: sometimes five-fold. In any case, how can we give a single solution to the problem of rent, when this depends on the length of leases; on the proportion of money payments as against payments in kind; on the "super-profits" of those who hold stocks in times of famine; on the progress of productivity; on the diminishing returns of newly colonized land, and lastly on the local variations in the evolution from feudal to capitalist rent which are affected by the differing reactions of the seigneurial community? Innumerable discussions show that 9-year leases favour farmers, 3-year leases favour owners at a time of price-rise. Labrousse has shown (what had hitherto been neglected) the immense importance of the periodic "crises de subsistances" [food shortages] in the history of class conflicts. Money-rent reacts towards price changes in the opposite way to rent in kind, and the struggle between landlords and tenants may modify the proportions of each. In Catalonia, in 1793,

a few steps from the French frontier, we read newspaper advertisements by lawyers offering to increase lords' feudal revenues by the mere manipulation of the old "capbreus" (land registers).

(4) *Commercial profits.* Until the establishment of a "world market," European mercantile capitalism gambled on the exchanges between scarce products (precious and exotic, or, in time of crisis, mass consumption goods like grain): i.e. on contracts between places whose conditions of production are in no sense comparable, and on the monopoly of the carriers. It is impossible to judge these profits by the price-wage gap in the merchants' own countries. Hamilton, by the way, overlooks the periodic super-profits which arose during crises, when commerce became monopolistic and wages slumped. Moreover, since these exogenous profits may be invested, they cannot be underrated in the genesis of the Industrial Revolution.

(5) *The price-wages gap.* Let us suppose, after all, that the price-wages gap remains the chief factor in accumulation, even in these old societies. Does the curve of the "general price-level" and that of the *individual daily money wage* really give us adequate information about "profit," when the "general price level" is made up of monopoly prices (Indian spices), of the market price of grains (agitated by the "crises" and burdened with seigneurial and ecclesiastical rents), of the price of cloth (of which it is difficult, in an artisanal and corporative economy, to calculate the labour cost in daily money wages)?

But even if we grant that the market-price has triumphed, that feudal payments have disappeared, that wage-labour predominated (and by then we should no longer be in the "formative" stage of capitalism), the gap between the market-value of goods and the remuneration of the workman-producer for those goods is not the gap between an abstract "price-level" and an abstract "wage-level." We must keep a strict account of the time of labour, wages in kind (common in the old economy). The effective yield of labour is not the same in out-work, in workhouses, in industrial colonies. Finally, machines make possible the substitution of cheaper labour (women, children) for dearer, and were indeed largely introduced for this purpose. How much reliance can we therefore place on daily-wages series—even of "real-wages"—based on a few categories of workers?

Admittedly the *global remuneration of labour* and *global capital accumulation* are antagonistic. But the entrepreneur who increases the time and intensity of labour by substituting one kind of labour for another through the introduction (late though it usually occurs) of machines, may easily raise his profits, even if the wage in money-units keeps pace with prices, as Simiand has demonstrated. Marx himself argued that the demand for higher money-wages did not necessarily inhibit capitalist prosperity, and was indeed the best method of forcing employers to undertake technical progress.

The stress on profit movements as the *only creative* and effective force may also imply the suggestion (conscious or not) that the "sacrifice" of the working class, *whatever the régime, is necessary.* Nevertheless, the theoretical confusion between "profit inflation" and the *profit drawn solely from inflation* leads us to attribute capital accumulation not to the exploitation of labour, but to a sort of Providence called "conjuncture" [market conditions].

(6) *The monetary thesis: inflation and quantity theory.* Moreover, the Keynesian historians also hold a controversial monetary theory. This is, in the initial stages, suggested metaphorically: thus we heard of "flux" of metals, "spur" of profit. We slip into the idea that abundance of metals, or any monetary abundance, *causes* the general price-rise. This is to direct attention to an important, but not the most important aspect, of price-movements.

For *similar* price-movements make less sense than *divergent* ones. There are the differences of *place*, such as those between regions. There are differences of *short period*, such as the "social gap" between wheat and rye prices, to which Labrousse has drawn attention. There are differences of *long period*, which reveal the uneven progress of productivity and bring about substitutions: wheat is grown instead of wine, coal substituted for charcoal, etc. Let us recall Colin Clark's and Fourastié's point about the difference between manufactured goods, which undergo technological cheapening, and services—which do not.

"General movements" smooth out these internal and contradictory variations. Let us imagine an index for recent years which was to combine the price of bread with that of aureomycin: originally scarcity price, then a high manufacturing price, then (as productivity leaped forward) a low manufacturing price. Retrospective computations are open to such confusions.

Naturally "general movements" are real. The cost of living "goes up" to-day as in the sixteenth century, i.e. money will progressively buy less goods. Our problem is thus largely one of money. But let us not make the simple assumption that prices rise *because* money is plentiful, as so many recent historical writings assume. Concomitance does not imply a single causal order. There is at least a dilemma; more probably, the two things *interact*. And it is curious that historians favour a universal "quantity" view, at a time when economic theorists increasingly believe, as did Marx, that the mass of money in circulation varies with the volume of transactions and the movement of prices, and not the other way round.

But let us turn neither to theory, nor to authority, but to history. There is no increase in economic activity or in prices without its accompanying buzz of monetary phenomena of all sorts. But *what is the order of the events?* If we inject money into or keep it within a closed and inactive system, one of two things may happen: if the money is "strong" and internationally negotiable, it will flow out; if it is "internal" money, a pure fiduciary symbol, whose relations with "strong" currency are unstable, there will be an *exchange crisis*. Moreover, "strong" money never "streams" into a system *unless attracted by production*. The old economists, theologians, and monetary technicians of the sixteenth and seventeenth centuries (often the same people) were not much mistaken on these points.

But strong and internationally valid money in that period meant gold and silver. Did they *create* activity or *reflect* it? Keynes suggests the former, on the basis of ill-considered examples of "looted treasures" injected into a vaguely defined "world" without any opposite flows. But he does also refer to *mining*. And mines are not sunk, closed, or reopened at any moment, as Marx pointed out, when criticizing Hume. Everybody knows that the "spur of profit" operated on mining entrepreneurs as elsewhere, and that the Discoveries corresponded to an increased demand for money. But if any psychological or sociological symbol might have created "profit-expectation," why the stubborn search for a *commodity*: gold and silver-money? Unless we accept the idea of *commodity-money*, we shall certainly be unable to understand history, and probably also theory. Gold, a commodity and as such exchanging for other commodities, goes only where these are produced. Even in Spain, when production ceased, gold ceased to arrive or flowed out, a fact which Hamilton, Keynes, Simiand cause us to forget, since they write as if they assumed that gold was not *"bought" with anything*. We may indeed have unilateral flows of gold; but these lead to hoarding, in which case we can forget about them, for hoarding is the very opposite of investment. This point was also anticipated by Marx.

We should, of course, study the historic routes of the precious metals, because these were pursued by the most active groups and moved along the great channels of trade, towards the most productive. The mercantilists saw this correctly. Long before Keynes, Marx "rehabilitated" mercantilism as the first, the crudest theory of the bourgeoisie, but not a "mistaken" theory, and one which did not conflict with its fundamental principle. In the capitalist system, the laurels go to the group which "makes money" as they do to the individual who "makes money." We are therefore not dealing with money as a sort of smoke, or product of the imagination.

Simiand imagined that money was a sort of myth, a "magic symbol," whose function was disturbed as soon as men sought for the reality of "purchasing-power" which lay behind it. But the men who really manipulated money always looked for this reality. The money-changer of the fifteenth century *weighed* his *écus*; for him they were a commodity. The royal official might see in money something *created by the State,* a means of policy. Only the "stupid and crude populace" incapable of finding its way among the 80-odd forms of coin which circulated in seventeenth-century France, had to put its trust in *denomination* alone, only to be robbed when one sort of coin was changed for its equivalent denomination in another.

This popular inferiority in monetary matters is what Marx attempted to combat in his 1847 lectures, by bringing out the concept of the workers' "real wage." The complete application of the "sliding scale of wages" would finally abolish it, though not capitalism. But if it is advantageous that money should be "a name" for the masses, for the capitalists it must nevertheless remain a commodity. Gold, silver, copper, have their value, founded on their cost. When the industrial cost of copper was such that, in seventeenth-century Castile, it became more advantageous to melt the metal in than to use it for coinage, the inflation of copper currency was arrested, as Hamilton has shown. How, then, could he study the "general movement of prices" without considering also the *conditions of production* of both the precious metals and the other commodities?

Let us suppose [wrote William Petty] that the production of a measure of wealth requires the same amount of labour as that of an ounce of gold . . . This is the real and complete way to determine the price of goods.

This conception of the old economists must, once again, become our point of departure.

## THE PROBLEMS RECONSIDERED

Hamilton's contribution to history has been admirable. We neither need nor should wish to reject or to overlook it. All I want to show is that, on the basis of the economic views of the old classics, the historian can undertake more complex and more fruitful researches than those which simple monetary models would suggest to him.

(1) *Wages and long-term trends.* Hamilton did not hesitate to claim that, if Petty had known his 1929 articles, he could not have put forward the subsequently so influential view that wages tended to fall to the minimum cost of living of the labourer. Since it is statistically proved that real wages can fall, he argued, they are obviously not minimum wages.

This is merely the old confusion between *individual daily wage* and the global remuneration of labour. In the pre-capitalist period, the number of labourers and the annual period of labour were both modest. The rising capitalism of the eighteenth century constantly demanded the employment of everybody, women and children included, for the longest possible hours and at the lowest wages. In how many families did supplementary wages, or more numerous and longer work-days compensate for the fall in the individual salary of the father? If this had not been so, how can we explain the fact that the number of men increased at the very periods when Hamilton proved that real wages were falling? Moreover, in the short run, the earnings of labour could fall well below the subsistence minimum: the crises of high grain-prices killed vast numbers of men. Why then did they become so much less murderous in the eighteenth century? Hamilton's curve can no more solve this problem than it can solve many others.

Clearly if research is to explain the possibilities of capital accumulation it must tackle problems of *demography*, the proportion of the *active population*, the *time of labour* and its *intensity*.

(2) *"Conjuncture" and "profit-inflation" or "surplus value" and "capitalist structure"*? A superficial observer might conclude that, by deriving the possibility of profit solely from the "price-wage" squeeze and by correlating capitalist accumulation and the pauperization of the labourer, Hamilton supported the Marxist concept of "surplus value."

But if he attempted merely to show that a certain gap between value produced and value consumed is essential to any expansion of production, he has merely proved an evident law of all societies. However, if value produced rises, nothing prevents consumption from also rising, while a margin for investment is maintained. Only when there is private property in the means of production and a permanent excess supply of labour does a tendency to skim off the maximum amount from mass consumption make itself felt through the operation of the free market. If we fail to define these specific historical conditions, we discuss wages without defining the wage-earners, capital without defining capitalism.

Hamilton asks us to seek the causes of the introduction and development of capitalism in "profit-inflation," the causes of profit-inflation in price-rises, and the causes of these in the accelerated production of precious metals. Nobody denies that periods of rapid monetary devaluation, whether in 1851–7, in the sixteenth or the eighteenth centuries, represented conjunctures favourable to capital and dangerous to real wages. But the historian's business is not only to discover favourable conjunctures, but to explain the appearance of economic "structures." The appearance of capitalism required a far more complex mechanism than the simple influence of American bullion on European prices. History does not start with Christopher Columbus.

(3) *Conditions of production and general price movements.* The Hamiltonian model rests on the observation of the "general movement of prices." But if all prices rise, it is logical to seek the cause of this in the cost (the conditions of production) of the precious metals which serve to measure them, while remembering that the conditions of pro-

duction of other commodities also change over time, and vary from one place to another. It may be useful to establish some elements of periodization for these changes.

(a) 1450–1525: *before the discoveries*. In Europe this was a period of major changes: of renewed population rise, after the great plagues and wars; of technical inventions (50 important ones, it has been calculated, against 43 in the eighteenth century), of social crisis, such as the struggle of peasants against lords, which prepared the subsequent contrast between Eastern and Western Europe, between Castile and Catalonia. In this period the current European products were cheap, metals and exotic products at a premium. Hence the passion for discovery and overseas trade. If Castile came to the fore then, it was because it was, from the fifteenth century on, a dynamic and creative country, with its association of sheep-breeders (the *Mesta*), its Andalusian and Basque navy, its fairs (e.g. at Medina). Thus the fact that the new metals arrived through Spain is consequence as much as cause.

(b) 1525–1600: *the price-rise*. We distinguish three elements in the conditions of production of American metals: (i) looting, (ii) forced labour and (iii) technical progress (the mercury amalgam process). This drastic fall in the cost of monetary metals corresponds well enough to their general devaluation.

However, if this inflationist invasion stimulated the production of certain countries, it finally destroyed that of Spain. Hamilton says that this was because the movement of wages kept pace with prices there. *But why?* Once again we must thus ask questions about population, emigration, hoarding, imperial indebtedness, investments in public securities such as the *juros* and *censos* which built a pyramid of parasitism, monopolies such as the Mesta and the port of Seville, the internal resistance of the feudalists, the existence in Spain itself of a quasi-colonial labour force (the Moriscoes). The problems, it is clear, are complex: economic structure counts for at least as much as conjuncture.

It is equally important to compare the conditions of production in Spain with those in other countries. For the metals which enriched Spain parasitically (and therefore in the end ruined her) flowed out into those countries *where its purchasing-power was greatest*. The market was thus unified, money redistributed. But the relations between the cost of production of the metals and that of other commodities were expressed *in terms of exchange-rates*, as the Spanish theologians who meditated on interest and usury understood, if they did not explain.

(c) *Seventeenth-century stagnation*. As the sixteenth gave way to the seventeenth century, the vertical drop in colonial population which has recently been demonstrated produced its consequences: mining profits fell, mines were abandoned for agriculture. This rise in the costs of silver production led to a fall in prices, in Spain from about

1600, elsewhere somewhat later. Spain attempted to meet this with a catastrophic inflation of *vellon* (mixed copper and silver, later copper) currency. Other countries reacted differently, though in general with some difficulty.

(d) *The eighteenth century.* Though its phases remain to be investigated in detail it is certain that the eighteenth century, with its price-rise and its favourable conditions for profits and capital, was also the century of revival for the Hispano-Portuguese colonial systems. Colonial mining once again profited from a numerous and available labour force. But Hamilton's model would lead us to confuse England, France and Spain, whose fortunes are not comparable in this period. If we wish to understand events in this century it is better to follow the structural analysis which Labrousse has made for France, demonstrating a dialectical process: bourgeois enrichment—popular impoverishment—revolution.

(4) *The "primary accumulation" of capital.* If capitalism is to function, moreover, capital must first have been accumulated before the establishment of a capitalist society properly speaking: private property in the means of production and the free market must have been established, the labour-force proletarianized. How could this have taken place?

The problem is thorny. If it is difficult to imagine a feudal society evolving "under its own steam" without the help of an exogenous urban or commercial factor, it is equally difficult to believe that in societies, ninety per cent of whose members were peasants, such transformations could have taken place as it were on the margin of agrarian society.

Research might therefore seek to elucidate certain key questions; the agrarian revolutions of the fifteenth and sixteenth centuries; the relative importance of feudal payments in money and in kind; the part played by the "super-profits" which agrarian sellers made during the periodically recurring famines; the problem of population and the vicissitudes of the landless labourer; and the appearance of agrarian undertakings requiring capital investment, such as irrigation arrangements, plantations, equipment for production for the market, all of which appear earlier than is often supposed. A question of particular relevance is how feudal revenues were divided, by means of the system of "adjudications" and in other ways, between an idle aristocracy and an intermediate class of "merchant-cultivators" or similar types who transformed seignorial revenues and held them ready for new types of investment; in other words how feudal revenues came to be mobilized for capitalist investment. My own work on Catalonia in the eighteenth century brings out the importance of these factors.

But if agriculture is perhaps the most obvious source of what Marx called "primary accumulation," there are others without which, he believed, the pace of capitalist expansion would have been slowed down considerably.

There is *loot* such as Spain drew from the Conquest of Granada, the African expeditions and her colonial conquests, and others from smuggling and piracy against the Spanish colonial monopoly. There is the *large-scale trade* which relied, as we have seen, on remote or temporary disequilibria of prices and not on the gap between realized values and wages. To regard mercantile enterprise in this period as a form of modern capitalism would be as mistaken as to overlook the part which "venturing" commercial capital played in the early stages of the first great productive investments. There is *the exploitation of colonial areas* by means of slavery, forced labour or quasi-feudal methods, which combined with profit by trade and profit by looting to extract wealth from the world outside Western and Central Europe for the benefit of the economically and politically advanced parts of our continent.

Such things are not merely more important than price-movements; they may provide clues to them. Thus the so-called "long waves" of prices and economic activities—the price-rise of the sixteenth, the deflation of the seventeenth centuries, etc., have long puzzled the student; some writers, like Marjolin, go so far as to regard them as "irrational phenomena." But might we not see them in terms of a historic alternation between an increase in the exploitation of colonial and European labour, recalling Marx' profoundly suggestive phrase: "The veiled slavery of the wage-workers in Europe needed for its pedestal slavery pure and simple in the New World."

It is not the business of this article to suggest positive solutions to the numerous problems I hope to have raised. Its purpose has been negative: to investigate the claims of one influential method of analyzing the rise of capitalism, and to demonstrate its failure to solve the problems it claimed to solve.

I would contend that the time is now ripe for erecting some sort of building from the enormous mass of facts accumulated by the German historical school, the enormous mass of figures accumulated in the past 25 years. This requires a theory of economic development; and though economists of all schools are to-day busily engaged on the attempt to construct such a theory, Marx, who first consciously faced our problem in its modern form, still provides the best guide to its solution.

# Christopher Hill

## 19

## Protestantism and
## the Rise of Capitalism

It is over 30 years since historical thinking in this country was stimulated by the publication of Professor Tawney's *Religion and the Rise of Capitalism*. Most historians would now accept the existence of some connection between protestantism and the rise of capitalism, though Professor Trevor-Roper is a conspicuous exception. But there is little agreement on the nature of the connection. Seventeenth-century protestants themselves emphasized the fact that godly artisans had been the backbone of the Reformation, and that protestantism in its turn had proved to be good for trade and industry; and they were right on both points. Nevertheless there are still untidinesses at the edge of the thesis. The object of this article is to try to clear away some of them, by developing hints given by Professor Tawney himself.[1]

One criticism, levelled especially against Weber, is that he made inadequate chronological distinctions, illustrating the causal influence of protestantism in moulding "the capitalist spirit" by quotations from 17th century writers; even Professor Tawney relies largely on Baxter and Bunyan in his discussions of English Puritanism. Another criticism is that some of the countries in which Calvinism developed in its classical form (Scotland, Hungary) were economically backward; many aristocratic supporters of, for instance, the French Huguenots, were not at all bourgeois in origin or outlook. A third criticism is that Weber and Tawney emphasised points of doctrine which would not have seemed central either to the reformers or to their critics. Protestant teachings on usury, callings, treatment of the poor, and so forth, were peripheral: granting that individual protestants contributed to the rise of a capitalist ethic by what they said on these subjects, it still has not been shown that protestantism as such is associated, either as cause or effect or both, with the rise of capitalism. If connections are to be established, they must be sought in the central doctrines of the

---

[1] R. H. Tawney, *Religion and the Rise of Capitalism* (Penguin ed.), pp. 101–3.

reformers, those which most sharply differentiated them from their Roman Catholic contemporaries. And then we have to face a fourth objection in the fact that the reformers thought they found their doctrines in the New Testament and St. Augustine. Are we to regard these writings as emanations of the capitalist spirit? If not, why not?[2]

The central doctrine of protestantism is justification by faith. The central target of the reformers' attack was justification by works. We must begin here.

When protestants criticised the doctrine of justification by works, they were not saying that charitable works should not be performed. They were attacking the purely formal routine actions by which many Roman Catholic theologians taught that merit could be acquired—telling of beads, saying of paternosters, giving of candles. Luther distinguished between "two kinds of works: those done for others, which are the right kind; . . . and those done for ourselves, which are of smaller value." "We wear and consume our bodies with watching, fasting and labour, but we neglect charity, which is the only lady and mistress of works. . . . Paul not only teacheth good works, but also condemneth fantastical and superstitious works."[3] "Fixed holidays and fasts, fraternities, pilgrimages, worship of saints, rosaries, monasticism and such-like" were the "childish and unnecessary works" which the Confession of Augsburg denounced in 1530 as having been exclusively emphasized by popular Roman Catholic preachers Tyndale, Foxe and other early English reformers delighted to draw up lists of these superstitious works, by which, they did not fail to point out, the church invariably drew money from the pockets of the faithful.[4]

These "extern matters and ceremonial observations, nothing conducing to any spiritual purpose" were what the reformers had most of all in mind when they denounced "works." In discussions between protestants and papists in England in 1559, the former singled out for

---

2 By "the capitalist spirit" I mean something more specific than a love of money, which can be found in earlier ages. I mean an ethos which, within the framework of a market economy, *emphasizes* productive industry, frugality and accumulation, as good in themselves. On this definition, banks and usury are not central to the problem, since they existed before the rise of capitalism. (See R. H. Hilton, "Capitalism—What's in a name?," *Past and Present*, No. 1.)

3 Ed. B. L. Woolf, *Reformation Writings of Martin Luther,* II, p. 110; cf. pp. 121–3, 293; Luther, *Commentary on Galations* (English translation, 1807), II, p. 216; cf. pp. 148, 270. In discussing theology, I have by preference quoted Luther, since he initiated the protestant break-through, and Calvin only secondly: for my concern here is with the *theological* distinction between protestantism and catholicism. I do not wish to imply that Lutheranism, as it came to exist in Germany and Scandinavia, contributed significantly to the capitalist spirit.

4 William Tyndale, *An Answer to Sir Thomas More's Dialogue* (Parker Soc., 1850), pp. 202–3; J. Foxe, *The Acts and Monuments* (4th ed., n.d., ed. J. Pratt), I, pp. xxii–iii, 61, 74–6, 85–6.

criticism the sermon on Candlemas Day, in which "there is also a history of a woman which never did good deed, but only that she had continually kept a candle before our lady," in return for which Mary saved her from hell. "What occasion of dissolute life and sin may be ministered to simple people by these and an infinite number of such like fables, it is easy to perceive."[5] The protestant objection was to mechanical actions in which the heart was not involved.

Where "good works" in the wider sense were concerned—acts of mercy or charity—a protestant thought that *what* a man did was less important than the spirit in which he did it. Justification by works led to a formal righteousness: by performing a round of good works, one bought oneself off from the consequences of sin. Grace came through the sacraments, through the miracle of the mass. Penance was imposed by the priest: it could be performed without true inner penitence. But protestants thought the effectiveness of the sacraments depended on the moral state of the recipient. Man was justified by faith alone: by turning towards God with the full consciousness of his moral being. He was saved not by his own righteousness, not by his own efforts, but by the righteousness of Christ imputed to the favoured few whom God had chosen. Once a protestant had acquired this sense of unity and close personal relationship with God, his attitude towards the world, to sin and to repentance was transformed. The goodness of an action depended not on what that action was (the pagan philosophers had attained to moral virtue) but on the conviction, the love of God, which inspired it. "Christ is eaten with the heart," said Cranmer in debate before Protector Somerset. "Only good men can eat Christ's body."

On Luther's visit to Rome, as he climbed Pilate's stairs on hands and knees, repeating a paternoster on each stair and kissing it, he wondered if this really did release souls from Purgatory. From Erasmus's Greek Testament he learnt that "penetentian agite" meant not "do penance" but "be penitent." This he described as a "glowing" discovery. In his consciousness of sin, Luther had come to hate the God whose commandments he could not keep: until his outlook was transformed by the Pauline sentence "the just shall live by faith." Henceforth, for him, external ceremonial, outward actions, were contrasted with internal conviction, a change of heart. God ceased to be an enemy to be propitiated: works flowed from grace, but man was not justified by them. He had been justified long before, or else his works were worthless. A good man made a good work, not a good work a good man. Faith was "nothing else but the truth of the heart."[6]

This insistence that each believer should look inward to his own heart contributed to give protestantism its fundamentally individualist bias. Papal doctrine since the 14th century had postulated a common

---

[5] Ed. E. Cardwell, *A History of Conferences* (1840), p. 90.
[6] Luther, *Galatians*, I, p. 230, cf. II, pp. 299–300.

store of grace, accumulated in the first instance by Christ, and added to by the merits of saints, martyrs and all who performed more good works than were necessary for their own salvation. Monks and chantry priests, by dedicating their whole lives to religious exercises, built up a superfluity of "works." "This treasure," said the Bull Unigenitus in 1343, "is . . . entrusted to be healthfully dispersed through blessed Peter, bearer of heaven's keys, and his successors as vicars on earth . . . to them that are truly penitent and have confessed." Individuals could draw on this treasury of grace only through the mediacy of priests, whose authority came through the hierarchy from the Pope. Indulgences, sold by papal permission, were cheques drawn on the treasury of merits: they could shorten time in Purgatory, for the dead as well as for the living. Thus good works were bought and sold, said Luther.[7]

Justification by works, then, did not mean that an individual could save himself: it meant that he could be saved through the Church. Hence the power of the clergy. Compulsory confession, imposition of penance on the whole population—the majority of whom were illiterate—together with the possibility of withholding absolution, gave priests a terrifying power. Obedience to the Church was an obligatory part of the virtue of humility. "If she [the Church] shall have defined anything to be black which to our eyes appears to be white," said St. Ignatius, "we ought in like manner to pronounce it to be black." Protestants would inculcate such blind faith in no earthly institution or man, but only in God; and fortunately God's pronouncements were more subject to argument than those of the Church. Even the Bible was checked by what the Spirit of God wrote in the believer's heart.[8]

Justification by works meant that salvation out of communion with the Church was unthinkable. For the reformers, the direct relationship of the soul to God was what mattered: the priest, the Church as an institution, were quite secondary. So from the very beginning the protestant revolt against the Roman Church was from the nature of its theology an individualist revolt. That of course was not how Luther and his contemporaries saw it. They began by criticising specific abuses —sale of indulgences, commutation of penance. But even when they went on to attack confession and monasticism, their starting-point remained the same: a rejection of outward ceremonial enacted without a change of heart. Here is Luther on monasticism:

"Hitherto it hath been the chief holiness and righteousness . . . [for a man] to run into monasteries, to put on monkish apparel, to be shaven, to wear a hempen girdle, to give himself to fasting and prayer, to be clothed with hair-cloth, to lie in woollen garments, to observe

---

[7] Luther, *Reformation Writings*, II, p. 214.

[8] Loyola, *Spiritual Exercises*, part ii, No. 13; Luther, *Galatians*, I, p. 284; Tyndale, *Answer to More*, p. 51; Jean Calvin, *Institutes of the Christian Religion* (trans. H. Beveridge, 1949), I, pp. 72–5.

an austere manner of living, and in fine, to take upon him monkish holiness and religion; and thus, resting in a show of good works, we knew not but we were holy from top to toe, having regard only to works and the body and not to the heart, where we were full of hatred, fear and incredulity, troubled with an evil conscience, knowing almost nothing rightly of God. . . . But there is another righteousness which God esteemeth and accepteth, which also we must consider; it consists not in a grey garment, nor in a black or white cowl, but in a pure conscience. . . . When the heart is pure, the house is unto it as the field, and the field as the house; the market is as much esteemed as the monastery; and on the contrary, neither remaineth unto me any work, place or garment which I count profane; for all things are alike unto me, after that holiness hath fully possessed my heart."[9]

Luther thus ended the dual morality, not merely by bringing the ascetic out into the world, but by telling him that his standards were all wrong. Monastic routine could be imposed only on men and women who did not know the direct relationship to God which Luther had experienced and taught. Once the heart was changed, it would leap beyond the formal confines of monastic restrictions into Christian liberty. "He that bideth in the world, as the monks call it," wrote Tyndale, "hath more faith than the cloisterer: for he hangeth on God in all things."[10] For Christians no action can be casual or perfunctory: the most trivial detail of our daily life should be performed to the glory of God, should be irradiated with a conscious co-operation with God's purposes. This was not originally to sanctify the life of all lay-men: on the contrary, Luther held that the world belonged to the devil. But the true Christian could live in the devil's world without being of it, because of his saving faith.[11]

But my motives, my intentions, the spirit in which I perform an action, are within my control. Philosophically, protestant theologians believed that the inclination of one's will towards God came from outside, from God; practically, as moralists, they emphasized the careful scrutiny of motives, the conscious attempt to see that one's will was turned in to the divine harmonies. "Impenitence is the unpardonable sin," declared Luther, for whom faith was "the most difficult of all works." Faith without a desire of repentance is as worthless as repentance without faith, wrote Calvin. No priest can search the secrets of my heart.[12] "Is there any angel," asked the Homily Concerning Prayer, "any virgin, any patriarch or prophet among the dead,

---

[9] Luther, *Thirty-four Sermons* (Dublin, 1747), pp. 76–7.
[10] Tyndale, *Doctrinal Treatises* (Parker Soc., 1848), p. 280.
[11] N. O. Brown, *Life against Death*, chapter XIV, *passim*. The Cathari, who also thought the world was the devil's, drew the conclusion that what happened there was a matter of indifference: trade and usury were therefore permissible.
[12] Luther, *The Bondage of the Will* (1823), p. 23; *Reformation Writings*, I, p. 259; Calvin, *Institutes*, I, p. 29.

that can understand or know the reason of the heart?" The question expected the answer No. I, and I alone, can know whether the illuminating contact with God has been established. If it has not, all the priests and all the ceremonies in the world will not establish it. Compulsory confession cuts across the individual's direct relation to God; it is "both tyrannical [to the sinner] and insulting to God, who, in binding consciences to his Word, would have them free from human rule."[13] For the godly, morality should be self-imposed: unquestioning obedience to the priest was a positive hindrance.

Protestants thus had a new measuring-rod. Duties, Calvin declared, are estimated not by actions but by motives. "There is nothing which God more abominates than when men endeavour to cloak themselves by substituting signs and external appearance for integrity of heart." To wear mourning apparel from mere social convention, without feeling real grief, was evil and hypocritical. Scholastic sophists, Calvin continued, "talk much of contrition and attrition, torment the soul with many scruples, and involve it in great trouble and anxiety; but when they seem to have deeply wounded the heart, they cure all its bitterness with a slight sprinkling of ceremonies." "There is nothing which gives men greater confidence and licence in sinning than the idea that after making confession to priests they can wipe their lips and say, I have not done it."[14]

Bishop Fisher regretted that he was not left time enough between condemnation and execution to perform so many good works as he believed to be necessary to salvation. Such good works no doubt included frequent repetition of the Lord's Prayer. Luther prided himself on having freed people from this mechanical repetition of the paternoster in the gabbling manner which has given the word "patter" to the language. "Neither words nor singing (if used in prayer)," said Calvin, "avail one iota with God, unless they proceed from deep feeling in the heart."[15] The Preface to the First Prayer Book of Edward VI complained that when men attended services in Latin "they understood not, so that they have heard with their ears only: and their hearts, spirit and mind have not been edified thereby."

Ceremonies are of value only in so far as they contribute to this edification of the believer, helping him to understand the act of worship he is taking part in. Hence Bible and Prayer Book in the vernacular; emphasis on preaching rather than on prayer and sacraments; music must edify and not distract—hence metrical psalms and hostility to organs, polyphony and choristers, dislike of images and gaudy

---

13 Calvin, *Institutes,* I, p. 555.

14 Calvin, *Institutes,* II, pp. 75, 465; I, pp. 534, 551; cf. II, p. 101, and Foxe, *op. cit.,* I, p. 77.

15 Calvin, *Institutes,* II, p. 180.

churches. All these sprang from the same concern with turning the heart of the worshipper towards God. The same principle opened the way to many of the heresies of later radical protestantism. The attack on set prayers, the desire of laymen to pray and preach, are natural extensions of Lutheran principles.[16] So was adult baptism.[17] So was Milton's demand for divorce where religious temperaments were incompatible.[18] Laud's attempt to revise ceremonies flew in the face of this long tradition. "The matter is not great which way we turn our faces, so the heart stand right," Raleigh had written in a phrase he later made famous at his execution. The chapel of Emmanuel College, its former Master told Laud, was "consecrated by faith and a good conscience," and so did not need the ceremony of episcopal consecration.[19] Many came to think tithes and the Sabbath mere ceremonies. And, since no one can judge the heart of another, we have in Luther's teaching the germ of the most subversive of all heresies, religious toleration, horrified though Luther would have been at the thought.[20]

It took time for such conclusions to be drawn. But in a society where custom and tradition counted for so much, this insistence that a well-considered strong conviction overrode everything else had a great liberating force. We see more clearly by the light of grace than by the light of nature, Travers told Hooker. We must, of course, take care that our inner light is not darkness. "Beware of thy good intent, good mind, good affection or zeal, as they call it," Tyndale warned. "Labour for knowledge, that thou mayest know God's will." So inquiry, searching the Scriptures, was stimulated. The godly man looked beyond ceremonies and sacraments to the thing signified, "and will not serve visible things," for that was idolatry.[21] As soon as protestantism established churches, it had itself to face the dissidence of dissent. The Calvinist discipline was one method of curbing the exuberant consciences of laymen, rather more doctrinally satisfactory than Luther's reliance on the secular arm. The Anglican *via media* [middle road] left room for men to have it both ways. "There is no religion

---

[16] Luther, *Reformation Writings*, I, p. 314; Tyndale, *Doctrinal Treatises*, pp. 118–19; *Expositions of Scripture* (Parker Soc., 1849), pp. 80–1.

[17] Luther, *Reformation Writings*, I, p. 255.

[18] Contrast Professor Boxer's agreeable account of a Jesuit who turned Protestant and married twice. He subsequently pleaded to the Inquisition that the ceremonies, being protestant, were invalid, and so he had been guilty only of "a sin of the flesh." His plea was accepted (C. R. Boxer, *Salvador de Sá and the Struggle for Brazil, 1602–86*, pp. 197–8).

[19] Sir Walter Raleigh, *History of the World* (1820), I, p. 78; H. R. Trevor-Roper, *Archbishop Laud*, p. 209.

[20] Luther, *Reformation Writings*, I, p. 180.

[21] R. Hooker, *Of the Laws of Ecclesiastical Polity* (Everyman ed.), I, p. xiii; Tyndale, *Doctrinal Treatises*, pp. 105, 362; *Answer to More*, pp. 6–7.

where there are no ceremonies," said Archbishop Bancroft. "The more ceremonies, the less truth," said the Puritan Greenham.[22]

Luther had started more than he knew when he laid it down that the heart decides for itself. "A man can form his own rule and judge for himself about mortifying his body." "Neither pope, nor bishop, nor any one else, has the right to impose so much as a single syllable of obligation upon a Christian man without his own consent, . . . for we are free from all things." This Christian freedom makes us "kings and priests with power over all things."[23] The important thing is not that Luther made such remarks, though that mattered; but that they flowed from the logic of his theological position. "To have faith," added Calvin, "is . . . to possess some certainty and complete security of mind, to have whereon to rest and fix your foot."[24] That is what protestantism gave to the 16th century man of scruple, tormented by a sense of his own sinfulness: an inner calm and self-confidence, intermittent perhaps, but firmly based on moments of elation which, once experienced, marked a man off in his own eyes from his fellows. (Hence the importance of the doctrine that the elect could never wholly fall from grace.) The tension between hyperconsciousness of natural sinfulness and the permanent possibility of God's grace expressed itself in exuberant efforts to do good works, which had nothing in common with formal righteousness. "We teach," Thomas Taylor declared, "that only Doers shall be saved, and by their doing though not for their doing. The profession of religion is no such gentlemanlike life or trade, whose rents come in by their stewards, whether they sleep or wake, work or play." The godly look often into their account books and cast up their reckonings. "But a bankrupt has no heart to this business."[25] For "the Papal doctrine of doubting of God's love cuts the sinews of endeavour."[26]

Luther was always very unwilling to apply this principle outside the purely religious sphere; yet its extension was inevitable. All action should rest on faith, he told the city of Nuremberg, when it was worried about the lawfulness of resisting the Emperor. Action taken in faith might be good "even though it were an error and a sin." "To

---

22 R. G. Usher, *The Reconstruction of the English Church*, II, p. 124; R. Greenham, *Workes* (1612), p. 653.
23 Luther, *Reformation Writings*, I, pp. 370, 268, 270. The Puritan representatives at the Hampton Court Conference in 1604 were supplied in advance with arguments against the ceremonial observances they objected to. "Whatsoever is not contained in the Word is burdensome to the conscience of Christians, who are set at liberty by Christ" (*Montague MSS.*, Historical MSS. Commission, p. 37).
24 Calvin, *Institutes*, II, p. 70.
25 Thomas Taylor, *Works* (1653), pp. 166–7.
26 Richard Sibbes, *The Saints Cordials* (1629), p. 92.

steal, rob and murder," Tyndale thought, "are holy, when God commandeth them." *Pecca fortiter* [sin boldly]: sin may not be sin after all if the heart believes strongly enough that it is commanded by God. And only the individual can decide this. He is therefore placed under a tremendous obligation to make sure that his heart is properly informed. But in the last resort conscience is the supreme court, from which there is no appeal.[27] Bishop Hall found it difficult to determine "whether it be worse to do a lawful action with doubting or an evil with resolution," since that which in itself is good is made evil by doubt. Oliver Cromwell was sure he should not accept the crown in May 1657 "because at the best I should do it doubtingly. And certainly what is so done is not of faith," and consequently is "sin to him that doth it."[28]

The danger of antinomianism [the belief that Christians are not bound by moral law] always lurked behind Lutheranism and Calvinism. "Whatsoever thou shalt observe upon liberty and of love, is godly," said Luther, "but if thou observe anything of necessity, it is ungodly." "If you have the true kind of Christian love and faith, everything you do is of service. We may all please ourselves what we do." Calvin agreed that, with safeguards, "the consciences of believers may rise above the Law, and may forget the whole righteousness of the Law." "The elect, having the Law written in their hearts, and loving it in their spirits," declared Tyndale, "sin there never; but without, in the flesh." "If an adultery could be committed in the faith," Luther reflected, "it would no longer be a sin." Barely a century later Laurence Clarkson acted on the principle that with God adultery and marriage are but one, "and that one holy, just and good as God."[29]

But the antinomians were a fringe, and can be disregarded for our purpose. What matters is the main stream of protestant thought. Luther and Calvin set men free from forms and ceremonies, and even from the law. It is essential to understand the release and relief which protestantism brought to ordinary men and women if we are to obtain any insight into the astonishing rapidity with which it spread. The political consequences of looking into the heart, of making integrity of intention the test, are clear. "If we deposed the said Queen Regent rather of malice and perverted envy than for the preservation of the commonwealth," said Knox, then God would prevail against us even if she deserved her fate.[30] But revolutions made with the right motives are godly. In October 1647 the members of the Army Council sought

---

[27] Tyndale, *Doctrinal Treatises*, p. 407; Sibbes, *The Saints Cordials*, pp. 41–42.

[28] J. Hall, *Works* (1625), p. 93; W. C. Abbott, *Writings and Speeches of Oliver Cromwell*, IV, p. 513.

[29] Luther, *Thirty-Four Sermons*, p. 281; *Reformation Writings*, II, pp. 115–16; Calvin, *Institutes*, II, p. 683; Tyndale, *Answer to More*, p. 114; Clarkson, *A Single Eye* (1650).

[30] J. Knox, *History of the Reformation* (1832), p. 162.

God in prayer before reporting to one another the inclination of their hearts towards Charles I. Ceremonies are the form of worship laid down by public authority. This authority is held to be inferior to the voice of God speaking within the pure heart. Strafford observed to Laud, of the Puritans, that "The very genius of that nation of people leads them always to oppose, as well civilly as ecclesiastically, all that ever authority ordains for them."[31]

Protestantism then was infinitely more flexible than catholicism. Catholicism had the iron framework of the hierarchy, headed by the pope. It had the machinery of confession, penance and absolution, and of church courts and excommunication, not to mention the Inquisition, with which to enforce traditional standards of orthodoxy. Protestantism lacked many of these barriers to change of moral attitudes. Some of the institutions and codes of the past were retained in the Lutheran countries and in the Anglican church. Efforts were made to erect new disciplinary institutions and codes in countries where Calvinism triumphed. Desperate attempts were made to compile a protestant casuistry. But the guides to godliness, the plain man's pathways to heaven, the practices of piety, were perforce addressed to the consciences of lay heads of households. The ministers may have helped such men to discipline and educate their families and employees. But the Roman Church was able slowly to adapt its standards to the modern world through a controlled casuistry guiding a separate priestly caste, which wielded the power of confession and absolution. Protestant ministers had to tag along behind what seemed right to the consciences of the leading laymen in their congregations.

It is here, through its central theological attitude, that protestantism made its great contribution to the rise of capitalism. What mattered was not that Calvin was a trifle less strict than the canonists in his approach to usury. What mattered was that protestantism appealed, as mediaeval heresy had done, to artisans and small merchants, whom it helped to trust the dictates of their own hearts as their standard of conduct. The elect were those who felt themselves to be the elect. What was astonishing was that so many people had at the same time the same miraculous experience of conversion: thanks to God's direct intervention, grace made them free. It would indeed be inexplicable if we could not see that the psychological states leading up to conversion were the effects of a social crisis which hit many unprivileged small producers in the same sort of way. There was no salvation in the old priestly magic, because that no longer gave them any sense of control over the world of economic fluctuations in which they now had to live. Only an assertive selfconfidence could do this, and that was so novel that it must seem to come arbitrarily from outside.

---

[31] Quoted by Tawney, *Religion and the Rise of Capitalism*, p. 213.

"Take me to you, imprison me, for I
Except you enthrall me, never shall be free,
Nor ever chaste, except you ravish me."[32]

The social situation set large numbers of men and women seeking answers to similar problems. As, thanks to a Luther, a Calvin, a Zwingli, groups of men realised that "the object of [Christ's] struggle was to raise up those who were lying prostrate,"[33] this in its turn redoubled their confidence. They were the elect, not only because they felt they were, but also because other people, good people, recognized that they were; and shared their views. So, once the religion of the heart spread (and the printing press, that technical triumph of the urban craftsmen, gave it a great advantage over mediaeval heresies), Lutheranism, and still more Calvinism, was a magnificent bond of unity and strength. Once touched with grace, the small group of the elect felt themselves to be unique, differentiated from the mass of mankind. Lack of numbers ceased to matter: if God was with them, who would be against them? So their numbers grew.

In the last resort, what comes out of the conscience of a man bears some relation to what goes into it: to the social environment in which he lives. Absolute individualism of conscience, paradoxically, means that society has a greater influence on conduct. So protestantism spread as a negative reaction to institutions and practices which large numbers of men and women felt to be abuses. But, for the same social reason, the positive forms which the protest took tended to vary from region to region, and in the same region from class to class. Belatedly, Calvinism tried by organization to impose homogeneity. But once the pamphlets and sermons had encouraged wide discussion of theology and church government, it proved as impossible to maintain unity as it was among English Puritans after 1640 or within the French Tiers Etat [Third Estate] after 1789. Unity existed only so long as there was an enemy to be overthrown. After that the voice of God said different things to different people. So the earnest minority which found the eternal decrees and the rule of the godly not unacceptable was challenged by those descendants of the mediaeval heretics who were prepared to contemplate the possibility of all men being saved: who wanted to be freed from the rule of new presbyter no less than of old priest.

From their different points of view both Hooker and Perkins showed themselves aware of this social background. Perkins asked how we should judge what is the measure of wealth which the master of a family may with good conscience seek. His reply was: not by the affection of covetous men, but by "the common judgment and practice of

---

[32] John Donne, *Complete Poetry and Selected Prose* (Nonesuch ed.), p. 285.
[33] Calvin, *Institutes*, I, p. 445.

the most godly, frugal and wise men with whom we live."[34] Hooker wrote ironically that "whosoever shall anger the meanest and simplest artisan *which carrieth a good mind,* by not removing out of the Church such rites and ceremonies as displease him, 'better he were drowned in the bottom of the sea.' "[35] Fulke Greville well expressed this sense of permanent criticism in protestantism, its ability to interpret even the Bible, when he made his chorus of priests conclude *Mustapha* with the words:

> "Yet when each of us in his own heart looks
> He finds the God there far unlike his books."[36]

For the protestant conscience there were no absolutes, no accepted infallibilities, though each sect as it arose tried to establish them. But there was no final court of appeal, not even the Bible. Even yesterday's conscience might be repudiated to-day. The religious radicals inherited from the mediaeval heretics the concept of the Everlasting Gospel, written in men's hearts; more respectable Puritans evolved the doctrine of progressive revelation: both allowed moral standards to be modified as society changed.

When the business man of 16th and 17th century Geneva, Amsterdam or London looked into his inmost heart, he found that God had planted there a deep respect for the principle of private property. The more sophisticated might express this in the 17th century by saying that respect for property was a fundamental law, or part of the law of nature (or reason): but it was easier, and more likely to overbear opposition, to say with Colonel Rainborough in the Putney Debates that God had commanded "Thou shalt not steal." Such men felt quite genuinely and strongly that their economic practices, though they might conflict with the traditional law of the old church, were not offensive to God. On the contrary: they glorified God. For here the protestant theologians had sold the pass, by their fundamental distinction between formal and charitable works, and by making the individual heart the ultimate arbiter.

The elect, Luther had said, must perform good works to help their neighbour, the community, the commonwealth, humanity; this prevents the doctrine of justification by faith giving "licence and free liberty to everyone to do what he will." Men serve God in their callings, however vile, because they serve their neighbour. "A cobbler, a smith, a farmer, each has the work and office of his task, and yet they are

---

34 W. Perkins, *Workes,* I, p. 769.

35 Hooker, *Of the Laws of Ecclesiastical Polity* (Everyman ed.), I, p. 406. My italics.

36 Ed. G. Bullough, *Poems and Drama of Fulke Greville,* II, p. 137.

all alike consecrated priests and bishops, and every one by means of his own work or office must benefit and serve every other, that in this way many kinds of work be done for the bodily and spiritual welfare of the community."[37] In this doctrine of usury Calvin always insisted that men must consider the good of the commonwealth before their own gain. It all depends on the attitude with which we go about our work. George Herbert derived directly from Luther when he wrote that labour was dignified or degrading according to the spirit in which it was done.

> "A servant with this clause
> Makes drudgery divine;
> Who sweeps a room, as for thy laws,
> Makes that and the action fine."[38]

The enthusiasm with which English Puritan preachers took up this point shows that it met a real need. It was very arguable that productive economic activity in the 16th and 17th centuries was a charitable good work in Luther's sense. The protestants' emphasis on hard work, which linked their reprobation of idle monks with their reprobation of idle beggars, sprang from the economic circumstances of the time as reflected in the thinking of bourgeois laymen. When Francis Bacon suggested that the age-old problem of poverty might at last be soluble if the resources of the community, including its labour, were rationally utilized, he was only developing an idea which he might have received from his very Puritan mother.[39] The ambiguity of the word charity helped. The law without charity was nothing worth. Fuller said that Edward VI's charity was no less demonstrated in his foundation of Bridewell for the punishment of sturdy beggars than of St. Thomas's Hospital for relief of the poor. Perkins thought the Poor Law of 1597 was "in substance the very law of God."[40] Professor Jordan's remarkable book on philanthropy in England shows how in the 16th and early 17th centuries sober and rational calculation of what was of advantage to the community replaced the mediaeval ideal of indiscriminate alms-

---

[37] *Thirty-four Sermons*, p. 215 and *passim*; cf. *Reformation Writings*, I, pp. 375–6; II, pp. 110–11, 121; Tyndale, *Doctrinal Treatises*, pp. 100–2; *Expositions*, pp. 125–6; *Answer to More*, p. 173.

[38] Cf. *Thirty-four Sermons*, p. 211; *Reformation Writings*, I, p. 276; J. Dod and R. Clever, *A Plain and Familiar Exposition of the Ten Commandments* (19th ed., 1662), p. 190.

[39] See my essay on "William Perkins and the Poor," in *Puritanism and Revolution*, p. 234; and a communication by V. G. Kiernan in *Past and Present* No. 3, esp. pp. 49–51.

[40] T. Fuller, *The Holy State* (1648), p. 144; Perkins, *Workes*, I, p. 755.

giving. The latter created beggars, and was self-regarding anyway; true charity was to encourage self-help in the deserving.

The preachers, and still more their congregations, might well be genuinely convinced in their hearts that industry was a good work, for the "common good," for "the use and profit of mankind"; that negligence in business harms the public state.[41] It is a duty to God and the commonwealth to use your talents, said John Preston. Provided you do not make gain your godliness, provided you do not seek riches but accept them as the blessing of God if they happen to come—then you may lawfully take care to increase your estate. "Ask thyself then," said Thomas Taylor, "what good doth my life to church, to commonwealth, to family, to men?"[42] It was in fact the labour of generations of God-fearing Puritans that made England the leading industrial nation in the world—God, as His manner is, helping those who helped themselves.

Through this emphasis on the inner conviction which inspired actions, bourgeois lay society could impose its own standards. "God's children look to the spiritual use of those things which the worldlings use carnally," said Greenham. The actions of the Scribes and Pharisees "were good in themselves, and for others," said Sibbes; "but the end of them was naught, and therefore both they and their works are condemned." "Man may with good conscience," Perkins thought, "desire and seek for goods necessary, whether for nature or for his person, according to the former rules: but he may not desire and seek for goods more than necessary, for if he doth, he sinneth." ("The former rules" include the convenient provision that "those goods without which a man's estate, condition and dignity . . . cannot be preserved" are necessary.[43]) The preachers attempted to spiritualize what men were doing away, by telling them to do it for the right reasons. One may suspect that their congregations paid more attention to the general permission than to the careful qualifications with which it was hedged around. "They are very hot for the Gospel," said Thomas Adams of such laymen; "they love the Gospel: who but they? Not because they believe it, but because they feel it: the wealth, peace, liberty that ariseth by it."[44]

Men are too ready to accuse Puritans of covetousness, observed William Gouge: we should be very cautious about this, since we can-

---

[41] Dod and Clever, *A Plaine and Familiar Exposition of the Proverbs of Salomon* (1612), Chapter IX, pp. 65–6; Chapter XVIII, pp. 10–11; cf. Chapter XIII, pp. 70–3.

[42] J. Preston, *Sinnes Overthrow* (4th ed., 1641), pp. 254–9; T. Taylor, *A Commentary Upon the Epistle of St. Paul to Titus* (1658), p. 183.

[43] Greenham, *Workes*, p. 20; Sibbes, *The Returning Backslider* (1639), pp. 451–2; Perkins, *Workes*, II, p. 125.

[44] T. Adams, *Workes* (1630), p. 389.

not read the hearts of others, or know all the extenuating circumstances. "Covetousness doth especially consist in the inward desire of a man, which is best known to himself . . . Observe the inward wishes of thine heart. If they be especially for the things of this world, they argue a covetous disposition." "When therefore thou thinkest of sparing," Dod and Clever advised, "let not the greedy desire of gathering draw thee to it, but conscience of well using that which God hath lent thee." "Seek riches not for themselves but for God," was Thomas Taylor's simpler formulation.[45] "We teach you not to cast away the bag, but covetousness," Thomas Adams reassured his City congregation. "O ye rich citizens," announced Joseph Hall, "we tell you from Him, whose title is Rich in Mercy, that ye may be at once rich and holy." When ministers went as far as that, we can imagine the simplifications and self-deceptions of laymen. The Presbyterian preachers, Hobbes noted two generations later, "did never inveigh against the lucrative vices of men of trade or handicraft."[46]

The Puritans tried to spiritualize economic processes. God instituted the market and exchange, Dod and Clever assured their large public. "He would have commerce and traffic to proceed from love," and He favours a fair bargainer. Greenham made unrepining acceptance of the market price evidence "that thine heart is rightly affected, both to God and to the brethren."[47] Emphasis on the motive of the heart is the key to the preachers' distinction between "biting" usury and legitimate commercial transactions,[48] no less than to their distinction between indiscriminate alms-giving and relief of the deserving poor, and to the protestant doctrine of the calling. All stem from the theology of justification by faith. Did adventurers sail to North America, "to seek new worlds for gold, for praise, for glory"? "If the same proceed of ambition or avarice," they were warned in 1583, "it cometh not of God," and will not prosper. But if men are impelled by zeal for the honour of God, by compassion for the "poor infidels captured by the devil," as well as by desire to relieve the poor of England and advance the interest of their honest and well-affected countrymen, then "so sacred an intention" gives them the right "to prosecute effectively the full possession of those so ample and pleasant countries." "If we first seek the

---

[45] W. Gouge, *A Commentary on the Whole Epistle to the Hebrews* (1866–7), III, pp. 293–5; cf. Greenham, *Workes*, p. 784; Dod and Clever, *A godly forme of household government* (2nd. ed., 1614), Sig. E. 6v–7; T. Taylor, *Works* (1653), p. 477.

[46] Adams, *Workes*, p. 862; J. Hall, *Works* (1808), V, pp. 103–4; T. Hobbes, *Works*, VI, pp. 194–5.

[47] Dod and Clever, *Proverbs*, XI, pp. 2–3; XX, p. 132; Greenham, *Workes*, p. 620.

[48] Cf. Bullinger, *Decades* (Parker Soc., 1849–52), III, pp. 41–2. Roman Catholic casuistry, on the other hand, by its emphasis on the formal and external, made release from the sin of usury depend to some extent on methods of accountancy (H. M. Robertson, *Aspects of the Rise of Economic Individualism*, p. 164).

kingdom of God," wrote Hakluyt with divine simplicity and prophetic accuracy, "all other things will be given unto us."[49]

This emphasis on the religious motive for colonization was often repeated. Historians looking only at the result have regarded it as gratuitous hypocrisy. Those who have tried to penetrate the hearts of the colonizers have seen it as a seriously-held intention, which for some reason was never carried out.[50] It was rather, I suggest, a necessary part of the thought-processes of men whose protestant training made secular pursuits possible only if entered into with the right motive. But the example of colonization shows how easily emphasis on godly motive could become a cloak for economic calculation. Protestants, said a preacher at Paul's Cross in 1581, are freed from the tyranny of the law upon the conscience. Hence we are prone to carnality, since "we live to ourselves."[51] Zeal-of-the-Land Busy, when asked about the lawfulness of eating a Bartholomew pig at the Fair, reflected that "The place is not much, not very much, so it be eaten with a reformed mouth, with sobriety and humbleness." The sin of Ignorance, Bunyan recorded 60 years later, was that he thought all problems of salvation were answered by saying "My heart tells me so."

Doctrines emphasizing the motives of the heart, allowing social pressures to influence individual conduct more freely, flourish especially, it may be suggested, in periods of rapid social change, and among those persons most exposed to its effects. Christianity arose in such a period; St. Augustine, on whose theology the reformers drew so heavily, also lived in an age when old standards were breaking down; and he too stressed inner motive rather than external action. "When it is plain to him what he should do and to what he should aspire, even then, unless he feel delight and love therein, he does not perform his duty." "If they said that any works of mercy may obtain pardon even for the greatest and most habitual sins, they would be guilty of much absurdity: for so might the richest man for his 10d. a day have a daily quittance for all his fornications, homicides, and other sins whatsoever."[52] There appears to be a permanent tendency for established churches to revert to ceremonial, and for opposition groups to stress the internal element. In the Middle Ages, after the Church had become institutionalized, those who laid the strongest emphasis on the intention, the purity of heart of

---

[49] R. Hakluyt, *Principal Navigations* (Everyman ed.), VI, pp. 3–4; *Divers Voyages* (1582), Dedication to Sir Philip Sidney.

[50] Perry Miller, *Errand into the Wilderness*, pp. 99–140.

[51] M. Maclure, *The Paul's Cross Sermons, 1534–1642* (1958), p. 126.

[52] Augustine, *De Spiritu et Litera*, 5; *The City of God* (Everyman ed.), II, p. 353. Cf. Samuel Baker's shrewd observation, "The Stoical necessity and Presbyterian predestination are the same" (*Characters and Passages from Notebooks*, 1908, p. 279).

ordinary lay Christians, were the heretics—Massalians, Paulicians, Bogomils, Albigensians, Lollards, to whom radical protestants from Foxe to Lilburne looked back for the true Christian line of descent. This age-old protest acquired a new significance as educated townsmen, trained by their mode of life in rational calculation and independent thinking, began to challenge the clerical monopoly of education and to assert their own standards of morality. The protestant emphasis on the heart helped to dissolve the hard crust of custom, tradition and authority.[53]

To summarize the argument, then: The appeal to inner conviction, and the rejection of the routine of ceremonies through which the priesthood imposed its authority, could have liberating effects in any society. The hold over men's minds of an established doctrinal system had to be broken before the political and social order sanctified by those doctrines could be challenged. The appeal to the heart was common to early Christianity and many mediaeval heresies. Its most obvious effects were negative. But, positively, it facilitated the evolution of more flexible doctrines. Since opposition to the Roman Church in the 16th and 17th century Europe drew its main strength from the big cities, protestantism could be developed in ways which favoured the rise of capitalism. But there is nothing in protestantism which leads automatically to capitalism: its importance was rather that it undermined obstacles which the more rigid institutions and ceremonies of catholicism imposed. The reformation mobilized masses of men against the Roman Church and the political authorities which protected it. Initial support for protestantism and especially Calvinism came from the educated minority, largely urban, which thought seriously about problems of church and state. But doctrines evolved by and for the middle class could appeal to other dissatisfied elements in the population, like the gentry of Hungary and Scotland, or the plebeians of the Dutch towns. By the same token, protestant churches were established —in Scandinavia, in central Europe—which made only slight and incidental contributions to the development of capitalism.

The protestant revolt melted down the iron ideological framework which held society in its ancient mould. Where capitalism already existed, it had henceforth freer scope. But men did not become capitalists because they were protestants, nor protestants because they were capitalists. In a society already becoming capitalist, protestantism facilitated the triumph of the new values. There was no inherent

---

[53] The failure of full-scale capitalism to develop in 14th century Florence may be connected with a lack of thorough-going heresy to unite its citizens against the Church. The heretical possibilities in the early Franciscan movement were tamed by the Papacy: the big bourgeoisie who came to rule Florence needed the Papacy, for this and economic reasons (Hilton, "Capitalism—What's in a name?," *Past and Present,* No. 1).

theological reason for the protestant emphasis on frugality, hard work, accumulation; but that emphasis was a natural consequence of the religion of the heart in a society where capitalist industry was developing. It was, if we like, a rationalization; but it flowed naturally from protestant theology, whose main significance, for our present purposes, is that in any given society it enabled religion to be moulded by those who dominated in that society.

"All external things [are] subject to our liberty," declared Calvin, "provided the nature of that liberty approves itself to our minds as before God." But Christian liberty was for the elect only. Professor Brown has argued that later Puritan attempts to spiritualize the market were the opposite of Luther's view that the world was given over to the devil.[54] Yet the transformation was due at least as much to the victories of the protestant outlook in the world as to an abandonment of its theology. When true religion had triumphed, the godly could hardly surrender the world so cheerfully to the devil. In a society run by protestants the ungodly must be disciplined; and the duty of performing good works for one's neighbour became a duty to the community. Hence the overwhelming emphasis of later Puritanism on the religious duties of industry, thrift and accumulation. As the bourgeois virtues triumphed, so the society of largely self-employed small producers was transformed into a society of domestic- and wage-workers, who could be profitably employed only by those who owned capital. In this society the few who climbed the social ladder did so at the expense of their neighbours. So the thought of the fortunate upper ranks came to stress more and more the vices and follies of the poor. Later Calvinism in England became harsher and more hypocritical, because of changes in society which it had helped to bring about.

Professors Haller and Jordan have stressed the importance of the Calvinist discipline and organization in giving a sense of status and self-respect to the unprivileged; and have suggested that Calvinism's spread, and its success in building revolutionary parties, owed more to this than to its theology. But the emphasis on motive also helped the theology to flourish among earnest, sincere and responsible men in any sort of environment; and the discipline, ideally designed for preserving the domination of a small nucleus, was adaptable to almost any form of revolt. The appeal of Calvinism in the 16th and 17th centuries was no more limited to the urban middle class than that of Marxism has been limited to the urban working class in our own day. In Scotland Calvinism became the bond of union between those who wished to be free of France and the French court, as well as of exploitation by the international Church. It was led by quite different social groups from those which dominated English Puritanism. The ministers were almost

---

[54] Calvin, *Institutes*, II, p. 135; Brown, *Life against Death*, Chapter XIV, *passim*.

its only intellectuals. Because the Kirk headed a movement for national independence, Calvinism drove far deeper roots than it did in England, where capitalism and the class divisions which accompanied it were much more developed. So in England, within little more than a century of the Reformation, Calvinists had led a successful revolution but had failed to monopolize state power because they could not hold together the diverse groups which had helped to make the revolution: whereas in Scotland Presbyterianism became a popular religion in the same sense as Catholicism did in Ireland, and in a way that Anglicanism never did in England. There were "nationalist" elements also in the Calvinism of Transylvania and the Netherlands.

So the fact that strong political feelings, of any kind, could express themselves, and be shared, through the emphasis on the heart, helps to explain the existence of sincere Calvinists among the aristocracy and gentry—themselves experiencing social crisis—in many countries from Hungary to France. But we should not be naive about this. Calvin deliberately set out to win the support of the high aristocracy in France; and the latter no doubt saw the use for themselves of a tightly-disciplined, wealthy and dedicated urban organization.[55] The godly in England also had few scruples about casting out devils with Beelzebub, in the shape of the Dukes of Northumberland or Buckingham, the Earls of Leicester or Essex.

An age of ignorance is an age of ceremony, Dr. Johnson correctly observed.[56] The victory of protestantism helped to end the animistic magical universe, and undermined the traditional popular conception of religion as propitiation. Henceforth God and the individual soul stood face to face. The sense of sin remained, became indeed more overwhelming, because sin had to be grappled with alone. But the sense of sin was now also a sense of potential freedom. No magician or priest or saint could help, but God could. His promises were free and sure. The Puritan remained terribly conscious of his own sinful nature, even whilst he tried, by careful scrutiny of motive, to identify his will with the will of God. "It does not need modern psychology to enable us to appreciate that the more bitter the internal struggle, the more complete was the assumption of identification with the Will of God in exernal activities."[57] The simultaneous conviction of depravity and righteousness does not make the most attractive characters in the world; but it gave a vital stimulus to productive effort in countries where capitalism was developing, at a time when industry was small-scale, handicraft, unrationalized. Successful mediaeval

---

[55] R. M. Kingdom, *Geneva and the Coming of the Wars of Religion in France, 1555–1563*, p. 56 and *passim*.

[56] Samuel Johnson, *A Journey to the Western Islands*, Raasay.

[57] John Marlowe, *The Puritan Tradition in England* (1956), p. 133.

business men died with feelings of guilt and left money to the Church to be put to unproductive uses. Successful protestant business men were no longer ashamed of their productive activities whilst alive, and at death left money to help others to imitate them. None were more industrious than those who had abandoned the concept of a work of supererogation.

> "Not the labours of my hands
> Can fulfill Thy law's demands."

The paradox of protestantism is that it eternally strives to fulfil a law which it knows to be unfulfillable. The paradox of capitalism is that production and accumulation become objects in themselves, losing sight of the end of consumption: just as the man whom Hobbes abstracted from this society sought power after power, ending only in death. Hobbist man is what capitalist man would have been if he had ceased to worry about his motives. At worst the preachers clothed his nakedness in a fig-leaf of hypocrisy; at best they humanized some industrial relations and directed energy towards public service as well as private profit.

# IX/THE REFORMATION IN GERMANY

THE Reformation, by which I mean the destruction of the Roman Catholic Church as the unique framework for the organization and practice of religious belief, was inevitable. In a society whose religious superstructure is the chief vehicle for the expression and defense of existing social relations, discontent with the latter was bound to have repercussions on the former. The Church, which was synonymous with Christianity, could not survive unscathed the transition from feudalism to capitalism.

From 1517, the date of Luther's Ninety-five Theses against the Church and the papacy, onwards, Europe was swept by successive waves of religious dissent such as had never been known before. First Germany, then Scandinavia, the Swiss cantons, England, and parts of the Czech and Hungarian lands rallied to the Protestant banner, while other countries, like France, Italy, and Poland, were infected, less successfully, by the virus of heresy. Besides being a religion particularly well suited to the new bourgeois morality, Protestantism became a means for kings and desperate men to challenge the universal, that is, supernational, authority of popes and emperors. For a century and more, the confrontation of Catholic and Protestant became the battle ground on which most of the issues of the day, however far removed from considerations of faith they may have been, were fought out and resolved.

The Reformation began in Germany, but there was nothing foreordained about that, nor about the forms it assumed. There is every reason to believe that, given the proper spark, England or Sweden or Bohemia (among others) might have had the honor of being the first to raise the banner of religious revolt. In Germany, the spark came in the shape of Martin Luther. He was not, however, predestined to restore the faith of the ancient fathers, his own opinion to the contrary notwithstanding. His personality was what is usually termed a historical accident. A man of talent afflicted with what appear to have been profound psychological problems, of which not the least was an overwhelming and inexpiable sense of sin and guilt, he found an outlet for his emotional needs in religious disputation, just as another man possessed of a similar psyche but operating in our own day might engage in a different kind of challenge to authority. So much for the kernel of truth in the oft-repeated assertion that a radical is a radical is a radical to the $n$th power.

If Luther was the spark that set Germany ablaze, what ought primarily to interest us is the kindling. What were the specific conditions that caused Luther's ideas to find an audience? The seamless robe of the Catholic Church had been rent many times before, only to be stitched up as good as new. But that task would henceforth be beyond the abilities of even the finest tailor. The difference was that where once rebels had expressed their protests and desires in religious terms, without necessarily attacking the Church as an institution, it was precisely the institution itself that was now repudiated. Still, that does not tell us the reason for the change. Similarly, to say, as the Catholic priest and historian Joseph Lortz does in the selection reprinted here, that the fundamental cause of the Reformation was the weakening of the "Catholic idea" promotes a symptom to the level of a cause without first explaining it. We have still to ask why that idea was no longer as attractive as it once had been. I suggest that the answer lies in an examination of the opposition among the classes of late feudal society, of their relations to one another within the reigning institutional structures.

Luther's ideas had an appeal because they represented one possible means of dealing with the problems at hand. Without the Elector Frederick of Saxony, a prince intent on increasing his power free of interference from pope or emperor, Martin Luther would quickly have been of the martyred and sweetly sanctified dead. Without the support of a section of the nobility and of the state apparatus, his church would soon have ceased to exist. Without the peasants to seize on his words as slogans, his impact would have been significantly more limited. But religious ideas are not mere epiphenomena, reflections of some deeper reality.

They exist, are believed in, have force. To explain their development in terms of social relationships is in no way to deny them significance, nor to reduce everything to the working out of a metaphysical force incorrectly labeled "economics."

Was the Reformation in Germany a bourgeois—or more properly—a prebourgeois revolution? It has been argued, especially by East German historians, that it was because it helped to prepare the way, under conditions of immature economic development and in the absence of a significant bourgeoisie, for the eventual accession of that class to power. That is, in fact, what is essential in the concept of a long-term bourgeois revolution: the gradual development by which capitalism became the dominant mode of production and the bourgeoisie took power in society and the state. In Germany, the process was particularly arduous. It may even be argued that the bourgeoisie was never strong enough to exercise power alone, but had always to share it with a state apparatus that at least partially escaped its control and with Prussian nobles, the celebrated Junkers. The Reformation (whose contents were, after all, primarily ideological) attacked not only the Church, but the entire world view of a society conventionally described as feudal, and by so doing added another element to the process of disintegration of a social formation in which the fundamental classes were lords and peasants and in which the bourgeoisie played only a minor and subordinate class role. Because the destruction of one social formation necessitates the emergence of another, and insofar as the bourgeoisie in the course of several centuries developed into the new ruling class, the Reformation must be considered as part of the long-term bourgeois revolution.

The growth of bourgeois power was challenged from below, as well. The militancy of the German proletariat in the late nineteenth and early twentieth centuries had a great tradition behind it, one that went back at least as far as the Reformation. In that period, Anabaptists and other religious radicals, the most famous of whom is Thomas Münzer, drew on a theological inspiration to formulate a program of utopian communism on earth. The Peasants' War of 1525 and the revolts that followed shortly afterward were brutally crushed, with Luther calling down fire and brimstone upon the rebels' heads, despite their belief that they were carrying his principles of freedom and true Christianity to their ultimate conclusion. Whatever else may have motivated him in this regard, Luther knew that he was dependent on kings and nobles for the survival of his church, and revolution was not to their liking. Luther decided then that Christian freedom existed only in the heart and mind of the believer but was not to be externalized in social practice.

It is to the analysis of this Christian communism that Ernst Bloch addresses himself in the selection from his book *Thomas Münzer, Theologian of Revolution*. Bloch is professor of philosophy at Tübingen University in West Germany. He previously taught at the University of Leipzig but decided to leave the German Democratic Republic about ten years ago because of political differences. Bloch considers himself a Marxist but is not in the current line of official Marxism. On the contrary, his work has always been marked by a certain utopian spirit and a rejection of dogmatic rigidity. That utopianism is particularly noticeable in this selection, both because of its subject matter and of the date of its composition, just after the end of World War I and the defeat of the German socialist revolution of 1919. Bloch's ideas are now enjoying a renewed influence among European, particularly German, students, one of whose most characteristic tendencies is to insist on the role of utopian thought and of intellectuals in a revolutionary socialist movement.

This is also the burden of the chapter reprinted here from Roy Pascal's *The Social Basis of the German Reformation: Martin Luther and His Times*. Pascal seeks to establish the class basis of Lutheran thought, and he provides an example of that sort of class struggle which, he says, is carried on as much in the realm of ethics as in politics. He demonstrates that once again Marxism, far from limiting itself to a simple and abusive theory of economic causation, is capable of accounting for the many-faceted complexities of social life.

# Joseph Lortz

## 20

# The Causes
# of the Reformation

Our problem is not simply to explain how Luther's personal development was possible but to show how this man was able to claim the allegiance of a huge section of the population of Europe, to show how the Reformation was possible as a world-historical phenomenon, capable of setting its imprint upon the whole range of life, religious and secular, in its own age and in the centuries which followed.

. . .

If we define "causes" as "presuppositions," there is indeed a summary, but penetrating and most illuminating formula which answers our question. The Reformation was caused by the disintegration of the basic principles and basic forms upon which the Middle Ages were built.

The principal question is that of the disruption of the unity of the Middle Ages; for the Reformation was without doubt essentially the break-up of this unity, or, better, the revolutionary consummation of this break-up.

The shortest formula for the empirical situation in so far as it appears as a preparation for the Reformation goes something like this: the unity of western Christianity had gone; the *una civitas christiana* [single Christian state] had already vanished. This meant that the unity of dogma and of Church life—still manifestly present— had surrendered in essence the substratum which supported their existence. The separation of the individual components of Europe and of the Roman Catholic Church (the rise of nations, in fact) had advanced so far that the lever could be applied with good prospect of achieving disruption. This state of affairs was brought to light by Luther, and he, indeed, was the first to allow it to lead right into schism.

Evidence for the pre-Reformation break-up of Christian unity or for the threat of its imminent disappearance is not difficult to produce.

(a) Avignon (the pope, formerly truly a universal figure, now very nearly became a French court bishop); the schism of the west (split of the entire western Church into two camps mutually excommunicating each other); the nationally conceived reform councils based upon a radically separatist idea of a council; the Renaissance popes as Italian princes. In contrast to the cohesion of medieval universalism these phenomena present a series of logically increasing expressions of religious nationalism.

(b) The national-political division of Europe, the rise of great national monarchies in the west, the emergence therein of national Churches, and, in Germany, the gradual tendency towards the erection of territorial Churches.

(c) The refusal of the west to respond to the papal call to war against the enemy of Christendom; the inevitable hardening of this refusal on account of the political relations of both popes with the Turks (Innocent VIII as paid gaoler of the captive brother of the Turkish sultan, and Alexander VI). The fall of Constantinople in 1453 was the expression of a Europe become disunited: it no longer mobilised its united strength towards a common end.

(d) The expulsion of heretical Bohemia from the common Christian heritage.

The beginnings of a new sense of unity which European humanism brought were powerless against the disappearance of western, Christian unity; they hastened it, in fact, for on the whole humanism moved towards secularisation, that is, the dissolution of the more spiritual Middle Ages.

.   .   .

The growth of the European nations was burdened, among other things, by a dangerous unevenness. The foundation was the linking together of religion and political-social life to become a single whole. With the co-operation and leadership of the Church in the course of many centuries secular society fought doggedly and consistently towards ever greater independence. This was in accordance with natural necessity and, as we have said, with the purpose of all true education. But the Church, although she had established and fostered this independence, was not entirely happy about it. By the Church we mean the socially and economically privileged priestly estate, the bishops, the church courts, the great religious orders, living and exercising their care of souls in the cities, and the Roman curia. Two classes within the same vital social organism grew at quite a different tempo and, to some extent, in different directions: a spiritual breach was easy, if not inevitable. On the other hand, the Church tolerated a carelessness in the expression of religious opinions, which gave too much latitude to freedom, and became a dangerous temptation. We must take account of certain dominant humanist views which were at work in this process.

The line of development is evident: the Reformation is an expression of Europe's attainment of intellectual and religious independence. It is the revolutionary declaration of the coming of age of the Christian people of Europe. As early as 1300 polemical writings on Church politics were full of the revolt of the laity in every form, and so basic that they simply could not be overlooked.

Not only did the basic mental and religious attitudes which characterised the Middle Ages change but so did the forms of expression they had known in the Church and the world. Medieval institutions were passing away. Concerning the Church, we think of everything that comes under the heading of the disintegration of its concept as an apostolic, religious entity, and under the heading of ecclesiastical abuses in the widest sense of the word. Concerning the world, we think of the colossal reorganisation in the social, cultural and political spheres. (Political: the impotence of the empire and the emperor, its diminution as a result of the loss of large frontier areas; the separation and enmity between countless emergent territories and regions.)

In the battle against this disorder and reorganisation in world and Church there arose those power currents which governed German history in the period of confessional division. But these did not arise merely from this battle. They arose essentially from their own roots. It was this latter fact alone which made the Reformation no mere episode, but an epoch in German history. The violence of its convulsion in the religious sphere even made it an epoch in world history.

In fact at the beginning of the sixteenth century this disintegration of medieval principles in every area of national-political, ecclesiastical, religious and scientific life had gone so far, reaching the Church and striking against her, that in broad outline the framework of the Reformation seemed to have been prepared. Seen as a religious and ecclesiastical event the Reformation is the denial of the visible Church, rooted and grounded in the objective teaching authority and in the sacramental priesthood; and it is the acceptance of a religion of conscience erected upon the judgment of the individual with regard to the biblical word. That is to say: along these two lines of its development, the Reformation replaced the basic medieval attitudes of objectivism, traditionalism and clericalism by those of subjectivism, spiritualism and laicism. This was a development, therefore, which took up, united, and carried on with surprising intensity tendencies of the late medieval interplay of forces. The Reformation was a revolutionary revolt against the papal Church by a theological lay movement. Everything which prepared the enmity of the laity against papacy and Church belongs to the causes of the Reformation.

In the intellectual sphere the most far-reaching effect was produced by that slowly emerging force which we like to call the subjectivist tendency, although it was still centuries removed from modern subjectivism. This development had begun in the moment when the western mind began to adopt its own independent attitude towards the Christian message, to pose bold questions and to give answers unheard of before. This happened at first within, but soon outside, the Church. The two epoch-making figures, both belonging to the high Middle Ages, are Bernard of Clairvaux and Peter Waldo.

An historical analysis of the intellectual, ecclesiastical, political and social situation at the turn of the sixteenth century yields, further, the precise reflection of this disintegration: a very strong, widespread and dangerous dissatisfaction with prevailing conditions and, moreover, strong agitation and a corresponding demand for reform that had already become violent. In reality the Lutheran Reformation, which grew into a denunciation of the former way of life, became an outlet for all this. But at the decisive point, namely, opposition to the Church as the supporting power of the Middle Ages, the demand for reform was expressed with extraordinary sharpness, and here it developed an unusually explosive power, which in its turn reverberated to unusual lengths.

The tension expressed vis-à-vis the Church possessed such great explosive power because a thorough reform had been due for three hundred years; indeed, Innocent III had made reform the theme of the fourth Lateran council. Furthermore, in spite of the manifestly great achievements and persons (in the papacy, episcopacy, clergy, monasticism, civil life, in piety, theology and art) a consistent decadence had set in within this development and, in spite of all the excellence, it could not be concealed or smoothed over. No matter how one may extol the value of fourteenth-century mysticism; no matter how we now concede many Christian features to the Renaissance, the sequence Avignon–schism–Renaissance is, seen as a whole, a development of religious debilitation, a dangerous disintegration of Christian and priestly life, a perilous eclipse of the Catholic idea. Indeed, when the Church was in danger of its life, in the two-, and then three-headed papacy, had not the self-seeking of the highest senate of the Church and of some of the popes prevented the initiation of the long-overdue reform? Certainly one can concede to Möhler that "by rebuilding upon the existent foundations (of the Church), according to the laws of continuity, a new and better time" could have been ushered in; but, in virtue of the inner consistency of the concrete situation at the beginning of the sixteenth century, there was not much prospect of this possibility becoming a reality. Conversely, the many, vain, centuries-old attempts at reform and the countless, frequently successful revolts against the Church's authority made things ripe for a radical break-through. People had had more than enough. They wanted to make an end of it. A radical revolution was bound to find many enthusiastic adherents.

The distribution of forces in seen even more in the fact that the absolute necessity of reform was a profound conviction in all trends and circles within the Church, all of whom were possessed by an intense longing for some sort of renewal.

The call for a reformation in head and members was, to be sure, vastly different from a merely polemical antipapal or anti-Church movement. It was first of all the positive expression of the conviction which penetrated to the very roots of western consciousness that the profoundest order of the Church had become distorted, and which imperiously demanded a transformation; there was also the conviction that this transformation would come through a tremendous revolution —an apocalyptic chastisement willed by God. This expectation was characterised by both longing and fear. From the most diverse quarters, in all spheres of life, this revolutionary mood had grown as a wish, a fear, a plan, as a prophecy, as an already living movement. Conditions were intolerable; a fundamental change had to come. The tyranny had to be broken. In a time of famine, with great frankness in his cathedral pulpit Geiler von Kayserberg (d. 1510) incited the people of Strasburg to take grain from the rich by force. It was this same, truly Catholic and deeply devout Geiler who knew that "Christianity was distorted from top to bottom, from the pope to the sacristan, from the emperor to the shepherd."

No revolution could be too radical to prevent many from finding at once, in this longing and fear, a proof of its justification. Luther, at first intensely earnest, then bold and obstinate, then reckless, in attack, found here an unusually well-prepared soil.

And yet, despite all we have said, the onset of the Reformation had not become self-evident. Its appearance and the world-historical shattering of Christianity which it precipitated, remain primarily a mystery. But we make a mystery no more accessible to understanding by hushing up whatever constitutes its incomprehensibility. It is better to emphasise the enigma which it conceals. By going beyond the quite inadequate forms of explanation hitherto provided, and realistically investigating the origin of the Reformation we are now, it is true, progressively illuminating its tragic genesis; but at the same time too much stress has been laid on one angle. It is time now to do justice to irrational factors. The complex of causes of the Reformation had so thoroughly come to a head that the breaking of a storm became almost an absolute necessity. But in spite of this, much of the undiluted essence of the Church, much of the heroic spirit of Christianity remained. It is false to describe the process as though the disintegration took place without any opposition, and even falser to trace back such a dissolution simply to an act of malice. The Reformation was a battle for the authentic form of Christianity; its emergence was not a self-evident fact; less still was it self-evident that the struggle was to be resolved by the greater part of western Christendom turning against the Church.

One of the indispensable preconditions of reaching an understanding of the development of the Reformation, and of assessing its value, is that we clarify the magnitude of the cleavage represented by the Reformation, in terms of these two problems. Only then will sufficient light be cast on Luther's responsibility for the Reformation schism.

There were two fundamental preconditions for the possibility of the Reformation: first, that the question be asked, whether the existent and ruling papal Church, believed to be of divine right, was in fact the true representation of Christianity.

We can sense at once the colossal development which was necessary before there could be any question of the Reformation. That is to say, doubt had to be raised not simply over this or that aspect of the ecclesiastical system: the whole presentation of the faith had to be rejected, and a fresh total conception of Christianity produced, capable of capturing the mind—almost overnight—of the majority of the members of the Church. For things to have reached such a state it was necessary that there should have been a prior, interior decadence in the religious and ecclesiastical heritage of the nations of Europe. Even the compelling power of Luther's oratory could not have found such an echo, had the beginnings of his views not somehow been familiar for a long time to the European mind.

It was, therefore, in the nature of things that this radical questioning should grow but slowly. Above all, before it had clearly emerged into consciousness, before it had been formulated, or grasped in its full import, it lay for long inarticulate within the secret, inner trend of the thoughts and deeds which determined the movement of history. From the awakening of the strongly personal piety within the Church in the twelfth century the way led through the destructive struggle of the Church with the "enlightened" Frederick II to the antipapal disintegration of the late Middle Ages. Ever more consciously, the contrast became expressed between the Roman Church and Christendom, between curia and papacy, between papal church and early Christian Church. To this one can add the name of Philip IV of France, the poverty controversy, nominalism Occam, *Defensor Pacis* [*Defender of Peace* by Marsilius of Padua, 1324], conciliar ideas, the Waldensians, the Cathars, Wycliffe, Huss, Hussites. What a vast, many-sided movement away from the Church then becomes visible.

And this movement of defection can be traced back to roots lying much further in the past.

Thus, for example, the whole tragic interconnection of justification, duty and fate in the course of the history of the world and of the Church had already become manifest in that great movement which the Church had been conducting—since the time of Gregory VII—for the liberation of its religious and spiritual principle from secular control. For this mighty process developed, at the same time, into a clericalisation of the Church, that is, to an exclusion of the laity from active participation in the government of the Church (strained relations with the ruling priestly caste arose and then changed to enmity), and to a de-sacralisation of the secular-political sphere. This process of secularisation contained also a bitter and self-perpetuating opposition between the Germanic and the papal, ultimately between Rome and Germany. From then on the interests even of the German Church were very often no longer those of the papacy. Pure faith, in terms of which it was possible to make a sharp division between papal politics and the papal, Catholic religion, provided a means of softening that opposition; but in real life this faith was not strong enough to keep friction permanently away from vital interests. Even at that time the great flight of churchmen and their concept of the Church into a "purely ecclesiastical" sphere (beyond real life in the actual political realm) was not particularly good for the Church.

The investiture controversy, in its broadest sense, inaugurated the rise of the medieval Church. Without it the great achievements of the Church in the high Middle Ages could scarcely have been realised. But, by the law of original sin, even the constructive elements in history are doomed to contain within themselves the seeds of their own corruption, which leads to new burdens, new trials and to new decisions. And so here too the investiture controversy became the cause of the decline of the Church, in the sense of a severe and lasting weakening of things papal and ecclesiastical.

This happened in a roundabout way through the concept of power which Gregory VII had introduced into the papal programme, but which so many of his successors had not succeeded in keeping on the high plane of heroic, religious devotion. Out of human weakness and egotism, by means of politics, law and greed they brought about that secularisation that led even further away from true Christianity, and which we know as the exaggerated curialism of the late Middle Ages, with its completely exaggerated views of direct papal jurisdiction over the temporal goods and laws of the Church and world.

In the meantime, the behaviour of the higher clergy had led the political rulers to turn a dangerous opinion into an axiom: the Church, that is its papal and episcopal incumbents, was to be fought like any other political, judicial and financial power. The battle against the pope, so often reckless in tone and in practical dealings (the pope figuring as "Antichrist," "son of wickedness," "blood sucker," "oppressor"), prepared the ground. As soon as this battle became allied with dogmatically false propositions people could easily, or at least more easily, find justification for false dogma in the long-familiar legitimacy of the battle. One cannot see, for example, how in 1412 in

Prague the papal bulls could have been consigned to the flames if people had not long been accustomed to that grim battle. The inner distortion (or emptiness) of the meaning of ecclesiastical institutions made independence from them easy, in spite of the fact that dogma was considered just as binding as ever. However, that this one-sided bond could never have developed and sustained sufficient strength to save the essential supreme authority of the Church, is taught by daily experience and proved extensively by history. This acceptance of dogma, and loyalty to the externals of the Church tend to be the last things to go, but once they do begin to go, their decline is very rapid. Suddenly they seem to lose their meaning. One day staunch Catholicism is there and is being emphatically lauded; the next day it is gone.

And hence it came about, that that fundamental doubt which had grown so slowly, spread out still more slowly into the masses. But in reality, as already indicated, in every sphere of life the ties with the Church became slacker and less absolute. That is to say, the impossibility of seriously calling the Church in question progressively dissolved, and the possibility of a radical transformation became more evident.

At the beginning of modern times the dissolution or obscuring of the Catholic idea assumed dangerous proportions, threatening life in two ways: it appeared first of all in the aggressive, heretical form of Hussitism and in the various, heretical (or quasi heretical) forms of apocalypsism, spiritualism and communistic socialism; and it also appeared under the guise of a scarcely perceptible, inner decomposition—in the indifferentism and immorality of Renaissance culture, in the secularisation of curialism, in the dangerous, intra-theological disintegration of what was Catholic in Occamism, and, most decisively, in the a-dogmatic and anti-dogmatic relativism of humanist, enlightened education and theology.

And yet it is precisely here that the mysterious element in the subsequent Reformation schism becomes evident. The Church was still the dominant power of the time, the acknowledged guardian and leader, the moulder, so men thought, of both public and private life. Proof of this can be adduced from many sides. The Christian faith was still the central point of all life, and it was taught and dispensed by the priests of the Roman pope; in science, theology, philosophy, law, as in social life, including the administration of justice, and charitable activity, the leadership of the clergy was not seriously called in question. Even the life of the state seemed conceivable only on a foundation of Church order.

And it is not as if this dominance was purely exterior. Precisely in this does the incomparably provocative and alluring paradox of the period fully disclose itself. We can sense this if we contrast the deep, truly evangelical, Church piety, the religious Church art of the years from 1500 to 1520, with the almost instantaneous defection of such wide circles to Luther.

At the same time we must interpret that proposition about the still unbroken dominance of the Roman Church over life in a very restricted sense, if we wish to avoid reaching an enormously false conclusion. In fact, fundamentally, the papal church was no longer the ruler and guide. Hussitism had torn away an entire country, Bohemia, from the western Church community and from the empire. But the decisive factor was that the visible and invisible foundations of life, out of which this dominance of the Church had first grown, had altered most radically. A breaking away from the Church on a gigantic scale, in part visible, in greater part invisible, had taken place; the power of the tradition of the Church as a demand for, and affirmation of, unquestioning obedience to the Church, had been essentially weakened.

Great revolutions are possible only where serious vacuums have formed within a dominant way of life. The vacuums suck alien, hostile forces in from outside, and these rush with elemental power into that which has become empty. The façade still stands, asserting its rights; but because it is itself in the wrong, and has become too superficial, the alien forces advance of themselves. Then there arises that apparently inexplicable, and yet basically natural process of the victory of new ideas over ancient, established power.

We will come to know the details of this process of undermining. Amongst the general causes we list, as always, the destruction of one's own substance by oneself, through the consumption of capital, instead of increasing one's substance and living upon the interest from capital. For example, spiritual capital was used up through the exaggerated use of spiritual weapons. This was one of the furthest-reaching causes, and one which had been longest at work in preparation. Here one must take account of the total process, extending over centuries, of the struggle between papacy and empire, with its excommunications, its antipopes and its large-scale invective. At the beginning of the preparation for the coming religious-ecclesiastical revolution stands the damage to the irreplaceable, religious, mystical aura which surrounded the pope as a completely other-worldly power. With every step into the sphere of politics, especially with every victorious step, the pope more and more became one ruler amongst many others. The twelfth and thirteenth centuries, too, contributed to this development, even although the life of faith was still advancing, and the purely spiritual substance of the hierarchy was still strong—as a result, maybe, of the mighty warnings uttered by St. Bernard and St. Francis. But then came Boniface VIII, Philip the Fair and the shattering incident of Anagni, after which, to all outward appearance, there remained in the most power-conscious of all popes, no trace of any likeness to God. Europe was left only with the profound experience that papal power, even in spiritual things, had very narrow limits. Then came the undignified haggling between Philip the Fair and Clement V—pope turned French court bishop and finally, Avignon, the emperor Louis the Bavarian and then the schism.

And we must not forget that not only the wholesale application of the highest spiritual punishments automatically diminished their effectiveness but that in the midst of a ceaselessly growing, extraordinarily rich self-awareness on the part of national states, provinces, and of the middle-class laity, Rome always linked very real political and economic demands with spiritual punishments. If the papacy, by an interdict on entire countries, could simply write them off (Bezold), then, whether this was formally justified or not, the situation had become quite impossible, so that the deepest, invisible foundation of faith, which presented Church and papacy as divine things, was severely threatened and dangerously weakened. Contemporaries knew well that in reality the papacy was identified with these things. The man, harshly affected by some punishment, distinguished between a secular and a dogmatic position, and yet did not distinguish. The wrath of the stricken was directed against individual popes, but very easily against the papacy as well.

In accordance with the universal character of the Church these developments applied almost equally to all of Europe. The Reformation, however, arose in Germany. Why?

The problem is very complicated and must, therefore, be approached from different angles. A provisional answer, leaving many elements (chiefly Luther) out of account, would run something like this: in Germany in the Catholic period there was never sufficient national fulfilment within the Church. What we mean is this: in Spain, France and England a present, although dangerous (cf. England) remedy against the common threat of an explosion in Church stability and European unity had been provided in time by the formation, with papal approval and within the unity of the Church, of national Churches, allowing considerable satisfaction of national interests within the Church. In these countries the explosive force was paralysed by this satisfaction, but the Germans were not satisfied and so the tendency towards rebellion in all the movements we have mentioned became, for the most part, concentrated in Germany. Because in Germany national interests had not been sufficiently satisfied by Rome there resulted a twofold intensification of the danger, making it easier for the breach to take place there than elsewhere. On the other hand, the political development in the kingdoms to the west made possible the political form of the Church just mentioned.

Roy Pascal

## 21

# The Social Basis
# of the German Reformation

In the face of the contradictions in Luther's theology and ecclesiastical policy, theologians have had to advance "excuses" for these inconsistencies. In particular, psychological explanations have been put forward to the effect that Luther was a man of a certain temperament, or was not able to foresee later developments, later interpretations of his doctrine. This would be all very well if Luther had not been the leader of a large and conscious movement, or if his thought and activity in other spheres belied the contradictions in his theology. It has been the purpose of this book, however, to show how Luther kept himself at the head of the reform movement, and how contradictions analogous to those in his theology appear in the rest of his thought. He destroys the authority of the Ecumenical Council and erects the Consistory, condemning the independence of thought of an Erasmus; he proclaims the integrity of the secular order and supports the princes in their struggle against the supreme secular head; he states that the commands of law have no divine quality, and yet promises that even heavenly rewards will follow on their observance; he knows that the princes are immoral and unreliable, yet puts in their hands, unreservedly, the material and spiritual welfare of the people; he opposes and accepts usury. With all this he shows himself to have been a man of great courage, perspicacity, integrity; these qualities distinguished him from his fellow-believers like Melanchthon and Bugenhagen, who were on many occasions ready to serve expediency when Luther insisted on principle. These contradictions cannot be overlooked. They cannot be ascribed to Luther's temperament or to his inadequacy to the task the times set him. The principle underlying them is fundamental to Luther's whole historical importance. This principle is not logical, it is not psychological; the repeated conflicts of Luther's life show it to have been sociological. The consistency amid all these contradictions, the consistency *of* the contradictions, is the consistency of class interest.

There are perhaps many people who are ready to grant that Luther's thought was guided into its peculiar lines by sociological moments, but who would not agree that the interest of any one class dominated his decisions. They might claim that he worked for the welfare of the German nation as a whole. If we examine his theory and practice in any one isolated sphere, this claim might seem persuasive. When Luther attacked the Papacy he was speaking for the whole of Germany; when he opposed the levellers and religious communists, the princes, nobles, and middle class united with him; when he finally sanctioned the struggle against the Emperor, most classes were with him; when he called for control of the financiers and monopolists, as when he scourged the morals of the princes, he represented a great body of opinion. Such was the constitution of society at that time . . . that any of these causes could count on the support of several classes. When we consider Luther's whole work, however, what is important is the highest common factor in the various bodies or groups who profited by his pronouncements. As far as practical action goes, there are two groups whose interests were continually advanced by Luther—the secular princes and that part of the middle class which had authority in the cities and the guilds but was not engaged in foreign monopoly trade or in finance. These two groups had by no means identical interests, but had common enemies, and each was a condition of the prosperity, of the existence, of the other. In England and France the alliance between the two had already shown itself to be the most powerful political force in society as it was then constituted. Owing to the strength of the territorial princes and the peculiar structure of the Empire, such a development had not been possible in Germany; the Emperor was not powerful enough to impose his will on the princes, nor had a constitutional monarchy as proposed by Nicolas of Cusa any reality. The consolidation of the absolutism of the princes, on the other hand, could not proceed in so simple a manner as that of the kings of England and France, for legally they were subject to the Emperor. The establishment of their independence needed a fundamental revision of the theory of society, so that while in England and France the growth of the monarchy meant in actual fact a continual gradual encroachment on the powers and rights of the Church, in Germany the theory of the Church, its theology, its political and legal theory, had to be revised in order to sanction such encroachment. This is the reason why Germany was the battleground of the Reformation, why the theoretical controversy there replaces the political struggle elsewhere as the focus of interest, why Luther is the German counterpart of Henry the Seventh or Louis the Eleventh.

Sanctions are not, of course, the affair of an all-powerful executive; its wishes are sufficient reason for its actions. Sanctions, which are simply the reverse of safeguards, are the affair of those who fear the power of others, whose desires have continually to be restrained by social necessity and who thus develop a theory of society and law to guarantee their own prosperity. Thus Frederick the Wise could remain a pious Catholic while placidly continuing with the expropriation of ecclesiastical property, and the bitter struggles of conscience were reserved to Luther and his associates. But Frederick and Philip of Hesse and all the other Protestant princes could not have acted as they did without the sanction and approval of the mass of the people. Although they possessed the most effective executive power in the Holy Roman Empire, they could use it only subject to the consent of the main body of their people, or to that, at least, of the authoritative leaders of the middle classes such as the town-councils. For instance, they more than once objected to taxes, which the Emperor Maximilian wished to impose, on the grounds that their subjects refused to pay and threatened rebellion. It was from these classes that the princes drew their power. Though their interests often clashed, they could both gain most from an alliance and a mutually favourable compromise. Thus the princes sustained Luther in his theological controversy as well as in his struggle with the Papacy as a temporal power and a Church. The complete revision of the social theory which this entailed gave them the support of all law-abiding citizens and contributed to their mutual advantage. Those princes who, on the other hand, claimed merely a reform of the Catholic Church, gained very little in comparison, and in particular could not later make their loss good for lack of a social theory which would justify such acts as expropriation of ecclesiastical property and centralisation.[1] A comparison between Frederick the Great and the Emperor Joseph the Second illustrates this, even so long after the Reformation as the end of the eighteenth century. The alliance between princes and middle class against the rest of the groups of interest in Germany was, then, no mere expediential matter, but a re-moulding of society and of its theoretical bases. Thus it is natural that Luther, who fashioned the shape social theory took in certain lands and preserved for three centuries, should have felt himself serving high ethical causes rather than the interests of a part of the middle class.

It is the necessary result of class conflict that the struggle is carried on in the ethical sphere as well as in that of politics. Where masses are engaged it is necessary that they should believe that certain guarantees accompany any alliance they make. And since, up till quite recent times, teleological guarantees were thought most binding, the struggle is waged over metaphysical as well as ethical issues. The pre-

---

[1] Of course the victory gained by the Protestant princes redounded to the benefit of Catholic princes too. The overthrow of medieval authority was general. The position of the Catholic princes became as absolute as that of the Protestant, except that formally the Church was an antagonistic force in Catholic principalities. Even the Jesuits avoided attacks on the established secular powers.

tended absoluteness of the resultant systems is the counterpart of the wish for the perpetuation of the respective political systems. Thus at any time there are a number of ethical systems, all differing and all claiming to be correct, all corresponding to the interests of particular political groups. An analysis of society according to the economic interest of several groups . . . is rightly considered inadequate, for a description of society does not assume resemblance to reality until groups are classified according to their ethic, to their general outlook on moral problems. Similarly, we cannot say definitely that Luther was the representative of the interests of a certain class until we have defined the moral outlook of this class and have proved Luther's to have been identical with it.

We can see in all ages that social classes produce an ethical system, or at least moral principles, which justify their economic and political rôle. The pious burghers of Muggleton, "mingling a zealous advocacy of Christian principles with a devoted attachment to commercial rights," are the rule, not the exception. This principle held in Luther's time as now, and the various social groups can be classified quite clearly according to their ethics. We need hardly consider the case of the Catholic Church in this connexion, since it defined itself primarily as a metaphysical and ethical system; it is enough to say that this system was developing into the rationalisation of the needs of the Papacy as a secular empire, with a supreme dogma of the infallibility of the Pope. All parties in Germany outside the Church opposed the imperialist policy of the Church and the principle of the identification of the secular and the spiritual worlds, but within this united opposition ideas as to what was right and wrong were varied. The concept of class gains in clarity if the various outlooks are described.

Among the Imperial knights, the remnants of the old fighting forces of the Empire, the idea of faithfulness to tradition and to the Emperor predominated. All the new developments in society were dangerous to them. Their property was expropriated by the larger secular princes. Their military services were no longer valuable in an age of mercenary armies and heavy artillery. The rise in prices which hit the peasants so heavily harmed them equally, for they lived on peasant labour. If they pledged their lands, they had no method of meeting their obligations, and were continually brought to penury. From a military point of view they were no match, even when they combined —a difficult matter, since their lands lay scattered all over Germany— for the armies of the princes, or for the forces organised by the larger cities. There was no independent career open to their younger sons, unless they became submissive courtiers at the court of a more powerful prince. It was natural that they should look back with longing on the times when they formed an integral part of the Empire, and that among them the concept of the "good old times" was current. Ulrich von Hutten was their spokesman. The virtues he praised were nation-alism, loyalty, freedom. The Emperor was the national hero, in spite of many clear proofs that Charles V, even Maximilian, were first and foremost dynasts interested chiefly in the glorification of their own house. Simplicity of life was a virtue in Hutten's eyes, and luxury meant for him the unpatriotic consumption of foreign goods, delicacies from the Orient, from France, and Italy. Trading he considered not merely a dishonourable, but also a dishonest and immoral calling, and said that the robber-knights were justified in waylaying the merchant caravans both for moral and practical reasons. The courts of princes were in his eyes hotbeds of luxury, the court officials sycophantic and lacking in the prime virtues of independence and honesty. His moral code is, indeed, convincing up to a point, and we can understand why he championed Luther, and why Luther felt in many things akin to him.

The international bankers and merchants also developed their moral code, which was not very different from that of Big Business today. A feeling of responsibility towards commercial and social obliga-tions, which was quite lacking in Hutten, is their basic principle. There is a noteworthy letter written by Jakob Fugger to Charles V (received by the Emperor on April 24, 1523)[2] in which this belief in the sacredness of a business obligation leads the financier to use the most outspoken language to his Emperor, language which would have seemed most presumptuous in any contemporary. Loyalty and honesty belonged naturally to the code of such a man. The class to which the Fugger belonged subscribed to more specifically Christian virtues, as their counterparts do today. That is, they exploited the community by all the commercial and financial tricks possible, and had no hesitation in stimulating wars, but joined with this a strong local patriotism and made charitable endowments on a large scale. While they could not be devoted allies of the Papacy, their peculiar enemies were the knights and the secular princes, who were not wealthy enough to give them room for operating and who put all sorts of barriers in the way of commerce. Thus on the whole they were loyalists, since the rule of the Emperor was the best guarantee for freedom of operation, though in this matter they were bound to be determined by particular business ties.

When we come to the broader masses of the middle class a different outlook appears. The moral code of the Imperial knights could be so clear because as a class their social function was clearly distinct from that of any other contemporary class, and they had a definite attitude towards contemporary society as a whole. The middle classes, on the other hand, affirmed social forms as they were, merely demanding

---

[2] Quoted by Ehrenberg, *Capital and Finance in the Age of the Renaissance*, p. 80.

modifications. In their morality, therefore, they dealt with individual failings and the duties of small groups, principles whereby society could be made more efficient from their point of view. In particular, the idea of work came to have a peculiar value. The general attack on the Catholic Church was delivered on the ground of the unproductivity of the institutions of the Church. There was immense moral indignation against the begging orders of friars, against begging of any sort, and one of the first tasks in towns which accepted the Reformation was not merely the organisation of charity, but the provision of employment for the unemployed. The two aspects of this principle of work—the obligation to work and the right to a proper reward for work—arose from two different social attitudes within the middle classes, as we shall see in a moment.

The main body of social satire and criticism rose from these classes, and was based on this idea of the moral value of work. One of the most popular works of the times was a modernised version of the medieval French epic of *Reynard the Fox*, in which efficiency is extolled at the expense of virtue. The famous *Ship of Fools* of Sebastian Brant satirises vices (follies as he significantly calls them) chiefly from the point of view of efficiency. Thus the parasitic Church, drunkenness, debauchery, idleness, unproductive professions like the law, come in for their full share of blame. But the idea of efficiency is not an abstract moral idea; it applies to a particular social form and is a form of propaganda for an existing order. Thus we find at this time a general satire by the citizens in the towns of the peasants, of their stupidity, avarice, even poverty; but the town-councils did not support the reasonable demands of the peasants put forward in the Twelve Articles, and acquiesced in their further suppression after the failure of the Peasants' Revolt. The peasants' conception of the proper conditions of work, of efficiency, was not shared by the town-dwellers. The limitation of middle-class ethic is shown most evidently in a passage in the *Ship of Fools* where Brant reproves those journeymen who, by working too much, cause over-production and break prices, so that the masters suffer:[3] he does not, however, criticise guild monopolies and control of price and production. On the whole, this moral outlook is based on the obligation to work; and the Christian virtues of love and submissiveness are adduced to sustain this system amongst those who do not profit by it. It is the outlook of a privileged class. In its attack on the privileges of the Church it needed some dogmatic authority which would guarantee its own privileges. Thus it upheld the idea of authority; and in the free Imperial cities the oligarchic despotism of the patriciate, which followed on the Reformation, was equivalent to the despotism of the princes in the principalities. The

---

3 Seb. Brant. *Narrenschiff. Ein gesellen schiff.*

sharp distinction drawn by Luther between the secular and spiritual sphere corresponded exactly to the needs of this privileged class. This theory justified privilege in the secular sphere, while freeing from its burden in the spiritual. Luther satisfied them, further, in that he attempted to dissuade from violence, which always means mob-rule, and to reform by the unanimous wish of the people, *i.e.* through existent authority. "Passive resistance" and the belief in the necessary victory of the true doctrine became articles of their moral code.

But not all of the middle classes profited by privilege, and not all subscribed to this moral code and the metaphysics on which it was based. Amongst those groups who suffered from ecclesiastical and secular privilege the idea of equality had subsisted since the introduction of Christianity. The principle of equality of conscience, which Luther enunciated as a polemical weapon, rallied round him the lower classes in the towns, and also the peasants. But workers in industry like the weaving, which was largely controlled by big merchants, and journeymen, for whom entry into the mastership was hindered by artificial restrictions, imagined that equality of conscience meant a real freedom for them. On one side they attempted to reorganise the Church on an equalitarian basis, each member taking the lead as the spirit moved him; on the other, their inspirations led them to devote themselves to the religious life, in which none took precedence of them, and to prophesy awful punishments to those who still were occupied with earthly business and self-advancement. They instituted common ownership of property, and put expropriated ecclesiastical property to the service of the whole community. Their principles were love and charity towards their neighbours and devotion above all to the life of the soul. But where they encountered the resistance and hard-heartedness of other classes they did not merely prophesy judgments from God. They found biblical texts enough, and inspirations enough, to justify the use of armed force against their unbelieving oppressors. Their aim became the immediate realisation of the kingdom of Christ, and their moral code embraced both mortification of individual desires and the unhesitating sacrifice of their lives. It was apparent to them, under Münzer's guidance, that while their doctrines were held by only a section of the community there could be no question of Christ's kingdom on earth. It was only later, after the cruel lessons at Mülhausen, Münster, and other places, that their doctrines took the idealistic form of pietism.

The peasants form the last group of interest we have to consider. Owing to the savage exploitation to which they were subject, their rising was of a more frankly economic nature than the movement of any other class. The anti-clericalism in the Twelve Articles is fairly obviously due to economic causes. But no peasants' rising during the Middle Ages had been free of communistic elements. The peasants had promised to retract any of the Twelve Articles which could not be justified by Christ's teaching, and in Christ's teaching they found many elements of agrarian communism. Equality of conscience meant for them equality of property, and they held a belief in the viciousness of towns and town occupations. It was this class-consciousness which led to the powerful uprising which threatened the princes themselves, not merely the economic demands peculiar to the situation of the peasants at that time.

In the organism of Germany at the beginning of the sixteenth century these were then the moral components, corresponding to the economic components. Any individual in any of these groups could consider himself working for the furtherance of high moral values and could justify antagonism against any other group on moral grounds. And moral principles, inculcated by education and environment, are as potent to move men to action and self-sacrifice as is economic advantage; further, being necessarily more vague and general than economic principles, they can unite together masses which have not necessarily the same ultimate aims. This was the strength of Luther's cause. By fighting the Papacy on metaphysical grounds he began at the right end of the stick. He rallied the whole of Germany, even foreign countries, on his side. From this beginning his doctrines narrow themselves down, repudiating alliances which had earlier been expedient. But though here and there his political and economic theory shows what class he represents, the struggle is mainly on a moral and theological level. He is convinced that he is protecting the Good and True. The analysis of his theology has shown, I hope, that the new elements in it were only such as allowed a new social order to be formed. His morality is everywhere marked with the standards of a particular class. His moral strictures on the peasants and enthusiasts bear in particular a class character. But the same signs are to be observed in his more general attitude. In his polemics against the levellers, as against the Turks, he stresses above all the danger threatened by these enemies of society to the family. He represents them as breaking up the home, sullying the purity of wives and maidens. Similarly, to describe religious experience he uses terms culled from the intimacy of family life. He believed that in the family the highest Christian virtues are cultivated, and wished to make it the model for the State. But the family is more than the fundament of the moral order: it was the basis of the state in which he lived. The preservation of the family is essentially linked up with the preservation and inheritance of private property. The enthusiasts and peasants were, of course, in the main quite innocent of the crimes against women which Luther imputed to them; but he was right in diagnosing their economic levelling theories as a threat to the family. It was a natural step to transpose the argument to the moral sphere. And the mass of supporters which followed Luther would not be misled by this method of attack, but rightly inflamed more hotly thereby.

There is no need to repeat Luther's values. He shared those of the settled, authoritarian middle class—the belief in "passive resistance," in the inevitable and pacific victory of the truth, in authoritarian methods, in the family, in Christian love and submissiveness, in the sanctity and necessity of work. Though he worked quite clearly for his own class in the economic sphere, he certainly had no consciousness of the class basis of these moral values. For this reason he was so dogmatic in maintaining them; Melanchthon, who was a finer and more rational mind, was led to waver this way and that through too rational an approach to Luther's dogmas. It must not be thought, of course, that this whole system was the abstract product of the middle class, simply and solely the rationalisation of the economic needs of the contemporaries of Luther. The metaphysical system, especially particular concepts, of such a class might be imagined in a different form than Lutheranism. They evolved, however, historically from a former state of society, together with the middle class itself. They are modifications of ideas and values which permeated the whole of society, and at no point in history is a complete revision of concepts possible unless a complete revolution in authority is aimed at. Luther's class enjoyed some part of authority before the Reformation, however, and consequently did not wish for a complete revolution. Indeed, it needed to sustain some authority in order to maintain its privileges against the claims of other classes. Thus Luther worked inside the traditional framework of ideas, and even preserved the traditional concept of dogma.

An analysis of a historical period such as this book attempts is, of course, inadequate without a wide perspective into the preceding and following times. Every aspect of the civilisation at a particular epoch arises from and is determined by the past. The materialistic conception of history must be distinguished from the crude theory that historical events are determined by economic conditions. The vital fact arising from the effect of economic moments on human beings is the creation of social and political forms, of class; and understanding of the nature of class is a presupposition for the understanding of history. The warring classes of the past, in competition for the hegemony of society, have created systems of metaphysics, of ethics, an art of their own. The idealism of individuals has contributed to the self-preservation, the self-assertion of the class. It is a complex task to penetrate to the heart of so elaborate a structure. It is hoped, however, that this book has not neglected any important aspect of the problem, and provides a clue to the meaning of the immense fermentation which was the Reformation.

# Ernst Bloch

---

## 2 2

# The Millenarianism
# of the Peasants' War
# and Anabaptism

Until a certain point, the peasant's fate had not been totally dreadful. His circumstances were bearable; they had even started to improve with monetary and urban development. This was so not only because the peasant delivered his goods to the city, thus obtaining the means to free himself from serfdom if the lord would agree to this redemption, but because even when he was not set free, he could find in the town a place of freedom, an ultimate haven.

Gradually, however, the problem ceased to be merely oppression by some landlord, which had still permitted the serf to manage; in time, urban development no longer provided any benefit to the rural population. It began to feel the weight of the economic results of the decision made by free townsmen to put themselves under the protection of a powerful lord who would defend them against violence and, if need be, represent them in the courts; the quit-rent they paid for this guarantee became a tithe which was more and more ruthlessly levied. Though it is true that the valuable town market—less and less able to provide for its needs within the town walls—had once supplied the peasants with currency and protected them against the insatiable greediness of the feudal lords (thanks to the principle that "the air of the town sets one free"), from the beginning of the fifteenth century, this was less and less true, especially in Germany. The main factors accounting for this deterioration were the growing importance of capital, especially commercial capital, but even more, the tremendously increased absolutism of the princes who allied themselves with capital.

Increasingly subjected to warlike lords, the petty bourgeoisie entered a period of stagnation. Futhermore, the development of corporatism, the increasingly strict barriers against the influx of new townsmen of rural origin, had already closed the peasant's access to the free communes. But the petty nobility was also experiencing hard times, and the peasantry under it felt the impact of its impoverishment. For the Junkers things had been going badly for some time already; gone forever were the days when the looting of convoys passing by their lairs assured them of daily spoils. Though deeply in debt, they dreamed of rivaling the luxury of the rich merchants and the princes. Moreover, knighthood had lost its importance because of the development of regular armies and the technology of firearms now available to the princes. These two factors increasingly reduced minor lords to greater and greater dependence upon higher nobility. Thus, from the fifteenth century on, knighthood was simultaneously subjected to a double pressure from above and below—from the peasants and from the princes (themselves linked with capitalism).

The landed nobility held its own as well as it could for a while, but after the defeat of Sickingen it had to surrender its autonomy completely to the princes in order to secure the right to oppress the peasantry without the slightest scruple and to fully enjoy the benefits of the land rent and the excess profits of agriculture. This is why, before the Peasants' War, but even more so afterward, the big urban bourgeoisie and landed nobility alone saw their power grow tremendously; this was the necessary result of the increased production and circulation of goods. While in France and England the development of trade and industry, by the interlocking of interests throughout the country, had resulted in political centralization, in a more backward Germany the same economic process resulted only in concentrating interests around local centers, and therefore in a political dispersion and a provincialization which, in a Germany excluded from international trade, could only become increasingly set and rigid. The old empire of a purely feudal type, based on outmoded economic patterns, fell to pieces. By the same token, the big imperial barons became almost independent princes, benefiting from and representing local and provincial centralization in a broken-up empire. The emperor, who once symbolized a status and a concept of the state no less universal than the status and the concept of the Church, descended more and more to the rank of a mere prince among the others of the empire, whose decadence he was utterly powerless to stop. Furthermore, the princes' need for money increased faster than commercial expansion; it increased because of the mercenary armies, the cost of a complex bureaucracy, and the luxury and growth of the courts. Because the cities as well as the minor and great nobility could solve their difficulties only through agricultural production and its excess profits, the whole weight of the pyramid corresponding to this new society ultimately fell on the peasants, on that central and defenseless mass, equally exploited by every state of the empire.

Faced with this oppression, and so long as it was not utterly intolerable, the peasants either bowed down silently or looked to the emperor to save them, in a dream that long paralyzed and deluded them. At the time of the Albigensians, Abbé Joachim de Flore had prophetically hailed Emperor Frederick II as the liberator of the "people"; when he died without having achieved this result, the peasants began to believe that Frederick was still alive, that he was in hiding and would come back to carry through the unfinished venture of the holy reformation.

Two royal legends thus took form: the French were expecting a new Charlemagne; the Germans, a new Frederick. The image of the Hohenstaufen was only later replaced retrospectively by that of Frederick Barbarossa, the emperor who appears on rare occasions, on his mountain and only before simple people, the one whose return will restore the greatness of the empire—not just any empire of the commonly known kind, but the very Kingdom of Christ, a communistic and apostolic one. The fact that the emperor would appear only in the heart of a mountain clearly shows that this legend is linked with ancient traditions; it harks back to a primitive and recurring myth, the image of the underground cave, of the Python, of the lunar divinities of matriarchal times, or that of the Hebrew Messiah hidden in a "bird's nest." The imperial legend, then, was clearly so deeply rooted that it was difficult at first for the idea of the "republic" to emerge from these muted or radiant astral dreams.

The day came, however, when the peasants got tired of waiting, when their legitimate anger could only explode. Secret meetings were held in isolated valleys, masses of people surged from dales and forests. In 1300, Lombard bands gathered; the lords felt the threat of the raised fist; and the insurrection was ruthlessly suppressed. Eighty years later, it was the French Jacquerie, just as rapidly and just as cruelly put down; now Germany was seething: throughout the fifteenth century, peasant revolts succeeded one another. First came the piper of Niklashausen, who demanded, in his Marian sermons, the total abolition of all duties, all rents, all corvées, the free and complete use of the forests, the waters, and the fields. In 1420, the Hussite War appears at the same time as the first sign of a general upheaval. Up until then, the heretics had remained in small groups, usually harmless because of their own weakness, the strength of their opponents, and the pacifist tendencies of original Christianity. But in Bohemia, where industry developed so early, a heroic era was inaugurated, the era of a communist and Christian revolution, whose power and impetus, as well as the consciousness of its aims, went much further than anything the heretics of the past had ever known, the Albigensians included. Here, the conflict within the ruling classes preceded the more basic conflict, accelerated by the torture of Hus and heightened by the national struggle of the Czechs against the privileged Germans. Thus there emerged—over and above the land-sharing ideal of the petty bourgeoisie, over and above the patrician-republican ideal of the high bourgeoisie and the aristocracy—the progressive and conquering communism of the Taborites, promoted by a radicalized peasantry and a powerful proletariat.

In Germany, a similar scandal was to break out only a hundred years later, when the sight of a weak monk boldly appearing before the emperor and the empire created confusion among the people, who were all the more confused and disturbed because they were unable to detect the interplay of interests underlying such boldness. Pure doctrine having thus proved irresistible, the outcast and Caliban mask could be dropped, and the door, even the most solid, opening to the kingdom of freedom seems to have been broken in. It is clear that to the economic factor was added, to set off the revolution, a political factor with mechanisms of a different kind: a desperate people and, at the same time, a conflict within the ruling classes who tore at each other with all their might. The whole structure tumbled all at once, and for the second time, the decaying Holy Roman Empire is assailed by all who are thirsty for land, all who are thirsty for happiness, by the religious and revolutionary will of the people, heralded by the frenzy of princes and capitalists.

That is why, beyond their economic aspects, the deepest roots of peasant upheavals have to be considered. If the circumstances and the possibilities of the time are to be grasped, it is necessary to take into account another need, another appeal. For if economic desires are the essential and constant ones, they are neither the only ones nor, in the long run, the most powerful; and they do not constitute the most direct motivations of the human soul, especially at times when religious feelings are uppermost. Opposed to economic events or parallel to them, acts of free will always intervene, as well as spiritual structures of universal significance whose reality, at least from the sociological standpoint, is undeniable. Whatever it may be, the state of the mode of production, as an economic attitude, itself depends on wider psychological and moral complexes that have a determining impact—especially, as Max Weber has shown, on religious complexes.

The economic factor itself is soon weighted with a superstructure, and its autonomous process of development conditions the emergence of cultural and religious configurations, but it would be wrong to believe that it can produce them all by itself, independent of the interplay of actions and reactions that link them to national character, to ideologies which survived former economic relationships, to the ideology of the developing society whose superstructure is often ahead of that of the economy, which has not yet reached maturity. To this should also be added the long-term influence, which every revolutionary class can perceive, of the spiritual and religious process (an often interrupted one) through which the human species educates itself—an autonomous process corresponding to historical necessity, if not itself historical, and belonging to the "philosophy of history." This is why a purely economic analysis is not only unable to explain thoroughly, with all its conditions and its causes, the mere emergence of so important a historical phenomenon as the Peasants' War, but such an analysis runs the risk of disintegrating, destroying, divesting of their original character by reducing them to the level of pure ideology the deeper contents of this seething human history, this daydream of the antiwolf, of the kingdom of brotherhood.

Marx himself gives religious raptures their due, at least during the first stage of every great revolution, to the extent that the new masters have felt themselves to be neo-Romans, neo-pagans; to the extent that the German peasants borrowed from the Old Testament its vocabulary, its passions, and its illusions (as the Puritans were to do later for their bourgeois revolution), to the extent that the French Revolution too donned the titles, the slogans, the costumes of Roman Consulate and Empire. In spite of the positivist spirit in which Marx removed communism from the domain of theology and confined it to that of political economy, thus depriving it of all its millenarian aspects (those it derives from history as well as those which are inherent in it), he does recognize that the "necromancies of history" have in reality a stimulating effect. In the particular case of the Peasants' War, with all its powerful imagery and spiritualism, it is all the more impossible (next to the economic factors that determined the unleashing of the struggle and the choice of its objectives) not to consider in itself its most essential and primary element: the familiarity with the oldest of dreams, the emergence and spread of the old heretical movement, the impatient, rebellious, and most serious ecstatic will for progress straight to Paradise. Inclinations, daydreams, most serious and purest emotions, enthusiasms directed to an end feed upon needs other than the most obvious one without becoming an empty ideology. They never disappear, having marked a prolonged period with their imprint; they spring up from a point in the soul where values originate and are defined; they survive all empirical disasters and retain their full strength, keeping forever present the millenarianism that so strongly inspired the sixteenth century, that of the Peasants' War and of Anabaptism.

So at that time, they wished, first of all, to do away with all adventitious constructions, to recover the state of youth. The peasants demanded a return to their former status. Things not only had to turn to their benefit but also to revert to the exact stage where they had once been when they were still free men, in free communities—when, in its original freshness, the countryside was open to all like a communal field. Despised, often contaminated himself by this contempt, the peasant had finally become proud of his status, proud of this humble condition that brought him so close to Christ's disciples, and the sweat from his work became a symbol in his eyes. It was the water that extinguishes the fire, that purifies, that justifies. A great pagan challenge was thus mixed with the apostolic era the best of them were dreaming about.

Second, however, their eyes were turned to the outside, to the far away; once again there was an attempt to read the stars. Even the common people endeavored to do so, now with fright and now with hope; the scene where Goethe, in his *Goetz*, has two peasant leaders converse illustrates this huge play of mirrors between heaven and earth:

Arise! Arise! We are off to Heilbronn. Sound the call all around.

The fire will still give us light for a good part of the way. Did you see the great comet?

Yes, it's a dreadfully dangerous omen. If we walk all night, we'll see it very well. It rises around one o'clock in the morning.

It shines for only five quarters of an hour. It looks like a bent arm holding a sword, the color of blood, a reddish yellow.

Did you see the three stars at the point of, and along, the sword?

And the wide cloud-colored spoke, with thousands and thousands of streaks, like a spear with, on the inside, little swordlike things?

I was terrified. What a pale red this whole thing is, with, underneath, so many firing flames and, inside, the dreadful figures, with their shaggy heads and beards!

Did you see that one too? And everything swarms as in a sea of blood, and doesn't stop moving, so much so that you lose your wits. Let's get up!

In Hungary too, they claimed to have seen, in the night, men fighting in the sky; on the banks of the Rhine, they thought they heard, in broad daylight, a big commotion and clash of arms in the air, like a real battle. Soon the rumor spread that two circles had formed around the moon, with a cross in the middle; around the sun, there were three circles, with a torch on the side, calling to mind the Johannine vision of the angel standing in the sun, shouting in a loud voice (*Apocalypse*, 19:17). The old prediction that accompanied Münzer from the start seemed on the point of fulfillment: the time was nearing when the waters would be full; in this year 1524, which the prophets had augured as a time of misfortune, all the planets were gathered in the house of Pisces. But Jupiter, the sparkling planet, looked hard toward Saturn, entered in conjunction with the peasants' star; the celestial clock rang to herald the day of judgment and the hour of the Messiah.

Wandering preachers were no longer satisfied with stirring up a few individual brothers by means of some timid symbols inscribed on doors and roofs; their appeal spread; they resorted to astrology in order to set dates, to promise signal victories. Enraptured, the people saw the advent of a shattering world, full of crushed lords and priests, submerged by an endless flood of water and blood; beyond, they set their eyes on the Kingdom of Heaven. Roughness and kindness, witches' round and coming triumph of sacred love, pagan cross lying in the abyss and cross held up high above the universe by the Chosen People, kingdom of Nimrod and kingdom of Christ—all this clashed, fought, hailed one another, reaching a functional correlation in a most dreadful division of moral and metaphysical powers. Add to all this the prophecy of Joachim de Flore, strangely instrumented, instigated, revealed, taught, demanded by the stars themselves—whose echoes seemed to pervade the whole world—announcing the impending arrival of a Third Gospel, the last in time.

The same Abbé Joachim who, in the twelfth and thirteenth centuries had prophetically hailed Emperor Frederick II as the savior of the people, exerts now, in the century of the Hussites and the Peasants' War, a great influence by prophesying a Third Empire (which will succeed that of law, i.e., of the state, and that of grace, i.e., of the Church). His writings describe the empire corresponding to this third and last Gospel as an impending and perfect Pentecost—that is, the enlightenment and freeing of all toiling and downtrodden people, thanks to the Holy Spirit and the communion in this Spirit. In the very near future not only God the Father, or the Law, but also God the Son, of the grace of love, will cease to reign and to impose their rule; the last Gospel, as the Holy Spirit of God, or *plenitudo intellectus* [completeness of understanding], needing neither state nor church, will burst into the now shattered prehistory which, until then, had been time. The prophecy interprets for its followers all the astrological signs in the sense of a change both of era and of humanity reduced to a puppet state; it heralds both the ultimate disaster and the miracle of Pentecost. And the feeling of finding one's place in the heart of the cosmos plays here its part as an apocalyptic intrusion in the genesis and the destruction of the universe, in the form of a twilight tearing away from Hell and of a victory. So the men who belong to this other facet of the Renaissance—dedicated to millenarianism and not to the Muses—have the impression of living under threat and at the same time, of being laden with honors; they fancy that nights of Advent are falling upon them, heralding the approach both of the thousand personifications of Evil—destructive genies, demons, astral spirits—and of the light of Christmas, nights where a purely astrological pandemonium mingles with a "pantheism" made up of a completely different theurgy, that of nostalgia and, at the same time, of faith in a secret path through which the old world and God himself will disappear to make place for the one and only Christian community.

Furthermore, the wandering preachers deal among the Christians with a third reality, the most important of all: not only the new challenge of the individual and pagan reminiscences, not only the astral and zodiacal conjunctions (historically effective, objectively problematical), but, at the same time, a great strengthening of human interiority, based on complete faith in the occurrence of a deep change in the most remote times. After a long era of preparation, living man now calls upon himself; it is through his own action that good will begin to be promoted. In spite of so much suffering, so much fear and trembling, the spark descended from above shines with a new brightness in every soul and communicates its fire to the wavering empire: "Through the advent of faith," says Münzer, "we, men of flesh and earthly creatures, thanks to the Incarnation of Christ, must all become gods." If God has become man, we must understand that it is true that the whole man, the abyssal man, becoming conscious of the image he carries in his innermost being, also becomes god. . . . The baptism of the true Reformation was possessed of the new infinity of human hope; from Münzer to Paracelsus and to Boehme, the only problem was, through the power of faith, to transmute into gold, into interiority, into a radiant Jerusalem, all the evil of earth and of "creatureness"— to prefer a utopian alchemy to a perfected and coercive astrology—to shatter God and drive him to love and to the coming Kingdom of the Spirit.

Thus, ever since the Brothers of the Valley, those mystical lay brotherhoods already active at the time of Eckhart and increasingly enterprising after Münzer and the Spiritualists, what started to emerge was the soul itself—freedom, as a new force, the ultimate force of salvation. . . . The soul now becomes the only thaumaturgical root, daughter and creator of the eternal Word which first in God reveals God; and this revolutionary magic of the object all at once overthrows the thing-idols, the astral idols, and the equally reified omnipotent Omni-God of the medieval Church—carrying God beyond things, beyond the world, and beyond God himself, all the way to the mystery of his own image, foreshadowed but not yet known. At this deep level ultimately lies the motive power and the content of the most spiritual revolution the world had ever known in its full scope; if it is a fact that Christopher Columbus was not seeking the road to the earthly Indies, but rather Atlantis or Paradise, it is even truer that Thomas Münzer's ark was aiming at nothing less than the ultimate of Christ and the Apocalypse.

No matter how strong the desire to renovate earthly life, it had to conform to these ultimate aims. To be sure, in their confusion the peasants remembered their former rights, and they mixed personal challenge with their need to recover the origins of Christianity. To be sure, the voices of the preachers, more widely heard every day, in calling the people to liberation, to stripping, to utter void, also directed them to earthly emancipation within an apostolic life. Even more so, the work of destruction of feudal society undertaken by the Humanists was aimed to secular ends; it involved the return to ancient sources, especially to those authors who had planned the application to the state of the basic principles of communism. . . . But all this returning to tradition of the Humanists, this engaging soul searching, in the face of Roman law and Pauline antitheses which had a meaning only in terms of absolute monarchy, all this returning would not have had any resonance if the people had not experienced precisely this strange, bewildering, millenarian intrusion, this fear of Judgment and of the Night, this unique prayer for the light of dawn to break.

But this movement restricted all will for earthly reform and revolution to a mere brief preparatory stage before the advent of the eternal Kingdom, so that Christ might find the world, when he would return to judge it and bring it back to himself, in an utterly apostolic era. The will to take root was therefore a superficial one among the broken people of the late Gothic era: the other tendency, the more basic one, was powerful among the masses and dominant among the Baptist leaders. In order to assess the extent to which it asserted itself at the time, one need only remember that Luther himself, though he refrained from any political and moral undertaking that might have served as a preparation for the Last Judgment, expected the end of the world, at the latest, toward mid-century.

It is, however, in the Bible that the Baptists found convincing evidence as to the omen of the end and the particular demands this end entailed. Since in the beginning of the world, up to the time of Nimrod, communism reigned; since it also reigned in the middle era, the time of the Apostles, it was imperative that it should reign as well at the time when the last days were believed to be near, for communism alone could enable the world to bear the dreadful questioning to which Christ would subject it on his return to earth. . . . So groups of people now started to assume a new shape; there were no longer just small secret meetings, pilgrimages, spine bent low, in the catacombs of the convents, nor even those free and peaceful communities of Beguines and Lollards, avoiding everybody, passionate, and purified by their faith in the coming advent of Christ; it was the time of the erection of the Tabor, of the city wholly devoted to spiritual communism. Finally Münzer appeared, crossing the threshold of the adventist city, extravagant, heading for disaster. The struggle here was not for better times, but for the end of time, strictly speaking, in an apocalyptic propaganda of action. The struggle was not to overcome earthly obstacles, openly, in a eudemonist civilization, but to derealize them through the intrusion of the Kingdom. Mankind had never known a deeper will or experience than in this baptism's aim for mystical democracy. What was yesterday a dream and a prospect must be achieved tomorrow; against this nostalgic aspiration, coercion is powerless, and so is darkness. Beyond the desert awaits the Promised Land, its splendor already exposed to view; for Münzer, God never ceased to be during the day a Cloud, and in the murkiest night, a Pillar of Fire.

. . . At that time, neither the aspirations of the peasants, nor the wishes of the progressive bourgeoisie, nor even the knightly dreams of a Hutten could be fulfilled in practice. Lasalle is not mistaken when he repeatedly remarks that, though the rebellious peasants considered themselves revolutionaries, all they wanted was to go back to an out-dated situation of small plots. They aspired to the division of the land. In any case, only the free and independent landlords were to be repre-sented in the Diets; they wanted an empire of small peasants, without nobility or princes. The reactionary character of the aristocratic upris-ing led by Sickingen can be even more clearly shown; as for the one instigated by Hutten, however radical it might have been on other points, it was not radical on the issue of serfdom: Hutten aimed at establishing a nobiliary democracy crowned by a monarchy. In his writings about the Peasants' War, Engels remarks:

Nobiliary democracy based on service, as it existed in Poland and as it persisted for several centuries, with minor variations, in the kingdoms conquered by the Germans, is one of the most primitive social forms, and its evolution usually results in the establishment of a highly developed feudal hierarchy, already representing a much higher level.

But for Lasalle, the failure of the peasant movement can be ex-plained mainly by its faithfulness to a principle valid only for an era which is in fact reaching its end:

In opposition to the revolt of the peasantry and the nobility, the rise of the territorial princes was based on the idea of a sovereign state independent of landed property; indeed, these princes represented a concept of the state as independent of all private property relations. In this sense, they constituted a relatively legitimate and revolutionary factor—and this is exactly what enabled them to develop successfully and to defeat the movements of the peasants and the nobility.

From this point of view, peasant democracy and aristocratic democracy *both* belonged to the past, and the will that inspired these two movements was therefore confused, sentimental, romantic, reac-tionary. To be sure, Münzer's preaching seemed to have aims still more remote and unreal: he calls upon the peasants to pool all their posses-sions; he leaps far beyond the shortsighted dreams of democracy and empire. Even nationalism is foreign to him; he boldly replaces a popu-lar emperor of a mystical type with Christ himself, a mystical universal republic, a theocracy, and something deeper yet: He demands com-plete common ownership, a return to Christian origins, a rejection of all public authority, the reduction of the law to Christian ethics and education. But all these demands imply a most unusual combination of forces. On the one hand, he consciously relies on the mining prole-tariat, while on the other he turns just as consciously to the spontane-

ity of the perfect Christian, completely freed of the dialectic of
economic determinism. He builds a kind of huge bridge linking what
is most effective on the plane of reality to what is most effective on the
plane of suprareality, and he places both at the very apex of the
revolution.

To be sure, the relations of production, such as they were at the
time, required private property (and, as opposed to the striving of the
peasants toward a system of small plots, they required, in the agricultural domain, and even more so in that of industry, a developing and
productive private property, and therefore economic inequality).
These relations of production also required and fostered the development of provincial centralization, the rise of those territorial princes
who were the biggest landowners and ultimately the owners of the
state itself, the representatives of the omnipotent "concept of the
State." . . .

If, in a country lacking the industrial conditions for Marxism, the
Bolsheviks succeeded in imposing by sheer will power the communist
ideal so closely linked to human nature, can Münzer be regarded as
Quixotic for totally ignoring, on the path to communism, the intermediate economic and historical step, for enlisting with equal determination the proletarian and millenarianist legions of the revolution?
True, an overburdened people could only answer this appeal in a far
too dispersed order; equally true, the princes were victorious on the
worldly and economic plane. But this is no objection, or only a minor
one, pitted against Münzer's impact, against the perfect tactical and
theoretical precision, the complete adequacy, the concreteness of his
fixed idea and of his idealism, his self-confidence, his conviction that
the time was ripe, his loyalty to the sovereign truth of the idea. Thus,
in his very failure, Thomas Münzer is in no way pathetic, episodic,
or ridiculous; he remains a fully representative, exemplary, tragic
figure. His failure was one more obstacle to the development of a
universal idea, genuinely incarnated, correctly presented, adequately
conceived.

On this point, we must admit that there is great divergence among
verdicts, particularly among the most sympathetic ones. Engels blames
Münzer for assuming responsibility for the movement at a moment
when it was not yet ripe enough to be assigned proletarian ends. On
the other hand, the bourgeois historian Zimmermann accepts, in the
last analysis, Münzer's entire endeavor, including the uprising of
Upper Germany, but nevertheless reaches, though with less class-
consciousness, a conclusion similar to that of Engels. He writes:

Münzer would have been a great man if, besides his imagination and
his multi-faceted receptivity, he had also possessed the necessary qualities for the achievement of his aims—if his talent for seeing things prac-

tically as they are and for carrying them out effectively had been equal to his poetical flights of fancy—and the skill to stir agitation and revolt in the deep layers of the population.

The same author stresses:

What Münzer lacked to be a Cromwell—a man who, though he had never been a soldier, suddenly emerged as a military genius—was to be endowed not only with inner enthusiasm, but also an iron fist and a clear view of all the demands of reality, whereas Münzer's view, which was never very clear when faced with reality, became blurred and strayed at the moment of danger.

Kautsky, on the other hand, expresses a value judgment on Münzer diametrically opposed to that of both Engels and Zimmermann, although, judging from a purely economic point of view and remaining on the level of purely practical politics, he gives little attention to ideas (and claims in fact not to have found "a single new idea" in Münzer, undoubtedly because for this "enlightened" man, these old mystical speculations have nothing new to tell us). He says:

His impetuosity, his power for action were unequaled. Yet he had nothing either of the bungler or the narrow sectarian. He was aware of the true relationship of forces in the state and society and, for all his mystical enthusiasm, he took those forces into account. The superiority of Münzer over his fellow-communists resulted less from his philosophical sense and his organizational ability than from his power for revolutionary action and especially his statesmanship.

This is a welcome corrective to overly one-sided views; the princes had good reasons indeed to demand that Münzer be turned over to them. In his conception of the revolution, the proletariat and millenarianism, raised like the two caryatids of the communist kingdom, constituted a combination that was by no means harmless. Without Münzer, the revolution would have lacked its sharpest sting and would not have created such a lasting spiritual upheaval. Ranke stresses Münzer's "strong position," and this purely political historian, who studies politics only in terms of ideas but limits the ideas to the realm of practical politics, reaches conclusions similar to those of Kautsky. He writes:

Münzer's inspirations, the Anabaptists' socialist endeavors, and the theories of Paracelsus constituted a very consistent whole; had they succeeded in combining, they would have changed the face of the world.

Münzer might have overestimated his own strength, and his constantly alternating boasts and faithful conformity to ancient models undeniably exhibit Quixotic features, and suggest that he paid his followers in a currency honored only in the Kingdom of God. This is true when he awkwardly identifies with Gideon; when, in his ecstasy, he sees himself as a new Daniel, a new Elijah, a Moses leading his people to the land of Canaan, convinced of having been endowed with a heavenly power which had not yet been granted to him, to which the right had not yet been conferred upon him. Nevertheless, he was indeed a tragic and earnest hero, endowed at times with messianic power. His aims were out of the ordinary, but in no way illusory; his outbreaks carried him to the shores of the satanic, but we would be mistaken to think that, like a Don Quixote with only negative traits, he was grounded there on a pure chimera. . . .

In concluding this sketch of Münzer, let us return once more to the figure of Luther and the role he played in the revolution. The appearance of this man who at first exhibited such boldness was long overdue. At the outset, he felt close to Münzer. . . . Indeed, it was almost the voice of Münzer himself that seemed to sound when Luther thundered his first revolutionary pronouncements, when he expressed his utter contempt for the princes, "the biggest fools and the nastiest boys on earth," when he showed how God had given them to the world as negative examples and how God would sweep them away together with the feudal clergy:

For as you know, dear lords, God commands that your fury cannot, will not, and must not be tolerated any longer. If these peasants fail, others will rise to take their place; and if you strike them all down, they will still not be vanquished. God will engender others.

In 1524, infuriated by the dissolution of the Nüremberg Diet, which was against the Great Reformer's interests, he still indulged in the most disloyal insults, going so far as to berate the emperor "as a miserable bag of maggots fated to die and in constant fear for his life." But this same prophet, at the beginning of the Peasants' War when the rebels turned to him, claimed at first to be neutral, posed as a pacifist, took refuge in verbal quibbling, dismissed both sides by proposing a stale compromise. Already he was not sincere; in fact, it was the peasants alone whom he held responsible for all the "sufferings" of Christianity: he ceased to conceal his thoughts in writing to his friend Spengler, secretary of the Nüremberg Council:

When they refuse to recognize the secular authorities and to obey them, they are guilty to the core, for their heart is certainly possessed by rebellion and murder, and it is the responsibility of the secular authorities to see to it that your lords take all necessary measures to preserve their power.

Luther's pacifist stand in connection with the Peasants' War shows that he is already going over to the princes' side, coming to terms with the princely establishment, and completely deserting the poor people. No sooner had the peaceful Elector Frederick died, no sooner had the ruthless Duke John ascended to the throne, than Luther, the very next day, began boldly renouncing his own legitimacy, all his expression of pity and understanding, all his former wrath against the princes. Surprising as it may seem, this brutal and sudden about-face can probably be explained by causes hitherto ignored: At that moment, Luther, for the first time since Worms, began to fear that he would be held responsible for the disorder. As a matter of fact, Duke George, a Catholic, stated after the Battle of Frankenhausen that in comparison with Luther, Münzer was only a small-time criminal. George concluded in no uncertain terms:

Since God permitted us to punish Münzer for his wickedness, he can now grant us permission to deal with Luther in the same way; in this task also we are ready to serve him, according to his will, as his unworthy instrument.

The battle itself, moreover, brought about a striking reconciliation between the Catholic and Protestant princes that paralyzed the further development of the Reformation. Not only would the Munich chancellor, at every sign of an uprising, declare to his master that "it is all the fault of the Luther clique," so that there, as well as in Austria, the Lutherans would be hounded and exterminated along with other sects, but the example of Bavaria clearly showed that with favorable treaties between the Elector and the Pope, and the participation of the crown in the clerical system of exploitation, faster and safer results could be obtained than through an ambiguous and complex secularization process.

. . . In the face of the negative and positive changes that were distorting his Reformation, Luther may well have felt strong anxiety for his own safety, his position, and his work. Whatever the pious sentiments of the new Elector John, other Protestant princes seemed less firmly attached to the new ideas; the solidity of faith of Albert of Brandenburg and Maurice of Saxony, for example, was not so reliable as their cynical cruelty, nor did it equal the former's incendiary lust or the latter's reputation as a Judas and his Machiavellian atheism. At the very outset of the Peasants' War, Luther may well have feared for himself a fate similar to that which awaited Münzer; at the least, he may legitimately have dreaded seeing his services become superfluous and witnessing the collapse of the political and economic substructure on which his dogma of the *sola fides* was based. This was why he preferred to act without delay, and so, playing his role of renegade to the bitter end, he wrote his vicious pamphlet "against the robbing and murdering peasants":

Let whosoever can do so sting, strike, and slaughter. If thou losest thy life, blessed art thou, no holier death canst thou know. The strange times are upon us when a prince serves heaven better by shedding blood than others do by praying.

Such is the language used by the frenzied Luther, who went so far as to glory in taking upon his shoulders all the blood of the peasants, and who did not even hesitate to approve the indiscriminate and loathsome massacre of all Anabaptists, including the pacifists and those who went like sheep to their martyrdom. This is what he gloried in, the mountain boy who had come up in the world, the Christian forgetful of the painful anxiety that once clutched at his soul, the dead earnest in which he once became conscious of sin. In fact, the monk of Wittemberg's amazing experience of faith will bear, together with the sinful nature of his *raison d'état*, even more astonishing fruits. This man, unfaithful to himself, sufficiently lax in worldly matters to authorize princely bigamy, so rigidly literal in his exegesis as to destroy the unity of the Reformation by his opposition to Zwingli, had wondered in his youth with what bitterness the first Christian martyrs would have looked upon the great bishops of the future, those who, forgetting the blood of Christ in their pursuit of temporal power, created martyrs in their turn. But Luther had now forgotten all that, thanks to his new two-facedness; worse, once Münzer's blood had been shed—Münzer who, up to the day of his martyrdom, remained faithful to the original Lutheran ideal—a new question sprang to his lips: "Where are your words now, where is he now, this God who, through the mouth of Münzer, proffered such promises a whole year long?" This as if, for the Christian Luther and at the very core of his doctrine, the Word of God did not basically imply that those who harken to it would be held in contempt and persecuted in this world—as if, for Christians, the world were not enemy territory! But Luther himself was to witness the decay of his work in the hands of the princes; it was of no avail to him to have first betrayed and then condemned the peasants, to have exchanged the role of an apostle for that of a Judas. While no compromise could probably have prevented the corruption of the movement, the refusal of martyrdom inevitably entailed, in addition, the corruption of the very principle.

This treason served the lords well, but Münzer disappeared, never to be heard of again. The rebel was forgotten, for history is written by the victors. Münzer endured for a longer time a fate worse than the one Sebastian Franck was threatened with by Luther, who declared that he felt for him "too haughty a contempt" to so much as mention him, that he wished to see him "covered with dirt and smothered by his own," and that he wanted every trace of him to disappear "like the curse of an evil one." It was his own youth that Luther thus thrust into the flames in this later atmosphere of falseness and confusion. It was in this despicably unscrupulous way that his original purity was tarnished by the beneficiaries of the status quo. of baseness and decay. It was a time when lies triumphed, when they alone were free to flourish. It was not enough for Münzer's hereditary enemy, the princely class, to survive; it also had to fatten on the burned castles and convents. For lack of a Cromwell or a Mirabeau, the German aristocracy enjoyed a most dangerous glory up until World War I.

# X/SOCIAL STRATIFICATION IN EARLY MODERN EUROPE

F OR our purposes, the early modern period in European history may be located between the end of the fifteenth century and the end of the eighteenth century, the time of transition from a dying feudalism to the kind of full-scale capitalism that was ushered in by the industrial revolution. It was also the era when the power of the feudal aristocracy as a ruling class was destroyed, to be replaced first by absolutist monarchy and a variety of hybrid classes like the bourgeoisie-of-the-old-regime (whom Régine Robin discusses in an article that follows) under the aegis of the state, later by a bourgeoisie in the modern sense of the term, the capitalist owners of the means of production.

The interpretation in the above paragraph is not universally accepted. Recent controversy among historians of modern Europe over the nature of the English civil wars (the role of the gentry) and the French Revolution (bourgeois or not?) bears witness to the fact that scholars of whatever persuasion are increasingly concerned with problems of social stratification. From having all too often ignored the matter or been content to adopt large and unconfining categories, they have now turned to an insistence on rigorous analysis.

But what principles of social stratification should be adopted as a means of analysis, and why? In contradistinction to class structure, the phrase has an air of objectivity. Is class the criterion? If so, what is a class, there being as many definitions as there are sociologists? If class will not do, then perhaps status groups or elites? Or the division between city and country, never a negligible force? Or perhaps that between the educated and the ignorant masses?

Even the existence of such controversies is evidence of the insidious penetration of Marxist categories into historical thought. The general problem of social stratification takes on meaning only in the light of the attempted refutation of Marxism. Alternate explanations are of course not to be dismissed out of hand, nor do I claim that Marx and/or Marxists are necessarily always right. It is, however, obvious that these shifts in approach have some connection with the coming to prominence of the Marxist mode of analysis.

For years a kind of vulgar Marxism, easy to confuse with almost any so-called social interpretation, had a large audience among historians both in the United States and elsewhere. Its partisans often confused the letter with the spirit, and the method with the specific analyses of this or that figure of Marxist scholarship or politics, never suspecting that the system was not a simple formula to be applied to textbook accounts, like dusting powder to fingerprints, in order for the truth to emerge. This "Marxism" was simplistic, mechanistic, and altogether uncreative. And no doubt there would have been a reaction against it, even in the absence of the political atmosphere of the 1950s that made all dissenting viewpoints suspect.

The reaction, whether based on structural-functional sociology or a belief that the past knows best what it was really like, has been salutary, for it has forced the abandonment of a theoretically unjustifiable mass of assumptions and a reexamination of some fundamental points of both historical reality and Marxist theory. The revisionist argument that emerged has two aspects. First, class is a category perhaps appropriate to highly developed capitalist societies, but not to earlier ones where status, honor, and precedence played the leading roles. Second, even if class exists, it is largely irrelevant for the purposes of explaining historical change. To demonstrate the last point, it is then shown that nobles and bourgeois were very largely engaged in the same kind of productive activity in the old regime and/or that the revolutions we call bourgeois ought to have another name, because they were not made by a small or nonexistent bourgeoisie. Roland Mousnier, professor of history at the University of Paris, in the selection from his book translated here argues both of these points, but with an emphasis on the former, in order to maintain that what really mattered in the old regime were the prestige groupings of orders and estates.

The revisionist position is in some ways a well-deserved thrust at Marxist analysis. Rarely have radical

historians had sufficient theoretical understanding to enable them to
seek the connections between status and other principles of stratification, both apparent and real, on the one hand, and class on the other.
Instead, they have too often been content to proclaim that they are all
a cover for a deeper reality. This sort of thing will no longer do. The
analysis of revolution must be conducted with the clear understanding
that the class position of the leading (or even of all) actors per se tells
us little, if anything, about the nature of the beast. Furthermore, class
is not just a collection of individuals, but is a category larger than the
sum of its parts. If the definition of class has first of all to do with
the social relations of production, it is nonetheless true that those
social relations of production cannot be defined in the abstract, in
isolation from other spheres of human activity. Class is man continually producing and reproducing himself and his relationships
within a general context that is at any given moment the result of all
previous historical development. Consequently, the bourgeoisie in the
old regime was not distinguished from the nobility exclusively by their
roles in the productive process (which may not always have been very
different) but by a whole series of attitudes, ethics, morality, options,
and plans for the future, with which the social relations of production
were in continuous and dialectical interaction. This, I think, is one of
the two main arguments put forth in the following selection by Régine
Robin, a young historian of the University of Paris-Nanterre.

Mme. Robin's language is some-
times difficult for the reader unfamiliar with the subtleties of Marxist
thought. This should not deter us, for she has a theoretical point of
fundamental importance to make. Social classes in general, she argues,
have tended to become confused with the social classes peculiar to
fully developed capitalist social formations. This confusion makes it
possible for Mousnier and others to argue against the existence of class
in noncapitalist societies. But the way in which classes are constituted
varies from one social formation to another, in the sense that the
relations of the several spheres of human activity—productive, ideological, legal, etc.—vary among themselves. In one time and place, the
superstructural elements (all those not directly concerned with the
economic base) will be of great importance, as was true of status considerations in feudal Europe. At another time, the exploitative relationships of one class to another will appear more direct, more naked,
and may seem to be exclusively economic. It goes without saying that
our task as students of history is always to seek the reality behind the
appearances, but with the knowledge that the appearances themselves

play a social role. In other words, we want to explain a society's own vision of itself, its professed system of stratification, with our own analysis based on the concept of class. It is with this end in view that Mme. Robin offers us a tentative picture of the class alignments in France on the eve of the Revolution.

Roland Mousnier

# 23

# The Society of Orders and the Society of Classes

## SOCIAL STRATIFICATION BY ORDERS

Social stratification by orders sub-divided into "estates" (German, *Stände*; French, *états*) is very frequent. It consists of a hierarchy of degrees ("estates," "conditions") distinguished from one another and determined not by the wealth of the members and their purchasing power nor by their role in the mode of production of material goods, but by the respect, honor, and dignity attached by society to social functions that may have no relation at all to the production of material goods. "The orders carry permanent dignity and are attached to the lives of the men so honored, if they are not forfeited," said the legal expert Loyseau of a typical society of orders in the seventeenth century. In India, at the beginning of the Vedic period we find in the Rig-Veda three orders or "colors" (*varna*): the *Brahma*, poet and priest; the *Kshastra*, warrior and chief; *Vis*, the commoner. In feudal France until the middle of the fifteenth century and in the France of loyalties that followed it, social esteem, honor, and dignity are attached to the profession of arms and the aptitude for command and to the protection which results from it. In China during the Ming and Ch'ing dynasties, from 1368 to the 1912 Revolution, social esteem, honor, and dignity were linked to the scholars who were successful in the examinations and who became public magistrates.

Thus, every society of orders rests on a consensus, a tacit agreement that arises from the circumstances in which that society at one point found itself. This consensus determines the most important social function, that which places one group at the top of the social hierarchy. The classification principle then may continue to exist for centuries and millennia apart from the circumstances from which it arose. Everyone's interest in maintaining the social order and the fear of the danger that might come with an upheaval coincide to perpetuate it; so do habit, which makes it very difficult to imagine another social order; the link fashioned little by little between the existing social order and the whole system of ideas that provides a rational justification for it; and the tendency of the dominant group to perpetuate the circumstances that gave birth to this type of social stratification—for example, wars in a feudal society.

Groups are arranged according to proximity or distance from the social function and life style of the dominant group, as well as according to the quality of service they render to it. In a military society, the command function and organization are essential. The social groups closest to the ruling military groups are those whose role carries a command function and who have the general and systematic knowledge that makes it possible: the magistrates, then the scholars, then the merchants. The military society needs a man of law who transforms into law the fact of power and legally orders social relations, thus assuring the equilibrium of the society. It needs the merchants to procure precious metals, rare and exotic goods, and materials for armaments. On the lowest rung of the social ladder are those who have a social function and life style most removed from those of the ruling group. In a military society, these would be wage-earning manual laborers. Peasants, artisans, scribes, process servers, and lawyers (prosecutors) render certain indispensable but common services that are considered vile and base. The ranks in the social hierarchy are numerous. It is incorrect to attempt a simple dichotomy or to reduce the stratification to two terms: those who free themselves from manual labor and those who are obliged to do it.

Each social group has imposed upon it by a consensus of opinion its social status—that is, its rank, dignity, honors, rights, duties, privileges, constraints, symbols, dress, food, coats of arms; its styles of living, upbringing, spending, entertainment; the profession(s) its members must practice and those which are prohibited; the behavior they must observe in regard to members of other groups in various circumstances of life and what they have the right to expect; the people they must be seen with and treat as peers and companions, and those with whom they should have relations only as a matter of social function or as a necessity of life, and so on. Social status determines, in principle, the degree of wealth or ease of each person, for status entitles one to receive a greater or smaller part of the social revenue in the form of wages, salaries, rewards, bonuses, indemnities, pensions, rents, services, exemptions from taxes or other public charges.

Each order can be composed of several social strata or "estates" or correspond to a single one. Generally, the strata are composed of several peer groups. In each of the estates making up the orders, there is a tendency toward inbreeding which is corrected by the multiple marriages of the women. (But it is a tendency rather than a rule.) In each of the estates making up the orders, there is a tendency to heredity. One may even speak of a tendency to caste when concern about the hereditary purity of blood appears. Social mobility is possible. On the average, three generations are needed to change the order and, sometimes, to change the estate. Social mobility is controlled and limited by society. The new arrival must have his worth tacitly recognized by his new estate by the behavior of its members toward him, and formally recognized by the state, which sanctions the change in status through an official act. Most of these characteristics are imposed by social pressure and consensus. Only a few generally receive legal sanction by custom and by law.

The society of orders can be changed entirely if the social esteem in which the different social functions are held happens to change. If in a military society the greatest social respect passes to the magistrates or, in general, to men of law, the entire social hierarchy changes and is then arranged in relation to the preeminence of the jurists who become nobles or the greatest among the nobles. In spite of this change, the society remains a society of orders if social classification is based on a consensus of opinion on the preeminence of a particular social quality, and not on religious purity or on the role played in the means of production of material goods.

Stratification by orders seems to me to be fundamental and frequent, to arise naturally as soon as the social division of labor causes a social differentiation to appear, to reestablish itself in the course of a prolonged social upheaval, to be the form to which every society tends to return when it has diverged from it, and the form that has a tendency to predominate in the second half of the twentieth century in which we live.

## MILITARY SOCIETY OF ORDERS: FRANCE IN THE 16TH AND 17TH CENTURIES

It is always necessary to return to Charles Loyseau, the magistrate who in 1610 published a kind of anatomy of French society in the sixteenth and seventeenth centuries that was reprinted many times, until in the eighteenth century attention turned to the society of classes then in the process of formation. Let us look at his *Traité des Ordres et simples dignitez*. For Loyseau, all of French society is divided into hierarchical orders. The order is "a distinction which confers public power," "and in French, it is specifically called 'Estate' as being the most stable distinction and quality and the one most inseparable from man." This distinction "of the same kind and same name belongs to several persons." At this time, "several" did not mean "a few," but "a great number or quantity." With the order, we thus are dealing with a social group.

French society was officially divided into three main orders. At the top was the ecclesiastical order—the clergy—for, by law, the "Ministers of God" must keep the "first rank of honor." Then, the aristocracy, either by "breeding," "ancient and immemorial," coming "from an old line," or nobility of distinction, arising from offices or seigneuries, which confer the same privileges. Finally, the third estate, which is made up of the rest of the people.

But each of these' main orders was subdivided into "particular orders" with hierarchies, into "ranks," "degrees," or "minor orders." The ecclesiastical order covers the hierarchy descending from cardinals, primates or patriarchs, archbishops, bishops; the three holy orders of priests, deacons, and subdeacons; the four minor orders of acolytes, exorcists, readers, doorkeepers; and finally, the tonsured clerics, for "the Tonsure . . . is the entrée to all the Ecclesiastical Orders and that which makes the cleric and which distinguishes the Clergy from the People." The aristocratic order is subdivided, from top to bottom, into princes of the blood, princes and relatives farther removed from the sovereign; the high nobility of knights, distinguished among themselves by their fiefs of dignity—in descending order, duke, marquis, count, baron, castellan; and finally, the lesser nobility of gentlemen, who were professional soldiers. The third estate is, in fact, composed of officers of justice and finance, although a few of them were noble by office and noble by dignity. In principle, at the head of the order were the "scholars," "doctors, masters and bachelors of the faculties of theology, law, medicine and the arts (grammar, rhetoric, and philosophy). Then came the lawyers. After them, the financiers, "all those who are intermediaries in the handling of money, that is to say, the funds of the King." Then came the "practitioners of legal agents"—those of the long robe: clerks, notaries, and solicitors; those of the short robe: sergeants, criers, appraisers, and auctioneers.

After them came the merchants, "as much on account of the utility, even the public necessity, of commerce . . . as for the usual opulence of the merchants, which confers on them credit and respect, and because the means they have of employing artisan and manual laborers gives them a great deal of power in the towns. So the merchants are the last among the people considered honorable, being qualified as 'honorable men' or 'honest persons' and 'bourgeois of the cities.'" With them are the apothecaries, silversmiths, jewelers, haberdashers, wholesalers, cloth merchants, hosiery merchants, and fur dealers, who are more merchandisers than manual laborers. All those mentioned above can carry the title of "bourgeois" if they live in privileged towns that have municipal rights, if they have a share in the city honors, in its rights and privileges, and if they have a voice in its assemblies.

Below the merchants are the tradespeople, "who live more by manual labor than by traffic of merchandise or by subtlety of mind, and they are the most vile." First, they are the laborers, "those whose ordinary task is to work for others as tenant farmers." They, like all village people or "peasants," are "vile people." However, under them are the artisans or craftsmen, "who practice Mechanical Arts, so called to distinguish them from the Liberal Arts. . . . Ordinarily, we say 'mechanical' for anything which is vile and abject," with their degrees of masters, journeymen, and apprentices. Even farther down, "those who are neither craftsmen nor merchants and who earn their living by the work of their hands, what we call unskilled labor or mercenaries, such as porters, mason's helpers, carters, and other people who do daywork; these are the most vile of the *menu peuple*" of the city and the country. Finally, at the very bottom of the ladder, the order of the "sturdy beggars" and "vagabonds and tramps," who live "carefree and in idleness at the expense of others."

Each order has "its particular badge, sign or visible decoration," that is to say, social symbols. The members of the ecclesiastical order wear the long robe and the tonsure. Moreover, those of the four minor ecclésiatical orders wear a surplice or the alb; the subdeacons have the fanon or manipule on the left arm; the deacons, the stole; the priests, the chasuble; the bishops, the mitre, cross, gloves, and ring; and the cardinals, the hat and scarlet robe. "Among the Nobles, the simple gentlemen have their coat of arms; the knights have their spurs and gilded harness . . . the Princes have Princes' capes. . . . Among the commoners, the Doctors, Masters, and Bachelors have different types of hooded capes according to the various Faculties, in addition to the long robe which they have in common with the Ecclesiastics; the lawyers have the cornet, the solicitors have only the long robe which differentiates them from the ordinary practitioners who are not bound by oath. . . ."

The orders hold "two other prerogatives of honor, to wit, title and rank." The titles are those of "knight" for the high noblemen, the high officials of the Crown, the members of the Council of State, the presidents and royal officials in the *parlement* of Paris, and the first presidents of other sovereign courts; of "noble man" for the officers of justice and lawyers who are not nobles, and that of "demoiselle" for their wives; of "king's counselor" for many officers, members of the *parlements,* bailiffs, seneschals, their lieutenants, and the treasurers-general of France. There are the "epithets of honor" "illustrious and excellent" for the princes, "high and powerful lord" for the knights and the great lords, "illustrissimo" for the cardinals, "reverendissmo" for the bishops, "reverend father in God" for the abbots, "venerable and discreet person" for other, lesser clerics, "noble man" for officers, and "honorable man" or "honest person" for the bourgeois.

Each order has its "rank, which is the prerogative to sit and to walk": "to wit, the Ecclesiastical Order is first, the Nobility next, and the Third Estate, last. Although there is no law to this effect, all is done by 'voluntary respect.'" The most minor priest ought to come before the greatest of the simple nobles. "But because the Ecclesiastical

Order is considered as an Exorbitant and Extraordinary Order in the temporal realm, Our Redeemer having Himself said that His Kingdom is not of this world . . . ordinarily one observes at present that those who have a degree of secular dignity do not want to yield to the priests, if they do not have a degree of ecclesiastical dignity." "The lowest noble must come before the most rich and honorable member of the Third Estate." But a difficulty arises if the member of the third estate is an officer of the king. In this case, the princes "do not yield to any officer whatever his rank"; the knights and other members of the high nobility yield only to officers who are also knights because of their office, as . . . "having the same rank as themselves and the office, in addition," like the chancellor of France, the councillors of the Council of State, the chiefs of the sovereign courts; the lesser nobles, gentlemen, and squires yield to the officers of the king who are magistrates, that is to say, the principal officials of the government and of justice "in the exercise of their power," even if they are commoners.

The orders have privileges. Only nobles have the right to carry a coat of arms stamped with a helmet or "lead armor." A number of offices are, in principle, reserved for nobles: Heads of offices of the royal household, many of the regimental offices, gentlemen of the privy chamber, gentlemen-in-waiting, equerries of the stable, gentlemen of the royal hunt and falconry: "All the principal military command posts either of a garrison or a regiment, notably those of the horse soldiers, even up to the ordinary positions of the ordnance companies, and as for captaincies of the infantry, nobles are preferred."

For ecclesiastical benefices, "several" churches, cathedrals, and "several" abbeys have their dignities, canonry, and posts for members of the regular clergy reserved for nobles. Generally, nobles were favored in the Church for dispensations of age, plurality of benefits, and length of time devoted to study.

As for the seigneuries, the fiefs were reserved for nobles. Commoners could acquire them only through dispensation and by paying the king the tax of Frank-fief. But only nobles were able to hold large and medium-sized seigneuries, duchies, marquisates, and counties, on one hand, and baronies, vicomties, vidameships, and castellanies, on the other. Commoners could obtain only ordinary seigneuries and high, medium, and lower rights of justice.

Only the gentlemen, excluding the nobles of the long robe, have the right to carry the sword "as being the sign and decoration of Nobility, even carrying it in France, into the King's Cabinet." All those of the high nobility have the right to the salute from commoners. Contributing their life for the defense of the state, the gentlemen were "exempt from taxes and all other personal contributions levied for war . . . from housing the constabulary." "In addition, gentlemen have the privilege of hunting . . . so that in peacetime, they may continue in an exercise resembling war."

For a simple crime, nobles were not punished as harshly as commoners and were never condemned to dishonorable punishments like the whip and the rope. But if they received less severe corporal punishment, they suffered harsher fines. And for crimes which are irreconcilable with nobility, such as treason, larceny, perjury, and duplicity, which are aggravated by the dignity of the person, they are more severely punished. Nobles have the right to resolve an affront by a duel, but the choice is theirs. They are not obliged to duel with commoners. The third estate benefits from a vast general privilege, that is, that the gentlemen, except for the glassmakers and a few others, cannot make profit on merchandise and by trade, cannot compete with the third estate.

Order is acquired—the ecclesiastical order by tonsure, which is a public testimony that one is dedicated to God; the order of nobility by birth, by letter of the king, "distributor anointed by God of the solid honor of this world," or by the provision, reception, and installation in ennobling royal or municipal offices. The high officers of the Crown, heads of offices of the royal household, heads of the sovereign courts, and the king's governors and lieutenants in the provinces become knights and thus members of the high nobility. Being of high nobility, simple nobility is conferred on their children. The secretaries of the king, the royal household and the Crown of France are the equivalent of nobles going back four generations; their nobility is handed down to their children, provided that they have resigned their office in favor of a son or son-in-law. The counsellors of the sovereign courts are nobles by personal title, but if grandfather, father, and son have exercised this profession without interruption, the title may be passed on to their descendants. By royal privilege, nobility is conferred on holders of municipal offices in certain towns. Finally, each person can have his quality of nobility recognized by decree of the Court of Excise (Cour des Aides) if he can prove that he, his father, and his grandfather have lived nobly, preferably on a seigneury or a fief, exercising a military profession and without having committed any act either vile or disgraceful to their quality. Later, these conditions were to be aggravated. The Royal Declaration of June 22, 1664 made necessary proof, by authentic title, of nobility dating from before 1560.

The orders of the third estate are acquired by receipt of a university rank; by provision, reception, and installation in various offices; by registration as a lawyer or as a solicitor in the various courts of justice; and by reception into a guild.

The order can be lost—the order of priest, in the rare case of degradation for infamy; nobility of dignity by infamy, which leads to the loss of office. Nobility of blood is lost in the case of lese-majesty or by treason when a gentleman is declared infamous and degraded from the nobility by his condemnation. But the other crimes and the exercise of mechanical or vile (that is, servile) arts for profit do not deprive gentlemen of their nobility, but only suspend it, for noble race is "innate to man." If the disgraced gentleman takes up his noble life again, it suffices for him to obtain rehabilitation letters from the king, which the latter never refuses. The gentleman can even do without them, for it is common law that the rights of blood and nature cannot be lost through civil means.

Professions derogative of Nobility are those of solicitor in the lower courts, record-keeper, notary, sergeant, lawyer's clerk, merchant and artisans of all professions. . . . It is understood that this applies when one exercises these professions for profit: for it is vile and sordid profit which disgraces the Nobility, whose proper occupation is to live on a private income or at least not to sell one's labor. Nevertheless, Judges, Lawyers, Doctors and Professors of Liberal Sciences do not lose the nobility that they have otherwise acquired, although they earn their living through their estate: because (apart from the fact it comes from mental work and not manual labor) it is more honorable than mercenary. . . . Tilling the soil does not cause loss of nobility . . . in so much as no profession that a gentleman exercises for himself and without taking money from others is disgraceful . . . it not being forbidden to Nobles to have small farms forever, for many years or for life: because in these leases, the real Seigneury is transferred to the lessee . . . so that henceforth the gentleman is said to work his land and not that of another. . . .

Such is the picture that Loyseau draws for us of the stratification by orders in French society. He describes for us primarily what has received legal validity from customary laws, edicts, ordinances, decrees of the council and of the courts of the *parlement*. Although his book contains observations taken from daily life, as a perceptive observer, the author does not give us a complete sociological description. He does not dwell on the tendencies toward endogamy in all degrees of the two secular orders, corrected by cases of hypergamy; on the general tendency toward heredity of order or estate, and on the tendencies toward the caste system which were beginning to make themselves manifest in the nobility; on the restrictions on social nobility derived from customs, for often many generations of living as a gentleman were necessary before ennobled persons were considered by the gentlemen as a part of their social group.

It is not surprising that he did not stress one essential principle, because it was evident: A family does not enter the upper degrees of this hierarchy by money acquired in activities having to do with the production of material goods, industry, commerce, agriculture, and the sale of goods. That is, the order in which one finds oneself is the cause of the quantity of worldly goods that one receives. For the clergy, nobility, and the upper ranks of the third estate, these came in the form of rents, seigniorial revenues, ground rent, and government annuities in the form of pensions, appointments, wages, and honoraria. Even payment for productive activities was sometimes regulated by status rather than by the state of the market. In fact, there were some poor gentlemen, graduates, and magistrates who, in general, were granted more respect than the richest merchant.

Many other texts throw rough light on what Loyseau has already shown. Juridically, the order of nobility was second; socially, it was the first and the one toward which everyone gravitated. The officers, bourgeois, and merchants called themselves "sieur" and took the title of squire, the first that a noble could have. Their wives took the name "demoiselle." The husbands also put helmets on their coats of arms, despite this being prohibited by the statutes of Orléans and Blois; carried a sword; and dressed in the costume of gentlemen. A contemporary of Loyseau, Montchrestien, moaned, in his *Traité de l'economie politique* in 1615: "At present, it is impossible to distinguish them on sight. The retail merchant is dressed like a gentleman. . . . As for the rest, who does not see that this conformity in dress introduces corruption into our ancient discipline?" By the profession of arms, a noble life on seigneuries and fiefs, and especially the exercise of an ennobling office, members of the upper levels of the third estate succeeded in having themselves legally recognized as noble, with all the privileges of the gentleman. But socially, these noblemen were not gentlemen. The men of the sword refused to recognize them as such. They refused them even the quality of nobles of dignity, of function, and of the robe. For the gentlemen of the sword, the gentlemen of the robe *(robins)* were only "bourgeois." Their sentiments are well expressed by a character in a novel:

I do not know by what quirk of fate the majority of these people [the *parlement* counsellors] are becoming half-crazy in their old age . . . the most probable reasons are that, first, they have abject souls, being born of lower-class parents, and that, in order to keep their foolish seriousness, they confine themselves out of reach of good company and spend their time doing things that make them all the more stupid, as they are the most vile in the world.

Jean-Louis Guez de Balzac, son of an ennobled man, but whose "quality" the gentlemen of Angoumois were to recognize in 1649, wrote to Chapelain on December 20, 1636:

I infinitely respect the person of our friend and I would desire her alliance passionately. But . . . the maiden has her head full of her nobility . . . hence . . . this scorn of all types of *bourgeoisie*, were it dressed in purple and sitting on the fleur-de-lys. Her mother may have thoughts less haughty and more favorable to the robe . . . [but] she is daily solicited by several persons of condition; and yesterday when I left her, I had the feeling the privy councillor would not be good enough for her daughter.

The bourgeoisie! That was all the nobility of the robe was for a gentleman. The Abbé François-Timoléon de Choisy, member of the Académie Française, goes further:

My mother, who was from the house of Hurault de l'Hospital, told me often: "Listen, my son, do not be proud, and tell yourself that *you are only a bourgeois.* I know well that your parents and your grandparents were *Maîtres des Requêtes* and Councillors of State; but let me tell you that in France, no nobility is recognized but that of the sword. The nation, martial in spirit, glories in its arms.

The military character of French society is underlined by the Archbishop d'Embrun, Master Georges d'Aubusson de La Feuillade, President of the Assembly of the Gentlemen of the Clergy, during the Fronde, when on March 15, 1651, he replied to the deputies of the Assembly of Nobles:

Thus, it is this nobility, not of blood but of your heroic souls, which is not buried in the tombs of your ancestors but is alive in the train of your generous actions, which inspired in you the thought of assembling for the preservation of your privileges. It is this ancient glory . . . which could not long suffer decisions to be taken without your participation in the affairs of a state that is military in its very nature and of which you make up the most brilliant and most powerful part. . . .

The gentlemen were pushing the nobles of the robe out of the nobility. Moreover, it is remarkable that in the 1614–1615 Estates General, most of the nobility of the robe sat with the third estate. Thus, a battle among the orders dominated French society. In the 1614–1615 Estates General, thanks to the procedural artifice of the government for the election of the delegates of the third estate, it was, in fact, the "fourth estate," that of the nobles of the robe. It was the battle between the orders, between the nobles of the robe and the other nobles, that allowed the king to keep the balance of power and led to the failure of the Estates General.

The order of the nobility blamed the higher levels of the third estate for stepping out of their proper sphere and for competing with it. It complained that by means of money made in commerce and financial activity, members of the third estate had acquired fiefs and seigneuries from a debt-ridden nobility and had cornered royal offices.

The latter had been, since the time of Francis I, officially sold or given away in return for loans never repaid. Rights of reversion and, above all, the *paulette*—the annual tax instituted in 1604 and constituting an insurance policy—were pointed to as the way in which these offices had become hereditary. Nonrobe nobles demanded the suppression of the annual tax and the end of venality among officials. They demanded that certain offices be absolutely reserved for them, together with at least one-third of the others. Thus, they clearly demanded the maintenance of their social preeminence not only through access to distinctions (the office is a "distinction with a public function attached to it"), but also through access to the honoraria, wages, and various payments that went with the offices. They even went further, and the members of the third estate became indignant at the nobles' demand that they be authorized to engage in large-scale commerce without disgracing their nobility, in order to make money.

But then, under these conditions, is it not money that classifies a man in the social hierarchy, and are we not dealing with a class society in the process of formation? Is not the struggle between the nobles of the robe and the other nobles a class struggle? I do not believe so. I am inclined to agree that there may have been, at the level of the merchants and farmers, a class society in the process of formation which was interfering with a status society because of the development of commercial capitalism. But at the level of the robe and other nobles, it seems to me always to be a question of orders and of a struggle between orders. Here are some of the reasons why I think so. Whatever the nonrobe nobles may have claimed, money alone did not permit entrance to the judicial offices. A grain merchant who had gotten rich could not buy the office of counsellor in the *parlement* either for himself or for his son. If he had managed to abuse the royal chancellor's good faith, he would not have been received by the sovereign court; the baseness of his origins would not have allowed it. It was usually necessary to rise by degrees—from a mercantile function to a financial one, from a financial one to a low judicial office or to the office of secretary to the king. Then one could hope to accede to a magisterial office, to the offices of lieutenant-general of a bailliage or of a sovereign court; then to those of the Maître des Requêtes and of the Council of State. Most often, it took two, three, or four generations—generally, four. It was the quality attributed by a consensus of opinion to the style of life of each degree that allowed a man to rise step by step, by means of resources acquired as a result of the level to which he had already risen in the hierarchy of orders. These resources had to be in the form of rents, fees, and honoraria, not in the form of profits. The nonrobe nobles were excluded from the judicial offices less by lack of income than by the enormous expenditures particular to a gentleman's way of life and by their contempt for learning.

We could say the same thing of the seigneuries and the fiefs. A grain merchant could very well force a gentleman who was his debtor to sell him a fief in exchange for settling the debt (although a gentleman would, more often than not, ask officers more highly placed in the hierarchy of orders for a loan). The merchant paid the tax of Frank-fief, for possession does not ennoble. He would merely be tolerated in possession of the fief. It would only be if he adopted the life style of the noble on his fief that after many years he, or rather his son, and most likely his grandson, might convince the local financial officers to strike his name from the *taille* rolls because they had lived nobly for a long time, with the sword at their side, and without "practicing the mercantile profession."

Again, it is noteworthy that what the nobles of the robe wanted was not so much to take up the life style of the gentleman, to adopt the profession of arms, and to spend money lavishly. Some did so, but they then experienced the same difficulties as the nonrobe nobles and often started their families on a decline. In general, the passage, by deliberate choice, into the nobility of the sword through a career as a professional soldier and accession to the higher ranks of the army and to the rank of governor of a garrison or a district was rare. More frequently, those who reached the offices of Maîtres des Requêtes or were named to the Council of State tried to establish their eldest sons in the functions of the Council of State with, for a few families like the Phelypeaux, access to the highest functions of secretary of state, controller-general of finances, and minister. The usual case was the consolidation of the eldest sons in the offices of *parlements,* which have "something holy and venerable" about them, or in those of the other sovereign courts, like the Nicolai family in the Chambre des Comptes. To esteem, and repose in the calmest, most regular, and most routine of functions, the sovereign courts added possibilities of keeping and improving one's fortune—of savings, commissions, loans, leases, and property speculations that the royal army did not offer.

The greatest number of *robins* consequently preferred the robe, the king's Council, and the sovereign courts, together with the high magistracies, the members of all these bodies making up a single social group and a single order with the nobility of function, legally similar to the nobility of the sword, but socially distinct from it. There were marriages between the sword and the robe, especially thanks to the hypergamy of the women. But what counted in this patrilineal society was the fate of the men, and particularly of the eldest sons. We should therefore not be misled by examples of the younger sons of *robins* who opted to become professional soldiers and by younger branches of robe families in which the men are of this profession from father to son. If one did not rise above the rank of *mestre de camp* and did not reach a high administrative post, it was not easy to enter the nonrobe nobility if one had not been born a gentleman. A family in which the eldest son and the oldest branch of the family remain of the robe is a family of the robe. But, as in all things, there can be exceptions.

Generally, the *robins* remained in their order. But there is a constant, obstinate effort, revealed by the attitudes and remarks of the third estate in the Estates General of 1614–1615, by the policy of the *parlement* of Paris, by its role and by that of other *parlements* during the Fronde, not to transform the society of orders into a class society, but to change the hierarchy of orders, to cause the order of magistrates and of "gentlemen of pen and ink" to be recognized as the first order, to change the principle of society and to make civil service to the state the most dignified, in place of military service. Magistracy, above all. Magistracy, the true first nobility. Loyseau, enlarging on one of the tendencies of French society, tells us this in all simplicity. He arranges everything in relation to the aptitude for the exercise of public authority. Thus, he divides society into two parts: those who command, and those who obey. Those who command are the king and the magistrates, his officers. Those who obey are the people, that is, everyone else: ecclesiastics, nobles, and the third estate:

The King has his general officers near him, who send his instructions to the provincial magistrates, who send them to those of the towns, and the city magistrates have them executed by the people. So much for those who command. As for the people who obey, because it is a body with several heads, it is divided into Orders, Estates, or particular functions. Some are particularly dedicated to the service of God; others, to protect the State by arms; others, to feed and maintain it by peaceful exercises. These are our three Orders or Estates General of France— the Clergy, the Nobility and the Third Estate.

In Loyseau's mind, for the magistrates it is not only a question of authority in the exercise of their functions by virtue of the power delegated to them by the king, but also one of social preeminence. Loyseau stresses the fact that the princes yield to no officer (which is normal since the princes are related, closely or distantly, to the king), except when those officers are engaged in the performance of their duties. This is clearly to distinguish between that which belongs to the political and administrative sphere and that which belongs to the social sphere. But all the other members of the high nobility, that is to say, the knights, must give way to the officers who are knights by virtue of their office, and this even when they are not performing their functions (chancellor of France, first presidents of the sovereign courts, presidents, attorneys and solicitors-general of the *parlement* of Paris). And all the lesser gentlemen had to give way to all magistrates, even if they were commoners, in their jurisdiction, even when they were not performing their duties.

Loyseau attacks the pretensions of the gentlemen to a superiority of race and purity of blood, an insurmountable obstacle to the claims of the gentlemen of the robe:

The rational soul of man coming directly from God, who created it specially when he sent it into the human body, does not have natural participation in the qualities of the generative seed of the body to which it is relegated. That is why I am astonished at the way in which almost all the highest Philosophers and Poets . . . have deluded themselves into believing that there are certain secret principles of virtue which are transferred from fathers to children by the act of generation; witness the sorites or inductions of Socrates, who concluded that as the most bounteous apple, wine, or horse was the best, so it was for the man of most noble race.

Aristotle in the eighth chapter of the third book of the *Politics* said that "among all nations, nobility is honored and respected because it is probable that he who is excellent is born of excellent parents," and therefore he defines nobility as "a virtue of race." Loyseau disputes this theory as false:

. . . so one sees often enough that the children of decent people are scarcely worth anything and that those of the learned are ignorant. . . . If sometimes their mores are found to conform to those of their fathers, that is not due to generation, which contributes nothing to the soul, but rather to education in which, if truth be told, the children of decent people [*gens de bien*] are much advantaged because of the careful instruction they are given, because of the constant and stimulating examples they have from their parents, because of the commitment they have not to fall into degeneracy and to belie their race, and finally, because of the credence and good reputation that the memory of their ancestors acquires for them.

Thus, everything depends on education, example, and heredity, not on blood. Everything depends on what a man can acquire for his children, not on what cannot be acquired.

Last but not least, Loyseau uses the old myth explaining the nature of French society by conquest in favor of the nobles of the robe. The origin of social stratification in France is the conquest by the Franks. The Frankish conquerors were noble; the conquered Gauls, commoners. The Franks subdued the Gauls, "and they retained this prerogative over them, that they alone could hold public office, bear arms, and possess fiefs, without being obliged to contribute any money either to the territorial lords or to the sovereign for the necessities of the state: instead, they remained obligated to fight wars." The conquered Gauls remained incapable of holding offices, of bearing arms, and of possessing fiefs; they were obliged to pay taxes to the lords and to furnish money for the needs of the state. As time passed, the two nations intermingled; the Gauls obtained the freedom of the Franks and with them, they formed the gentry (*gentilhommerie*), which kept the privileges of the conquerors. Some Gallic commoners were no longer absolutely excluded from offices, arms, and fiefs. But they remained deprived of the principal offices of the Crown and the king's household, of government, of ordnance companies, of principal fiefs and seigneuries, and they remained subject to the Frank-fief for ordinary fiefs.

Loyseau does not consider rejecting this myth since, for him as for all his contemporaries, it was history itself. But he does not draw the usual conclusion, to wit, that the social stratification of France was just and reasonable, since it derived from right of conquest. He draws from it a completely different conclusion—that the nobility was born of "public and general law," that it is a matter of "common law," that it comes not "from the law of nature, like freedom, but from the ancient law and disposition of the state." And one sees what this reflection suggests: Natural law is immutable, but law that arises from the state can be modified. If a law of the state established the soldier as a noble, another state law can ennoble the magistrate, not only at the same level as the soldier, but above him. A very small change reaching upward from society to the state could, in the same society of orders, with the same forms of nobility, make of the magistrate the noble par excellence in place of the soldier.

The nobles of the sword fought against this tendency of the nobles of the robe. They called the nobles of dignity, the nobles of function, "bourgeois." The historian thus has the right to do the same thing, if he specifies precisely what he is talking about. What is this "bourgeoisie"? The words "bourgeois" and "bourgeoisie" have, as always, several meanings. They can designate "the assembly of people who live in a town," the town dwellers as opposed to the country dwellers. They can also define the people of the third estate as distinguished from the gentlemen and the clergy. Or, they can mean the person for whom a worker works. The epithet "bourgeois" can be a simple legal title designating one who lives in a town, participates in its financial burdens, is part of its militia, and has been recognized as a bourgeois by the municipality. In this sense, a humble cobbler can be a "bourgeois of such and such a place." In certain towns, it was necessary in addition to satisfy conditions of wealth, income, and housing. The principal master craftsmen and merchants can even be considered as the only bourgeois. But there is a very remarkable meaning found frequently in the works of authors of town histories in the sixteenth and seventeenth centuries: The bourgeois is the commoner, a town dweller who lives nobly on his income, exercising no profession or trade, and who, in addition, has the right to the title of "bourgeois of such and such a town," with participation in its honors and privileges, a voice in its assemblies, and eventually, the possibility of becoming a municipal magistrate. These latter bourgeois are not at all a social group of capitalist entrepreneurs taking part in the production of material goods. It is probable that our nobles employed the word "bourgeois" in this last sense. In any event, these terms "bourgeois" and "bourgeoisie," scornful in the mouths and beneath the pens of gentlemen, do not take us out of the society of orders. But this variety of meanings, so different from that which prevailed in the nineteenth century, invites us, when we find these terms in a document, to look at it carefully in context and to see exactly what social group is being described. Some historians have not taken this precaution.

We will not call this society "feudal," although fiefs and manors are abundant and play a rather important role in social relations. It is even possible that this role developed anew in the great economic recession of the seventeenth century. But we are no longer dealing with the type of society in process from around 850 to around 1250, between the Loire and Meuse rivers, which is the true feudal society. We find ourselves in the presence of a society in which the contracts of fief and manor no longer dominate social relations. The latter are dominated by the hierarchy of dignities and loyalties. The loyalties have no legal sanction, and that is why the official texts do not speak of them, and why one can easily underestimate their importance. Within the order of nobility, and also between the third estate and the nobility, men offer themselves to a "protector," a patron, and become his "creatures." They give themselves to him; swear their entire loyalty and absolute devotion to him; consecrate their service to him; fight for him in duels, brawls, and regular battles; speak, write, and intrigue for him; follow him in misfortune, even to foreign lands; go to prison for him; and kill for him. In return, the master and "protector" clothes, feeds, and relies on them, advances them in the world, marries them, helps them to obtain posts, protects them, and gets them out of prison; if he is a prince, he obtains for them the treaties with the king that end revolts. The king himself can compel obedience only through the intermediary of such "faithful" who are his "men" and who have in their turn their own "faithful." Louis XIII had Richelieu, Richelieu had Séguier, Bouthillier, and Sublet de Noyers, who in turn had their "faithful." But the "faithful" did not bind himself through an act of faith and homage and did not expect a fief as compensation. Thus, there is no feudalism here. There can, however, be no doubt that these "loyalties" derived from the feudal epoch and the period of vassalage that preceded it. But let us not confuse origin and nature. Loyalties were not bound to the feudal system. They existed in societies that did not know and had never known a feudal regime. They were something else, and they characterized another type of society, at least a species in the great genus of societies of orders.

What, then, was the role of the fief and the manor in this society of dignities and loyalties? Probably, it was above all that of a social symbol. Fiefs and manors seemed to bring relatively little income to the "direct seigneur," at least in a number of provinces. They seemed in any case to have been the cause of a failure to earn. It is probable that the possession of a fief was a matter of dignity and prestige in the society of orders, an instance of a sentimental survival.

# Régine Robin

## 24

## On the Definition
## of the Prerevolutionary Bourgeoisie

If the idea of "bourgeois," as the term was used by the men of the seventeenth and eighteenth centuries, is ambiguous and inadequate, what is the definition of the "bourgeoisie"? The question has some importance, since it dominates all interpretations of the French Revolution. In this bourgeois revolution, where is the bourgeoisie? The answer to the problem can only be given after the solution of another problem, which at present constitutes a real bottleneck in historical research, that of class. Class is defined by a complex relationship of exploitation which does not have to do only with economic life.

It is not the existence of classes which poses a problem—assuming that they have been identified—in the society of the *ancien régime,* although the forms of social inequality are structured according to orders, estates, or conditions. Why orders? That is the crux of the matter. The problem is not one of historical origins but rather of why is it necessary to construct the society in orders. This is another problem. The majority of current historians admit the existence of "class" where capitalist society is concerned, class governed by economic relations, but deny it for all other modes of production and, by extension, all the social formations not dominated by the capitalist mode of production.

In fact, a real misunderstanding is woven around the notion of social class in its current usage. It is a vulgarized definition, exclusively economic, which is not correct. This conception rests on a Hegelian reading of Marx that modifies its data and concepts. In the capitalist mode of production, there is no separation in time and space of labor and surplus labor; surplus value is not immediately visible, it is hidden. It requires rigorous analysis to identify it. Moreover, in the legal and ideological structure, class is no more directly visible than is surplus value, and the domination of class is masked by legal equality. . . . In the capitalist mode of production, the operation of economic, political, legal, and ideological levels is characterized by relative autonomy. Economics in this mode is not only determinative but also plays the dominant role. The result is that the ties of dependency can appear to be essentially economic. Besides, there is the possibility of relatively easily identifying the social classes with economic level. Thus, when Mousnier writes:

Class society appears in a market economy when supreme social value is placed on the production of material goods, when supreme social esteem, honor, and dignity go to the entrepreneur of such production, when it is the role played in the production of material goods and, secondarily, money earned in this role which places individuals at various points in the social hierarchy. A social class is composed of those who play an analogous role in the mode of production, who have similar sources of revenue, secondarily fortunes or incomes of the same order of importance, similar life styles, common interests, etc., . . . in the nineteenth century, typical class societies existed in Europe, in particular, in Northwest Europe, around the North Sea and the Channel, and in North America

he identifies the notion of class with the classes formed by the capitalist mode of production. Now, these classes, such as they are, are distributed in a social formation. . . . It is in the identification of the concept of social class with specific social classes in a well-defined socioeconomic system that the misunderstanding rests.

In fact, in what Marx calls the feudal mode of production, . . . the connection between various areas of activity is altogether different. The economic determination in feudal society exists, but through delegation, by representation. It would be erroneous to think that the difference between the capitalist and feudal modes of production resides only in a different kind of liaison of legal and economic structures, construed as always identical concepts given once and for all and of which it suffices to vary the combination to obtain the various modes of production.

In the two modes of production, it is the nature of economics and the nature of law that are fundamentally different. In the feudal mode there is a separation in time and space of labor and surplus labor, contrary to the capitalist mode. Besides, the surplus value is immediately visible; it is not masked as in the capitalist mode. Appropriations are made and continued for centuries, thanks to legal and ideological sanctions. These are the "extra-economic reasons" of which Marx speaks, the relations of personal dependence codified and legalized, relations of dependence at one and the same time legal and economic.

In all forms in which the immediate worker remains the "possessor" of the means of production and means of labor necessary to produce his own subsistence, the relation of property must resemble the relation of master to servant; thus, the immediate producer is not free; but this servitude can dwindle from bondage with obligation of forced labor to payment of a simple rent. We suppose that the direct producer possesses here his own means of production and the material means necessary to carry out his work and produce his means of subsistence. He practices, in an autonomous manner, the cultivation of his field and the domestic rural industry which is attached to it. . . .

Under these conditions, there must be extra-economic reasons, of whatever nature they may be, in order to oblige him to work for the benefit of the landowner. . . . There must thus necessarily exist personal relations of dependence and a privation of personal liberty, whatever may be the degree of this dependence.

The production process then supposes the existence of extra-economic links [between the cultivators who have a property right in the land they work and the lords who have rights of eminent domain, that is, who have a call on the product of the land]. Consequently, it is absolutely impossible to identify social classes solely at the economic level, since the mode of production will not exist without these extra-economic links, which lay the foundation for it. Not only can the classes of the feudal mode of production not be the same as those of the capitalist mode of production, they must necessarily be of a different nature. In the capitalist mode individuals are defined not only by an economic-social function, but by a status, an "estate," and condition codifying duties and privileges. It is the fusion of an economic-social function and an unequal legal status that characterizes the classes of this mode. Their form of dependence is at one and the same time legal and economic. I do not say, however, that the orders or the estates are classes of the feudal mode of production, but that they fulfill the function carried out by classes in the capitalist system. This stratification makes possible the reproduction of types of appropriation and of surplus value characteristic of this [i.e., the feudal] mode.

This point is all the more important because Marxist historians do not hesitate to write that the order is only a legal and ideological superstructure. . . . Such a formulation may be ambiguous. It would not be wrong to lead us to believe that there is, on one hand, the superstructure, a simple legal mask, and on the other, the profound reality, the class. If the order is the superstructure, it is so in a mode of production in which that superstructure plays a fundamental role.

The problem posed in the beginning is, however, far from resolved, since a complex social formation cannot, in any case, be identified with a mode of production. The original social formation called the *ancien régime* is not made up of the simple overlapping of the feudal and the capitalist modes of production, because the very large penetration of capital into the feudal mode of production gave rise to a complex transitional whole.

Let us return to our problem of definition. Georges Lefebvre proposed to include in the bourgeoisie:

The justice and finance officers, even if they have personal nobility, since at the time of the elections to the Estates General, they had been excluded from the assemblies of the nobility; the persons living nobly, that is to say, on the income from real estate or their rentes; the shipowners, the large-scale merchants and chief artisans of the workshops, and the retailers, grouped or not in guilds; state officials or similar persons: officers, retired persons, agents of the farms and tax administrations, employees of the *Intendance* [royal administration in the provinces], of provincial estates, of communal administrations; the liberal professions: lawyers, doctors, surgeons and apothecaries, professors and schoolmasters.

Such a definition does not break completely with the conception that men of the seventeenth and eighteenth centuries had concerning the bourgeois, since it leaves aside the problem of the rural bourgeoisie and peasantry. Moreover, it means defining the bourgeoisie in a very negative fashion. Just as the third estate ended up resembling those who were neither clerics nor nobles, the bourgeoisie thus conceived includes all those who, in the town milieu, are neither clerics nor nobles, on one hand, nor poor, on the other hand. Moreover, such a definition is ambiguous. It wishes to be inspired by Marxism, since the lower limit of this bourgeoisie—the chief artisans of the workshop —seems to correspond to the lowest level of persons having control over the means of production, since the other artisans who sell their labor power are not part of it. It is only partially inspired by Marxism, however, since it mixes elements whose positions in the process of production are greatly diversified (real estate income, profit, interest and corporative framework).

At the International Congress of Historical Sciences in Rome in 1955, Pierre Vilar placed himself more systematically in the Marxist framework and proposed a definition of the function of the bourgeoisie that I shall give here:

1. To dispose freely of the means of production.
2. To apply to these means through free contract a work force that possess only its labor power.
3. To appropriate in this way the difference between the value realized by the merchandise and the remuneration given the work force.

Those who do not live directly or indirectly on social appropriation thus defined are not bourgeois. . . . The liberal professions, because they perform certain services in any society remunerated by the upper classes, do not seem to me specifically "bourgeois." And as regards the bourgeois-officers, the bourgeois-clerks and (under certain conditions) the bourgeois-rentier, they are only temporarily bourgeois. A fruitful career would make them noble. A devaluation would ruin them. . . . The merchant himself, the typical bourgeois of the Middle Ages, is in a sense the antithesis of our bourgeois. His fortune was adventurous, monopolistic, and usurious. Now, capitalism could only develop if it destroyed, by extending the market, these rather limited opportunities for getting rich. Certainly, the last adventures of merchant capital give rise to "the primitive accumulation" of modern capital, but investment immediately changes its nature. Thus, the clear definition of bourgeois is all the more necessary because the same word designates contradictory objects which mutually destroyed each other. . . . Without definition and without theory, no description can create a science.

In its very formulation, this effort at definition runs into an obstacle. It presupposes conditions proper to the capitalist mode of production. Points 1 and 2 are not realized in *ancien régime* society. The free contract is, by definition, a condition of a capitalist society. The process of pauperization, however complete it may be, did not categorically deprive the direct producers of the means of production. However far the process of primitive accumulation may have gone, it could not alter the fact that the corporative, artisanal, and even manufacturing structure still had not created the general conditions for free contract. Certainly, capital as a social relation existed well before the specific form of real appropriation corresponding to the capitalist mode of production. Marx said it many times: "Capital first takes hold of labor in the technical conditions given by historical development. It does not immediately modify the mode of production." This is what Marx calls the formal subjection of labor to capital. The process of production at this stage maintains the unity of the work force and the means of production. The passage from manufacturing to big industry transforms the particular workers into a collective worker and inaugurates what Marx calls "the specific mode of production" of capitalism; the real subjection of labor to capital then replaces the formal subjection.

Vilar's definition could doubtless have been expressed differently, as in the following manner: The bourgeoisie, in the framework of the *ancien régime,* would be the class whose legal status is that of commoner, which, in the town as well as in the country, groups together all those who are in a position of socioeconomic domination in the sphere of capitalist social relations (although the capitalist mode of production still has not reached the stage of extended reproduction); which is antagonistic toward the privileged persons not engaged in these same social relations insofar as it desires consciously or unconsciously another kind of state and in time another productive framework; which is capable, however, of integrating itself into the seigniorial system by breaking out of its sphere and by entering the landed, officer, or seigniorial nobility through a more or less complicated *cursus honorum* [political career]. By breaking out of its sphere, it reinforces this particular type of interpenetration of social relations that constitutes the society of the *ancien régime*. By remaining in its sphere, it saps that society. The possibility of its accession to the dominant class, having the state apparatus in its hands, implies the destruction of the previously dominant relationships and the establishment of a new social formation where the capitalist mode of production prevails. This would not arise full-blown from the old formation after a social revolution, but would be realized progressively, after a more or less long transitional phase.

This definition designates precisely all the elements which, at the stage of formal subjection of labor to capital, participate directly or indirectly in capitalist social relations, although—let us repeat—the social formation considered here, the *ancien régime*, is not yet at the stage of the capitalist mode of production in its extended phase. In this perspective, a certain number of categories that present historiography qualifies as bourgeois for various reasons are excluded. First, all the nonnoble seigneurs who are directly part of the legal-economic exploitation at the antipodes of capitalist social relations, even if the demesne constitutes the essential part of their holdings and seigniorial dues bring in almost nothing. Then, the landowners, rentiers, officers who are rentiers of the land—all the categories that live nobly from landed income or on the interest from state bonds. They do not belong to forms of profit, but to forms of interest. Looking for a functional model of the society of the *ancien régime*, Quesnay had grouped into an indistinct whole "a propertied class" comprising the king, the nobility, the clergy, the rentier officers, and the commoner seigneurs—a class whose revenue is composed of the "net product" of agriculture appropriated from the mass of the "productive class which furnishes the net product to the propertied class." In so doing, he conceived that the only form of surplus value was ground rent: "It is in this way that the first prophets of capital saw as representatives of bourgeois wealth only the noncapitalists representing the feudal landowners. Consequently, they placed all taxes as a charge on ground rent, which is wholly to the advantage of bourgeois capital" [Marx]. If we do not want to commit an error similar to that of Quesnay, it is necessary to differentiate between the bourgeoisie and the nonnoble nonseigniorial rentiers among landowners. The latter should be called the bourgeoisie-of-the-*ancien-régime* with hyphens between the words, making of it a concept properly designating this essential class in that society.

This does not mean that the landowner-rentiers of the land disappeared with the revolutionary turmoil. We know that, on the contrary, this class went on to form a considerable body and together with the "capacities" (that is, the liberal professions) played a political role of the first order. This key class is the effect of the transition created by the penetration of capital into the feudal mode of production, and it plays a considerable role as long as the capitalist mode of production is not generalized. This class is characteristic of the transition phase. After the Revolution, the class of former seigneurs will blend into it (a number of seigneurs even before the Revolution are on the verge of doing so), differentiated by political and ideological cleavages inherited from the recent past (noble or nonnoble character of class position) and revitalized by the Restoration. This class was the pillar of the social order in France from approximately 1815 to 1860. . . .

Other categories, strictly speaking, cannot be part of the bourgeoisie according to our definition, notably the classes engaged in the guilds. There is nothing further removed from the capitalist framework than the guild defined by Coorneart as "an economic group of quasi-public (or semipublic) law submitting its members to a collective discipline for the practice of their profession."

The guild framework partakes of another structure than that of the capitalist social relations. As Marx says, "we would not be able to conceive of money without the prior activity of urban professions which rest neither on capital nor on wage labor, but on the organization of work by guilds." Further on in the same text, he shows the specific characteristics of guild organization in relation to capitalism:

The urban artisan group, although it is based essentially on exchange and on the creation of exchange values, has for its main and immediate goal the maintenance of the artisan and the master-artisan as such, in other words, use value and neither enrichment nor exchange value. Consequently, production is always subordinated to preexisting consumption, and supply follows demand and grows only slowly.

If certain categories cannot, as we have seen, be defined as bourgeois, others, on the contrary, do not figure as such in the definition of Georges Lefebvre. I refer to all those who in the countryside are engaged in capitalist social relations (farmers who gather up leases on the great plains in the Parisian basin, rural merchants, merchant farmers, farmers who have sufficient surplus of stocks and are able to speculate on the high price of grain, who have at their command temporary or permanent workers, a labor force of semi- or purely salaried workers).

However, the bourgeoisie, somewhat apoplectic in the Lefebvre definition, becomes anemic in ours. How then can the Revolution be called bourgeois if the bourgeois are so few in number, with the exclusion of the guild classes and the commoner-landowner classes? This is because the character, bourgeois or not, of the Revolution is not measured essentially by the social position of this or that group which has taken this or that decision. The bourgeois revolution in England could be led without paradox by a part of the nobility.[1]

The French Revolution rendered possible the generalization of the capitalist mode of production, not on a short-term but on a long-term basis (sometimes with contradictory features like that of the stabilization of small holdings), by the untangling of economic, legal, and even political structures which formed the real obstacle to establishing a national market and free contract. This is the role of guild, seigneury, office, and order.

The order is much more than a nonegalitarian legal structure. Lousse defines it as "groups of persons designated to perform certain social functions and having an appropriate legal status." Order associates status and social function, setting up distinctions, privileges, and status differences at all levels. The guild associates status and function in the framework of artisanal production. Similarly, in the field of agricultural production, the seigneury integrates the bond of economic dependence, codified and consecrated by the customary law and religiously kept up to date in land registers, with the bond of legal dependence. The seigneury is a judicial power of a particular type. Economy and law are here in the same relation of association as function and status are at the level of corporation and order. There remains the office, which is at once a share in public authority and venal property, the integration of judicial administration and, by extension, political power, of public authority and a particular type of property and privilege, with the right to transmit position through heredity. Now, office, guild, seigneury, and order are so many elements that hinder the formation of the "free individual" and the free contract. It is easy to show this in regard to the guild. The seigneury, insofar as it maintains the peasant in useful possession of a small landholding and in enjoyment of multiple rights of usage, prohibits him from being free in the sense that it does not deprive him totally of all the means of production. It protects him from complete destitution and keeps him from finding himself in a position in which he would have no other recourse but to sell his labor power. The seigneury is exclusive

---

[1] The bourgeois sector in the strictest sense is itself complex. It would be necessary without doubt to define the mixed types, since under the *ancien régime* the same individual often participates at one and the same time in real estate, finance, and industrial profit. Where the financial sector is concerned, the distinction made by Lüthy between financiers and bankers seems fertile to me: "More than any other institution of the *ancien régime,* venal financial office was a heavy and inadaptable monster of another age." The financiers were not at all characteristic of the bourgeoisie. Jaurès remarked that the general farmer formed "a hybrid social force at the point of contact of the *ancien régime* and the new capitalism." Hybrid forces, mixed types, and combinations of sources of income are without doubt the most widespread in a society in which capitalism has still not made "personal dignity a simple exchange value."

of capitalism. It is, however, a form of property; hence, the hesitation of the revolutionaries to abolish it.

The order which establishes differences in distinction and legal status among the subjects of the king constitutes an impossible condition for a free contract, the foundation of capitalist social relations. In order for these social relations to take place, it is necessary that men who find themselves face to face in the sphere of circulation, buyers and sellers of labor power, be formally equal; that the worker be bereft of all links of personal dependence, that he be personally free. "The transformation of money into capital demands thus that the possessor of money find on the market a free worker, and free from two points of view. First, the worker must be a free person, disposing of his labor power as he wishes " [Marx]. If the worker is not the free owner of his labor power, of his own person, if he sells his labor power once and for all, he makes himself a slave, he enters into a completely different productive structure than that of wage labor. The temporary sale of labor and the freedom understood in this sense is an unvarying feature of the capitalist mode of production.

The office is joined to the state through a precapitalist corporate framework [i.e., a framework of relationships such as in the guilds]. Now, ideology and mercantile law cannot permit that justice, the basic sphere in which capitalist exploitation is both established and masked, be both a piece of property and a function. If justice is the same for everybody, the judge cannot belong to a caste which owns the legal function relatively independent of the state. The office, a function-property, kept the buyers of venal posts relatively sheltered from "royal absolutism." In the same way, the order, privileges, and fundamental laws of the kingdom transcended the monarchy. The nation-state, guarantor of "the general interest," cannot tolerate, as Voltaire said, these "states within the state." Capitalist relations of production postulate a different social space, a linear, horizontal space, not this vertical, partitioned space of guilds and communities, offices, seigneuries and, above all, of distinct orders.

A single text, furthermore, a preamble to the Constitution of 1791, abolished the distinction of orders, the venality of offices, guilds, and seigniorial justice:

The national assembly, wishing to establish the French Constitution on the principles that it has just recognized and declared, irrevocably abolishes the institutions which were prejudicial to liberty and equality of rights. There is no longer any *nobility* or *peerage* or any hereditary distinctions or distinction of *orders* or *feudal regime,* no patrimonial justices nor titles, denominations and prerogatives which derive from them, nor orders of knighthood, or corporations or decorations, for · which there was demanded proof of nobility or which supposed distinction of birth, or any other superiority than that of civil servants in the exercise of their duties. There is no longer *venality* or *inheritance* of any public *office*. There is no longer for any part of the nation nor for any individual privileges or exceptions to the law common to all Frenchmen. There are no longer *guild-masterships* or guilds of professions or crafts, the law no longer recognizes religious vows or any other engagement which would be contrary to natural rights or to the Constitution.

There it is in the text; aside from the delicate problem of the seigneury, the Revolution had been made on September 3, 1791. It remains clear, however, that a text does not establish a new order and that the French Revolution, begun in 1789, really ended only in 1830.

Thus, the Revolution untangled the intertwined elements that hampered the establishment of new legal relations. Whether those who were at the origin of this untangling were conscious of it or not, whether they were bourgeois according to our definition or not, is of little importance. . . .

It remains true that a part of the nobility was engaged not only in the ideology of liberalism and universality [doctrine of legal equality of all members of society], but in the new social relations. Pierre Goubert underlines the fact that in the eighteenth century, "financiers could no longer stand to be commoners. In its turn, industry, especially new industry, was full of nobility, especially of old nobility." Out of the 603 iron masters in the census taken at the end of the eighteenth century in 21 generalities, the Church had 57 enterprises or 9.4 percent, and the nobility had 304 (50.5 percent), so that 361 factories or nearly 60 percent were in the hands of the privileged. The Montmorencys and the Ségurs dominated Saint-Gobain. The Duke of Penthièvre in Champagne, the Marshall de Lorges in Bourgogne, the Wendels in Lorraine were in the forefront of industrial organization. Jean Meyer has recently shown that the largest shipowners in Nantes at the end of the eighteenth century were nobles; Francois Bluche, that the Parisian parliamentarians of high nobility were numbered among the greatest property speculators of the capital, almost all united by matrimonial ties to the financial or banking milieu. These examples do not constitute exceptions adopted to artificially establish a paradox, but aim at specifying that a part of the nobility is ready, even unconsciously, to establish itself in the bourgeoisie, in another social structure. This process would go forward throughout the nineteenth century.

Therefore, I agree to call "bourgeoisie" (in quotation marks) every group which is found thus designated in the texts written during the *ancien régime,* the bourgeoisie-of-the-*ancien-régime,* that class of commoner landowners, land rentier officers, of "capacities" with landed income; and *bourgeoisie* (in italics) those elements already engaged in the capitalist social relations, insofar as they are not nobles.

The fundamental classes of the *ancien régime,* very schematically, seem to be the following:

The seigniorial class with distinct subgroups (the privileged seigniorial class, the privileged seigniorial class whose major source of income is ground rent nonseigniorial in nature, and the commoner seigniorial class). A large part of the nobility and a good part of the clergy belong to it. It exercises legal-economic control over the nonfreeholding peasantry. . . . It is the lord-peasant relationship which fashions cultural models of social success, since the dream of every rich commoner is to belong to the privileged seigniorial class, even though a seigneury brings in a poor return; it maintains the force of the notion of the order. Not that the seigneury is synonymous with nobility! Not at all, but the nobles who in the Estates General of 1614 wanted to prohibit access to the seigneury by nonnobles, felt, in a confused way but with profound affective logic, the connection between the two ideas. The fact that the seigniorial and peasant classes constitute the principal social relationship and are constantly battling one another both within and without the framework of the village community explains Albert Soboul's use of the word "feudal" to designate French society in 1789.

In the same way, the classes engaged in the guild framework, in which great social tensions reign, are to the town what the seigniorial relationship is to the country. Classes defined within the seigneury or the guild are characterized by the fact that they are realized in institutions where law and the production process are joined in a highly complex manner. These classes will disappear as classes at the moment of the French Revolution. The former, thanks to the tidal wave of peasant agitation; the latter, by the Allarde Decrees of March 2–17, 1791.

The elements that make up these classes were restructured in various ways. The seigneur became part of the mass of large landowners; master artisans, journeymen, and apprentices swelled the ranks of the bourgeoisie, the salaried working class, or the more or less independent artisans who continued to exist for a long time and are still very much alive in our own day. As for the peasantry, it ceased to exist as a class the moment the seigniorial-peasant relationship was untangled. It swelled the bourgeois or salaried categories or more generally (and this fact weighed heavily in the political evolution of France) formed the familial and small landholding peasantry that Marx speaks of in the *18 Brumaire of Louis-Napoleon Bonaparte* and that, from Bonapartism to radicalism, continues to play a decisive role in French political life.

The bourgeois and the wage-earning classes, much in the minority, needed another structure, another combination of social elements in order to develop. In this connection, I would like to digress for a moment.

Using the celebrated passage by Marx on the necessary correspondence between productive forces and social relations of production, taken from *The Introduction to the Critique of Political Economy*, and

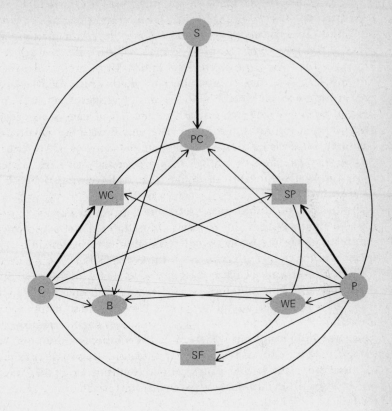

The dissolution and restructuring of social classes as a result of the French Revolution
(heavy arrow denotes major destination)

Classes which disappeared after the Revolution:

- S   Seigneurs
- P   Peasantry
- C   Corporate framework composed of masters, apprentices, journeymen, etc.

Classes which existed both under the Old Regime and after the Revolution, although
transformed by the latter:

- PC   Propertied classes (bourgeois-of-the-old-regime)
- B   Bourgeoisie
- WE   Wage-earning class

Classes which emerged as distinct classes from the Revolution:

- SP   Small-landholding peasantry entirely free of the seignorial system
- WC   Working class outside the guild framework
- SF   Various surviving forms, such as sharecropping outside the seignorial system

noting that in 1789 economic development was not such that a social revolution ought to have taken place, thus acknowledging the advance of "mind" over "economics," some scholars make an attempt to see Marx as a primitive of historical science—in any case, as a mechanist. The procedure seems to me very summary. Marx broke with the evolutionist language (degree-level) he used in this text. In *Das Kapital*, productive forces and social relations are not things measurable in the light of technical progress, but a combination of factors engaged at a given time in technical and social relations. Productive forces are not measured in terms of constant and successive progressions which, at a certain moment, find themselves confined in the social ensemble and cause the whole thing to burst, like a chrysalis leaving the cocoon at its appointed hour.

Productive forces and social relations depend on the mode of production dominating a given social formation, in the sense that the dominant mode of production determines their rhythm. The consequences in the eighteenth century are these: the [primary role played by] the seigniorial and peasant classes, the corporative framework, the statist organization, and the nonegalitarian legal structure impose a very slow rhythm on productive forces. There were so many chains to break, and they were broken not to liberate a confined capitalism, ready to emerge full-blown, but by virtue of a revolutionary situation. Moreover, it is not the social revolution that transforms the rhythm of productive forces, for it constitutes only a condition of possibility; it is the Industrial Revolution, the passage from formal to real subjection [of labor to capital], which does so, much after the social revolution.

When I write that the social revolution creates the possibility of the generalization of the capitalist mode of production, I do not wish to be misunderstood. The social revolution performs this function at the level of its law and reason, in the long term. In reality, in the short term, the contradictions into which men find themselves plunged slow down the free development of productive forces. Moreover, the social revolution may not take place for lack of a revolutionary situation. . . . Germany, which saw the generalization of the capitalist mode of production in the second half of the nineteenth century, had not known social revolution as had England or France. Even in France a vast movement developed that could have brought about the abolition of those elements which obstructed the generalization of economic liberalism. The suppression of forced labor [corvée], of guilds; the great Maupeou reforms which suppressed the venality of offices at the same time as the *parlements*, those citadels of the maintenance of privilege, and created free justice depending on the state; the authorization to enclose land, to sell the common lands; the attempts at fiscal reforms which were, initially at least, to apply to landowners, privileged or not; the land survey projects—all were so many points in a program that might, through other historical forms and doubtless with as many ups and downs, resistances and contradictions, have realized the work accomplished by the Revolution.

Between the classes that disappeared as classes (seigneurs, peasantry, classes engaged in the guilds) and those that were "bearers of the future" (the bourgeoisie and the wage-earning class), we find a class characteristic of the *ancien régime*; that is, that bourgeoisie-of-the-*ancien-régime* with landowner, officer, and commoner bases. Of course, we are speaking only of fundamental classes. We still have to understand in all their complexity the mixed categories participating in several social relations, the future "capacities" not directly productive in their complicated relations with other social categories, and all those popular elements that form "the people" without being wage earners, journeymen, or apprentices. The immense problem of the clergy still remains, a product of the [dominant role played by] the structure of orders. I realize what learning would be necessary to solve the few problems I have formulated. I had only one other ambition, to clarify the problem of this somewhat "catchall" category that one commonly calls the "bourgeoisie" before 1789.

# XI/MENTALITÉS COLLECTIVES IN EARLY MODERN EUROPE

I T is now generally accepted by historians that the first half of the seventeenth century witnessed a general crisis of European society. It was, of course, a crisis of growth, in the sense that history did not then come to an end, nor did Europe as a whole enter into an irreversible decline. On the other hand, people suffered greatly from economic difficulties (inadequate production, famine, pestilence, unemployment, price decline, taxation) and political upheaval (revolutions in England and the Netherlands, rebellions in Spain and France, the Thirty Years War in Germany and Central Europe). The Spanish Empire began to fall apart, and the Mediterranean states were at the end of their epoch of glory. Whereas in England and the Netherlands the conquest of political power by the bourgeoisie and the gentry made it possible to absorb the ill effects of the crisis and to overcome them, in Spain the crisis meant the end of any hope for the establishment of a significant level of capitalist enterprise and a productive ethos.

The crisis was general, but each social class and each nation lived it in a different way. Both terms are necessary if we are to grasp the meaning of the crisis in all its complexity: It is not sufficient to speak of the nobility, the bourgeoisie, and the peasantry, but of the French or Spanish noble, or even the Castilian or Rhenish peasant. The port workers of Venice and Rotterdam were likely to have radically different reactions to the crisis for reasons only partially having to do with the decline of one city and the rise of the other. It is in crises that we can best see the results of the cultural conditioning to which men are subject, the weight of tradition and social practice, phenomena which do not cut across or go beyond classes so much as they form an integral part of them.

In the articles that follow, Pierre Vilar, the author of a vast and very important work on the history of Catalonia and professor of economic and social history at the University of Paris, investigates the reasons for the crisis in Spain and the reactions of retreat and disillusion that then took shape. His colleague Robert Mandrou, a specialist in the relatively new discipline of historical psychology, attempts to describe some of the basic components of the mind of the average Frenchman in the same period. One must beware here of the concept "average," bearing in mind the abuses to which it may give rise. Hypersensitivity and emotional instability, and even more so the sense of impotence before the world of nature, will vary as a function of social position, at least at the level of the collectivity, if not of the individual. This said, there is no reason not to seek for patterns that may apply to all members of a society in one degree or another.

Pierre Vilar

## 25

# 1598–1620: The Crisis of
# Spanish Power and Conscience

It has often been said that it would be useless to ask Cervantes for an interpretation of the decadence of his country because he could not have foreseen it. This is to betray a strange ignorance of chronology. For if the word "crisis" means the passage from a period of ascension to a period of decline, then it is certainly between the years 1598 and 1620, between the moment of grandeur and the moment of decadence, that we must locate the decisive crisis of Spanish power, as well as the first great crisis of uncertainty among the Spanish people. The two parts of *Don Quixote* are, in fact, dated 1605 and 1615.

Of course, there is room for discussion here. Castilian money collapsed only in 1625; Iberian unity, in 1640; the "illustrious infantry," in 1643. On the other hand, it was a whole century earlier, in 1558, following a famous state bankruptcy, that Luiz Ortiz in his memorial formulated the first (and not the least vigorous) of the pessimistic prognostications concerning the health of Spain.

But the reign of Philip II was characterized by that alternation of storms and fair weather that often pushes frightened peoples to a belief in miracles. Saint Quentin enabled the people to forget the country's bankruptcy; Lepanto, the revolt of the Moors and of the Beggars. When the Armada was disbanded, the Hispano-Portuguese Union—the Empire of the Three Oceans—was hardly ten years old. Spain appeared to be, if not in the morning, at least at the high noon of her adventure. Silver was pouring in from the Indies in greater quantities than ever. To aristocratic ears, the complaints of the Cortes [legislative assembly] must have sounded like so much petit bourgeois quibbling.

Such symptoms, however, always have a meaning. No sooner had the old king passed away at the Escorial in the autumn of 1598 than far-sighted Spaniards already ventured to confess that the decline had come; some even said the abyss. The preamble to a Memorandum presented to Philip III in 1600 states that since the virtues of the new prince are equal to those of the late king, the recovery of the republic is assured, "however low it may have fallen." Was this merely an impertinent remark? In the context, no. But this way of destroying an entire oratorical flourish with six simple words was to become the favorite technique (a very deliberate one) in *Don Quixote*. The time was coming when, in laughter or in tears, Spain was to confront her realities with her myths.

The realities of 1600 were harsh indeed. At the highest points of the sixteenth-century inflation, in which Spain took the lead, prices leapt abruptly skyward. Andalusian wheat climbed from 430 *maravedis* the *fanega* in 1595 to 1,041 in 1598; Castilian wheat, from 408 to 1595 to 908 in 1599. And this is an underestimation of the real scope of the increase. Taxes, so often flouted, were sometimes necessary. But then it was the producer who suffered. In the last five years of the century, lampoons abounded for or against the *tasa del pan* [the fixing of the price of bread], or the public granaries, or the *montipos*. Doctor Cristobal Perez de Herrera, a galley doctor, wanted to organize relief for the poor. Instead, all that was organized was the repression of vagrancy. From 1599 to 1601, "the hunger spreading from Andalusia" joined the "plague descending from Castile"—the bubonic plague, the most terrible of all, although it did not originate this time in the Mediterranean, but simply, as Dr. Herrera related, "among the poor, deprived of all the necessities of life." "Nearly all of Spain," especially inland Spain, "was devastated by it."

Such bloodlettings were common in the old economies, where they were usually easily compensated for, but the plague in this case attacked a worn-out population living in overcrowded cities and arid countrysides. The human deficit was a lasting one. After 1600, the Spanish depopulation, a familiar theme, was recorded in figures—mainly in the census and in wages. A Castilian gardener who was paid 3,470 *maravedis* in 1599 received 9,000 in 1603. The real wages of the Spanish worker, between 1601 and 1610, registered an unprecedented leap. Was this a Golden Age for the workers? No, there simply were no more workers— no wage earners, that is. For the Castilian tenant farmer or the Moorish semiserf still scratched a capricious soil; grain prices continued their crazy dance; the *fanega* of Andalusian wheat went from 204 *maravedis* in 1602 to 1,301 in 1605: it was again a time of famine. But the dearness (or rather the absence) of a labor force was the Castilian economy's death warrant. In 1620, the lampoons that proliferated were no longer about the bread tax, but about the disturbing invasion of foreign goods.

This was all the more true in view of the fact that the general level of prices descended after 1601. Silver from the Indies arrived more slowly—or rather, it arrived at a higher price. There, too, in Mexico and Peru, the exploitation of man reached its limits. A terrible drop in the population now forced the mine owners to turn to the semifeudal agricultural domain. The rise of silver prices was about to stop, first in Spain. One of the mechanisms of colonial parasitism that had enabled her until then to live artificially above her means had just jammed.

Could she adjust to this change? She was prevented from doing so by the consuming habits of the rich, the enormous state expenses, the widespread indebtedness. Receiving less good money and throwing it away abroad, she made bad money for domestic use. In this century began the large-scale minting of pure copper, the paper money of the time. Between 1600 and 1610, the Cortes and the monetary theoreticians ceaselessly criticized this policy and predicted disaster.

To the economic narcotic of inflation was added, in 1609, the social narcotic. The anxious public was offered a diversion: the expulsion of the Moors. These were the remnants of the defeated Moors, converted by force but still unassimilated. They were often peddlers, shopkeepers, or more frequently peasants living in closed communities, in the service of the great lords of the Reconquest—a colonial problem on her own soil that Spain dragged along for two centuries without finding a solution. By 1600 the danger of an uprising was probably mythical, after so many rebellions, repressions, expulsions, and mass displacements. But the distrust of the false Christian, the *mala casta* [evil race], the spy, the marauder, the ducat-grabbing trafficker made the Moor a convenient scapegoat in time of crisis. He was said to "be too prolific" and to "live on nothing," and such were in fact the real complaints against him. The Castilian middle class, on the verge of bankruptcy, was jealous of the colonial labor force available to the big lords. But by way of compensation for the expulsion of the Moors, the lords won the annulment of their debts. Rather than striking at the feudal economy, the expulsion measure therefore hit its creditors instead: the rich, bourgeois farmers. Because of that, and because the figure of 500,000 departures has to be accepted, the significance of the expulsion, once called into question, must now be admitted. The Kingdom of Valencia lost a good third of its inhabitants. Once the operation was completed, the public, which had demanded it and proclaimed it a holy necessity, nevertheless felt anxious.

It is easily understandable that such upheavals should be accompanied by an equally profound crisis of the state apparatus. Don Quixote awakens one morning beneath a cluster of hanged bandits and surrounded by forty living ones, "which made me think that I must be approaching Barcelona," he said. A fairy tale? No, an exact description of the reality. The high point of Catalonian banditry was reached between 1605 and 1615. The Viceroy Almazan, not wishing to be taken for a spineless weakling (*por un palo*), burned and hanged; but the bandits in their prison cells made deals for money with his own wife and daughter. His successor, Albuquerque, "doomed the principality to the galleys," but he had to go to Barcelona by sea; by land, "the bandits were more in control than the king," as the bishop of Vic expressed it. Pushed to that extreme, banditry almost amounts to a form of dissidence. The people, like Don Quixote, felt sympathy for the leaders of the robber bands, who were never taken by surprise during the repression. Also, foreshadowing the coming secessions, Madrid was suspicious of Barcelona, and Barcelona criticized Madrid. Thus spoke her envoys to the court:

That our country is infested by bandits, who have even established their headquarters at the gates of Barcelona—this is what we are accused of here, and we are treated like Negroes . . . our affairs are in the hands of people who have no love for us, and who understand nothing. . . . They spend their time at parties and festivals; they hunt and play, and let the world and business go to the dogs. . . .

These were the words of Brother Franch in 1614. In 1615, the lawyer Rosell had this to say:

The king and his ministers act so slowly in all matters that it is the world's greatest pity. They importune the Ambassadors of the Pope, of the King of France, of the Venetians, of the Emperor, and others still, in an effort to settle the conflict in Italy; and they never make up their minds; some day they will have to, and on less honorable terms! . . . For the past two years the enemy has been harassing the Philippines. . . . No decision was made, and now we hear that they have taken all the Islands, destroying an important garrison. In short, our good King is a real saint, but he never manages to overcome his scruples. His ministers prefer playing all night and getting up at noon to waging war. Today they are talking of nothing else but the parties of the Duke of Lerma. And whoever hurts, let him groan!

To reach these "gentlemen," it takes three days in the antechamber working on their confidants and confessors. Not to mention the bureaucracy!

The amount of paperwork they do here is beyond words! And not one person in ten knows what it is all about!

Here we touch upon a well-known disease: the mania of memoranda, or "projecting." This is not to be confused, however, with the "tip" sold for one *real* on the street corner (this was common), the technician's formula, the corporation's complaint, the ideas of the "republico" nurtured in the lawyer's office or the monk's chamber. But from all this outpouring, one thing emerges clearly: the crisis was as sharp in the minds of the people as in reality. To blame the historian for attributing contemporary preoccupations to the people of another time is to think that the merchant must read the *Konjunkturforschung* [economic analysis] to realize the anguish of bankruptcy, and the unemployed worker must learn about hunger from a trade-union journal. As much ink was spent in dispensing economic advice in the Spain of 1600 as in the United States of 1930. There was a great deal of rubbish, and a few bright ideas. And in the last analysis, the true interpreter of the times was Cervantes in one case, Charlie Chaplin in the other. The short-sighted arbitrarian takes a short-term view of the crisis. But the ship-wreck of a world and its values belongs to the domain of a brilliant tragicomedy.

For the drama of 1600 transcends Spain. It heralds the difficulties of seventeenth-century Europe, which are recognized today as the general crisis of a society. Cervantes said an ironic adieu, tender and cruel, to this way of life with its feudal values—a way of life whose death throughout the world was unintentionally prepared by the Spanish conquerors, who also assured, paradoxically, its survival inside the mother country, but only at the price of its ruin. In this original dialectic of Spanish imperialism lies the secret of *Don Quixote*.

## SPANISH IMPERIALISM: THE HIGHEST STATE OF FEUDALISM

It was in the last third of the fif-teenth century that the rhythm of development of productive forces in Western Europe set the requirements for basic social changes. Popula-tion increase, extension of the area under cultivation, new techniques—all were combined in different ways in different countries, but with one overall result: a devaluation of ordinary commodities in comparison with rare goods and precious metals. A double race then started: a race for treasure and a race for territory. Portugal seemed to win the first, but in the end it was Spain that won them both.

The conquest of Granada, the African raids, the discovery of the Islands had already brought treasure, lands, and a subservient labor force to the Castile of the Catholic kings. Ferdinand, Machiavelli's "Prince," established a modern, mercantilist state. The empire "on which the sun never set" added to the fine Italo-Flemish inheritance both the mines of America and the spices of the Orient. The poor and backward Spain of today makes us forget the great Spain of old, center of one of the most powerful imperialisms that ever existed.

But why this decline, still more rapid than the rise? Has anyone had more to say on the subject, from Montesquieu to the modern scholars, than the "projectors" of 1600? Aridity, deforestation, the decline of agriculture, emigration, expulsions, an excessive amount of *morte-mains*, of alms, and of clerical vocations, vagrancy, contempt for work, the nobility craze, entailed properties, high prices, high wages, taxes, wars, the weakness of kings and their favorites: these "causes of decadence" are too numerous to miss seeing in them the interrelation of cause and effect, the general crisis in which political impotence, productive incapacity, and social corruption are indissolubly linked.

Cantillon, in his schematic analysis, went to the heart of the matter:

When the excessive supply of silver from the mines reduces the population of a State, accustoms those who remain to excessive spending,
raises the prices of products of the land and labor to new heights, ruins
the state manufactures through the use of foreign products by the
landlords and the miners, the money from the product of the mines
will inevitably flow out of the country to pay for foreign purchases:
This will gradually impoverish the State. The heavy circulation of
money, general at first, will cease. Poverty and misery will follow. This,
more or less, is what happened to Spain after the discovery of the
Indies. . . .

An impressive analysis, but one that does not go beyond purely economic mechanisms. For a truly social analysis, Marxist concepts must
be applied.

The Spanish conquest laid the foundations for a new society because
it established a world market and made possible the primitive accumulation of capital by spreading cheap silver all over Europe. But that
new society could develop only on the basis of increased productive
forces and new social relations. This was to happen in northern Europe.
In Spain, on the other hand, or rather in Castile, the ruling classes
carried out the Conquest as they had the Reconquest: in a feudal manner. To occupy the land, enslave the people, take its wealth—all that
does not facilitate "investment" in the capitalist sense of the word. But
that is what a rising bourgeoisie could do. And between 1480 and 1550
it did not fail to do so. Owing to its position in the silver circuit, it at
first tried its hand at only the unstable capitalism of the ports and fairs.
On the other hand, the productive forces available to it—lands, people,
technical inventions—very soon encountered the law of diminishing
returns on the Castilian plateaus. Hence the sterilizing effect of monetary injections after 1550. There was much spending, much importing,
much lending at interest, but little production. Prices and wages rose.
Parasitism developed, and the enterprising spirit died out. All this
spelled disaster for the future.

Let us not forget, like Cantillon, another cause of ruin. Imperialism
is also a political reality. If the silver imported privately from the
Indies paid only for foreign imports, that which came for the king was
already pledged in advance to the bankers of Augsburg, then to those
of Genoa. Big-power politics also deflected from Spain the flux of silver
that financed rising capitalist production in Europe. And by 1570 it
was necessary to fight the king's own subjects. By opening up the abyss
of the Flemish wars, the Beggars threw down the gauntlet of the then
most advanced bourgeois nation to the Catholic and feudal "Empire"

of Philip II. Thus, Spanish imperialism was indeed the highest stage of the society it helped to destroy. But on its own soil, in Castile around the year 1600, feudalism entered its death agony before anything was ready to replace it. This drama was to continue, and it is still continuing today. And that is why *Don Quixote* remains a symbol.

## THE PARADOXES OF A DOOMED SOCIETY

If we are to be accused at this point of engaging in abstract dialectics, the same charge will have to be made against contemporary commentators.

"Thus," said the scholar Martin Gonzales de Cellorigo, "if there is neither gold nor silver money in Spain, it is because she has too much of both. Her poverty is caused by her riches, and this imparts truth to two conflicting propositions which, though they cannot be formally reconciled, must both be considered true in our Spain."

Is the scholasticism of this "projector" of 1600 shaken only in its form by the impact of historical fact? Not at all. This man, even more than Cantillon, has penetrated to the very core of the problem. He shows the opposition between the productive mass and the parasitic mass. And if he no doubt exaggerates the relative importance of the latter, at least he reveals clearly the role of public debts (the *juros*) and private debts (the *censos*) through which the interest from the silver of the Indies brought about an inflation of stocks and bonds in Spain. Anticipating Lenin, he describes what happens to coupon-clipping peoples:

And all the trouble comes from the disdain for everything that constitutes man's natural sustenance, and from an attitude that is fatal for any Republic—the idea that wealth consists merely in money and in interest on money. The stocks and bonds which yield this interest have plunged the country into the depths of misery, as a widespread plague might have done. For all the Spaniards, or most of them in any case, preferred to live on their interest, or their dividends, without considering where the means could be found for supporting such a way of life. . . .

In other words, when the merchant, under the spell of the guaranteed profits his stocks bring him, leaves his business, when the artisan leaves his trade, the farmer his fields, and the shepherd his flock, when the nobleman sells his lands to obtain stocks and bonds of five times their value, they do not realize that if everyone did the same, the real income of the national patrimony would be exhausted, and all the money would go up in smoke.

For example, a single farmer has to support not only himself, but also the lord of the domain, the title-owner, the tax collector, the tax-farmer, and all others who have claims on the land, so that from the bottom to the top, it can be said that the proportion of those who work to those who do nothing productive is about one to thirty. Hence the legal actions against creditors, the increasing number of people who are forced to borrow, or else fail to meet their obligations because they cannot. This system of rents provides for a million executive agents, many of doubtful integrity, who only bring ruin upon the nobility and the entire body of the state. . . .

The wealth has not taken root because it has remained, and still remains, dangling in the air in the form of papers, contracts, titles, bills of exchange, gold and silver money, and not in the form of goods capable of bearing fruit and attracting foreign riches thanks to the domestic wealth.

Cellorigo ends on this note:

It seems indeed as if they wanted to turn this country into a republic of charmed men living outside the natural order of things.

These words were written in 1600: "A charmed man living outside the natural order of things." Cervantes, in 1605, was to give that man an immortal name. But Cellorigo deserves credit for so forcefully connecting the illusory, mythical, and mystical superstructure of his country and his time with the parasitic character of the society, the gap between its way of living and its way of producing.

This coincidence is no accident. Once the illusion nurtured by the silver of the Indies and the resulting inflation ran up against the hard reality of the crisis at the turn of the century, writers began playing the game of contradictions: Spain is rich; Spain is poor. She has the Indies; she is "the Indies of others." She feasts; people are dying of hunger. She hangs on to an empire; she has no more people. The dangers of such antitheses for a rhetoric nurtured on a mixture of scholasticism and Latin memories can easily be imagined. But what saved the "projector," for a time at least, from banality was his touching love for the "republic" and his naive faith in a return to reality.

His bleakest pages suddenly brighten with anxious tenderness when he writes of "our Spain," and it is in fact with him (and not before, despite a few early diagnoses) that we witness the triumph of the Spaniard's passion for analysis, and his feeling of vital insecurity toward his country, so well described, but wrongly dated, by Americo Castro. Here as elsewhere, the task of the historian is to date exactly rather than to generalize hastily. Around 1600, a series of texts, the only reliable collective testimony, continually glorified the three creative realities: population, production, labor. After 1620, and especially after 1626, thought increasingly tended to seek refuge, on the contrary, in mysticism or in theorizing, in the *laudatio temporis acti* [in praise of time gone by], and sometimes in defiance or absurdity. At the summit that separates these two currents, Cervantes took his place and smiled.

## THE SOCIAL FOUNDATIONS OF SPANISH UNREALISM

Space does not permit it, but it would be interesting to analyze in detail the social foundations of this Spanish "unrealism."

The polarization of wealth at various levels permitted nothing to crystallize that did not quickly evaporate. The great feudal and colonial incomes made it possible for some to live in insane luxury; when they declined (as in fact they did), the lord went into debt, as did the masters of the Moors and the duke who was the ostentatious host of Don Quixote and Sancho.

In the bourgeois society, little remained by 1600 of the bankers' and big merchants' fortunes of the sixteenth century that "embraced a world, and an ocean, but had them so little in their grasp that everything was engulfed in the abyss at once." Already the son of the bankrupt, Guzman de Alfarache, became a *picaro* [rogue] and ended in the galleys.

The case of the village potentate deserves special mention. Several of Cervantes' villagers bore the nickname "the rich," which described a typical exception: the peasant who knew how to accumulate wealth, the usurer, the tax-farmer, the profiteer who took advantage of the famine. But the universal *kulak*, as everywhere a potential bourgeois, was now condemned by inflation to the role of the perpetual *nouveau riche*, whose money is so swiftly won and devalued that he decides to spend it in gargantuan feasts. Or else he lends it out at high interest but to people with bad credit: either the impoverished (the poor peasant *must* go into debt) or the powerful (including the king himself). Enterprise did not pay, so the "rich man" ate, was waited on, invited, gave, robbed, let himself be robbed, all in the old style. By position and circumstance (rather than by religion or temperament), the Spanish society of 1600, the very antithesis of the Puritan society, turned its back on saving and investment.

The "rich man" ate. He ate so much that the doctors were concerned. But Dr. Herrera, "doctor of the galleys, the king, and the kingdom," as he called himself, dared do no more than prescribe a limitation of the meals to four or six main dishes, an equal number of entrées and desserts. Some limitation! Unfortunately, few participated in these feasts. The hungry masses could only dream of picking up the crumbs, or of coming upon such a feast by accident as Sancho did when he became governor (and he was understandably vexed by the presence of the doctor keeping watch over the dinner table!) The two obsessions—feast or famine—were the two poles of the *picaro*'s dreams.

The Spaniard, even if less rich, was waited upon. The blind beggar has always had his domestic servant. The humanist confined to a convent by the Inquisition has four servants at his beck and call. The "projectors" regarded the wearing of the white ruff as a curse, since it required the care of highly paid, specialized valets, and its original cost (250 *reals*) was doubled by five or six unfoldings and ironings. "Serving master" paid as well as "plying a trade," and many trades were merely services. It would be interesting to calculate exactly the massive transfer of the active population of the sixteenth century to the nonproductive sector, this tertiary sector so often cited today as a measure and result of progress, although in that period it meant only social parasitism and the accompanying decadence.

The Spaniard gave. And the accumulating wealth of the Church maintained an increasing number of nonproducers. But the emergence of capitalism requires the conversion of the beggar into a wage worker. This transformation failed in Spain, although not a few Spaniards would have welcomed it. It was not the Spanish temperament that prevented it, but an economic climate in which it was easy for the rich man to be generous and in which the poor man had more to gain by living from day to day than by working steadily for a wage that looked very meager in contrast with the prevailing prices and the promises of adventure.

And the Spaniard robbed and let himself be robbed. The *sisa*, the servants' levy on the master's income, existed on every level: the family, the community, the administration. Cervantes, a war veteran rewarded with a post as tax collector, practiced it so clumsily that he went to prison. As he himself said, either necessity or accident could lead to the galleys. That is why Don Quixote freed the galley slaves. In Catalonia, a more dynamic (and less charitable) border country, social dissidence produced bandits rather than *picaros* or beggars. The gangs, linked to the aristocratic clans, had their agents in the banks and offices who notified them of the approach of convoys of good money (counterfeit money [*boscatera*] was produced in the woods).

In all, it was a picturesque society and more pleasant, in many ways, than the Puritan society; but in other respects, it was rotten and, in any case, doomed. The production principle, which in other places encouraged more rapid growth, is inexorable. Detached from reality, the Spain of 1600 preferred to dream.

Cellorigo, Deca, and Cervantes tell us that people were so hard pressed that, to live better, they even dared bank on the expulsion of the Moors or the Black Death, and on their neighbor's inheritance. Probably because the rich uncle from America was becoming less generous! And everything, of course, had come from the great mirage of the Indies. Spain, wrote Deca, really prospered only when its inhabitants, from the Pyrenees to the sea, "had no reason to rave, or to put their hopes in new adventures, but only in cultivating their *own* lands, tending their *own* sheep, catching their *own* fish, plying their *own* trades, minding their *own* business." This is what the governess of Don Quixote shouted to Sancho: "Go cultivate your plot, and take care of your own house, and cease to dream of the Islands and the Islanders!"

Cervantes' lesson is for Sancho, for the Spanish people who thought they had something to gain from the ambitions of their masters, as well as for Don Quixote, a master who finds in books an idealized version of the adventures of his ancestors.

In books: This is the last point to consider. The inflation of the nonproductive tertiary sector in Spanish society was not limited to material services; it also applied to the intellectual "charmers," in the best as well as the worst sense of the word. There were the lawyers, the "projectors," and the bad ones had a larger audience than the good. There were also the storytellers. The Madrid of Philip II was shaken by a storm of literature. There we find Gongora, the finest of the pure poets, who belonged to just that period. We also find the greatest master of the "dark" novel: Mateo Aleman published the first two parts of his *Guzman* in 1599 and 1604. There we find Lopé, too, and the theatre was indeed the only national production that happily met the needs of its market. Not only the elite and the Court, but also the masses and the provinces showed their eagerness, but for lack of anything better, they were enchanted by cheap picaresque novels, idyllic love stories, and knights' adventures. And the Spanish villages responded enthusiastically to the puppet shows, as people do today to the most outdated Westerns. Any kind of evasion was welcome; and the craziest men are the most idle. That is Don Quixote.

So this masterful word picture of the tragicomic encounter between mythical superstructures and the reality of human relations made its appearance in the midst of a declining society worn out by history, in a country at the climax of its contradictions, at a moment of sharp crisis baring all its blemishes, at a time when the idle rake, the bankrupt rentier, the attractive gangster, the unemployed beggar ran through the streets and the highways, when the scholar drew inspiration from pure art and the average man from two-penny literature. The work is a game, full of old anecdotes, classic grimaces. It is also a parody, outdating its models on every theme of the arts of evasion. It does not "paint" the world, but takes apart its mechanisms better than any learned treatise, so clever are every one of its touches. And also because the "soul of this soulless world" is this puppet laden with suffering and full of dreams, in the torn costume of yesterday's respectability, who lives twenty lives (and a single love), defends honor, weakness, friendship, the motherland, captures princes, makes big speeches to the world. Anachronistic, and therefore ineffectual, this work is also an affirmation of good will, a vast reserve of human sympathy, which augurs well for the future. And the old world—from the delicate connoisseur of pure poetry to the poor man fighting against hunger—can recognize itself in this work, and identify lovingly with its hero. The crisis produced an interpreter worthy of itself.

# Robert Mandrou

## 26

## Some Characteristics
## of Mass Psychology in
## Early Modern France

To stress the dominant conditions for the totality of French society is to describe not an average mentality (which is meaningless), but fundamental traits which are valid for any mentality of the time.

We should rank first among these general characteristics of a modern collective psychology the hypersensitivity of temperaments: It is the result both of the chronic undernourishment from which most human beings suffer and of the insufficient technical and intellectual means available to them for the control of a too often hostile nature; it is also the result of partly legendary verbal traditions that foster violence, fears, and emotional instability. This hypersensitivity, this emotionalism, is a constant and universal trait, for rare indeed are the individuals or groups who seem free of it. To describe it requires a thousand observations that disclose, at the very moment when an emotional shock is felt, the vivid reactions, the straightforward show of feelings by men of that period: pity for a slow-moving chain gang; dramatic displays with twisted fists and arms to indicate mourning or grief. But it does not mean that this emotionalism amounted to sentimentalism. They certainly had a strong enough taste for thrill-seeking at times, which resulted in a somewhat disconcerting mixture of pity, vivid displays of grief, and apparent cruelty. On the hunting grounds, the game was slaughtered, one might say, with gusto; in town, capital punishment was a choice spectacle that attracted crowds, whatever the form of torture. This especially high receptiveness implies, in short, a propensity for emotional shock.

However, the best evidence in favor of this first trait is probably a multiform fear so ubiquitous that a mere listing of the occasions and motives for fright in everyday life would require pages. Let us give only a few examples: We know that night provided a thousand grounds for it, because it is dark; but there was also the fear of wolves and of bandits on the highway and especially in the woods; comets and every kind of eclipse were astonishing and frightening, since they were believed to portend some evil, for the good reason that these men did not understand such phenomena; even the learned prophecies of the almanacs caused panic fears. Then, they lived in everyday fear of the mad dogs who infested the countryside and the city streets. They dreaded the plague and all the contagious diseases that recurred from epidemic to epidemic and were never controlled by the physicians. Everything contributed, so to speak, to create fear: material life conditions, the shortage of food, an inadequate environment, and—above all—intellectual conditions. The approximate state of knowledge created its own fears: it added to the fear of the wolf that of the werewolf, a man changed into a wolf by a diabolical hand, and all the phantasms of imagination played their role here.

This explains, at least partly, I believe, the powerful collective movements of fear: the panic of epidemics and wars, the Jacqueries, the urban riots. We should also perhaps include ultimately within this framework, at least so far as their primary motivation is concerned, the satanic fears of the witchcraft epidemics. When the satanic fear descended upon a village or a district with the help of some high judge, no one escaped its hold, which spread the vilest suspicion on men and things, and incited whole communities to denunciation and ritual crime. In contrast, we perceive in this atmosphere of constant threat the meaning of the moments of relaxation in temporary security, the joy of momentary freedom; the most beautiful of all peasant festivals is the harvest, when nights are short and granaries temporarily well-stocked.

The second trait, social antagonism—or rather social aggression—is the reverse of the solidarity whose components we have analyzed. This aspect, which the accepted terminology—a thoroughly inadequate one —would lead us to call negative, is part and parcel of solidarity in the true context of collective life. Social groups such as parishes, classes, and youth societies, are largely formed in terms of the vital hostilities they must face: solidarity is a defense, a protection, and also a collective weapon. This is only too obvious in the case of the family group, whose biological necessity supports and fosters (through the concept of the blood relationship) the ideal of a unit that puts its internal solidarity to the test whenever it comes into contact with others; marriages, partitions, inheritances are so many acts bearing proof—in the smallest details of the observed legal tradition—of the mistrust with which relationships between families are handled. The parish or the village, geographically determined by the lands of the village, deliberately seeks to be a tightly knit community, hostile to "strangers." We are immediately reminded of the old troopers, the vagrants, the plague carriers, who were undoubtedly dreaded breeds. The same is true of the peaceful travelers, the merchants or the tourists: they too were suspect. But this reflex also operated, though to a lesser extent, toward peasants from neighboring villages, in spite of their being more or less familiar people. It also operated toward city people, who, because they too often happened to be tax farmers, landlords, or titleholders, were even more apt to be kept at a distance.

This aggressiveness is also obvious in the case of larger groups such as classes. There is no need to reopen the well-stocked record of the class struggle. Though the Marxist model does not exactly fit the various kinds of social conflicts that seem to be the hallmark of modern times, who could affirm with a straight face the nonexistence of social antagonisms pitting against each other the nobility, the bourgeoisie, the peasants, and the craftsmen, to mention but a few examples?

Political solidarity, as expressed in the modern state, fosters national feeling through battles against foreigners. For a great many centuries, the English in the west (from Normandy to Guyenne) and the Germans in the east have provided staunch prototypes of hostility; the sixteenth century added choice recruits, the Spaniards, anathematized with remarkable eloquence in the *Satyre Ménippée*. Let us leave aside the strong religious antagonisms engendered by the lightning progress of the Reformation in François I's and Henri II's France; forty years of armed struggle bear witness here. Moreover, religious wars whose determining aspects are purely religious and political also provide evidence (from the details of raids against castles, towns, and villages, and against isolated troops) of the virulent conflicts between social groups that we observe here at the very heart of war: the nobility against the peasants, the nobility against the bourgeoisie.

We can even recognize this aggressiveness in temporary social groupings that seem by definition the least apt to perform vital protection functions: the youth societies (groups of youths who liked to caper at the city gates) bear witness to the same effect in their own way; they disclose the weight of the patriarchal domination imposed by their elders, by parents and grandparents. They are, to a great extent, that era's expression of the constantly strained dialogue between fathers and sons.

To illustrate social tensions with a list of conflicts would not provide an exhaustive definition of this aggressiveness. We think it can also be seen in a different form in the mimicry created around the dominant class: the old nobility—whatever its real status—continues to represent, for all other groups, a behavior to be imitated. This does not concern only its original raison d'être, the military function, which is still displayed in tournaments, duels, and hunting (not to mention the taste for looting and disorder); it would be too much to claim that the imitation the nobility elicits makes of the tournament or the hunt a prototype of all struggles—for example, the opposition of Catholic to Protestant groups. It might be one, at most, for the parades of the youth societies or for the rough "big games" that pitted against each other the champions of adjoining villages.

This mimicry, however, is perceptible, in a subtler fashion, in the hierarchy of dominant collective feelings. Feudal honor, that emotional "reflex" of nobiliary ethics, found its match, more and more during the Middle Ages, in each of the other social classes: the idea of the group's honor—whatever the group—molds both written constitutions and customs. Lesdiguières said once that it is unworthy of a nobleman to go and cut to pieces peasants rebelling against a salt-tax collector; it is unworthy of a bourgeois, an administrator once said, to lend a hand to an urban rebellion. Thus the rights and duties of each group were gradually defined on the model of the nobility. It served as the model, though it may seem paradoxical to assert it so bluntly, even for highwaymen, who did not rob just anybody, did not spare indiscriminately the life of a monk or of a bishop, and who became quite successfully, at times, administrators of justice and righters of wrongs, avengers of the oppressed, protectors of the weak. In reading the rules of the guilds and the writings of memorialists, we find this concept of honor peculiar to each group and suitable to its function. This multiple sense of a moral hierarchy is expressed through a thousand shades of meaning. To mention only one example, let us quote the lawyer who, in describing the society of his time, used an expression involving both his social ideas and his view of the world to describe manual workers, artisans, and laborers: "vile people."

A third general characteristic appears just as clearly as the previous two: man's feeling of impotence in the face of the natural world. Here again, two facts contribute to this: physical and biological nature was, from an intellectual standpoint, an unfathomable mystery; moreover, the tools of the technicians who strove to control it had very limited effectiveness. Sixteenth-century men neither understood with their intelligence nor controlled with their hands and tools the world in which they lived.

We could almost suggest that, by contrast, social relationships, with their sometimes challenged subordinations, with their often violent clashes, reveal a much better control of man over man. Indeed, though the king, the bishop, the squire were not always obeyed to the letter, they had at least been able to devise laws, in the form of ordinances or mere customs, that governed a human order. Customary relationships and written law indeed represent a rather successful effort to regulate human relationships. On the other hand, there was as yet no *corpus* of laws of nature. . . . Even more, the Copernican revolution had just played havoc, at least superficially, with the one system in which medieval and sixteenth-century men believed they had found perfect stability without any mystery.

Faced with nature, that realm of inexhaustible wealth extended by discoveries of the new wonders of the tropics and the Indies, the sixteenth- and seventeenth-century French felt therefore somehow defenseless; even the monsters, the prodigies that filled their bestiaries, do not matter so much. These "phenomena," accepted as strange but endurable products of a nature whose purposes are unfathomable, mainly provide an evidence of their "receptivity" to the natural-supernatural and to miracles, or to be more exact, their receptivity through acceptance of experiential facts. Prophetic dreams whose prophesies were alleged to have come true, long-distance communication, haunted houses, and many more phenomena were believed genuine on the testimony of witnesses whose word could not be doubted. Nature, this creation of God, can produce and create everything.

It is probably more important here to dwell on the paucity of means available to them to transform this natural world, to use it for their own benefit. We will not waste time listing twentieth-century scientific techniques of which they had not the faintest idea; it is easier to draw up the balance sheet of their resources. They are essentially limited in this field to agricultural techniques that draw from the land, from the flora and fauna, the totality of their food. To be sure, empirical applications of these techniques did get substantial results. To graft apple trees and achieve twenty or thirty different varieties was a favorite pastime of the lord of Gouberville that brought prosperity to a whole district, and the art of taming wild animals for domestic needs was also quite remarkably perfected. Inherited through centuries-old traditions, these agricultural techniques seem quite inadequate to us today, considering the progress achieved by animal and vegetable biology within the last two centuries; and in spite of the achievements of which we have given only a few examples, they were also considered inadequate by the men of that time. Their agriculture was hardly sufficient to ensure the subsistence of rural and urban communities: a bad frost in March, a July thunderstorm were enough to annihilate not only the hopes of the peasants, but also the vital resources of a whole area. The inadequacy of agriculture no doubt suffered further interference at the distribution stage from a social organization that increased the technical weaknesses at the production stage. This strengthened all the more the natural feeling of insecurity.

Techniques of confrontation with nature other than in agriculture (crafts and, before long, manufacturing) also offer a contrast between the remarkable perfection of empirically acquired skills and a centuries-old stagnation that made it impossible to achieve complex changes and especially to speed up production. Working stone and wood; spinning, weaving, dyeing wool, silk, or hemp; tanning leather were so many techniques thoroughly mastered by rigidly controlled corporations. Technological progress was circumscribed within the very framework of these corporations, which valued more highly achievements and "masterpieces" reproduced a thousand times than methods making it possible to speed up production and increase productivity. Verbal or written customs perpetuated, so to speak, technological tradition; nothing instigated or stimulated innovation.

In short, therefore, it was a very limited technical mastery of the natural environment that did not satisfy its users any more than did scientific knowledge. The accumulation of a nomenclature made all the more shapeless by the fact that it rejected no evidence, the impossibility of distinguishing the natural from the supernatural made of these sciences whose only method was compilation a limited tool for investigation. No one, not even the greatest minds, possessed a method that could make it possible to refine the amazing mixture displayed by every science of half-seen truths, inherited errors, and accepted fancies; no one had an all-embracing view of things and of the inexhaustible and mysterious world, a view that would have made it possible to relate and integrate the fragmentary solutions that had been found for specific problems. The fears of the fifteenth-century sailors that disappeared only as they reached the new continent are hardly a symbolic image of this confusion. The alchemist searching for the secret of secrets is an even clearer illustration of the scientist's impotence.

Unable to master or understand the world (or rather creation), these people turned to God all the more fervently. Explanations, interventions, gifts were requested of God, creator of all things, and if not of God himself, then of his saints—and of his fallen angels. This is not, of course, the only reason for the fervor displayed by the believers of these times. There are certainly other explanations—and other emotional impulses—that drove them along the difficult path of faith. On a different level, it could be shown that there is a relationship between the difficulties encountered in mastering the natural world and the enthusiasm displayed in gaining power over other people. But the very predominance of the supernatural within nature itself confirms our point of view. The recourse to an all-powerful divinity, into whose hands men and things are at every moment confided, is a basic intellectual process. It enables the believer to appeal to God, or some other intercessor, for goods—"benedictions"—that men are unable to provide. The approach is essentially the same when the appeal is to Satan, or to one of his malevolent henchmen or tempters.

Constantly present in mind and heart, the Christian faith provided people (quite aside from the social reality, the control of the individual "from the cradle to the grave") with a frame of reference characterized by the predominance of this divine force that is constantly appealed to, constantly present, and ever ready to intervene in the affairs of the world. As everyone knows, the Christian's faith also provided him with a moral code. But perhaps its main function—at a time when the long doctrinal disputes between the orthodox and the heretics had managed to muddle the simplest dogmas—was to create a sense of, or rather a sensitivity to, the precariousness of human destiny on an unexplored planet full of plagues as well as benefits. This sensitivization was, of course, a long-range affair. It developed throughout the Middle Ages, beginning with the first large-scale introduction of Christianity in the Merovingian period, but it achieved its aim in the fourteenth and fifteenth centuries, when religion itself became more human and less dogmatic. After the era of doctrinal definition, after Saint Thomas and Saint Bernard, it was precisely the confidence of a deeply humble humanity in a God full of compassion for the sufferings of this world that found expression in the numerous representations of the Passion, the Virgin, the Christ on the Cross. They signified for everyone— Catholics, Protestants, and even the few libertarians in the years 1610– 1640—a concern, now considered "natural," for human suffering, for piety, for a sincerity of faith that was mainly a confidence in the supernatural omnipotence of God. The Frenchmen of modern times derived from this religious emotion not only hope for eternal salvation, but also a sense of humanity that permeated even the most tormented existence.

# XII/MOMENTS OF BOURGEOIS CONSCIOUSNESS

O NE of the most difficult tasks facing the emergent bourgeoisie of early modern Europe was the construction of an ideology consistent with its class interests. On a general level, the bourgeoisie, in the course of its struggle to break the bonds imposed on it by a feudal society, opted for the principles of rationality, individualism, universalism, (limited) equality, and the notion of contract. But the ideology of each national segment of the bourgeoisie developed in accordance with specific historical circumstances, even as the class itself was the expression of concrete relationships in a particular setting. Class is never an abstract category.

The growth of bourgeois ideology was, then, very largely determined by the nature of the adversary. In France, and for that matter in most Catholic countries, the Church was so intimately concerned with the maintenance of the feudal status quo, with order (in reality, stasis), that it came into open conflict with the aspirations of the new, revolutionary class. (It is often said today that the bourgeoisie has forgotten its revolutionary origins. I think it is more accurate to say that it remembers, but does not like to think of them.)

There is nothing inherently impossible or even unusual about an alliance between Catholicism as a religion and the bourgeoisie. This has been amply demonstrated through time, but especially since the nineteenth century, when the bourgeoisie began to emphasize the utility of religion as a rampart against revolution, a point of view it had never wholly abandoned and was ready to express at the drop of a popular revolt. What brought Catholicism and the bourgeoisie into collision in the earlier period was the role of the institutional Church, a role which was, however, always expressed in terms of religious principle. The desire for a career open to talent cannot be reconciled with the preaching of an immutable and rigid order of things. The bourgeois might well want to serve God, but in his own way and time. The Church said: "A man is nothing before God when he is not what he is supposed to be." And the *honnête homme* answered: "I am what I am, and not what I am supposed to be." As the late Swiss historian Bernard Groethuysen explains in the following selection, the bourgeois shared neither the need to believe that characterized the majority of the ecclesiastical community, nor the respect for traditional morality that was so closely tied to it: He had become the eternal outsider. So long as birth remained the criterion of distinction for the Church and one could not be born twice into the same world, a clash between itself and the bourgeois was inevitable.

In England, where the Reformation and the rise of Puritanism had made it possible to justify bourgeois man to God (and God to bourgeois man), the problem was rather different. The secular values of the bourgeoisie were elaborated more in the margin of the churches than in strict opposition to them. But de-Christianization was nonetheless real for all that, even when it took the form of outward conformity accompanied by a strict division of property and function between God and Caesar. Moreover, there was no massive return to religion by the bourgeoisie as a class in the nineteenth century, perhaps because the working class got there first, whereas in France the secular tradition of the workers made right-thinking Christianity attractive to the bourgeoisie.

But all that is to run ahead of our story. In seventeenth-century England, with Catholicism defeated, Puritanism in the minority (and, in addition, ambiguous about what it wanted), and Anglicanism too deeply involved in the service of the state, an increasingly atomized society needed to establish a principle of political obligation, the expression in the state of a secular morality universally applicable to all citizens. Thomas Hobbes in his *Leviathan* (1651) and John Locke in his *Two Treatises on Government* (1690) both developed contract theories to act as a surrogate for the "authoritative allocation of work or rewards" common to societies where custom and status reign supreme. The former argued that in making themselves into a society men abdicated their natural rights to the will of a single sovereign, who came from outside their ranks. The latter insisted on a contract that tied each man to all of his fellows, so that sovereignty could be said to reside in the people and was best exercised by some mixed form of government and in particular constitutional monarchy. Despite their differences, there was much they shared in common, like opposition to the theory of divine right monarchy and a tendency to a materialist theory of knowledge, the latter, to be sure, more pronounced in Hobbes than in Locke. Both theorists assumed that men were constantly struggling to appropriate a part of the real world for their own enjoyment and consequently wished to protect their acquisitions (and the right to acquire) from the predatory activities of others. They were describing a reality they found to be increasingly present in seventeenth-century English bourgeois society. C. B. Macpherson of the University of Toronto shows in the selection from his book reprinted here that their assumptions required a certain vision of society, a model of social relations, upon which to found a theory of political obligation. This model, he argues, can be discovered in complete form only in what he has christened a "possessive market society." This he has defined as "one in which, in contrast to a society of independent producers who exchange only their products in the market, there is a market in labour as well as in products. . . . Possessive market society also implies that where labour has become a market commodity, market relations so shape or permeate all social relations that it may properly be called a market society, not merely a market economy." This analysis is wholly compatible with Marxism, for it places the accent on the social relations of production; it offers us a view of the function of contract theory radically different from the shibboleths usually poured forth about the Lockean tradition of democracy and the nastiness of Thomas Hobbes. This attempt to bring the abstruse assumptions of political philosophy down to earth I find very exciting.

So long as it was possible to maintain the fiction of the autonomy of isolated individuals all equally subject to the play of free market forces and representing a cohesive set of interests, contract theory worked well enough. But the increasing difficulty with which individuals crossed class barriers and the consequent rise of class consciousness would seem to indicate that theory and reality have not gone their separate ways. Macpherson thinks the answer to the current dilemma of liberal democracy may lie in a call upon the rational faculties of individuals to recognize that unity and mutual aid are the only alternative to universal destruction—independent of any change in the nature of possessive market relations. Perhaps this may be so, but the very class relationships that grow up in a possessive market society make this view appear too sanguine by half.

# Bernard Groethuysen

---

## 27

## The Bourgeois Order

THE BOURGEOIS JUSTIFIED

The whole "course of the centuries, covering the life of all Christians and all men, is but a great caravan," says Nicole. There was therefore no point in attempting to outdistance others, which, in any case, ill befitted Christians who could not forget where they were going. Sometimes those who made up the caravan were arranged in one order of precedence, sometimes in another. It was of no great moment, since all, whether first or last, would reach the same goal. What mattered was that there should be order, that some should walk at the head, and others follow, so that everything might be done according to rule.

Thus all things here below had been ordained beforehand. Divine Providence had marked the framework within which the life of each individual must develop. The social order indicated to each his place, so that there might be no confusion. Divine Providence, in marking each one's destiny beforehand, had assigned him a particular station and a particular vocation. If the social structure with its various divisions were to collapse, it would have to be rebuilt. And everything would then revert once more to the same order, and the inhabitants would take up their various occupations once more, each according to his vocation; thus life here below, which for a Christian could be only a constant expectation of the next, would resume its regular course.

"It was by the most wise and most adorable of all counsels that God, in creating the world, and desiring to establish a society of men living together and destined to converse with one another, distinguished various conditions within it, and assigned them their functions and duties. Under this dispensation, there are superior and subordinate conditions, brilliant ones and obscure ones, all ordered by divine wisdom, and necessary for the maintenance of peace on earth and good order. For without that diversity which sets one in a position of command and keeps another in dependence, which causes one to appear in splendor, and reduces another to obscurity, what confusion there would be in the world, and what would become of human society!"

God had thus willed that there should be different conditions in society; he had placed each man where he was, and, to please God, men must remain where they were and fulfill the duties of their station. There was no other way to salvation. "I say that man's whole prudence, even in the matter of salvation, may be summed up under two headings," explains Bourdaloue, "to advance in the perfection of his own station, and to avoid any other perfection, or any perfection contrary to this one, or one which prevents its practice." For that was God's will. "I have told you, Christians, that God's will is that each should be what he is in the world perfectly; that a king should be perfectly a king; that a father should perfectly fulfill the office of a father, a judge the function of a judge; that a bishop should perfectly exercise the ministry of a prelate; that all should walk perfectly in the paths marked out for them; that they should not be mingled, and that none should interfere in what is within the competence of another; for if things were so, and each was willing to be merely what he ought to be, we can say that the world would be perfect."

Thus each individual, by perfectly fulfilling his own particular duties, would advance in Christian perfection and at the same time contribute his part to the maintenance of the social order. "There is no condition authorized by law," says Père Haineuve, "that is not in the order of Providence, which has ordained this diversity of conditions, without which the world and human society could not subsist. . . . Hence no one embraces any state, or is born in any condition of civil life, save by the order or permission of this same Providence, which has established inequality and subordination, as well as a diversity of conditions among men."

Thus everything had been disposed to uphold the social order. "But this general disposition of Providence did not suffice, and a more specific one was required," insists Père Bourdaloue. "I mean that, among these different conditions, it was necessary that God, according to his designs . . . of predestination, should mark out for each man and should determine for him the particular station to which he was called. And that is what God did; so much so that there is no man who does not have his own specific vocation, which he must try to know well, and which he is necessarily compelled to follow."

Every man who exercised a function, however humble, exercised it by order of the Lord. The Divinity had appointed him to his task, and saw to it that he carried out his duties. To carry out his duties well was to pray. "I maintain that to perform all one's duties faithfully; to work, to act in one's station in accordance with God's will and good pleasure, is to pray. . . ." "If God committed a task to you," says Père Bourdaloue, "and you carry out its functions assiduously, then, in so doing, you are praying. If Providence committed to you the conduct of a household, and you give it your care, then, in so doing, you are praying. The same applies to everything else." Religion hallowed all the social duties; it sanctified all conditions. "Duties of state are thus in a sense true duties of religion; and if they differ from them in their object, they do not differ from them in the obligation which they impose on us. The sovereign on his throne, the father in his family, the master in his house, the judge in his court, the warrior at his post, the pilot on his ship, the farmhand in the field he cultivates, the artisan in his workshop—all in carrying out the duties of their state are discharging a true duty of religion."

It would thus be a grave error to seek to oppose duties of state to those of religion. "True piety," writes Massillon, "is the order of society; it leaves to each his own place; makes of the state in which God has placed us the sole way of our salvation; does not place a chimerical perfection in works which God does not ask of us; and considers as vices virtues which do not belong to our state. Everything that disturbs public harmony is an excess of man, and not zeal and a perfection of virtue. Religion disavows the most saintly works which one might substitute for duties; and a man is nothing before God when he is not what he is supposed to be."

Order was always of divine institution, however imperfect and unjust it might appear. Some gained from it greater advantages than others. It could not be otherwise. There were rich men who enjoyed the good things of this world and lived in opulence; there were the poor, deprived of everything and living out their lives in penury. So it must be, if there was to be any order at all. "Thus there had to be a diversity of conditions, and especially there had to be poor, so that there might be subordination and order in human society," says Père Bourdaloue.

Order was the all-important thing, and not the greater or lesser advantages that might accrue from it to this or that particular individual or class. Hence the Christian must carefully refrain from anything that might upset the established order. Was not religion itself, asks Massillon, "necessarily linked with law and order? It falls and is weakened when law and order breaks down. . . . As soon as the order of civil society gives way, all religion totters."

Order was thus its own justification; that, for the Christian, must suffice. Men should abide by the established order and conform their lives and actions to it. This applied not only to injudicious reformers and seditious minds, who sought an imaginary perfection for the things of this world, but also to all those who on their own account wanted to get ahead and rise from their condition. The ambitious upset the social order, for ambition "carries us to a level to which we should not aspire, since it is above our condition," says Bourdaloue. Ambition operated in contradiction to the designs of Divine Providence, which had ordained everything beforehand; it caused man to take God's place; it caused man to go his own way, instead of the way marked out for him by Divine Providence.

If the bourgeoisie pondered the teachings of Père Bourdaloue, it must have found its own condemnation in them. The bourgeois, according to Bourdaloue, could not claim that "natural and legitimate greatness which is established by God," and which belonged only to "princes, and all those who derive their superiority from birth or blood." He, personally, would never know any greatness but "an artificial one, whose only support is industry and human ambition." In trying to rise out of his condition, the bourgeois was seeking to correct the defect inherent in his birth; he was taking it upon himself to improve the designs of Divine Providence; he lacked humility and was entering into contestation with God. "There are two types of greatness, that which God has established in the world, and the other which is set up, of itself, the former being the handiwork of Providence, the latter the products of human ambition." God had no part in bourgeois greatness. So long as the bourgeois remained in his own sphere, he was there by divine right, in the same way as all who had a rank or a place in society; but this ceased to be the case as soon as he lifted himself up. At that point, he was acting on his own responsibility. He was constituting himself his own providence; he was putting himself in the place of God. The movement which urged him on was a perpetual defiance of the Church, which maintained that it was his binding duty to confine his existence within the narrow limits which Divine Providence had set for him.

Was the bourgeois, then, no more than a climber, the spawn of sin, bearing within himself, under new forms, the ancient marks of mankind's corruption? No, he was not, or, if he was, he would always be ignorant of the fact. If he was ambitious, he was so in perfectly good conscience; he was ambitious as a matter of duty. His law was to get ahead, always to move forward. Therefore everything in this bourgeois life was carried out in the most orderly manner. Where, then, were the ambitious men of old times, courtiers without scruple, glorying in brilliant but short-lived successes? The Church's grandiloquence lost its edge when it addressed the bourgeois, who walked on with assured step, moved by an irresistible force that drove him onward.

Why was he portrayed as a depraved sinner, a man corrupted and succumbing to the temptations of self-love? In seeking to improve his position, he asked, was he not working for his children? That was his great argument; he justified himself in his children. If the clergy preached to him about the temptations of riches and accused him of being laggardly in the use of the means of salvation which Divine Providence had placed at the disposal of the rich, namely, almsgiving, he pointed to his children. "I have children, and for them I need all my wealth." It was not for himself that he had got rich, he explained; he had worked for his family, for his posterity. Père Griffet puts his argument as follows: "But I am no longer master of the riches which you ask me to give to the poor; I owe them to the children whom God has given me; I have many of them, and I have in the first place to think of raising them, and then of settling them in life. . . . Must not everything give way before the call of blood? Must not paternal love have priority over the love of a neighbor whom we don't know?"

Your children, the clergy replied, "will be rich enough, and you will leave them a large enough heritage, if you make them heirs of the prayers of the poor, and of the favor of Jesus Christ, which the infallible action of those prayers cannot fail to obtain for them." But the bourgeois did not want to entrust the care of his family to anyone, not even God. "It will not be your ability, or your foresight, which will ensure these rich heritages for your children," says Père Croiset. "Alms have more virtue than all the glosses and contracts." But the bourgeois could not believe this. His duty, he felt, was to be prudent and far-sighted, so that his children might later bless him and so that, in the meantime, he might enjoy the esteem of his neighbors. What argument could be advanced to convince him of his errors? What could be said to awaken in him the pangs of remorse of the sinner? He was working for his family, for his class; was he not in security of conscience?

"What does the world tell you? What does it require of you? What sentiments does it inspire in you? Lift yourselves up, get richer, amass goods, buy offices, acquire honors, flee humiliations and poverty as the greatest evils on earth! That is what the world says. Read the Gospels, and see whether they do not teach us precisely the opposite." But the bourgeois was not converted. Not from weakness of the flesh, but because he believed himself to be in the right as against the Church. He knew what he wanted and why he was entitled to want it. He, too, wanted order, a new order, which would be born of the efforts of his class and which the Church could not recognize.

"Today," says Père Croiset, "all conditions seem to be mixed together. The bourgeois who has just made his fortune is often indistinguishable from the man of quality, save by more brilliant luxury. . . . A propriety of order and Christian courtesy used to distinguish stations and conditions, even down to their clothing, in accordance with the spirit and moral teaching of Jesus Christ." Now, however, "confusion and disorder" were rampant.

How, in all this, was a divine order to be recognized? God, we know, "ordered all conditions and placed a wise difference among them." Consequently, when "he has placed us in a position, our business is to remain fixed there, as a saint says, like statues in the niches in which the craftsman placed them; if he considers it fitting to move them, they suffer themselves to be moved; if he leaves them, they do not budge.

There, Lord, that is how we should be in your hands! That is order, and nothing is more reasonable."

But the statues had budged, and the Church lamented the confusion of conditions. Men were no longer following their vocations. They were seeking places here and there, according to their whim. Where was Divine Providence? How was one to continue to believe that God had some part in a social order where everything was topsy-turvy and where the bourgeois, born yesterday, and the product of his own industry, lifted himself above those whose rank was of divine right and whom Divine Providence had singled out above their peers?

Order, for the Church, was the *status quo*, which everyone could recognize because it was self-evident. Any constituted society had its order; men must respect the established order. For, once order had been instituted, God, "the first founder of all the states which make up the world and constitute human society," forbade its violation on any pretext. The generations which succeeded one another must always be able to find the form and the rule of that order, so that the Christian might follow the path traced for him.

As a result, once transformations began to take place from within and values shifted, the Church, by identifying its God with an order that no longer had any justification for existence, was to compromise him, and the adherents of the new order, feeling that the Church merely protected abuses, ceased to ask its advice. Incapable of perceiving any order but that which existed and only very dimly perceiving the order which was emerging, what answer could the clergy give to those who were keeping abreast of the times?

There must be harmony between the Christian and the man who carries out the duties of his profession, Bourdaloue had said, "so much so that . . . the Christian cannot be separated from the trader, the Christian from the working man or craftsman, the Christian from the army officer, the Christian from the prince or monarch. For all these states, and every other state, if I may put it so, must be Christianized in our persons."

The Church did not succeed in establishing harmony between the bourgeois and the Christian. The individual bourgeois might remain a Catholic; the bourgeoisie, the bourgeois State, did not. The bourgeois, seeing himself abandoned by the God of the Christians who appeared never to approve of him save to the extent that he stayed prudently within the narrow confines of his sphere, went on to the conquest of power without the cooperation of the Church and, without asking the advice of the God of the Christians, he asserted what he called his rights and established a new order.

THE TRIUMPH OF THE RESPECTABLE CITIZEN
                              On the ruins of the Gospel of Jesus
Christ, "there arises a gospel of worldly probity, embracing all the
duties of reason and religion. The Christian people are to be turned
into a people of philosophers; all the virtues are summed up under
the headings of the public weal, the proprieties of civil life, law and
order, social tranquillity; no other laws, principles, norms of manners
or conduct are known or recognized; people make it a point of honor
to abandon the title of Christian and to merit the title and sustain the
character of an upright man." Thus Père Charles Frey de Neuville
accuses his fellow citizens of seeking to limit "all the duties of religion
to the duties of probity" and of imagining that "the true Christian can
add nothing, or almost nothing, to the qualities of the upright man."
"When a man wants to speak highly of another," says the Pastor of
Gap, "he says of him that he is an upright man; he does not say, and
dare not say, that he is a genuine Christian, as though there were something discreditable in being a Christian."
    The bourgeois aimed at being an upright man, and nothing more.
"You will tell me, no doubt, that you are upright men, but that you are
not religious fanatics," says Abbé de Boulogne; "for that, my brothers,
is the eternal refrain, the favorite maxim which, according to the self-
styled sages of the times, will solve everything. You are not religious
fanatics! No, indeed, since you are not Christians, since God is no
longer anything for you!" This was why, as the Pastor of Gap says,
"most upright men in whom the so-called philosophical spirit has not
absolutely extinguished the light of faith . . . have nothing now but
a sterile faith which normally plays no part whatsoever either in their
virtues or in their good deeds. Instead of Christian virtues, they have
only moral virtues, like those of wise pagans; virtues, consequently,
which are unavailing for the next life." The education which they gave
their children was proof enough. "I would wish," says the Pastor of
Gap, speaking to his parishioners, "that you would season your conver-
sations with a few words bearing some relation to religion and piety,
words which *felt* Christian, if I may so express myself, and made it clear
that you were Christians. . . . I will allow, Monsieur, that you give your
children fine instruction on the way they should behave in the world.
'My son, have a sense of honor; be upright; . . . take care to earn a good
reputation for yourself. . . . Be gentle, honest, courteous, considerate,
serviceable. . . . My daughter, be modest and reserved. . . .' Those are
certainly very wise counsels, and thoroughly worthy of an upright man;
yes, indeed, but a pagan father said the same things to his children.
Why has religion no part in these instructions which in other respects
are so excellent?"

The bourgeois was an upright man without being a Christian. "Every day," says the Pastor of Gap again, "we see persons otherwise estimable, and leading well-ordered lives, who are basically nothing more than honest pagans, and have no Christian virtues at all." The upright man knew his duty without asking the God of the Christians. He knew how to be "moral" without having to ask the Church.

To finalize his independence and prove conclusively to himself and to others that he knew how to order his life, the bourgeois would have liked to have his moral code set down in the form of a catechism. "For some time, now, we have been constantly hearing about the need for composing a catechism of morality, in which no use would be made of religious principles—antiquated incentives which it is time to set aside," says Necker, who did not share this view, whereas Rivarol, who did, asserted that "a catechism of morality is today the first requirement of the nation. . . . The wise await it, the religious fanatics fear it, the government has made it necessary."

But what did the bourgeoisie want to include in its catechism? A secular morality, of course, which would be that of the whole human race, the assumption being that "the civilized nations of the world are agreed on the essential points of morality, just as they differ on those of faith." "It is said, and that is the fashionable sentiment nowadays," says Caraccioli, "that, independently of all religion, there is a certain love of justice which nature inspires in us, and which suffices at least to form an upright character." Thus the bourgeois morality was of general human application. That was the interpretation which the bourgeois found on rereading the works of the philosophers, when he felt himself to be man, and not simply a bourgeois. From that sentiment he was to draw new strength to assert himself. Good sense, reason, nature, and humanity, he felt, were on his side.

Nevertheless, the eighteenth-century bourgeois was not the reasonable being whom he often represented to himself. He was not man in the abstract, he was a man of a particular period, the product of a particular set of economic and moral circumstances. Consequently, when he talked about man as he was and as he should be, it is man seen through bourgeois eyes that we recognize in the image he presented of the human condition . . . not man as such, but the respectable citizen, the representative of a certain class. Hence, too, his morality could not be of universal application, without distinction of social class. This, in any case, the eighteenth-century bourgeoisie came increasingly to realize; not everyone could be a pillar of society.

There must be "a religion for the people, and Christianity is without question the best that can be given them." That was the view of the respectable citizen, as the Pastor of Gap has already told us. The bourgeois recognized without difficulty that the moral autonomy which he had gained for himself was not for everyone. For the populace, everything must remain as before; they must remain believers. We should have no illusions on this subject, explains Necker in his book, *De l'Importance des Opinions religieuses*. Social order required the existence of poor people.

"It is unavoidable, in the best regulated societies," writes Necker, "that some should enjoy, without labor and without trouble, all the conveniences of life, while others, in far greater number, should be forced to seek the most meager subsistence, the most limited reward, in the sweat of their brow." Or again, "Will it be said, imprudently, that if distinctions of property are an obstacle to the establishment of a political morality, we should strive to destroy them? . . . One may dream of a state where things would be otherwise, and where equality reigned among men, but would one imagine that these primitive relations can be restored at a time when the disparity of means has considerably increased, and when all the superiority of state and power is consolidated by the immutable force of disciplined armies?"

That, too, was why religion could not be dispensed with. "The successive abuses of force and authority, by undermining all the relations originally existing among men, have raised so artificial an edifice in their midst, in which there is such disproportion, that the idea of a God has become more necessary than ever, as the leveler of this confused assemblage of disparities of all kinds." In the emerging nations it might be different, "but in our old states of Europe, where the growth of wealth is constantly widening the differences in fortunes and the gap between conditions, . . . where poverty constantly jostles magnificence, a morality backed by religion is essential to hold back the multitudes who behold so many good things, so many objects of envy, and who, standing so near to everything they call happiness, may never aspire to it."

We should therefore recognize the utility of religion. The rich had property which religion protected far better than could any emancipated morality. "God, giving his laws on Mount Sinai, has only to say, 'Thou shalt not steal' and, with the exalted idea of this God, . . . this commandment preserves sufficient authority for all time; but if political philosophy says, 'Thou shalt not steal,' it must add to that precept a series of arguments on the laws of property, on the inequality of conditions, and on the various relations of the social order." It was therefore much safer to stick to religion and to entrust the defense of property to God rather than to philosophy.

Thus, in order to be able to profess a secular morality, the citizen must already possess some property; otherwise he must be content with the religion reserved for those who possessed none. And the more impoverished the latter became, the greater the efforts that must be made to preserve their faith. Necker says as much, "The more the weight of taxation keeps the people in a state of prostration and desti-

tution, the more indispensable it is to give them a religious education."
But was this not an admission that religion was never more than an
expedient, a lesser evil which men cannot do without if those who are
unable to become pillars of society are to be kept to the straight and
narrow path? That is what Rivarol says, in his letters to Necker. "I
feel," he writes, "that if religion is necessary to the people, it is less to
make them happy than to make them capable of enduring their misfortune. For it is the extreme disparities in wealth that must be blamed
for the expedient of religions; when this world has been rendered un-
bearable to men, they must be promised another." Or again, "If my
lackey doesn't kill me in the depths of a forest because he fears the
devil, I am not going to withdraw such a brake from that brutish soul
any more than I would want to take from him his fear of the gallows;
since I cannot make an upright man of him, I'll make him a religious
one."

Thus the bourgeois, having learned prudence, proposed to reserve
his morality for himself; the rest might remain religious until further
notice. This suffices to show the closeness of the link between the new
morality, whatever the general forms in which it was clothed, and the
spirit of a class. Not that the respectable citizen, as he developed his
principles, always realized the boundaries that would confront him
once he attempted to apply them. The bourgeoisie had created a new
conception of life for itself. It was quite natural that, to ensure the
triumph of that conception, its authors should present it in generalities
and relate it to a universal order. They sought to broaden it rather than
to delimit its boundaries. The bourgeois spoke of "man" and "humanity"; he tended to invoke "nature." However, if a man were to be
"upright," he found it very useful, if not essential, to be propertied. In
any case, was it not altogether natural to own property, and did not
the bourgeois condition correspond to the intentions of nature, which
desired its children to be happy and provided them with the necessary
means to that end?

In reducing bourgeois morality to its social and economic dimensions,
it has not been our intention to detract from its value. It was precisely
because the respectable citizen was but a sublimation of the honest
bourgeois, and not an abstract figure produced by a moral catechism,
that he constituted a reality: the new man of the modern bourgeoisie
as contrasted with the man of former times, as conceived by the Church.
This new man had proved himself; his own existence was to be his
supreme argument. He had proved what only life itself could bear out:
that by living as he had, one could succeed. He could point to flourishing towns and villages; he could show that well-being had spread wherever he had been allowed to use his abilities unimpeded. And it seemed
that a jealous God no longer reserved happiness for the next life alone,
now that his children were capable of conducting themselves as reason-

able and enterprising men. The world which the bourgeois had created testified in his favor. It was his world. It was not the product of the churchgoers. He had created it in defiance of the godly, who spoke to him only of the vanity of human efforts in the face of death. He, personally, had believed in life and had succeeded.

"Everywhere one could hear the sound of chisel and hammer, and not even darkness could quell the eagerness of those who were having splendid mansions built for themselves. All along the streets you could see wood being polished, marble being cut. Floors were being raised upon floors, as though to create a rampart against death." So a writer of the period, who took the part of the Church, describes the activity he witnessed in Paris around 1772. The bourgeois had been confident of his own strength and had become master of the world. The great and the poor, the former to justify their rank and wealth, the latter to console themselves for having none, turned to the church and rendered it homage; but what reason had the bourgeois for doing likewise? A child of this world, he had grown up without the assistance of the Church. The God of the Christians had never wanted to recognize him; what he was, he owed to himself; he had appointed himself his own providence, and was not prepared to recognize any other.

# C. B. Macpherson

## 28

# The Political Theory
# of Possessive Individualism:
# Hobbes to Locke

MODELS OF SOCIETY

### i. *The Use of Models*

The construction of models of society is an unusual, and may be thought an unnecessary, procedure in an analysis of political theory. What value it has must be left to the reader's judgement of its results, but its probable usefulness in analysing Hobbes's theory is suggested by Hobbes's own method. He constructed a model of man, which he built up carefully by logical connexion of postulated elements of human nature. He constructed also a notable model of relations between men, the state of nature, which he deliberately set up as a limiting case. It might be called a model of non-society, and it is so impressive as to overshadow the model of society contained in his discussion of power, honour, and value. The fact that Hobbes had, in effect, a model of society other than the state of nature is often quite overlooked. His model of society is not as explicitly constructed as his other models, but it is fully as important in his argument. We may therefore hope to make a more precise analysis of his argument than would otherwise be possible, by comparing his model with models of society more explicitly constructed. By so doing we should also be able to test the consistency of his model, and its degree of approximation to actual societies.

These purposes have determined the nature and the number of models here constructed. The problem was to construct the fewest possible models to which all known kinds of society could be assimilated and which would isolate their features in such a way as to permit comparisons with Hobbes's model. Three models appear to be sufficient. It need scarcely be said that the models used here would not be sufficient or appropriate for general sociological or historical analysis. The first model, for instance, which I call customary or status society, is drawn broadly enough to include societies as widely different as the ancient empires, feudal societies, and tribal societies. The second model, the simple market society, is drawn very narrowly; it is less a model of any historical society than an analytical convenience for isolating certain features of the more fully developed market societies of modern times. The third model, which is intended to correspond to modern market societies, I have called the possessive market society. Its essential difference from the other two models may be indicated here, before it is more fully examined, partly in order to explain why that name has been chosen.

By possessive market society I mean one in which, in contrast to a society based on custom and status, there is no authoritative allocation of work or rewards, and in which, in contrast to a society of independent producers who exchange only their products in the market, there is a market in labour as well as in products. If a single criterion of the possessive market society is wanted it is that man's labour is a commodity, i.e. that a man's energy and skill are his own, yet are regarded not as integral parts of his personality, but as possessions, the use and disposal of which he is free to hand over to others for a price. It is to emphasize this characteristic of the fully market society that I have called it the *possessive* market society. Possessive market *society* also implies that where labour has become a market commodity, market relations so shape or permeate all social relations that it may properly be called a market society, not merely a market economy.

The concept of possessive market society is neither a novel nor an arbitrary construction. It is clearly similar to the concepts of bourgeois or capitalist society used by Marx, Weber, Sombart, and others, who have made the existence of a market in labour a criterion of capitalism, and like their concepts it is intended to be a model or ideal type to which modern (i.e. post-feudal) European societies have approximated. It differs from theirs chiefly in that it does not require any particular theory of the origin or development of such society. It is not concerned about the primacy or relative importance of various factors such as Marx's primary accumulation, Weber's rational capital accounting, or Sombart's spirit of enterprise. Its use does not require acceptance of the whole of any of these contentious theories. And it may claim the positive merit of drawing attention directly to two essential features of such society, the pre-eminence of market relations and the treatment of labour as an alienable possession.

## ii. Customary or Status Society

The essential properties of a customary or status society may be defined as follows:

(a) The productive and regulative work of the society is authoritatively allocated to groups, ranks, classes, or persons. The allocation and performance are enforced by law or custom.

(b) Each group, rank, class, or person is confined to a way of working, and is given and permitted only to have a scale of reward, appropriate to the performance of its or his function, the appropriateness being determined by the consensus of the community or by the ruling class.

(c) There is no unconditional individual property in land. Individual use of land, if any, is conditional on performance of functions allotted by the community or by the state, or on the provision of services to a superior. There is hence no market in land.

(d) The whole labour force is tied to the land, or to the performance of allotted functions, or (in the case of slaves) to masters. The members of the labour force are thus not free to offer their labour in the market: there is no market in labour. (There may be a market in slaves, but a market in slaves comprises only an exchange relation between masters, not between slave and master, and is therefore not a market relation between all the persons concerned.)

From these properties of a status society certain characteristics follow. In the absence of markets in land and labour, individuals (except in the upper ranks) have no means of continually seeking to alter their place in the scale of power, that is, of changing the amount of their natural power that is being extracted from them or the amount that they are extracting from others. There is room in this model for men at the upper levels of power, who want more delights, to invade others at those levels forcibly, and so to compel others at those levels (including any who would otherwise be content) to enter the competition for power. There is room, that is, for dynastic struggles, palace revolutions, and baronial conflicts. But this is competition between rivals for the benefits already being extracted from the subordinate population. It cannot be general throughout the society, because the existence of the society, and the continued extraction of the benefits being fought for by the rivals, require that the customary allocation and enforcement of the productive and directive work of the society be maintained. The bulk of the society must be confined to ways of working and living which are set by the contribution they are required to make to the society, and these allow them no general opportunity of invading or subduing their fellows. Since there is no free market in individuals' labour, i.e. in their natural powers, competition between individuals for acquiring some of the natural powers of others cannot permeate the whole society. There is room in the model too for those at the bottom to resist, by force, increases in the exactions demanded of them by their superiors. Such resistance will be infrequent if it is assumed that the level of exactions embodied in custom is normally as high as is safe and profitable for the ruling class. In any case, combined resistance by members of a lower class is not in itself, and does not produce, a general pattern of invasion of each individual by his fellows.

In short, the model of a customary status society, while it permits perennial forcible invasion between rivals at the top, and occasional forcible invasion between classes or sections of classes, does not permit perennial invasion, either forcible or otherwise, of individuals by individuals throughout the society. The model neither permits nor requires the constant search for power by individuals over individuals, of such extent that all individuals must seek more power in order to protect what delights they have. It is apparent that the model of a status society does not meet Hobbes's requirements. The essential shortcoming is that in the status model the natural powers, i.e. the labour, of individuals are not freely transferable. Only in a society in which every man's labour is an exchangeable commodity can the transfer of control of individuals' powers be as ubiquitous as is required by Hobbes's assumptions.

### iii. Simple Market Society

The simple market society also falls short of the requirement, for we define it as a society in which the production and distribution of goods and services is regulated by the market but in which labour itself is not a market commodity. It is doubtful if a society closely approximating to this model has ever existed for very long. But the model is introduced in order to separate the features common to all market societies from those which are found only in full market societies. The separation is useful in drawing attention to features of the full market society which are not emphasized in the familiar economists' models. For purposes of economic analysis the most essential features may be those common to all market societies; for purposes of political analysis the most essential features are those peculiar to the full market society.

The simple market society has the following properties:

(a) There is no authoritative allocation of work: individuals are free to expend their energies, skills, and goods as they will.

(b) There is no authoritative provision of rewards for work: individuals are not given or guaranteed, by the state or the community, rewards appropriate to their social functions.

(c) There is authoritative definition and enforcement of contracts.

(d) All individuals seek rationally to maximize their utilities, that is, to get the most satisfaction they can for a given expenditure of energy or goods, or to get a given satisfaction for the least possible expenditure of energy or goods.

(e) All individuals have land or other resources on which they may get a living by their labour.

From these properties of the model certain consequences follow. In search of the means to live, individuals will deploy their energies, skills, and material resources in ways which the society (i.e. the same individuals as consumers) is willing to pay for. The productive and other functions of society will thus be performed by individuals in search of rewards that can only be had by using their energies and resources. Since individuals seek the maximum return for their work, and since division of labour is more efficient than is each doing everything for himself, individuals will exchange products of their labour and resources for goods produced by others. There will thus be a market in products. Prices will be determined by competition between sellers and between buyers, and will determine how individuals allocate their labour and resources between different kinds of production. The market is self-regulating in that prices will move so that what is offered for sale will be bought and what is wanted will be produced and offered for sale.

There is no reason in this model for the market in products to be extended to a market in labour. To rule out a market in labour absolutely a further postulate would be necessary:

(f) That the satisfaction of retaining control of one's own labour is greater than the difference between expected wages and expected returns as an independent producer.

Since in the simple market society individuals retain the control of their own energies and skills, and exchange is only between products, market exchange cannot be a means by which individuals gain by converting some of the powers of others to their use in such a way as to require the others to change their ways. It is true that everyone in this model exchanges products in the market, and may be said thus to convert indirectly some of the powers or labour of others to his use. And everyone enters the market for gain, and does gain by entering the market. But the gain each gets in this market is the greater utility he gets by producing one thing for exchange rather than everything for himself. No one's gain is at the expense of others; no one converts more of the powers of others to his use than they convert of his. If there are some men who want more than they have, who want to increase the amount of satisfactions they enjoy, they can do so by exerting more energy or skill and so producing more and getting more in exchange. But in doing so they are still not converting more of the powers of others to their use than others are converting of theirs. And their action does not require any counteraction by the others who are content with the level they have. The simple market society therefore does not meet the requirements of Hobbes's society. Individuals who are content with their existing level of satisfactions are not pulled into competition for more power in order to protect the level they have.

The model of the simple market society obviously falls far short of correspondence with modern market societies. If we dropped postulates (e) and (f) and simply added the stipulation that there is a competitive market in labour, we would have a sufficient model of a fully competitive market society. But rather than simply stipulating that there is a market in labour, it will be more useful to see what further postulates are required to bring about a market in labour. We shall therefore construct the model of a full market society by adding the postulates which are necessary and sufficient to bring about a transformation of the simple to the full market society.

## iv. Possessive Market Society

The model of the simple market society is transformed into the possessive market model by retaining the first four postulates of the simple model and adding four more. We thus have the following postulates:

(a) There is no authoritative allocation of work.
(b) There is no authoritative provision of rewards for work.
(c) There is authoritative definition and enforcement of contracts.
(d) All individuals seek rationally to maximize their utilities.
(e) Each individual's capacity to labour is his own property and is alienable.
(f) Land and resources are owned by individuals and are alienable.
(g) Some individuals want a higher level of utilities or power than they have.[1]
(h) Some individuals have more energy, skill, or possessions, than others.

When the four new postulates are added to the first four postulates of the simple market society, a full market society follows. Those who want to increase their level of utilities or power, and who have either greater possessions which they can use as capital (and the skill to use them profitably), or superior energy and skill by which they can accumulate capital, will seek to employ the labour of others for a price, in the expectation of getting from the labour they employ a value greater than its cost. Individuals who have less land or resources, or less skill, than can regularly give them a subsistence by their independent production, will accept wages that will give them a subsistence.

The greater efficiency of combined labour organized by men of

[1] Since postulates (d) and (g) are superficially similar it is perhaps worth emphasizing their difference. Postulate (d) stipulates that everyone wants to get as much as possible for as little as possible, but not that anyone wants to get more than he has.

superior skill, energy, or resources will, in the competitive market, drive down the prices of the products, so that increasing numbers of solitary producers find it impossible, or less profitable, to continue independently, and therefore offer their labour in the market. Thus, in a society where labour is alienable, and where there are different levels of desire and of ability or possessions, a competitive market in products brings about a general competitive market. Labour, land, and capital, as well as products, become subject to the determination of the market: prices for all of them are set by competition between sellers and between buyers so that what is offered will be bought and what is wanted will be offered.

We thus have the essential features of a modern competitive market society. Without any authoritative allocation of work or rewards, the market, responding to countless individual decisions, puts a price on everything, and it is with reference to prices that the individual decisions are made. The market is the mechanism through which prices are made by, and are a determining factor in making, individual decisions about the disposal of energies and the choice of utilities.

Exchange of commodities through the price-making mechanism of the market permeates the relations between individuals, for in this market all possessions, including men's energies, are commodities. In the fundamental matter of getting a living, all individuals are essentially related to each other as possessors of marketable commodities, including their own powers. All must continually offer commodities (in the broadest sense) in the market, in competition with others.

Competition in this market, unlike that in the simple market in products, is a means by which men who want more may convert more of the powers of others to their use than others convert of theirs. For the effect of competition in this market is to compel entrepreneurs (who must have had some capital initially, with which to hire labour) to use increasing amounts of capital as a means to more efficient production. The greater the capital required in order to stay in the market, the less possible is it for men of little property to enter into, or stay in, independent production. As the greater efficiency of more highly capitalized production permits the population to increase, such production becomes indispensable for the larger society. And as the land runs out (which it does the more quickly because land has become a kind of capital), an increasing proportion of the population becomes dependent on selling its labour. Thus a class division between those with land and capital, and those without, sets in (if it was not in existence already). When land and capital are all owned by one set of people, there is a permanent change in the distribution of the whole product between persons, to the disadvantage of the persons without land and capital. Since the latter cannot resort to independent production, they cannot demand in wages an amount equal to what would ᵇᵉ the product of their labour on land or capital of their own. Those who have the capital and land can therefore, by employing the labour of others, get a net transfer of some of the powers of others (or some of the product of those powers) to themselves.

In speaking of this process as a net transfer of some of the powers of one man to another, we are taking the powers of a man to be (following Hobbes's definition) the whole of a man's present means to obtain future apparent goods. The powers of a man therefore include not only his energy and skill, or capacity to labour, but also his access to the means (land, materials, or other capital) without which his capacity to labour cannot become active labour and so cannot produce any goods. No narrower definition of man's powers is consistent with a model of a society of *men*, at least with any society in which men must produce in order to eat. For if a man, to remain a man (i.e. to continue to exist), must produce, then he must, to remain a man, have bòth the capacity to labour and access to the means of labour. The powers of a *man* must therefore by definition include access to the means of labour.[2] A man's powers are therefore reduced when he has less than free access to the means of labour. If he can get no access, his powers are reduced to zero, and in a competitive society he ceases to exist. If he can get access, but not freely, his powers are reduced by the price he has to pay for access, and that price measures the amount of his power that is transferred to another.

As between the simple market model (where everyone has land or materials to work on) and the possessive market model (where some men have no land or capital of their own), what some men have lost is free access to the means of turning their capacity to labour into productive labour. Having lost this part of their powers they must continually sell the remainder of their powers to those who have the land and capital, and must accept a wage which allows part of the product to go to the owners of land and capital. This constitutes the net transfer of part of their powers to others. It is a continual transfer, since it proceeds as production takes place. Its amount is not fixed, but fluctuates in the competitive market with changes in the supply of labour and of capital.

A net transfer is, of course, not unique to the full market society. For while it cannot exist in the simple market society, it does exist in all those customary and status societies where a ruling class maintains itself by tributes, rents, or slavery. What is unique about the transfer in the market society is that there it is maintained by continual com-

---

2 A narrower definition of a man's powers is possible only in a model of an *economy* which abstracts so far from man's human quality as to consider him not even as a system of matter in motion which must be in continual motion, but merely as the owner of a factor of production called labour.

petition between individuals at all levels. Everyone is a possessor of something, if only of his capacity to labour; all are drawn into the market; competition determines what they will get for what they have to offer. Their net return registers the net amount of their own powers that has been transferred to others (or whose benefit or product has been transferred to others), or the net amount of others' that they have transferred to themselves. Since this is determined by the impersonal operation of the market, in which relative prices change in response to changes in wants, changes in energy and skill expended, innovations in production, changes in the ratio of labour to capital, and other factors, everyone is potentially in movement up or down the scale of power and satisfactions.

The possessive market model requires a compulsive framework of law. At the very least, life and property must be secured, contracts must be defined and enforced. The model also permits state action much beyond this minimum. The state may control land use and labour use, may interfere with the free flow of trade by embargoes and customs duties, may assist one kind of industry and discourage another, may provide free or subsidized services, may relieve the destitute, may require minimum standards of quality or of training, and may by these and other kinds of interference prevent prices (including wages) reaching the levels which an unregulated or less regulated market would produce. What the state does thereby is to alter some of the terms of the equations each man makes when he is calculating his most profitable course of action. But this need not affect the mainspring of the system, which is that men do calculate their most profitable courses and do employ their labour, skill, and resources as that calculation dictates. Some of the data for their calculations is changed, but prices are still set by competition between the calculators. The prices are different from what they would be in a less controlled system, but as long as prices still move in response to the decisions of the individual competitors and the prices still elicit the production of goods and determine their allocation, it remains a market system. The state may, so to speak, move the hurdles to the advantage of some kinds of competitors, or may change the handicaps, without discouraging racing. The state may, of course, deliberately or otherwise, by the same sort of intervention put racing out of business. But it need not do so. One cannot infer from the fact of intervention that the intention is, or that the effect will be, to weaken the system. The possessive market model thus does not require a state policy of *laissez-faire*; a mercantilist policy is perfectly consistent with the model and may indeed be required at some stages in the development of a possessive market society.

Whatever the degree of state action, the possessive market model permits individuals who want more delights than they have, to seek to convert the natural powers of other men to their use. They do so through the market, in which everyone is necessarily involved. Since the market is continually competitive, those who would be content with the level of satisfactions they have are compelled to fresh exertions by every attempt of the others to increase theirs. Those who would be content with the level they have cannot keep it without seeking more power, that is, without seeking to transfer more powers of others to themselves, to compensate for the increasing amount that the competitive efforts of others are transferring from them.

The possessive market society, then, does meet Hobbes's requirements. It is a society in which men who want more may, and do, continually seek to transfer to themselves some of the powers of others, in such a way as to compel everyone to compete for more power, and all this by peaceable and legal methods which do not destroy the society by open force. The possessive market society is the only one of our three models which does meet Hobbes's requirements. And it is difficult to conceive of any other model which would do so. Only in a society in which each man's capacity to labour is his own property, is alienable, and is a market commodity, could all individuals be in this continual competitive power relationship.

The fact that the possessive market model meets (and is the only model that does meet) Hobbes's requirements may of course be attributed to the fact that we put in that model (and excluded from the other models) certain postulates which Hobbes explicitly makes about his society. Certainly, postulates (g) and (h)—that some individuals want more delights than they have, and that some have more abilities than others—are explicit in Hobbes, and it might be thought that they were not really needed to produce our model. It is important to notice, therefore, that both these postulates, and indeed all the four postulates stipulated for converting the simple market model to the full market model, are needed to produce a model that corresponds in essentials with actual competitive market societies.

Postulate (e), that each individual's capacity to labour is his own property and is alienable, is self-evidently required: without it, one of the essential features of modern competitive market societies would be impossible. The same may be said of postulate (f), that land and resources are owned by individuals and are alienable. This postulate is not required for, although it is consistent with, the simple market society: the simple market in products could operate even with fixed and inalienable rights in land. But it is required for a full market society. For unless land and resources can be transferred through a market, and so be combined with labour in the most profitable way, full advantage cannot be taken of the availability of labour. Postulate (g), that some individuals want a higher level of utilities or power than they have, is equally required for a modern competitive market society.

For without this postulate there would be no incentive to accumulate capital and use it to employ labour, and hence no general market in labour. This postulate, like (f), is not required for, although it is consistent with, a simple market society; but it is required for a full market society. Finally, postulate (h), that some individuals have more energy, skill, or possessions than others, is required for a modern competitive market society. For unless some individuals have more possessions than others to begin with, or have abilities to acquire more than others, there could be no accumulations of capital, without which there could be no general employment of labour.

All four of the postulates that distinguish our full market model from the simple market model are needed to produce a model that corresponds in essentials with actual competitive market societies. And it is these postulates which, by producing a market relationship in labour as a commodity, produce the essential requirement of Hobbes's society, namely, the mechanism by which those who want more power or delight than they have can engage in continual, non-violent competition for the power of others, which compels the others to enter the competition.

. . .

## POSSESSIVE INDIVIDUALISM AND LIBERAL DEMOCRACY

### i. The Seventeenth-Century Foundations

We are now in a position to consider the extent to which some identifiable social assumptions are common to the main seventeenth-century political theories, and how they are relevant to the problems of later liberal-democratic society.

The assumptions which comprise possessive individualism may be summarized in the following seven propositions.

(i) What makes a man human is freedom from dependence on the wills of others.

(ii) Freedom from dependence on others means freedom from any relations with others except those relations which the individual enters voluntarily with a view to his own interest.

(iii) The individual is essentially the proprietor of his own person and capacities, for which he owes nothing to society.

Proposition (iii) may appear in a theory as an independent postulate, or as a deduction from (i) and (ii) plus a concept of property as an exclusive right. Thus: since the freedom, and therefore the humanity, of the individual depends on his freedom to enter into self-interested relations with other individuals, and since his ability to enter into such relations depends on his having exclusive control of (rights in) his own person and capacities, and since proprietorship is the generalized form of such exclusive control, the individual is essentially the proprietor of his own person and capacities.

(iv) Although the individual cannot alienate the whole of his property in his own person, he may alienate his capacity to labour.
(v) Human society consists of a series of market relations.

This follows from the assumptions already stated. Since the individual is human only in so far as free, and free only in so far as a proprietor of himself, human society can only be a series of relations between sole proprietors, i.e. a series of market relations.

Or proposition (v) may appear in a theory not as a deduced proposition but as the primary or even the sole social assumption. This is possible because propositions (i) to (iv) are contained in it. The concept of market relations necessarily implies individual freedom as defined in (ii) and proprietorship as defined in (iii) and (iv); and the postulate that human society consists of market relations necessarily implies that an individual's humanity is a function of his freedom (proposition i).

(vi) Since freedom from the wills of others is what makes a man human, each individual's freedom can rightfully be limited only by such obligations and rules as are necessary to secure the same freedom for others.
(vii) Political society is a human contrivance for the protection of the individual's property in his person and goods, and (therefore) for the maintenance of orderly relations of exchange between individuals regarded as proprietors of themselves.

These assumptions are present in one form or another in each of the theories that have been analysed. And it appears from the analysis that the strength of each theory is due to its having incorporated these assumptions, and the weakness of each to its having failed to deal with some of their implications.

The assumptions are clearest and fullest in Hobbes. His model of man, as the sum of a man's powers to get gratifications, reduces the human essence to freedom from others' wills and proprietorship of one's own capacities. His model of society, which follows from his model of man plus the assumption that every man's powers are opposed to every other man's, we have seen to be a full possessive market model. The political society whose necessity he deduced from these models is an artificial device, calculated to provide the maximum security that could by any means be provided for the individual's exercise of his capacities.

For Hobbes the model of the self-moving, appetitive, possessive individual, and the model of society as a series of market relations between these individuals, were a sufficient source of political obligation. No traditional concepts of justice, natural law, or divine purpose were needed. Obligation of the individual to the state was deduced from the supposed facts, as set out in the materialist model of man and the market model of society. The models contained the two suppositions of fact which Hobbes thought sufficient for the deduction of right and obligation: equality of need for continued motion, and equal insecurity because of equal liability to invasion by others through the market. The system, both mechanical and moral, was self-moving and self-contained. It needed no outside mover or outside standard of right.

I have argued that it was Hobbes's possessive market assumptions which gave his political theory its extraordinary strength and consistency. I have argued also that it was one flaw in his market model that made his political theory inapplicable to the possessive market society. The flaw was his failure to see that the market society generated a degree of class cohesion which made possible a viable political authority without a self-perpetuating sovereign body.

When we turn to the theory of the Levellers we find again the main assumptions of possessive individualism, but now differently formulated, and with their implications not as fully worked out. The human essence is freedom from the wills of others, and freedom is a function of proprietorship of one's person: "every one as he is himselfe, so he hath a selfe propriety, else he could not be himselfe." Political society is a contrivance for securing individual natural rights, that is, individual freedom and proprietorship. No individual can alienate the whole of his property in his person, but anyone can alienate his property in his own labour; in doing so he gives up his natural right to a voice in elections but not his natural right to civil and religious liberties.

The strength of the Leveller theory may be variously assessed. Its powerful appeal, for those in the Leveller movement, may be ascribed to its insistence on individual freedom, both religious and secular, and to the skill with which history and Scripture were marshalled in the cause of freedom for the men below the wealthy and above the dependent poor. Its theoretical strength is attributable in large measure to its realistic recognition of the position of the individual in a market society. The Leveller writers saw that freedom in their society was a function of possession. They could therefore make a strong moral case for individual freedom by defining freedom as ownership of one's person.

The theoretical weaknesses of the Leveller position can all be referred to their failure to see the full implications of their possessive individualist assumptions, which failure may in turn be referred to the limits of their vision as members of an intermediate class. They

did not see that if you make individual freedom a function of possession, you must accept the full market society. If you insist that a man
is human only as sole proprietor of himself, only in so far as he is
free from all but market relations, you must convert all moral values
into market values. But the Levellers wrote as if there were no difference between the market morality of possessive individualism and the
Christian social ethic which they also upheld. They brought in, over
and above the individual right of self-preservation and self-advancement, a concept of "humane society, cohabitation or being" as "the
earthly sovereigne good of mankind," with a consequent obligation
on everyone to work for "communitive Happinesse." They wavered
between a view of a man's labour as a commodity and a view of it as an
integral part of his personality. They asserted the right of individual
appropriation of land and goods, but denied the rightness of its consequence, the greatly unequal distribution of wealth.

While the Levellers treated the class structure of seventeenth-century
society more seriously than did Hobbes, and so avoided the error into
which Hobbes had been led by his neglect of class cohesion, their treatment of class was also faulty. In excluding wage-earners and alms-takers
from political rights they recognized one of the prevailing class divisions, and in denouncing the conspiracy of the rich against themselves
(the intermediate class of small independent producers) they recognized another. Their demand for a political voice for themselves was a
demand that the second dividing line should be erased. The implied
assumption was that all those above the dependent poor were capable
of enough cohesion to support a single elective political authority.
There was no such cohesion, as events were to show. This error of the
Levellers, which appears as a fault of empirical judgement, may be
traced to the imprecision of their theoretical grasp of market society.
They did not see that a possessive market society necessarily puts in a
dependent position not only the wage-earners but also all those without
a substantial (and, by the natural operation of the market, an increasing) amount of capital.

Harrington's theory stands somewhat apart from the others. Less
concerned with right and obligation than with empirical uniformities
of political change and stability, Harrington gave less attention to
moral principles than the Levellers, and less to psychological analysis
than Hobbes. While his concern for civil and religious liberties puts
him in the liberal tradition, he is not as pronounced an individualist
as the others. Working mainly by comparative and historical analysis
he does not appear to rely on postulates about the moral or behavioural
nature of the individual. Yet [discussed elsewhere] he did postulate
that every man seeks power over others, and that power is a function of
property. He recognized that these postulates were necessary for his
theory of the balance. And if he said little about human nature, it was

because he fully endorsed Hobbes's analysis: "his treatises of human nature, and of liberty and necessity, are the greatest of new lights, and those which I have follow'd, and shall follow."

What most clearly entitles us to describe Harrington as a possessive individualist is his assumption that seventeenth-century English society was a possessive market society. His whole case for erecting an "equal commonwealth" in England depends, I have argued, on that assumption. He both assumed the existence and accepted the morality of bourgeois society. The behaviour of both gentry and people was brought under one general theory of possessive and accumulative motivation. The institutional balance he proposed between gentry and people would work, and the agrarian law which was to stabilize the balance would be indestructible, only because both classes accepted the market relations which Harrington assumed would henceforth permanently prevail.

He did not read market relations back into the very nature of man, as Hobbes had done. But though he did not penetrate as far as Hobbes into the nature of bourgeois man, he avoided the error into which Hobbes had been led by such a high degree of abstraction. Harrington saw the reality of class structure. He allowed for, indeed built upon, the possibility of class cohesion, as Hobbes did not. And he avoided the opposite error of the Levellers: he did not assume an improbable degree of cohesion or identity of interests between the greater and the meaner sort of freemen, but tried to arrange a balance of power between them.

The main weakness of Harrington's theory, I have suggested, was due to his insufficient logical ability, which led him to contradict himself in his use of the principle of the balance. Had he sharpened his assumptions and been more careful in his deduction he could have avoided those contradictions. Thus we may say of Harrington that the theoretical strength of his system lay in his recognition and acceptance of possessive market relations and motivation, and its theoretical weakness in his failure to see fully or state clearly all the assumptions that were involved.

With Locke we are again in the realm of moral rights and obligation derived from the supposed nature of man and society. As with Hobbes, Locke's deduction starts with the individual and moves out to society and the state, but, again as with Hobbes, the individual with which he starts has already been created in the image of market man. Individuals are by nature equally free from the jurisdiction of others. The human essence is freedom from any relations other than those a man enters with a view to his own interest. The individual's freedom is rightly limited only by the requirements of others' freedom. The individual is proprietor of his own person, for which he owes nothing to society. He is free to alienate his capacity to labour, but not his whole person. Society is a series of relations between proprietors. Political society is a contractual device for the protection of proprietors and the orderly regulation of their relations.

But the assumptions of possessive individualism are not unalloyed in Locke. He refused to reduce all social relations to market relations and all morality to market morality. He would not entirely let go of traditional natural law. He used both Hobbes and Hooker to establish his political obligation. His main theoretical weaknesses might be traced to his attempt to combine these two sources of morality and obligation. The weaknesses are better traced, I have suggested, to his inability to surmount an inconsistency inherent in market society. A market society generates class differentiation in effective rights and rationality, yet requires for its justification a postulate of equal natural rights and rationality. Locke recognized the differentiation in his own society, and read it back into natural society. At the same time he maintained the postulate of equal natural rights and rationality. Most of Locke's theoretical confusions, and most of his practical appeal, can be traced to this ambiguous position. The ambiguity was less a result of his imperfect logic than of his trying to cope with a contradiction in market society of which he was not fully aware. He did not analyse that society as clearly as Hobbes but he did take into account a problem that Hobbes had neglected, that is, the complications raised by class differentiation in an atomized market society.

It may be too much to say that it was because Locke kept these complications in mind that he did not produce clear models of man and society, and reason from them as rigorously as Hobbes. But it may be said that the effective reception of Locke's theory owes much to his having kept the complications in mind and dealt with them, however confusedly. At least his having kept them in mind enabled him to avoid Hobbes's error, and to produce a political system without a self-perpetuating sovereign.

In making the one structural alteration in Hobbes's theoretical system that was required to bring it into conformity with the needs and possibilities of a possessive market society, Locke completed an edifice that rested on Hobbes's sure foundations. Locke's other contribution, his attaching to this structure a façade of traditional natural law, was by comparison unimportant. It made the structure more attractive to the taste of his contemporaries. But when tastes changed, as they did in the eighteenth century, the facade of natural law could be removed, by Hume and Bentham, without damage to the strong and well-built utilitarian structure that lay within. Hobbes, as amended by Locke in the matter of the self-perpetuating sovereign, thus provided the main structure of English liberal theory.

The basic assumptions of possessive individualism—that man is free and human by virtue of his sole proprietorship of his own person, and that human society is essentially a series of market relations—were deeply embedded in the seventeenth-century foundations. It was these assumptions that gave the original theory its strength, for they did correspond to the reality of seventeenth-century market society. The assumptions of possessive individualism have been retained in modern liberal theory, to an extent not always realized. Yet they have failed as foundations of liberal-democratic theory. The trouble is not that they have been kept after they had ceased to correspond to our society. They still do correspond to our society, and so must be kept. The trouble with some liberal theory is that it does not recognize this, and tries to do without them. But the real trouble is that one change in possessive market society—a change which does not alter the validity of possessive individualist assumptions, since it is a change in an aspect of market society that was not reflected in those assumptions—has made it impossible, on two counts, to derive a valid theory of obligation from the assumptions.

The change was the emergence of working-class political articulacy. It has not altered the validity of possessive individualist assumptions for possessive market societies, because those assumptions reflect or state the atomized rather than the class nature of that society. We have seen that a possessive market society is necessarily class-divided. We have also seen that a possessive market society is a series of competitive and invasive relations between all men, regardless of class: it puts every man on his own. It is this second aspect of possessive market society that was and still is accurately reflected in the assumptions of possessive individualism. The assumptions remain indispensable, but no sufficient principle of obligation can now be derived from them.

# GLOSSARY OF MARXIST TERMS

*Accumulation.* The acquisition of capital necessary for the development of production. Before the capitalist mode of production can become dominant, capital has to be available and concentrated in the hands of the potential employers of labor, and a work force dependent on wages has to be created. *Primitive accumulation* refers to the process by which the capital necessary for capitalist development is acquired. The process varied from country to country, the wealth coming sometimes from agriculture, sometimes from mercantile activity. But on the whole it was marked by a high degree of violence, directed against both the feudal system and the resisting peasants and urban wage-earners. *Capitalist accumulation* refers to the process within the capitalist mode of production whereby wealth is acquired through the creation of profits.

*Appropriation.* The term refers to the proceeds (or surplus value) from the product of the workers' labor taken over by the capitalist after wages have been paid.

The *bourgeoisie* is a social class, that is, a group of men defined by the role they play in the relations of production. By definition, a class cannot exist by itself but only in relation to another class. Nor is a class strictly and solely an economic category, for men, as they engage in the productive process, develop all sorts of characteristics affecting all areas of social life: the way they think, express themselves, make war, build political institutions, etc., *ad infinitum*. It is the sum of the interactions of all these areas, as well as the dialectic of the struggle between the classes, that defines each of them.

As is true of all other classes, the bourgeoisie has had a long history. In classic feudal societies, the bourgeoisie was those persons who were engaged in trade and who were outside the dominant lord-peasant relationship. We therefore speak of the *commercial bourgeoisie,* at a point in time before capitalism had penetrated all aspects of production. In France before 1789 there were other types of bourgeoisie, such as the financiers who collected the taxes and dealt in state finance, and the office holders who occupied the higher echelons of state administration. Under fully developed capitalism, the bourgeoisie is defined as the capitalist owners of the means of production.

All revolutions bring about a change in power relations in a society. In a *bourgeois revolution* the dominant class is replaced by the bourgeoisie. But a revolution of this sort may take years before it is completed, and it may be more or less successful, that is, the class seeking power may be forced into a whole series of compromises with both the older and newer opposition, and the particular shape taken by the new regime will be much affected by the balance of forces so realized. A *pre-bourgeois revolution* is one that takes place when the bourgeoisie is still relatively undeveloped and in conditions of economic backwardness. The term has been applied to the history of sixteenth-century Germany in particular. It is to be noted that a revolution identified with a given social class is not necessarily the conscious work of all, or even some, of its members. Rather, it is the result of the revolution and the place it occupies within a precise analytical framework that determine its class character.

*Capitalism* is that mode of production characterized by the pursuit of profit (rather than the satisfaction of social needs), where capital is concentrated in the hands of the owners of the means of production and where profit is realized at the expense of the workers (proletarians) who are dependent on the sale of their labor power for a living. Emphasis must be placed on the notion of production and its subordination to capital. Insofar as this does not exist, neither does the capitalist mode of production. Care must be taken not to confuse *capital investment*, which has always existed, with capitalist production. Hence, the expressions *commercial, financial,* or *speculative* capitalism which, applied to medieval or early modern Europe, refer to marginal capitalist practices subordinated to the needs of feudal society and its dominant class. They had little or nothing to do with the productive sphere, although their existence was not without importance in the process of primitive capitalist accumulation.

The phrase *rationally acquisitive capitalism* is associated with the names of the German sociologists/historians Max Weber and Werner Sombart. Writing in the first decades of the twentieth century, both thought that what distinguished the medieval from the early modern economy was a new spirit of desire for gain and rational organization, quite independent of the ownership of the means of production as Marx would have it.

*Determinism.* The term refers to any system of historical or philosophical analysis which subordinates human action to external forces, whether material or spiritual. Marx has often been accused of being an economic determinist, but in reality he was not. Marx wrote that "the mode of production of material life conditions the process of social, political, and spiritual existence as a whole," and he sought to discover the laws according to which the *capitalist* mode of production functions. This said, he never established an automatic correspondence between the economic sphere and any other sphere of human action. Nor did he deprive men of the possibility of making their own history. On the contrary. In short, if the general shape of historical development is determined (for instance, the destruction of capitalism and its replacement by socialism), the way in which this may take place is totally undetermined. The timing of events, the ups and downs of the process are so many unknowns, and men are free, within the bounds of certain material constraints, to act as they will. Similarly, one sphere of human action—economic, social, political, intellectual, military—may at any given moment assume greater importance than, or be in advance of the development of, the rest, precisely because of the existence of significant human freedom.

*Hegemony.* According to Antonio Gramsci, a class is said to exercise hegemony when it has seized the initiative in the process of social change.

*Neo-Marxist* describes any thinker or theory that accepts Marxist principles as a point of departure but rejects certain of their component theses.

*Production.* For Marx, it is productive activity that distinguishes men from other animals. It is in the course of producing that men create the basic relationships that bind them one to another, the characteristics that give their societies shape and consistency.

The *means of production* refer to the items that make possible the creation of material objects: land, capital, tools, raw materials. The *productive forces* or *forces of production* include the means of production together with the labor of the workers and the techniques applied. The *relations of production* or *social relations* are the ensemble of relations into which men enter in the process of "producing and reproducing real life." Specifically, these include the system of property holding (of the means of production), the distribution of material goods, and the class structures that are their expression.

A *mode of production* is the total of the forces of production and of the relations of production. But it is an abstract category not meant to describe reality. A *social formation* is the expression used to describe a concrete historical moment in which elements of one or more modes of production may be present and interacting with one another, thus creating a unique situation. Each social formation encompasses activities directly economic in nature, as well as ideologies, beliefs, and institutions.

*Revisionism.* A school of thought which rejects most of the fundamental notions of Marxism, particularly the dialectic and the analysis of capitalist development, making of the little that is left a series of ethical recommendations. The revisionists favor using parliamentary reform to pass from capitalism to socialism, and reject both revolutionary violence and the dictatorship of the proletariat.

*Surplus value.* In the capitalist mode of production, the relationship between the owner of the means of production and the worker (proletarian) is an exploitative one. The capitalist buys the worker's labor power. The labor power is used to create products sold on the market as commodities. Surplus value is that part of the proceeds which remains in the hands of the capitalist after deducting payment to the worker, a payment which permits the latter to survive and renew his labor power. But the amount of the wages paid the worker does not affect the fact of his exploitation.

THIS BOOK was set on the Linotype in Baskerville. The punches for this face were cut under the supervision of George W. Jones, the eminent English printer and the designer of Granjon and Estienne. Linotype Baskerville is a facsimile cutting from type cast from the original matrices of a face designed by John Baskerville, a writing master of Birmingham, for his own private press. The original face was the forerunner of the "modern" group of type faces, known today as Scotch, Bodoni, etc. After his death in 1775, Baskerville's punches and matrices were sold in France and were used to produce the sumptuous Kehl edition of Voltaire's works.